IRONY'S EDGE

The often "cutting" edge of irony, says Linda Hutcheon, is always a social and political edge. Irony depends upon interpretation; it "happens" in the tricky, unpredictable space between expression and understanding.

Irony's Edge is a fascinating, compulsively readable study of the myriad forms and the effects of irony. It sets out, for the first time, a sustained, clear analysis of the theory and the political contexts of irony, using a wide range of references, mostly from contemporary culture.

Examples extend from Madonna to Wagner, from a clever quip in conversation to a contentious exhibition in a museum. And the stakes are high – many radical artists and cultural activists consider irony to be usefully subversive; others see it as more suspect. After all, irony can just as easily legitimate as undermine relations of power.

Irony's Edge provocatively builds upon all the major existing theories of irony, providing the most comprehensive and critically challenging theory of irony to date.

Linda Hutcheon is Professor of English and Comparative Literature at the University of Toronto. She is the author of a number of related books including *The Politics of Postmodernism* (1989); *A Poetics of Postmodernism: History, Theory, Fiction* (1988); *A Theory of Parody: The Teachings of Twentieth-Century Art Forms* (1985); and *Narcissistic Narrative: The Metafictional Paradox* (1984).

IRONY'S EDGE

The theory and politics of irony

Linda Hutcheon

London and New York

First published 1994
by Routledge
2 Park Square, Milton Park, Abingdon, Oxon, OX14 4RN

Transferred to Digital Printing 2005

Simultaneously published in the USA and Canada
by Routledge
270 Madison Ave, New York NY 10016

© 1995 Linda Hutcheon

Typeset in Baskerville by Solidus (Bristol) Limited

British Library Cataloguing in Publication Data
A catalogue record for this book is available from the British Library

Library of Congress Cataloging in Publication Data
A catalogue record for this book has been requested

ISBN 0–415–05452–4 (hbk)
ISBN 0–415–05453–2 (pbk)

Printed and bound in Great Britain by
Antony Rowe Ltd, Chippenham and Eastbourne

CONTENTS

ILLUSTRATIONS

ACKNOWLEDGEMENTS

This book is dedicated to the members of WIPE (Work in Progress in English), a group of both junior and senior colleagues at the University of Toronto who read much of this manuscript over the last few years. Their helpful suggestions, devastating criticisms, and general enthusiasm and support were all equally important in making this study possible in this form.

In a field where there is so much fine work, it is hard to know where to start to pay one's intellectual debts. While the works of many critics have been crucial to my thinking (and the references to them in the text bear witness to their number and impact), a few names stand out: Wayne Booth, Ross Chambers, Joseph Dane, Peter Hagen, D.C. Muecke, Allan J. Ryan, Alan Wilde, and Hayden White. Some of these have generously and critically read parts of this work, but my debt to all is a more general and deep one. To Sharon Butler and Alain Goldschläger, the first people with whom I ever thought through some of irony's problems, go thanks for stimulating me to start on this topic over a decade ago; gratitude for helping me work through some of the thornier issues goes to the students and faculty in my 1988–89 irony seminar at York University and in the 1990 International Summer Institute for Structural and Semiotic Studies course, and to the graduate students in the 1989–90 and 1993–94 graduate seminars at the University of Toronto's Centre for Comparative Literature. To the university departments and conference organizers over the last few years who bravely let me try out some of these ideas on a live audience go my thanks for their indulgence and for making possible important interactions that often changed utterly the direction of my thinking. A special thanks goes to those colleagues and students at the University of Puerto Rico and University of Victoria, with whom I was fortunate enough to spend more extended periods of time. And, without the bibliographical and technical expertise of Christine Roulston, Russell Kilbourn, and Catherine Lundie, this book would literally, physically, never have been possible.

Many friends, students, and colleagues (besides the WIPErs) read parts of this book or provided examples or references that have been particularly helpful. I have endeavored to incorporate their criticisms and suggestions as much as possible. Warm thanks to Susan Bennett, Victor Burgin, Bill Callaghan, Mark Cheetham, David Clarkson, Melba Cuddy-Keane, Chandler Davis, Christopher Douglas, Heather Dubrow, Rebecca Duclos, Len Findley, Mark Fortier, Ken Frieden, Susan Gingell, Carol Greenhouse, Marjorie Halpin, Adrienne Hood, Anne Lancashire, Michael Levin, Jill Levinson, Beauvais Lyons, Katie Lynes, Tim McCracken, Eva Mackey, Robert Martin, Peter Narváez, Shirley Neuman, Kristin Roodenburg, Margeret Sinex, Joey Skaggs, Bob Wallace, Richard A. Watson – and to any of you I have inadvertently omitted. Full credit for any errors or infelicities of any kind in this text goes, of course, solely to me.

A special debt is owed to my husband, Michael Hutcheon, whose own "sense of irony" is likely the reason why I had to figure out how irony worked: theory as self-defense. But our collaborative research projects and common interests also provided the perfect "discursive community" in which to try out ideas and to explore possible attributions of irony.

At Routledge, I must thank Janice Price for her encouragement, her faith, and her friendship; Talia Rodgers for the enthusiasm, expertise, unfailing patience, and good humor that kept me and this book going; Tricia Dever for her generous assistance and efficiency; Bill Germano, for conversations about opera and books, as well as valuable advice.

In these times of economic recession that place increased pressures on universities and their teachers, it is the release time made possible by the generosity of funding organizations that makes research even possible for many of us. Because of this, my sincere gratitude is to the Connaught Foundation at the University of Toronto and the John Simon Guggenheim Memorial Foundation.

Very little of this book has appeared in print in any form: some of the general ideas and part of the discussion of the work of Anselm Kiefer appeared as the "E.J. Pratt Memorial Lecture" published by Memorial University of Newfoundland; an early version of what was to become, in a different form, section II of Chapter 2 appeared as "The Complex Functions of Irony" in *Revista Canadiense de Estudios Hispánicos*, vol. 16 no. 2 (1992): 219–34. A much longer and differently focused discussion of the "Into the Heart of Africa" museum exhibit featured in Chapter 7 was given as the "1993 Routledge Lecture" and appeared in *Textual Practice* (Spring 1994).

The ironist is a vampire who has sucked the blood out of her lover
and fanned him with coolness, lulled him to sleep and tormented him
with turbulent dreams.

Søren Kierkegaard, *The Concept of Irony*

L'espèce de gens à qui l'ironie est antipathique éclaire aussi sa nature.
Ce sont les femmes et le peuple. Le peuple ne comprend pas l'ironie; la
femme non plus. Le peuple voit sous l'ironie un orgueil de l'intelligence,
une insulte à Caliban. Quant à la femme, elle est peuple par son
incompréhension et par son mépris de l'intelligence. . . . La femme est
surtout une physiologie et une sensibilité, non un cerveau. L'ironie,
attitude de cérébral en qui s'affirme le primat de l'intelligence sur le
sentiment, lui est suspecte et antipathique. La femme est et reste un être
passionné dans sa chair et dans ses nerfs.

Georges Palante, "L'ironie: étude psychologique"

. . . women, children, and revolutionaries hate irony, which is
the negation of all saving instincts, of all faith, of all devotion,
of all actions.

Sophia Antonovna, in Joseph Conrad's *Under Western Eyes*

NOT!
Wayne's World

INTRODUCTION
The "scene" of irony

With 1445 entries listed under "irony" in the *MLA Bibliography* for only a single decade, why might the world need yet another book about irony? And that listing tells just part of the story – the literary part: this topic has been tackled by scholars in fields as diverse as linguistics and political science, sociology and history, aesthetics and religion, philosophy and rhetoric, psychology and anthropology. Irony has been located and explicated in literature, the visual arts, music, dance, theater, museum displays, conversation, philosophical argumentation, and the list could go on and on. Even granted that most of those 1445 entries are for articles about "irony in . . ." some text or artist's *oeuvre*, the sheer amount of energy expended in trying to figure out how and why people choose to express themselves in this bizarre way remains astonishing to me. There seems to be a fascination with irony – one that I obviously share – whether it be regarded as a rhetorical trope or as a way of seeing the world.

My own particular interest was triggered by the fact that irony appears to have become a problematic mode of expression at the end of the twentieth century. It has never been without its problems, of course, but lately the various media seem to be reporting an increasing number of cases of the more or less disastrous misfiring of ironies. Magazine articles appear, exploring the prevalence of irony (*Spy*'s March 1989 issue's cover featured Chevy Chase as "That Ironic Guy" and the heading, "Isn't it ironic?"). Or else they lament its rumored outmodedness (*Esquire*'s September 1991 front page told us to "Forget Irony – Have a Nice Decade!"). And, certainly, if the newspaper and television coverage can be believed, today the public consequences of misunderstanding seem more serious, or at least more visible. Therefore, it is this – its perceived politics – that has determined my particular "take" on irony and has provided the focus for my attempt to theorize irony's social as well as formal dimensions. My aim has been to build upon that vast corpus of work done by others (or rather, upon what part of it I could manage to read in the last decade), using a collaborative rather than oppositional model of scholarship. The result is that you will not find here any detailed refutation of any other theory (or theorist):

1

there are many other books and articles available which do this with both rigor and gusto. Instead, this study incorporates the work of others and builds upon it, focusing on the issues, not the personalities. It is heavily "referenced," in the sense that it provides many references (in parentheses) to that work upon which it has built, so that those who wish to explore in more detail the context of a particular argument can do so.

What this book tries to do – with a lot of help from a lot of others – is to figure out how and why irony comes about (or doesn't), with a particular interest in the consequences of interpreting a text (in any medium) as "ironic." Why should anyone want to use this strange mode of discourse where you say something you don't actually mean and expect people to understand not only what you actually do mean but also your attitude toward it? How do you decide if an utterance is ironic? In other words, what triggers you to decide that what you heard (or saw) is not meaningful alone, but requires supplementing with a different, inferred meaning (and judgment) that would then lead you to call it "irony"? Unlike metaphor or allegory, which demand similar supplementing of meaning, irony has an evaluative edge and manages to provoke emotional responses in those who "get" it and those who don't, as well as in its targets and in what some people call its "victims." This is where the politics of irony get heated. That affective dimension of irony's edge is the starting point of this study; it is also its (deliberate) limitation.

Given that vast amount of previous work on the general topic of irony, my choice has been to look at what might be called the "scene" of irony: that is, to treat it not as an isolated trope to be analyzed by formalist means but as a political issue, in the broadest sense of the word. The "scene" of irony involves relations of power based in relations of communication. It unavoidably involves touchy issues such as exclusion and inclusion, intervention and evasion. Because of training and temperament, no doubt, I have shied away from focusing on irony as a way to achieve any kind of "truth," freedom, or a host of other ineffables that have been claimed for it over the centuries. In other words, I don't think irony has been a terribly significant force in the evolution of civilization or anything grandiose like that. But it does seem to have been around for a long time, in Western culture at least, and it certainly has been the object of much attention.

Many have written of the shift over time from seeing irony as a limited classical rhetorical trope to treating it as a vision of life.[1] The focus of this study, therefore, will not be on Socratic irony[2] or romantic irony.[3] As you can see from the notes (p. 206), many others have treated these aspects already. Nor will this book focus on the plural heritage of that influential romantic view of irony as the perception and transcendence of the epistemological, ethical or experiential paradox of appearance vs. reality, a heritage to be found – through the mediation of such figures as Kierkegaard, Schopenhauer and Nietzsche – in such diverse places as Marxist

2

theory[4] and deconstructive aesthetics,[5] not to mention American New Criticism.[6] What appear to me the exaggerated claims made in the past and present for the power of romantic irony (in terms of freedom, pleasure, psychic health, intellectual stimulation, and so on) will be dealt with where relevant to the discussion of irony's politics, as will assertions regarding irony as the defining characteristic of modern culture or society,[7] art,[8] or criticism.[9]

In short, this study does not treat irony as a keystone of poetics, a paradigm of criticism, a mode of consciousness or existence that raises questions about the self and the nature of knowledge, a philosophical stance *vis-à-vis* the universe, an informing principle of personality, or a way of life.[10] Its aims and focus are much more modest: to try to understand how and why irony is used and understood as a discursive practice or strategy, and to begin to study the consequences of both its comprehension and its misfiring. My approach, therefore, will not be taxonomic: I have tried to "resist the list" as much as possible, but this is a field of research which has spawned what one critic accurately called a "cottage industry in taxonomy."[11] My concern here is simply with verbal and structural ironies, rather than situational irony, cosmic irony, the irony of fate, and so on. That is another reason why the philosophical focus that has been so important to discussions of irony from the romantic period through to the current neo-pragmatic "ironism" of Richard Rorty is not necessarily my own.

This study is also not organized along historical lines, partly because many fine historical studies already exist[12] and partly because, as you will see, the particular way I have chosen to think through the problems of irony demands that I work from the present, from my own act of interpreting – attributing – of irony and move outwards from there to try to understand how and why irony comes into being. While my examples are taken from my own recent experience, my hope is that the personal and the contemporary provide the ground for theorizing irony as a discursive strategy in such a way that it has meaning for others besides myself. What this book is not, however, is yet another book on postmodernism (see Hutcheon 1988a, 1988b, 1989). (In fact, if you look in the index you will find only this reference to that word.) Though current debates on that topic have provoked renewed interest (including my own) in irony, the problems encountered in trying to discern the functioning and politics of irony go back much further. To limit an analysis of irony to one cultural enterprise would be unnecessarily restrictive – and, as I've learned, an utter red herring.

In *A Theory of Parody* (1985), I tried to think about parody "outward" from texts, trying to learn from the example and teaching of a variety of twentieth-century art forms. As the title of this book hopes to suggest, this is both a continuation and a revision of that earlier work. I never felt that I had figured out, even to my own satisfaction, how irony worked in parody, partly because my earlier modeling of their interrelations at that time was in terms of microcosm to macrocosm: irony seemed to me to be structured as a miniature (semantic) version of parody's (textual) doubling. Here, I have tried to work through how and why irony's edge gives parody its "critical" dimension in its marking of difference at the heart of similarity. But my interest here is not in parody alone but in all or any uses or attributions of irony, especially those that have caused problems either through their misunderstanding or their understanding. And, despite those frequent denials of the possibility of theorizing irony,[13] I join the others who have rushed in, for not everyone has feared to tread into this potential quagmire.

Irony's Edge: The Theory and Politics of Irony, like its predecessor, then, "theorizes" from examples, or more accurately from the interpretation of examples. It is irony *in use*, in discourse, that is its primary concern: the "scene" of irony is a social and political scene. While formal issues will be investigated, it is their functioning in context(s) that is my main interest. Therefore, there are inevitable continuities with the semiotic methodology of *A Theory of Parody*, but as supplemented by a conjunction of theoretical perspectives united by "family resemblances": Bakhtinian dialogism, social semiotics, speech-act theory, Burkian dramatism, enunciation theory, pragmatic as well as syntactic and semantic analysis, and a range of poststructuralist and feminist insights. In addition to "resisting the list," I have tried, as much as possible, to resist both neologisms (on the grounds that the long history of writing about irony should provide us with more than enough useful terminology) and those complex semi-mathematical or logical formulae that some theorists favor as ways to explain how irony works. What I have done, however, is separate the inseparable: I have artificially isolated, for purposes of discussion, a series of elements that, in practice, work together to make irony happen: its critical edge; its semantic complexity; the "discursive communities" that, I will argue, make irony possible; the role of intention and attribution of irony; its contextual framing and markers. This order was arrived at by starting with what seemed to distinguish irony most from other discursive practices (its "edge") and moving through the major elements that stand out for me as important to think through on a theoretical level, while being aware always that "[n]aming the parts does not show us what makes the gun go off" (Mahood 1979: 19). My focus is always on how irony comes into existence (or does not) for me as an interpreter: your response to the examples is no doubt going to differ – sometimes more and sometimes less – and for a complex of reasons that this study also seeks to address.

Chapters 1 and 2, because of their introductory function and broader focus, offer a series of relatively brief examples, but Chapters 3 through 6 are divided into an initial theoretical discussion and a subsequent detailed textual analysis. Chapter 7 uses the public controversy over the interpretation of a particular cultural text (a museum exhibition) as a way both to summarize and to problematize the various points raised in the study as a whole. A warning: not very many of these ironies are particularly "funny" ones. One of the misconceptions that theorists of irony always have to contend with is the conflation of irony and humor. I should also mention that the examples discussed in detail or in brief come from a range of media – music, fiction, academic discourse, film, opera and popular music performances, visual art, museum exhibits. This choice represents my recognition of the fact that irony "happens" (and that's the verb I think best describes the process) in all kinds of discourses (verbal, visual, aural), in common speech as well as in highly crafted aesthetic form, in so-called high art as well as in popular culture. Therefore when it comes to the politics of irony today, the scope of possible examples is going to be enormous and daunting. I have sometimes chosen ironies with public and discernible consequences to supplement my own response and interpretation. Hence, the emphasis on performances, because of the overtly public and social nature of their reception. While any description of a performance is already an interpretation (Alter 1990: 132), of course, the point of the analyses of my own attributing of irony will be precisely that act of interpretation.

In a study of the discursive politics of irony written in the 1990s, you might well expect to find a concentration of examples of irony focused on issues of gender, race, class, or sexuality. While the first chapter does indeed deal with such ironies and the theories that have developed around them and the last chapter directly engages the postcolonial context in which irony might be deployed, the extended *analyses* in Chapters 3 to 6 deliberately do not focus on these issues, although the *theory* always does. The reasons for this decision are multiple, though not the least of them is my desperate need to put some (albeit artificial) limit on the possible examples, if not on the theory. As the next chapter will explore, feminist and gay and lesbian criticism has taught us much about the textual complexities of the gender and sexual politics involved in studying discursive strategies in specific texts by both men and women; and postcolonial analyses have explored at great length the textual specificities and particularities of the colonial and postcolonial conditions. Therefore, it would be almost impossible to do justice to any of these specific complexities and their political intricacies in a book that offers a gener-alized theory of irony. But, another perhaps even more compelling reason for this limitation in the examples (though, once again, not in the theory) is the fact that many fine analyses of precisely this particular political dimension of feminist, gay, lesbian, or postcolonial irony in specific texts exist already and, indeed, have informed much of my own thinking on this topic.

In order to cast a different historicizing light on these sorts of issues, then, I have selected instead, for a number of my examples, contemporary

5

texts that invoke a history that is more or less familiar to most of you reading this book: World War II and the context of Nazi Germany. It is this very familiarity that enables certain cultural texts (performances, paintings, photographs, music compositions, literature, as well as critical discourses[14]), to call upon public memories of National Socialism's history in order to provide a shared discursive context for many in Europe and North America even today. And it is the still potent emotional force unleashed by those memories that makes irony's edge so tempting for both ironists and interpreters. Whether irony is appropriate or not when dealing with such material is one of the questions these analyses explore.

The music dramas of Richard Wagner are a recurring point of reference in this book for both personal and political reasons. I have spent much of the last five years studying Wagner's work – for another research project as well as out of that kind of passionate curiosity that often follows upon previous adamant rejection. Therefore, it was available, so to speak, in my mind as a possible source of examples. But there are other reasons for considering it as well. No one would deny the impact of the man who, as poet, librettist, composer, conductor, director, producer and "master of the revels" (Lindenberger 1984: 276), changed the face of music in the nineteenth century, offered aesthetic analogues for writers as diverse as Joyce and Mallarmé, Swinburne and Mann, Wilde and Proust, Baudelaire and Zola, and for painters from Fantin-Latour to Cézanne to Dali. But against all that has to be weighed Wagner's influence on one of the most influential men of the twentieth century, an influence Wagner has never been able to live down: that upon Adolf Hitler. It is impossible to listen to or see Wagner's music-dramas today outside of the context of the Nazi appropriation of their Teutonic mythology and their composer's own anti-semitic views. The fact that Wagner died well before Hitler used his work for his own purposes is not the point here: the point is that the context in which I hear or see Wagner's music today has to include Hitler, and that is a fact with which I (and perhaps you too) must deal. Likewise, when a contemporary text invokes Wagner, such is once again the political context in which I inevitably interpret that work and its possible ironies. Or when a production of a Wagnerian opera invokes Hitler or the Nazis, this is the broader historical context of reception in which I experience the work.

It has been said (Suleiman 1976) that there are books about irony (e.g. Muecke 1969) and books about interpretation (e.g. Booth 1974), but for me the two cannot be separated: irony isn't irony until it is interpreted as such – at least by the intending ironist, if not the intended receiver. Someone attributes irony; someone makes irony happen. For the examples offered here, that "someone" is me, but *your* reading is likely to be quite different, either in its general decision about the attribution of irony or in its specific sense of where and how the irony comes into play. While it might well be argued that this is so for any interpretation offered of any text, I think it is even more the case for irony. Part of the purpose of this study is to examine why this might be true.

Among the other difficulties faced in writing about irony is the decision about *how* to do so. Critics agree that the analysis of irony is usually complex and laborious (Pronger 1990: 107), while the practice of it appears deft and graceful. It's not unlike the difference between a joke and explaining a joke: irony "cancels itself out the moment it adds a word of interpretation" (Adorno 1974: 210). I hasten to add: this is a book *about* irony, and not an ironic book. I have taken to (ironic) heart the injunction of the "Teachers for a Democratic Culture" in their "Regulations for Literary Criticism in the 1990s," intended to restore public confidence and sidestep further press attacks on the profession. Regulation VII is "*No irony*":

> The lesson is clear. Employing irony, speaking tongue in cheek, talking wryly or self-mockingly – these smartass intellectual practices give our whole profession a bad name. If there's one thing calculated to alienate an otherwise friendly and helpful press, it's irony. As Dan Quayle once put it, irony is an ill wind that bites the hand that feeds our fashionable cynicism.
>
> We cannot mince words about irony. Knock it off, and knock it off now. In the first place, nobody understands your little ironies but you and your theorymongering friends. In the second place, even if someone *does* understand your ironies, they still won't translate into newsprint and you'll wind up looking foolish anyway. In the third place, great literature demands of us a high seriousness of purpose – not disrespectful laughter and clowning around. So just wipe that smirk off your face.
>
> (Bérubé and Graff 1993: 3)

Nevertheless, some commentators (in the past, of course) have written about irony in a deliberately and polemically unsystematic and ironized way.[15] Because of both personality and what the French would call my own "déformation professionnelle," I admit that, even without Regulation VII, I'm not terribly comfortable with that mode of writing, and so I have chosen a more systematic approach, while acknowledging throughout the artificial and even, to some extent, arbitrary separation of aspects which, in actual fact, work together simultaneously to make irony "happen."

There are perhaps even more personal reasons for choosing to tackle this topic that so many others have already addressed. There is a long history of argument[16] that the key to the Canadian identity is irony, that a people used to dealing with national, regional, ethnic and linguistic multiplicities, tensions, and divisions have no alternative. Since I live and work in a city that Wyndham Lewis, in the 1940s, called a "sanctimonious icebox" and in a country Fredric Jameson defines as "the semi-periphery of the American core" (in Stephanson 1987: 46), perhaps irony *does* have an attraction for

7

me. But as the epigraphs to the book suggest, there is also a curious gendering in the discourses about irony and its politics. When irony is seen as something debilitating, it is figured as a vampire – a feminine vampire (Kierkegaard); when it is considered the mark of the intellect, woman is denied access and understanding (Palante); when its negativity is deemed counter to instinct, faith, devotion and action, women join children and revolutionaries in hating it (Conrad).

I offer, as an initial and partial response to these engenderings, that irony-marker (recently developed by a Canadian actor) for a world that seems to be growing deaf to the unsaid, if not to its power:

"Not!"

1

RISKY BUSINESS
The "transideological" politics of irony

There is no correct understanding of the word irony, no historically
valid reading of irony . . .
Joseph Dane, *The Critical Mythology of Irony*

The word "irony" does not now mean only what it meant in earlier
centuries, it does not mean in one country all it may mean in another,
nor in the street what it may mean in the study, nor to one scholar what
it may mean to another.
D.C. Muecke, *Irony and the Ironic*

I begin with these daunting assertions as a kind of warning, to myself as
much as to you. I am obviously neither the first nor the last to show an
interest in irony, the mode of the unsaid, the unheard, the unseen: in
Western cultures it has always fascinated theorists, critics, and artists alike.
Its history has been rehearsed often, as I suggested in the introduction, and
there is surprisingly little disagreement as to its basic definition (see
Karstetter 1964: 162–70; N. Knox 1973), both in classical rhetoric and in
subsequent literary and philosophical extensions of the term (see Dane
1991; Schoentjes 1993). Irony has certainly been called the "child of Janus,
god of beginnings, and without doubt the most ill-behaved of all literary
tropes" (States 1971: 3). Nevertheless, ours joins just about every other
century in wanting to call itself the "age of irony," and the recurrence of
that historical claim in itself might well support the contention of
contemporary theorists from Jacques Derrida to Kenneth Burke that irony
is inherent in signification, in its deferrals and in its negations.

Yet most people feel there is something faintly (or even strongly) suspect
about irony, at least as *others* use it. Is that because verbal irony is "language
giving the lie to itself yet still relishing its power" (Hartman 1981: 146)? The
suspicion of deceit that accompanies indirection, especially when
combined with the idea of power, understandably makes for a certain
unease. That irony can be used as a weapon has always been known: the
social put-down and the satiric barb have their corollary even in the critics'
wielding of authority over texts (and especially over previous imperceptive

9

readers) through their attribution of irony (Dane 1991: 6, 156–7; Booth 1970: 329). Perhaps it is what I want to call the "edge" that irony possesses in its verbal and structural forms that makes the stakes higher here than, say, in the use of metonymy. Even situational irony (and, with it, things like the irony of fate, cosmic irony, and so on) would not seem to provoke quite the same worries (cf. Glicksberg 1969), but verbal and structural ironies seem to be either deplored or prized, depending on how and in whose interest they are seen to operate. This too makes people uneasy, for if "[i]rony's guns face in every direction" (D.J. Enright 1986: 110), then anyone might come under fire. It is almost as though, in ethical terms, irony were inscrutable (Tittler 1984: 20). But it might not hurt to recall that no epistemological (Kenshur 1988: 347) or ideological (Hirst 1976: 396–7) position is ever *intrinsically* either right or wrong, either dangerous or safe, either reactionary or progressive. And the ironic stance is no exception.

There is nothing *intrinsically* subversive about ironic skepticism or about any such self-questioning, "internally dialogized" mode (LaCapra 1985: 119); there is no *necessary* relationship between irony and radical politics or even radical formal innovation (Nichols 1981: 65). Irony has often been used to reinforce rather than to question established attitudes (cf. Moser 1984: 414), as the history of satire illustrates so well. And this, the "transideological" (White 1973: 38) nature of irony, is the focus of this book: irony can and does function tactically in the service of a wide range of political positions, legitimating or undercutting a wide variety of interests. It is this focus that has determined what, in the Introduction, I called the "scene" of irony in this particular study.

Ever since irony as a word and concept came to the attention of ancient Greek culture, there have been arguments about how irony works and what its scope is or could be. Does "irony" refer to a word with implied different meaning or is it an entire manner of speaking? In other words, is it a trope or a figure? Could it be both? (See Quintilian 1977: 9.2.45–6.) My particular interest in the transideological politics of irony is what suggested to me the need for an approach to irony that would treat it not as a limited rhetorical trope or as an extended attitude to life, but as a discursive strategy operating at the level of language (verbal) or form (musical, visual, textual). This choice of *discourse* as the scope and site of discussion is also intended to ensure a consideration of the social and interactive dimensions of irony's functioning, whether the situation be a conversation or the reading of a novel (Krysinski 1985: 1; Warning 1982: 256).

But who are the participants in this social act called "irony"? The party line says that there is an intending "ironist" and her/his intended audiences – the one that "gets" and the one that doesn't "get" the irony. What do you do, then, with the obvious fact that ironies exist that are not intended, but are most certainly interpreted as such? Similarly, there are ironies you might intend, as ironist, but which remain unperceived by others. Irony's indirection complicates considerably the various existing models of intersubjective communication between a speaker and a hearer (see Hernadi 1988: 749; Adams 1985: 1). With irony, there are, instead, dynamic and plural relations among the text or utterance (and its context), the so-called ironist, the interpreter, and the circumstances surrounding the discursive situation; it is these that mess up neat theories of irony that see the task of the interpreter simply as one of decoding or reconstructing some "real" meaning (usually named as the "ironic" one) (Booth 1974; Karstetter 1964), a meaning that is hidden, but deemed accessible, behind the stated one. If this were actually the case, irony's politics would be much less contentious, I suspect.

The major players in the ironic game are indeed the interpreter and the ironist. The interpreter may – or may not – be the intended addressee of the ironist's utterance, but s/he (by definition) is the one who attributes irony and then interprets it: in other words, the one who decides whether the utterance is ironic (or not), and then what *particular* ironic meaning it might have. This process occurs regardless of the intentions of the ironist (and makes me wonder who really should be designated as the "ironist"). This is why irony is "risky business" (Fish 1983: 176): there is no guarantee that the interpreter will "get" the irony in the same way as it was intended. In fact, "get" may be an inaccurate and even inappropriate verb: "make" would be much more precise. As I will argue in Chapter 5, this productive, active process of attribution and interpretation itself involves an intentional act, one of inference.

The person usually called the "ironist," though, is the one who intends to set up an ironic relation between the said and the unsaid, but may not always succeed in communicating that intention (or the relation). The complex reasons why this might occur form one of the subjects of this book. Irony, then, will mean different things to the different players. From the point of view of the *interpreter,* irony is an interpretive and intentional move: it is the making or inferring of **meaning** in addition to and different from what is stated, together with an **attitude** toward both the said and the unsaid. The move is usually triggered (and then directed) by conflictual textual or contextual evidence or by markers which are socially agreed upon. However, from the point of view of what I too (with reservations) will call the *ironist,* irony is the intentional transmission of both information and evaluative attitude other than what is explicitly presented.

It is not without nervousness and self-consciousness that I raise issues of intentionality in a post-Derridean, post-Barthesian, and post-Foucaultian age. But in the study of irony's edge, it seems to me to be unavoidable. After all, the touchy political issues that arise around irony's usage and interpretation invariably focus on the issue of intention (of either ironist or interpreter). And it is because of its very foregrounding of the politics of human agency in this way that irony has become an important strategy of

11

oppositional rhetoric. Much previous theorizing of irony's functioning has been done, explicitly or implicitly, primarily from the point of view of the ironist (Muecke 1969 and 1970/1982; Booth 1974; Hirsch 1971: 1193). When irony is considered as a speech act, it is once again the role of the intending speaker that tends to ground analysis (Grice 1975; Amante 1981; Groeben and Scheele 1984; Bach and Harnish 1979). And yet, both intention and agency are involved in the activity of the interpreter as well. One of the significations of the verb "to mean" is "to intend" (Wilson 1992: 165), but *interpreters* "mean" as much as *ironists* do, and often in opposition to them: to attribute irony where it is intended – and where it is not – or to refuse to attribute irony where it might be intended is also the act of a conscious agent. This agent is engaged in a complicated interpretive process (Hagen 1992: 11, 20) that involves not only the making of meaning but the construction of a sense of the evaluative attitude displayed by the text toward what is said and what is not said. The interpreter's job, therefore, cannot simply be one of somehow "rightly comprehending" (Furst 1984: 14) the ironist's intention or the text's signals. Whether irony is "present" in a text or "found" there (Steig 1989: 21) is another question this study explicitly addresses.

The interpreter as agent performs an act – attributes both meanings and motives – and does so in a particular situation and context, for a particular purpose, and with particular means. Attributing irony involves, then, both semantic *and* evaluative inferences. Irony's appraising edge is never absent and, indeed, is what makes irony work differently from other forms which it might structurally seem to resemble (metaphor, allegory, puns). As the second part of Chapter 2 explores, this is the case whether its tone be gently teasing or devastatingly harsh, whether its inferred motive be benign playfulness or corrosive critique. The semantic dimension of irony is difficult to treat in isolation, without keeping not only "one eye on the receiver, but the other on the surrounding tension-filled environments" (Collins 1989: 79). From the point of view of its discursive politics, the one thing irony would *not* seem to be is what it is usually claimed to be: a simple antiphrastic substitution of the unsaid (called the "ironic" meaning) for its opposite, the said (called the "literal" meaning) – which is then either "set aside" (Fish 1983: 189; Searle 1979b) or sometimes only "partially effaced" (Tittler 1984: 21). Once again, I think the political problems of irony would be relatively straightforward if this were in fact the case.

The third chapter will argue in detail that irony "happens" – and that is the verb I think best describes the process. It happens in the space *between* (and including) the said and the unsaid; it needs both to happen. What I want to call the "ironic" meaning is inclusive and relational: the said and the unsaid coexist for the interpreter, and each has meaning in relation to the other because they literally "interact" (Burke 1969a: 512) to create the real "ironic" meaning. The "ironic" meaning is not, then, simply the unsaid

12

meaning, and the unsaid is not always a simple inversion or opposite of the said (Amante 1981: 81; Eco 1990: 210): it is always different – *other than* and more than the said. This is why irony cannot be trusted (Kenner 1986: 1152): it undermines stated meaning by removing the semantic security of "one signifier : one signified" and by revealing the complex inclusive, relational and differential nature of ironic meaning-making. If you will pardon the inelegant terms, irony can only "complexify"; it can never "disambiguate," and the frustration this elicits is among the many reasons why it is difficult to treat the semantics of irony separately from its syntactics or pragmatics (Plett 1982: 76), its circumstances (textual and contextual) or its conditions of use and reception.

The story – of both chapter and book – thus far, then: the attributing of irony to a text or utterance is a complex intentional act on the part of the interpreter, one that has both semantic and evaluative dimensions, in addition to the possible inferring of ironist intent (from either the text or statements by the ironist). This study argues that irony happens as part of a communicative process; it is not a static rhetorical tool to be deployed, but itself comes into being in the relations between meanings, but also between people and utterances and, sometimes, between intentions and interpretations. Like me, you will be able to provide many personal examples of the complexity of this process and the possible consequences of that complexity, examples from your daily lives that vary from misfired quips to serious puzzlement over, say, an art exhibit you visit. I recall seeing the large-scale, parodic paintings of Attila Richard Lukacs for the first time and, despite having read about his work (Dompierre 1989), I truly didn't know how to "read" the gay artist's large, irreverent tableaux that figure more or less naked skinheads within visual contexts borrowed from both Nazi iconography and the history of art. I knew that the resulting clash of cultures and associations was almost invariably seen as ironic by reviewers, but I didn't know how to go about interpreting the specific meaning of these ironies. For one thing, the cultural connotations of skinheads were plural and even contradictory for me – and possibly for you too. Do you think of racist violence and white supremacism? I did, especially in a contemporary German context – and, though Canadian, Lukacs lives and works in Berlin. Or are your associations more with the rebellion born of the hopelessness of economic deprivation? As one critic put it: "are they neo-nazis, proletarian heroes, gay-bashers or available homosexuals?" (R. Enright 1992: 14). Lukacs may insist on his intention to be critical: "I know my work deals with elements of fascism but I think if anyone with a two-bit mind looks at the work, he would see that it's more of a comment against it" (in R. Enright 1992: 25). Fascism, he says, is associated with violence, power and evil; it is out there and has to be dealt with. And so it is. But *how* the resulting work is interpreted by viewers like me is not totally within the artist's control, whatever his intentions. Where one viewer saw "criticality and radicalism" (Dompierre 1989: 11) in his work, another saw it as "part fetish arena, part history painting" (R. Enright 1992: 14).

I should have thought that I was primed, in a way, to make irony happen in Lukacs's work by the similarities between his strategies (of size and choice of gay-coded intertexts) and those of other artists, such as photographers Yasumasa Morimura and Evergon, who also recall the history of art in their work and, through ironic alterations, recode its gendered representations in gay male terms. And, after all, the relation between irony and "gay sensibility" has been argued frequently (see Sontag 1982: 105–19; Pronger 1990: 104), though today some see the irony of camp as "cheap," as more "an excuse not to grow up" than any form of protest (Headlam 1993/1994: 88). It was the juxtaposition of the formal echoing of previous art (some of it, like that of Caravaggio, with clear homosexual connotations) with the neo-Nazi associations of the subject matter that proved intractable for me, however. What might indeed have been intended as ironic critique remained for me merely ambiguous and unsettling, though none the less powerful for that.

When the political dimensions are as overt as they are in Lukacs's even more recent homoerotic work which echoes the visual style of National Socialist "worker" art, the potential problems that collect around attributing and intending irony are pretty evident, even if they are also complex. But I think there are *always* going to be potential problems with *any* use of irony: "between the intended irony that goes unperceived and the unintended that becomes irony by being perceived, there is room for many kinds and degrees of misunderstanding, misfire, and fizzle, as well as of understanding and complicity" (Chambers 1990: 19). With irony, you move out of the realm of the true and false and into the realm of the felicitous and infelicitous – in ways that go well beyond what is suggested by the use of these terms in speech-act theory (Austin 1975; Felman 1983; Pratt 1977). Irony removes the security that words mean only what they say. So too does lying, of course, and that is why the ethical as well as the political are never far beneath the surface in discussions of the use of and responses to irony. It has even been called a kind of "intellectual tear-gas that breaks the nerves and paralyzes the muscles of everyone in its vicinity, an acid that will corrode healthy as well as decayed tissues" (Northrop Frye, cited in Ayre 1989: 183). Irony obviously makes people uneasy. It is said to disavow (Kaufer 1981a: 25) and to devalorize (Ramazani 1988: 12), usually because it distances.

In fact, perhaps the most oft-repeated remark about irony – made both by those who approve and by those who disapprove of it – is about its emotional ethics, so to speak. They say that it is a mode of intellectual detachment (Schoentjes 1993: 153–86), that "irony engages the intellect rather than the emotions" (Walker 1990: 24). But the degrees of unease irony provokes might suggest quite the opposite. Irony is said to irritate

14

"because it denies us our certainties by unmasking the world as an ambiguity" (Kundera 1986: 134). But it can also mock, attack, and ridicule; it can exclude, embarrass and humiliate. That too may irritate, and not at a terribly intellectual level either. Yet, irony has consistently been seen as a favored trope of the intellectual and, therefore, a commentator on Irish nationalism can assert that "it is hard to summon much of it [irony] when you have been blinded by a British army rubber bullet," and ask: "How is such irony not simply to defuse our anger?" (Eagleton 1988: 8). But the very long history of irony's deployment in satire and invective might suggest the possibility, less of a *defusing*, than of an *engaging* of precisely that anger. Irony always has an edge; it sometimes has a "sting" (Gutwirth 1993: 144). In other words, this study argues that there is an affective "charge" to irony that cannot be ignored and that cannot be separated from its politics of use if it is to account for the range of emotional response (from anger to delight) and the various degrees of motivation and proximity (from distanced detachment to passionate engagement). Sometimes irony can indeed be interpreted as a withdrawal of affect; sometimes, however, there is a deliberate engaging of emotion. As the final chapter will show, any use of irony or, for that matter, any discussion of the politics of irony that ignores either irony's edge or this wide and complex range of affective possibilities does so at its peril.

Unlike synecdoche, say, irony always has a "target"; it sometimes also has what some want to call a "victim." As the connotations of those two terms imply, irony's edge is often a cutting one. Those who might not attribute irony where it was intended (or where others did) risk exclusion and embarrassment. In other words, even the simplest social dimensions of irony frequently involve an affective component. And, of course, irony might be deemed appropriate only for certain topics or certain audiences; it might not be accepted as fit for use in a particular place or at a particular time. Again, as the final chapter's examination of a contentious museum exhibition will illustrate, any such violation of (even unspoken) conventions can also result in strong reactions with serious consequences. And yet, there are many situations in which it might actually be prudent and tactful to use indirect forms of address like irony (Holdcroft 1976: 147), just as there are others in which they would be provocative and transgressive.

Needless to say, irony can be provocative when its politics are conservative or authoritarian as easily as when its politics are oppositional and subversive: it depends on who is using/attributing it and at whose expense it is seen to be. Such is the transideological nature of irony. Since this is the focus of the entire study, a few examples and an overview of the different ways in which irony can be considered transideological in its politics are in order. My operating premise here is that nothing is ever guaranteed at the politicized scene of irony. Even if an ironist intends an irony to be interpreted in an oppositional framework, there is no guarantee that this

15

subversive intent will be realized. In a totalitarian regime (or simply in a repressive discursive context), to use or attribute irony in order to undermine-from-within is relatively straightforward, if dangerous (Benton 1988; Dines-Levy and Smith 1988: 245): the rules or norms are known and adhered to in the letter, though not in the spirit, of the ironizing utterance. The dangers only materialize if the authorities also attribute irony and the protective cover of indirection is blown. In a more democratic situation, where different positions or "truths" theoretically coexist and are valued, irony is actually even riskier – though less materially dangerous. Those whom you oppose might attribute no irony and simply take you at your word; or they might make irony happen and thus accuse you of being self-negating, if not self-contradicting. Those with whom you agree (and who know your position) might also attribute no irony and mistake you for advocating what you are in fact criticizing. They may simply see you as a hypocrite or as compromised by your complicity with a discourse and values they thought you opposed. They might also, of course, attribute irony and interpret it precisely as you intended it to be.

Risks like these, though, are part of the double bind of democratic discourse. In other words, it is not simply repressive governments or "established authority and those who feel a need for its blessing" who might suspect or have cause to suspect irony (Muecke 1969: 246). Fredric Jameson has interpreted what he refers to as Paul de Man's early and "notorious 'anti-semitic'" article, "Les Juifs dans la littérature actuelle" as "the ingenious effort at resistance of a young man altogether too smart for his own good" (1991: 258) – that is, as simultaneously self-protective and resistant irony that was so "disastrously misunderstood and misread" that de Man spent the rest of his career articulating and teaching the "rigors of deconstructive reading" in order to form readers "capable at least of resisting this kind of elementary interpretive blunder" (ibid.: 258).

But it isn't only in contentious examples like de Man's wartime journalism that the political risks of irony are made evident: "Politically speaking, the ironist is extremely hard to assail precisely because it is virtually impossible to fix her or his text convincingly. In the ironic discourse, every position undercuts itself, thus leaving the politically engaged writer in a position where her ironic discourse might just come to deconstruct her own politics" (Moi 1985: 40). Why, then, bother using irony? The usual response given is that, despite the risks, the indirection and critical edge of irony still make it a "possible model for oppositionality whenever one is implicated in a system that one finds oppressive" (Chambers 1990: 18). A possible model, yes; but never an unproblematic one. The transideological politics of irony at once force a distinction between irony that might function constructively to articulate a new oppositional position, and irony that would work in a more negative and negativizing way. In the latter case, according to this argument (Chambers

16

1990), it would be the *product* of that system that would be negatively ironized, from a point of view exterior to the system. The ironist would stand outside, in a position of power (or at least masking any vulnerability). By contrast, the more constructive or "appropriative" function of irony would target the *system* itself, of which the ironist was also a part. It would endeavor "to use that system, with all the play the system allows, to produce different ends, that is, to change the products of the system" – even if the changes can only be "local and sporadic" (Chambers 1990: 21).

However you might choose to talk about the difference between irony that is seen to exclude and finalize and irony that is seen to relate and relativize, the politics of irony are never simple and never single. Unlike most other discursive strategies, irony *explicitly* sets up (and exists within) a relationship between ironist and audiences (the one being intentionally addressed, the one that actually makes the irony happen, and the one being excluded) that is political in nature, in the sense that "[e]ven while provoking laughter, irony invokes notions of hierarchy and subordination, judgment and perhaps even moral superiority" (Chamberlain 1989: 98). More is at stake here, in other words, than may be the case with other discursive strategies, and that "more" has a lot to do with power. This is why the language used to talk about irony – here, as elsewhere – is so often the language of risk: irony is "dangerous" and "tricky" (Lejeune 1989: 64) – for ironist, interpreter, and target alike.

Because irony, as defined in this study, happens in something called "discourse," its semantic and syntactic dimensions cannot be considered separately from the social, historical and cultural aspects of its contexts of deployment and attribution. Issues of authority and power are encoded in that notion of "discourse" today in much the same way that, in earlier times, they were encoded in the word "rhetoric" (Burke 1969b: 50). To discuss irony as a speech act but outside of this broader political frame is to risk idealizing communication as a reciprocal, utopic exchange and thus minimizing the workings of power by downplaying something crucial to irony's complexity: the fact that agents do not characteristically engage in speech acts "from positions of equal advantage or conduct their transactions on an equal footing" (B.H. Smith 1988: 111). Communicative exchange (or discursive activity) is a form of social activity (Godzich 1986: xxi; Stewart 1978/79: 13; Halliday 1978: 10), and it therefore involves relations of not only real but also symbolic power, not to mention relations of force, as well (Bourdieu and Passeron 1970: 116; Hodge and Kress 1988: 4).

Whether you see the power of irony working to exclude and to put down or, instead, to create "amiable communities" (Booth 1974: 28) between ironists and their intended audiences, the social nature of the participation in the transaction called "irony" should not be ignored. From the point of view of the intending ironist, it is said that irony creates hierarchies: those who use it, then those who "get" it and, at the bottom, those who do not. But from the perspective of the interpreter, the power relations might look quite different. It is not so much that irony *creates* communities or in-groups; instead, I want to argue that irony happens because what could be called "discursive communities" already exist and provide the context for both the deployment and attribution of irony. We all belong simultaneously to many such communities of discourse, and each of these has its own restrictive (Hagen 1992: 155) but also *enabling* communication conventions. To pick a few relatively innocuous examples: the jokes shared by those who are parents are often lost on people like myself who do not have children, and a lot of British political satire is baffling to me as a Canadian. This is not a matter of in-group elitism; it is merely a matter of different experiential and discursive contexts. In a way, if you understand that irony can exist (that saying one thing and meaning something else is not necessarily a lie) and if you understand how it works, you already belong to one community: the one based on the knowledge of the possibility and nature of irony. It is less that irony creates communities, then, than discursive communities make irony possible in the first place. As later chapters will explore in detail, the more the shared context, the fewer and the less obvious the markers needed to signal – or attribute – irony.

The multiple discursive communities to which we each (differently) belong cannot be reduced to any single component, such as class or gender. They certainly involve openly held beliefs, but also ideologies, unspoken understandings, "assumptions – about what is possible, necessary, telling, essential, and so on – so deeply held that they are not thought of as assumptions at all" (Fish 1983: 190). Of course, things like class, race, ethnicity, gender, and sexual preference are involved, but so too are nationality, neighborhood, profession, religion, and all the other micro-political complexities of our lives to which we may not even be able to give labels. The relational and dynamic model of overlapping discursive communities that will be suggested in Chapter 4 is offered as a different way to address what is usually called interpreter "competence" – a term which has, for me, uncomfortable connotations which bespeak the exclusion (as this book's epigraph by Palante shows) of those who cannot see through to the "depths" (Chambers 1991: 53) of intended meaning or climb to the "heights" of superior knowledge (Booth 1974: 44). If, as psychologists (Winner 1988) assert, irony is learned at a young age, then how do you explain the fact that young students, who "speak the language of irony all the time" (Chamberlain 1989: 102) and who see it in popular culture, fail to attribute and interpret it in literary texts studied in the classroom? One way is to argue that it is, at least in part, a matter of different discursive communities, and not a question of competence in the understanding of irony itself.

As is often the case, I can better explain this with an example: take the various possible ways of interpreting that much cited moment in Francis Ford Coppola's film, *Apocalypse Now* (1979) when a military helicopter flight in Vietnam is accompanied by the music from Wagner's music drama, *Die Walküre* (1870) known as the "Ride of the Valkyries." Whether or not you know the precise source of the music or its particular context within the opera, you may well have heard it before, either "straight" or in one of the many parodic, mass-media versions of it that have made it into a kind of aural cliché today. Hearing its rhythmic power and strong dynamics while viewing a military maneuver might suggest to you a certain appropriateness, either because of vague suggestions of war or because the characters' response on screen reveals it as functioning "as an aphrodisiac designed to release aggressive and destructive tendencies" (Müller 1992: 389). Yet, in the context of the film, this "high-art" music is highly incongruous and clashes with the rock music that has dominated the sound-track to this point. What if, in addition to this, among your many discursive communities there was one framed by some knowledge of Wagner's work, and therefore you knew that this was called the "Ride of the Valkyries" and perhaps even that, in Wagner's mythic universe, the Valkyries were supernatural women? Then, suddenly out-of-place suggestions of the feminine and the otherworldly might well intrude on your viewing of what has so far in the film been a very male and material, not to say earthy, world. If you know even more about this, the second opera of the cycle known as *Der Ring des Nibelungen*, you might add to these now multiple incongruities, the fact that this music is used in the opera to accompany the warrior maidens as they search the battlefield for the dead bodies of those fallen heroes worthy of being taken to Valhalla, the home of the gods. However, the male-piloted helicopter, you may then notice, is just going into battle in the film: this is a killing mission, a conscious attempt to create – and not reap and redeem – dead bodies.

I have been writing "you" here but, of course, I mean "me," for this is how I attribute and interpret irony here. For me, it is the superimposition or rubbing together of these meanings (the said and plural unsaid) with a critical edge created by a difference of context that makes irony happen. But that productive and spark-causing rubbing together is made possible in part by the context provided by my awareness of Wagner's work. Irony does not create any community here; the discursive community makes the irony possible in the first place. An American male soldier may well interpret that scene very differently; so may a Vietnamese, whether either knows Wagner's work or not. And irony may not figure in their interpretations at all.

The various possible ways of interpreting the work of some contemporary African American visual artists can further illustrate the inclusive function of discursive communities. Many critics see an ironizing of the exclusive realities of both Western art and racial stereotypes in Carrie Mae Weems's *Ain't Jokin'* photo-text series. Without going into too much detail, I should

19

explain that these works repeat – with ironic differences – white racist stereotypes of and jokes about blacks in such a way that white viewers, like me, are made uncomfortable, as we are no doubt intended to be. But these works might also make blacks uneasy, for they specifically target the black internalization of white racial stereotypes. Differences in discursive community based on race (and, in many of the photographs and their accompanying texts, gender as well) will therefore determine differences in attribution and interpretation of ironies. Weems foregrounds the issue of power in representation and in humor and, because her reference points are things like American verbal and visual clichés, folklore, and oft-repeated jokes, her photo-texts permit access to (or contact with) many American discursive communities across cultural, racial and even educational lines, though with very different results.

This is not the case with the work of another African American artist, Robert Colescott. In order to interpret a painting like his *Eat Dem Taters* ironically, what is needed is a knowledge of both the history of art and the history of racist representations of blacks. Let me describe this for you: the work echoes, in title and formal composition, van Gogh's canonical portrait of peasant poverty, *The Potato Eaters*. But those white European peasants have been replaced by blacks who have been drawn in an exaggerated version of that stereotypically racist cartoon-style of the "happy darkies" (Johnson 1989: 149). The ironies suggested by what ends up being – for the viewer who recognizes them – almost a superimposition of racial colors and drawing styles point up both the visual stereotypes still with us, in comic form, and also the invisibility of blacks in the European painting tradition. (See Gilman 1985: 76–94 for a discussion of the politics of the places where blacks *do* appear.) In addition, the manner in which van Gogh's painting is "copied" appears to be deliberately crude in brushstroke and form, another incongruity that has been read ironically and interpreted by one viewer as suggesting that "[e]sthetic discrimination is a metaphor for racial discrimination" (Johnson 1989: 152).

As these few examples try to suggest in their very different ways, the overlapping of discursive communities does not necessarily involve "compelling consensus" (Adorno 1974: 210), but does provide at least some similarity of concern, interest, or simply knowledge (of context, norms or rules, intertexts) that enables the participants to perform "moves of indirect communication" (Randall 1988: 47). I think interpreters of the work of Colescott or Weems have attributed irony and even ironic intent differently – or not at all – according to (among other things) their discursive communities. It is the overlapping of some of the communities of ironist and interpreter that sets the stage for the transmission and reception of intended ironies. Here, the textual markers (which may also vary from community to community) function in metacommunicative ways (Bateson 1972: 178), offering implicit signals and information about how

20

the relationship between the participants should work within this interpretive frame called "irony." In certain contexts, then, incongruities or seemingly inappropriate details are not interpreted as signaling deception or error – these are our normal "default assumptions" – but as marking ironies to be inferred (Winner 1988: 142).

The existence of a discursive community can activate a variety of markers that function in different ways, however. There are those that work to spark in the interpreter some sense that irony may be intended (in some cultures, a wink or quotation marks around a word in a text); then there are others that direct the interpreter to the specifically intended unsaid meaning. In both cases the signals must probably be socially agreed upon. Again, an example may clarify: a recent work by Victor Burgin (see Plate 1.1) presents two black and white images of the Australian continent, but in the first (dated 1788), the country's shape is black on a white ground, and in the second (dated 1988), it is white on a black ground. The very repetition of the simple, strong image is perhaps the initial marker, alerting the viewer to the possibility of double meaning; the color and date changes direct the interpretation of irony – at least, if you know that Australia, once a penal colony of Britain, celebrated its bicentennial of white settlement in 1988 without having come to terms (historically or in the present) with its colonized aboriginal (non-white) peoples.

Plate 1.1 "Untitled," by Victor Burgin. Computer-generated graphic provided by the artist.

The complicated – and politicized – interrelations of discursive community, intention, textual and intertextual context, and these metacommunicative signals are dealt with in detail in Chapters 4, 5 and 6. At this point, however, a somewhat briefer discussion of a complex (but I hope also clarifying) example might give you more of a sense of what is at work here as well as what is at stake. In the fall of 1989, the English Stage Company (also known as the Royal Court) came to Toronto, as the guests of the Canadian Stage Company. A single cast performed two plays, on alternate nights. One was a contemporary historical play by Timberlake Wertenbaker, called *Our Country's Good*, whose plot revolves around rehearsals of George Farquhar's eighteenth-century play, *The Recruiting Officer* (which was the second play performed by the company). But the rehearsals in question are those conducted by prisoners in that 1788–89 Australian penal colony to which Burgin's work alludes. The story of the rehearsals is historically validated, and was also the subject of a fictional account in Thomas Keneally's *The Playmaker.*

This Royal Court two-night production was metatheatrical in two senses: the obvious one, in which, as a member of the audience, I was watching rehearsals of the very play I was going to see on the same stage the following evening; and secondly, because the actors in Wertenbaker's play who (as convicts) rehearsed the roles in Farquhar's play actually took those same roles in the eighteenth-century play the next night – but the performance I saw bore little resemblance to the rehearsals I had watched in Wertenbaker's play. *Our Country's Good* presented the convicts before and during casting and rehearsals, in fact right up to the moment the curtain rose. The next evening, the curtain went up again, but on such a different version of *The Recruiting Officer* than the first play had suggested that, for me, the contrasts played ironically with and against the words of the text, the portrayal of characters, the style of acting, and the ideological and historical frame.

In Wertenbaker's 1988 play about 1788 Australia, one of the actor-convicts has seen Garrick on stage and wants to deliver his lines in that famous actor's gestural style and verbal manner. The differences in context (the London stage vs. the Australian rehearsal) and in manifest acting talent make for ironies whose edge cuts against both the pretensions of the would-be thespian and the late eighteenth-century "extravagant, stylized acting" (Wilson 1990: 148). But there were further ironies: here was what the audience knew (or guessed) was a very skilled actor playing a character who is an avid but rather inept performer. The next night, when the same actor played this same role in *The Recruiting Officer*, the Garrick style was nowhere to be seen: the entire production was spare and understated rather than at all extravagant or stylized. It foregrounded the political background and social reality of a particular place (Shrewsbury) at a particular time (1704) right after the Battle of Blenheim – the decisive battle of the War of Spanish Succession in which the Duke of Marlborough and the Austrians won over the Franco-Bavarian forces. This victory had meant the saving of Vienna and the checking of Louis XIV's territorial ambitions in Europe – something always of interest to the British. The society that the director (Max Stafford-Clark) chose to portray in *The Recruiting Officer* was one preoccupied with money and politics. So when Wertenbaker's play ended with the opening lines of Farquhar's, what were marked for me were disturbing continuities, not differences:

> If any gentleman soldiers, or others, have a mind to serve Her Majesty, and pull down the French King; if any prentices have severe masters, any children have undutiful parents; if any servants have too little wages or any husband too much wife; let them repair to the noble Sergeant Kite, at the Sign of the Raven, in this good town of Shrewsbury, and they shall receive present relief and entertainment . . .
>
> (Wertenbaker 1989: 39)

The plot of this (not quite typical) restoration comedy conflates politics, economics and the erotic. But, in this production, the laughs never masked the brutal and brutalizing society I watched at work and at play. The working-class servants and farm folk were presented, not as caricatures, but as fully rounded characters, and the "misogynist and homosocial dynamics" (Wilson 1990: 145) of social relations were underscored, not ignored. Within some discursive communities, there would have been an added layer of potential ironies because this interpretation of the play was very different from a legendary one within the Royal Court's own history: the famous 1963 Maggie Smith/Laurence Olivier one, directed by William Gaskill. The new *mise-en-scène* differed from the norm of restoration comedy performances in general and also from the normative expectations of London audiences familiar with that earlier production, thereby underlining the major changes in the company and in the public temper over time. To do this play, its members researched the social conditions of the time, visited Shrewsbury, watched a play in a prison with convicts as actors; in short, they "workshopped" the production.

But even for spectators (like myself) who saw only the two presented plays, many said and unsaid meanings rubbed together through mutual contextual framing. First of all, the incongruities created by the convicts playing roles that are those of different class stations and social positions worked to reinforce *similarities*, rather than *differences*: they suggested that Farquhar's characters were considerably less "worthy" than they would have liked to see themselves and, on the contrary, that the convicts were more dignified and noble than their criminal status (and their treatment by the authorities) would perhaps have implied. Some viewers felt this "humanization" of the convicts was sentimental, but for me the double cutting edge

23

of irony prevented that. Like all of you, I too see plays, just as I read books, in a certain broader context: cultural, yes, but also social and political. My way of interpreting Wertenbaker's message was certainly to read it as a positive and basically humanist one, affirming the social value of theater in transforming people's lives. The ambiguity of the title, *Our Country's Good* revolves around the apostrophe in *Country's*. Does it signal a possessive? In other words, are the convicts sent to Australia for their country's (Britain's) good, as the play text suggests? Or does the apostrophe mark a contraction and thus an assertion: our country is good? If so, *which* country is in question? And who constitutes the first-person plural? When the play's text suggests that Britain is good because of its love of and respect for the power of the dramatic word, irony may well happen for some viewers, depending on their interpretation of the speaker of those sentiments as well as on their own beliefs about the power of theater. For a Canadian audience, a further ironic frame slipped into place simply because this message about the civilizing force of the dramatic word came from a British company playing to Canadians: the long reach of cultural imperialism and colonialism was felt in other parts of the Empire besides Australia.

But this was the autumn of 1989; the Royal Court had come out of Thatcherite Britain. What looked indeed like a traditional message – drama changes lives, makes for better people – became, for me, in this historical and political context, a radical ironic indictment of cuts in arts funding by conservative governments there and elsewhere. Within Wertenbaker's play, the Governor of the colony, with the full weight of his implied authority, puts the message this way: "The theatre is an expression of civilisation. We belong to a great country which has spawned great playwrights: Shakespeare, Marlowe, Jonson, and even in our time, Sheridan. The convicts will be speaking a refined, literate language and expressing sentiments they are not used to" (Wertenbaker 1989: 9). Yet, when the Farquhar play opens the next night, that "refined" language is shown to hide brutish sentiments and actions where money, and not high moral tone, characterizes all. Here too, the Thatcherite context offered new ground for possible ironies.

Performance ironies are not the only possible ones, of course, and the published version of *Our Country's Good* offered two further contextual frames that made other ironies happen for me. There is an epigraph from R. Rosenthal and L. Jacobsen's *Pygmalion in the Classroom* which tells of an experiment in which 20 percent of the children in elementary schools were named to their teachers as "showing unusual potential for intellectual growth." Not surprisingly, perhaps, teachers gave these students more attention and eight months later their IQ scores were indeed higher; teachers described them as "more interesting, as showing greater intellectual curiosity and as happier." But these children were, in fact, chosen by a table of random numbers; they were only "special" in that their names came up. But they did improve (according to test results) when more was

24

expected of them and when encouraged by teachers. And a shift in teacher expectation changed not only what they did with the students, but perhaps what they perceived about them as well. In other words, the changes were not only in the charges, but in those in charge. To frame a narrative about convicts as actors in relation to authority and power in this way might well guide readers to look for ironic discrepancies between words and deeds, as well as between expectations and results.

The Royal Court director, Max Stafford-Clark, kept a journal during the researching and rehearsing of the two plays. It was published in the form of a series of letters to the (obviously, now deceased) playwright, George Farquhar. One (printed with the play text) is a letter about that research trip taken by the company to a prison to watch a play performed by prisoners. The parallels with the situation in Wertenbaker's play are obvious: the convicts act with varying degrees of skill, but always with intense focus and commitment, and they are proud of their achievement. This performance, like the rehearsals in *Our Country's Good*, is sexually charged. All such dramatic performances would be, suggests Stafford-Clark, because sex is one of the few expressions of independence left to convicts: the rehearsals in Australia must have been "crackling with sexual energy," he speculates. The prison guards, like the British military in eighteenth-century Australia, distrusted all of this: the men were there to be punished, not to have a good time. In Wertenbaker's play, a hanging is referred to as the prisoners' idea of theater – to which the Governor replies: "I would prefer them to see real plays: fine language, sentiment." These words echoed in my mind with certain sad ironies, when I later read the letter (also published with the play) written to the playwright from one of the prisoners who had performed in the British prison play: "Drama, and self-expression in general, is a refuge and one of the only real weapons against the hopelessness of these places."

I should admit something that is probably all too obvious to you: that I am finding the process of writing about the complexity of this (transideological) politicized interaction of contexts and discursive communities a somewhat daunting experience. While this would theoretically be true for interpretation of any kind, I persist in thinking that it is even more difficult – because of the risks involved – with irony. Here, you cannot help but be aware of the limitations of your own perspective. Whether you are British, Australian or Canadian, free or in jail, male or female, working class or not, socialist or conservative in politics – all these factors will condition whether or not even those seeing (or reading) the same play will attribute irony; the interpretation of the specific function and meaning of the irony will also differ, of course.

None of these ironies will likely be, in this particular case, very funny. As I mentioned in the Introduction, the relationship between irony and humor is a vexed one (see Schoentjes 1993: 99–100), but none the less not

25

one that can be ignored in dealing with the politics of irony. Not all ironies are amusing (cf. Freud 1905: 175) – though some are. Not all humor is ironic – though some is. Yet both involve complex power relations and both depend upon social and situational context for their very coming into being (Lewis 1989: 35–6; Walker 1988a: 25; Barreca 1988). If, as has been claimed, there has been a paucity of major scholarly work on the language of humor (Chiaro 1992: 1), perhaps it is in part because the language of irony has seemed a somewhat more appropriately "serious" object of academic study. But there do exist theories of humor as incongruity, disparagement and release that find their echoes in those elements of irony that its politics foregrounds (see Gagnier 1988: 135–6). The affective dimension of irony (its link to fear, unease, superiority, put-down, control) and its formal dimensions (juxtaposition, incompatibility) find their way into theories of humor as well (Paulos 1980: 2–8). The attribution of mocking intent (Bennett and Woollacott 1987: 165) has often made theorists generalize and see all irony as characterized by "painful" laughter (Palante 1906: 149). On the other hand, irony as a form of humor has also been seen as what "disarms" and therefore offers access to material that is not, in fact, very funny at all: like the racial stereotypes in Weems's photo-texts (Felshin 1991: 11) or Colescott's paintings. Just as irony comes into play because discursive communities exist, so humor too is said to reinforce already existing connections within a community (Barreca 1992). Both are situational, communal, "social, choral" (Bakhtin 1986: 135). But it is irony's edge that appears to be what gives certain forms of humor, such as that in recent North American Native writing (like that of Thomas King), its status as a "survival skill, a tool for acknowledging complexity, a means of exposing or subverting oppressive hegemonic ideologies, and an art for affirming life in the face of objective troubles" (Fischer 1986: 224). That may sound like it's claiming a lot, but the history of both humor and irony bears witness to many similar statements about their perceived function and significance throughout the centuries.

Many of the extended examples of ironies discussed here and in later chapters are not particularly droll, though. This is not intended to take away from either the power or the presence of humorous irony, but is the result of my conscious desire to short-circuit that knee-jerk rejection of irony (and irony theory) – as trivial and trivializing – that characterizes so many critiques of contemporary culture. Of course, even humorous ironies can be deadly serious. To offer another quick example, Lucien Pintilie's production of the opera, *Carmen* (which played in the 1980s in Cardiff and Vancouver) dealt ironically with the cliché some of Bizet's music has become today by deliberately pointing to precisely that fact: when Carmen began her "Habañera" or Escamillo started to sing his "Toreador Song," the on-stage audience (for this was a reflexive performance played within a performance) burst into applause and cheers. Interrupted not only by this

26

but by the theater audience's laughter, Carmen started again, this time switching from the French text she had begun with to the English of her listeners (both those on stage and most of those in these particular audiences): perhaps if people actually understood what she was singing about, this implies, the clichéd music and its words about love might take on new meaning – in this narrative about a woman's sexuality and independence and an abusive male's possessive and fatal jealousy. None of this interpretive potential would take away from the delight in the humor caused by the reaction to Carmen's song; indeed, the reflexive moment is what set up for me a specifically ironic frame for understanding the gender-related continuities between fiction and fact, between the past and the present. The authority of clichés sometimes rests precisely on the fact that there may be something in them that still speaks to us, if we stop and think about it for a moment.

Not all serious or humorous ironies work to demystify or subvert authority like this; some wield power to different ends. As I have been arguing, the transideological nature of its politics means that irony can be used (and has been used) either to undercut or to reinforce both conservative and radical positions. But I cannot complete these introductory and orienting remarks without pointing out that irony might be seen as transideological in at least two other senses as well. In the extensive critical literature on irony, the debates often center on whether irony is political *at all*. To this political/apolitical question must be added another pointed and politicized one: does irony function primarily affirmatively or destructively?

To take this latter opposition first, the terms are, I think, interdependent rather than opposed: the position that irony works in a positive and constructively affirmative way is usually held by those who also see irony as a powerful tool or even weapon in the fight against a dominant authority – which irony is said to work to destroy. Most recently, it is feminist, post-colonial, gay and lesbian theorists who have argued this position in different but related ways. The contrasting view of irony as negating, as largely destructive, appears to be held, at different times, by almost anyone who has been on the receiving end of an ironic attack (or missed the irony completely) or by those for whom the serious or the solemn and the univocal are the ideal. Obviously, this last group would include not only the humorless, but those whose political commitments lead them to desire, perhaps for didactic purposes, an unambiguous discourse of engagement. So, *pace* Bakhtin, it is not necessarily only those "dogmatic and authoritarian cultures" that are "one-sidedly serious" (Bakhtin 1986: 134). But again, the affirmative and the destructive political functions cannot really be separated one from the other because those who see irony as primarily destructive also tend to see it as totally complicitous – and thus hypocritically affirmative.

27

This is likely why, most often, theorists trying to account for a range of possible functions of irony decide that irony is *both* "affirming and negating" (Culler 1974: 25). At times, the claims for these dual and contradictory functionings are rather extreme, as in the view that irony is what allows one to "see where God is to be found in a world abandoned by God," yet is in itself "demonic" (Lukács 1971: 92). At other times, this particular articulation of transideological duality is put in somewhat more modest terms, and angled slightly differently. On the one hand, irony is said to function as the "ultimate form of recuperation and naturalization": "We reduce the strange or incongruous, or even attitudes with which we disagree, by calling them ironic and making them confirm rather than abuse our expectations" (Culler 1975: 157). On the other hand, it is said that irony can also be used to "avoid premature foreclosure, ... to give the benefit of the doubt by allowing [a text] to contain whatever doubts come to mind" (Culler 1975: 158). Which evaluative position you hold usually depends as much on your perspective on the issue under review as on your personal view of irony. For example, when irony came to be associated with Derridean *écriture*, it was interpreted by its opponents as frivolous, deviant, and perverse and by its adherents as playful, reflexive, and liberating (C.D. Lang 1988: 4–7).

The other way, mentioned earlier, in which thinking about irony as transideological might help explain arguments about its politics is by clarifying the framing of the most basic debates over whether irony is even political at all (see Conway and Seery 1992: 1–2); the next step would be to lay out what is at stake in the decision as to whether the position then taken is a positive or negative one. Is the "ironic perspective" essentially philosophical and therefore private (Rorty 1989: 73)? If so, is that dissociation from what is deemed the political and the public good or bad (see McCarthy 1990a; Rorty 1990; McCarthy 1990b)? Or, to come at this issue from another angle, it has been suggested that academic interpretations of texts that show how "the forces of oppression are subverted by the boundless powers of irony and allegory that no prison can contain" (Gates 1991: 18–19) risk rendering their perpetrators complacent and smug: irony becomes a kind of surrogate for actual resistance and opposition. Ironists have been accused of smugness before, of course (Booth 1974: 249–50), but this time it is the interpreter too who is not being let off the hook. Even worse, irony is seen by some to have become a cliché of contemporary culture, a "convention for establishing complicity," a "screen for bad faith" (Lawson 1984: 164). What was once an "avenue of dissent" is now seen as "a commodity in its own right" (Austin-Smith 1990: 51). This position is usually articulated in terms of contrast: the "authentic" or "sincere" past versus the ironic present of the "total ironist" (see Gitlin 1989) whose use of what is interpreted as a mode of "monadic relativism" (Jameson 1991: 412) prevents taking any stand on any issue. The Hegelian and Kierkegaardian position on irony as negation is at the base of this position (Warning 1982: 263), as, in a very different way, it also underlies what has been called a contemporary post-apocalyptic, "ironic-nostalgic" retreat from a world of "progress" in ruins (Vattimo 1992: 84).

Nevertheless, even those who hold the view that recourse to irony's multivocal instability is usually at the expense of "necessarily univocal social commitments" (Eagleton 1986: 152) have felt obliged to admit that there can exist ironies that point to the "necessarily unfinished, processual, contradictory nature of historical affairs" (Eagleton 1986: 162). Some go even further to assert that irony not only works to point to the complexities of historical and social reality but also has the power to change that reality – at least for a time: "During the revolutionary struggle irony is made welcome for its thrusts at the . . . enemy. Once the revolution is in the saddle, irony gets a prompt and dishonourable discharge" (D.J. Enright 1986: 108–9). Such a shift is only possible because of irony's transideological nature: while irony can be used to reinforce authority, it can also be used to oppositional and subversive ends – and it can become suspect for that very reason.

Almost any book or article on irony written before the last decade or so will articulate the history and continuing strength in the Europeanized West of the idea that irony is a conservative force, used to "shore up the foundations of the established order" (Elliott 1960: 273). Sometimes this is argued in terms of its deployment in satire or sometimes in terms of more general social associations that date back at least to Aristotle's notion in his *Rhetoric* (1419b: 9) that irony better befits a gentleman than buffoonery, and that take on significant weight in, for example, eighteenth-century British concepts of urbanity and wit. Most accounts – whether approving or disapproving – see satire and its irony as siding with authority in this period, and many feel that "as prisoner of its own form, it never entirely divested itself of its authoritarian inheritance, its unrebellious malice" (Adorno 1974: 210). Irony is "no less authoritative because its meanings are implicit rather than explicit" (Belsey 1980: 72). The negative connotations of irony (deception, disparagement, destabilization), which enter theoretical discourse with the word and its derivation from the Greek *eiron* figure, are never totally absent from these discussions of irony's normative politics, but their force depends upon the evaluation of whether this conservatism is a good or bad thing. As the next chapter explores, it seems that no matter what role is granted to irony, by either ironists or interpreters, there will always exist both a negative and a positive perspective on it.

The opposite to the "conservative" view – in other words, the theory that irony is really subversive and oppositional – also has a long (and parallel) history in which satire's deployment of it plays an important part as well. And, similarly, the range of evaluations of its function and efficacy can be seen in statements that run the gamut from enthusiastic endorsement to vituperative condemnation. This is what makes irony's transideological politics so difficult to sort out. The subversive functioning of irony is often connected to the view that it is a self-critical, self-knowing, self-reflexive mode (White 1973: 37; B. Bennett 1993) that has the potential to offer a challenge to the hierarchy of the very "sites" of discourse, a hierarchy based in social relations of dominance. Such a challenge, such an ability to undermine and overturn, is said to have "politically transformative power" (Stallybrass and White 1986: 201). The concept of irony as "counter-discourse" (Terdiman 1985) has become a mainstay of oppositional theories that take on such hierarchies – be they based on race, ethnicity, class, gender, sexuality . . . and the list could continue. A "mode of combat," irony becomes "a *negative* passion, to displace and annihilate a dominant depiction of the world" (Terdiman 1985: 12), a passion that is seen to be especially crucial when the dominant, established discourses show great "absorbtive capacity" (ibid.: 13). In this view, irony's intimacy with the dominant discourses it contests – it uses their very language as its said – is its strength, for it allows ironic discourse both to buy time (to be permitted and even listened to, even if not understood) and also to "relativize the [dominant's] authority and stability" (Terdiman 1985: 15), in part by appropriating its power (Chambers 1991: xvi).

This intimacy, then, is what makes irony potentially an effective strategy of oppositionality. But intimacy can also be seen as complicity: one is always "vulnerable to being reassimilated to the modes of power and knowledge which one seeks to disrupt" (Siegle 1989: 390) – or one is vulnerable to being interpreted that way, at any rate. South African novelist, J.M. Coetzee's novel, *Foe*, for example, has been hailed for its critical engaging of both feminist and postcolonial political contexts (Dovey 1988: 11), but has also been attacked for its choice of the indirect mode of allegory for that engagement, one that does not address the immediate, "daily, grubby, tragic consequences" (Gordimer 1984: 3) of apartheid and racial inequality in his country. Instead, *Foe* offers as allegory the story told of a female castaway on Robinson Cruso's [*sic*] island and of her return to London with Friday, who becomes her responsibility when Cruso dies. Or, more accurately, *Foe* tells of Susan Barton's attempt to get Daniel Foe (who added the *De* to his name in 1695 [Gallagher 1991: 171]) to tell *her* version of the story of that famous castaway island.

It is the irony that literary history bears with it – we never did hear this version from Defoe – that suggests a way to make irony happen. What if you see *Foe* as ironizing both allegory as a genre and also a set of specific intertexts, including *Robinson Crusoe*, "one of the founding narratives" of "colonial storytelling and its prototype" (Atwell 1993: 6)? To read the novel as simply allegorical might be to risk agreeing with those who see such a use of allegory as the sign of some "stately fastidiousness" (Gordimer 1984: 3) in refusing to confront openly the economic and racial conditions of oppression in South Africa and to project the defeat of the oppressors (see

Vaughan 1982; Rich 1982). Instead, perhaps the ironizing of allegory in that novel (and thus its *double* indirection) could be at least one way for a white, South African, male writer to try to approach – without bad faith and without appropriating – the silenced stories of the woman and the black who have been written out of both literature and history. How can their stories be told, by him, without acknowledging the inevitable distance that biology and history entail, that culture and ideology construct and reflect, but that irony can embody and enable? Instead of the expected similarity of allegory, this ironized version can point to difference, in an attempt to avoid *both* imperial and simply oppositional single-voicing. Language can allow for what have been called "alternities of being" (Steiner 1975: 473) through alternities of saying. But when irony is used to do so, there is no doubt that the risks appear to be greater. For some, even "to pronounce the word 'irony' is to find the thing itself, with all its impossible lived tension, has vanished into thin air" (Jameson 1988a: 3).

In spite of this injunction and in spite of the evident political risks, the last few decades have seen many claims made for irony as a most appropriate mode not only for those in political opposition but, more generally, for those with the "divided allegiance" (Sollors 1986) that comes from their difference from the dominant norms of race, ethnicity, gender, or sexual choice. Bringing together DuBois's early idea of black double consciousness and Bakhtin's notion of double-voiced discourse, African American theorists have indirectly theorized irony in their discussions of "signifying" (Mitchell-Kernan 1973). This idea of an irony that functions to repeat and yet to revise the white discourses in which North American blacks perforce operate allows "negotiation along two axes of power, the social and the mental, the public and the covert" (Cooke 1984: 15). The marginalized can be heard by the center, and yet keep its critical distance and thus unbalance and undermine. The complexity and multivocality of signifying are seen as a means of critique of the metaphysical presuppositions both of Western white culture (which either absented blacks completely or valorized them as "natural") and also of any black notions of the "transcendental black subject, integral and whole" (Gates 1984: 297). But, as this suggests, there is far from agreement on the value of ironic signifying, especially among those for whom a firm and stable racial subject position is seen as a political necessity, if not an existential reality (see West 1990).

Similar debates have occurred in feminist circles, where the suspicion of irony's instability is frequently countered by the realization of the power that lies in its potential to destabilize. Sometimes this power is directly harnessed to oppositional and critical ends; sometimes it is more an indirect attempt to "work" ideological contradictions and not let them resolve into coherent and thus potentially oppressive dogma. As such, irony has been seen as "serious play," as both "a rhetorical strategy and a political

31

method" (Haraway 1990: 191) that deconstructs and decenters patriarchal discourses. Operating almost as a form of guerrilla warfare, irony is said to work to change how people interpret. The operating premise here is that "[s]ingle vision produces worse illusions than double vision" (Haraway 1990: 196). While it is important to keep in mind that irony's transideo-logical nature has meant that it has often been used as a weapon of dominant cultures to keep the subservient in their place (Walker 1990: 22), strong arguments have also been made for irony as something that "springs from a recognition of the socially constructed self as arbitrary, and that demands revision of values and conventions" (Walker 1990: 4). This can be seen in feminist "revisionist mythmaking" (Ostriker 1986: 11): the retelling of familiar folk narratives in works as different one from the other as Margaret Atwood's *Bluebeard's Egg* (1983), Suniti Namjoshi's *Feminist Fables* (1981), Angela Carter's *The Bloody Chamber* (1979) and even Laurie Anderson's *United States* (1984). In this latter case, the ironic retelling of the Adam and Eve story through the conventions of ethnographic discourse "makes strange" both the so-called "primitive" authenticity of anthro-pology's "native informants" and the mythic and religious authority of the "Western narrative of origin" (McClary 1991: 133). This is the irony feminist theorists see as working to deprive "hegemonic culture and its critics of the claim to naturalized or essentialist gender identities" (J. Butler 1990: 138).

The epigraphs to this book notwithstanding, women have also occasionally been granted privileged status *vis-à-vis* irony. They are said to be able to use irony as a particularly potent means of critique of (Barreca 1991; Agress 1978) or resistance to patriarchal social restrictions or even "essential" male claims to "truth" (Derrida 1974: 209–10). Irony has been seen as both empowering (McClary 1989: xiv) and "empleasur-ing" (Brownstein 1988: 68). And it is often the transideological nature of irony itself that is exploited in order to recode into positive terms what patriarchal discourse reads as a negative. So, the silencing of women's voices is transformed into the willed silence of the "ironic and traditional feminine manner" (A.L. Rosenthal 1973: 30). As in theories of black signifying, women's marginalized and "divided self" (Ostriker 1986: 11) is interpreted as the enabling precondition of irony's distance (Walker 1988b: 208), doubleness (Walker 1988a: 12), and even duplicity. This (strategically essentializing) reading (see Fuss 1989) includes mimicry – as staged re-presentation – and mimicry is said to come easily to women (and those in postcolonial circumstances [Bhabha 1984]), who can replay the original discourse with ironic differences (Irigaray 1985). But it also includes the "deceptive powers of the feminine" (Zeitlin 1985: 75) which, it is claimed, make the indirection of irony attractive and efficacious (Gilbert and Gubar 1979: 80). Given the binaries of deceit and piety, it would seem that women are often happy to pick the former (Ellmann

1968: 93) and rely on the "feminine resources of evasiveness" (Spacks 1976: 24).

Because of this, the argument goes, women may be more open to or tolerant of "ambivalence, ambiguity, and multiplicity" (Flax 1987: 643). But, for some, irony – with its emphasis on context, perspective, and instability – is simply what defines "the present conditions of knowledge" (Fischer 1986: 224) for *everyone*, and not only for women. In this light, the recent revival of interest in rhetoric, for example, becomes "one sign of a loosening of the bonds that bind us to the single and the singular track, to a paranoid obsession with certitude and fixed and single destinations" (Hebdige 1991: 225). It is not that I would disagree at all that irony can be this kind of general reflexive mode, one that has the potential to reflect and model "the recognition that all conceptualizations are limited, that what is socially maintained as truth is often politically motivated" (Fischer 1986: 224). But the transideological message that a historicized perspective on irony suggests is that "it ain't necessarily so."

We don't have to look to the past, of course, to complicate the picture of the rewards as well as risks of irony. Entire careers are being made to this day on the ambiguities provoked by the attribution of irony: is Madonna the Empowered Woman-in-Control or the Material Girl, Complicit-with-Patriarchy-and-Capitalism? The exact same evidence is always used to argue both sides: Madonna on the cover of *Vanity Fair, Elle,* and *Vogue* in the fall of 1992, publishing *Sex* along with the recording of *Erotica* with a $60 million contract with Time Warner. Those who interpret her as ironically subversive see her in control of her own plural representations/masquerades – be they of vamp or virgin – through irony and artifice (Birringer 1991: 216), though few seem willing to grant her quite the total self-ironizing camp of a Mae West. Those who refuse to attribute irony see only complicity with patriarchal representations and a desire to milk them for all the (considerable) money they are worth. Madonna has attacked feminists for missing her ironies: "Irony is my favorite thing. . . . Everything I do is meant to have several meanings, to be ambiguous" (in Ansen 1990: 310). But ambiguity and irony are not the same thing: irony has an edge.

From the choice of name on, the construction of "Madonna" as performer would appear to have much ironic potential, none the less. If you want to attribute ironic intent, however, you have to begin with the fact that "Madonna" is her given (or, more aptly, her Christian) name, rather than an assumed stage name, but that alone would not prevent irony from happening in the space between religious associations with the name and popular culture. The Western iconographic tradition – in which the paradoxically virginal Madonna is often figured with Child – sets up a further intertextual context within which the singer's self-representations in film, video, song lyrics, and live performance are transgressive and perhaps, to some, ironic. In Italian, "madonna" is also the word used for the

33

representation (the statue, the picture) of the Virgin Mary. Is it appropriate or ironic that, perhaps in Madonna's case too, icon and referent share the same designation? Historically, "Madonna" is the medieval and renaissance title of respect given to a high-born woman, and for an Italian-speaking discourse community, the added subliminal idea of "ma donna" (my woman), in terms of either possessiveness or material/sexual possession, is likely ironizable, no matter what stand you take on her personal politics. Would the potential for irony be altered, however, if her birth name were not Madonna, but Mary Magdalene ... or Marilyn? Or would the ironies simply be different ones? Certainly, the "modest proposal" (Stevens 1992) that Madonna help out the American economy even more by getting pregnant – because a Madonna and Child would sell even better than a Madonna – would have to be shelved.

Those who see irony rather than complicity in Madonna's "engagement with traditional musical signs of childish vulnerability" (McClary 1991: 155) see her playing with patriarchal expectations in a knowing and – for herself and other women – empowering way, citing the singer's statement: "Everything I do is sort of tongue in cheek" (McClary 1991: 209, n.40). For those who refuse to attribute politicized irony, it is that "sort of" that disturbs: how far can you appropriate without buying into certain conventions of desire? Or must a woman deliberately assume the representations of patriarchy in order to uncover how these function? Irony has a long history, of course, of being one of the weapons in the arsenal of the "culture of resistance" (Stimpson 1988: 227) of the powerless, and it is this history that the Madonna-as-Ironist camp invoke. This is what Luce Irigaray has called "mimicry":

> One must assume the feminine role deliberately. Which means already to convert a form of subordination into an affirmation, and thus to begin to thwart it. Whereas a direct feminine challenge to this condition means demanding to speak as a (masculine) "subject".... To play with mimesis is thus, for a woman, to try to recover the place of her exploitation by discourse, without allowing herself to be simply reduced to it. It means to resubmit herself – inasmuch as she is on the side of the "perceptible," of "matter" – to "ideas," in particular to ideas about herself, that are elaborated in/by a masculine logic, but so as to make "visible," by an effect of playful repetition, what was supposed to remain invisible: the cover-up of a possible operation of the feminine in language. It also means "to unveil" the fact that, if women are such good mimics, it is because they are not simply resorbed in this function. *They also remain elsewhere*: another case of the persistence of "matter," but also of "sexual pleasure."
>
> (Irigaray 1985: 76)

This long passage seemed worth citing in full because, if you do attribute to Madonna political agency through irony, this is the kind of argument you

34

would likely want to use. The control suggested here – over self-representation, over the maleness of the gaze (Tamburri 1992: 1) – is what is represented as a spectacle in itself in the film *Truth or Dare* (Pevere 1991: C3). But the ambiguities never totally go away: is it irony's subversive edge that is so unsettling about Madonna's performances or is the disturbing fact the obviousness of her act of buying into "female commodity fetishism" (Marcus 1988: 281), an obviousness that not everyone is willing to read as irony? Those who will grant her the control of erotic self-representations still question the maleness, the patriarchal nature of those images: "Madonna the producer may have chosen the chain, but Madonna the sexual persona in the video is alternately a cross-dressing dominatrix and a slave of male desire" (Paglia 1992: 4). Is it somehow fine to be "behaving in a stereotypical way" (Madonna, in McClary 1991: 149) as long as you are "masterminding it"? Commentators have claimed that it is "the protective shield of irony that renders every Madonna move ambiguous" (Ansen 1990: 310), but once again, irony is not ambiguity.

Is Madonna so successful because of her irony or her complicity? Or is that the very point? It would seem that the inability to make a clear distinction might well be what has allowed her to attract multiple audiences: those who see her as totally dominated by the masculine gaze (and either approve or disapprove); those who see her as utterly "in charge" (a positive no matter what her actual choice of self-representation); those who see only her canny commercial instincts (and, again, either approve or do not); those who see her as subversively, flamboyantly, provocatively deconstructing the "traditional notion of the unified subject with finite ego boundaries" (McClary 1991: 150) through irony.

It is irony's transideological identity as much as its "protean polymorphism" (Tittler 1984: 16) that raises these questions of risks as well as rewards. It is true that the word "irony" has been extended and overused so much that there is a danger that it will lose its effectiveness altogether (Booth 1974: 2). But the more difficult problem for many today resides in the fact that irony can obviously be both political *and* apolitical, both conservative *and* radical, both repressive *and* democratizing. Of course, all discursive strategies can be described in these exact same terms, but more does seem to be at stake with irony – perhaps because of its edge. No one seems to see metaphor as something that is associated with anything as vast as "the collapse of belief in the possibility or desirability of global political transformation" (Callinicos 1990: 22), but irony is seen in precisely these terms. And few seem willing to make the opposite and positive kinds of politicized claims about anything but irony: witness one feminist view that a "political movement possessed of reflexivity and an ironic spirit would be formidable indeed" (Riley 1988: 98).

It is for these complicated reasons that I want to suggest, in concluding, a kind of symbolic "sign" under which a theory of irony might be written: let's call it, quite simply, the IRON. Suggestions of the familiar household pressing and smoothing device do not so much point to the incommensurability of the domains of ironing and irony (as suggested by Lori Chamberlain [1989]), but rather to the appropriation of irony's transgressive, provocative, and subversive potentialities into women's domains. But the transideological politics of irony are also encoded in such a "sign," for (as my friend, David Clarkson once suggested) the IRON can also be a branding device, one that hurts, that marks, that is a means of inflicting power. To resolve the opposite connotations of these two IRONs into a third, however, you need only think of irony in the symbolic light of the non-domestic and somewhat less violent golf club known as the IRON: it has an oblique head (the greater its number the greater its obliqueness); it is subtle (compared to the alternatives); it works to distance objects. But, it can also miss.

2

THE CUTTING EDGE

I EMOTIONS AND ETHICS ON EDGE

Attempts to theorize irony usually begin with some semantic definition of irony as involving saying one thing and meaning another. While the next chapter will deal with this obviously important relationship between the said and the unsaid, there seems to me to be something else that characterizes irony even more particularly, something that makes it even more distinctively different from other figures of speech, from other rhetorical strategies or structural devices: what I've been calling its "edge." Unlike metaphor or metonymy, irony has an edge; unlike incongruity or juxtaposition, irony can put people on edge; unlike paradox, irony is decidedly edgy. While it may come into being through the semantic playing off of the stated against the unstated, irony is a "weighted" mode of discourse in the sense that it is asymmetrical, unbalanced in favor of the silent and the unsaid. The tipping of the balance occurs in part through what is implied about the attitude of either the ironist or the interpreter: irony involves the attribution of an evaluative, even judgmental attitude, and this is where the emotive (Meyers 1974: 173) or affective dimension also enters – much to the dismay of most critical discourse and most critics.

The tendency in deconstructive criticism has been to take the edge off irony, in a sense, to remove it from its familiar historical realm of association with authority (as in Deleuze 1967: 77, 106; Kierkegaard 1971: 341; C.D. Lang 1988): "Irony is the mode of language which cannot be mastered. It cannot be used as an instrument of mastery. It always masters the one who tries to master it or to take power with it" (Miller 1982: 106). Nevertheless, if the long tradition of both commentary on and use of irony is to be believed, evaluation (if not mastery *per se*) has formed part of irony's intentional framework – to the extent that irony has usually been regarded as allowing quite unproblematic inferences about the attitude of ironists (Sperber and Wilson 1978: 403). The terms in which intentionalist theories present this view are those of the ironist's negative judgmental stance, as inferred through a tone of mockery or ridicule or contempt. And it is this tone that is said to suggest to interpreters that these attitudinal positions

37

are, in fact, emotional ones, that they could be read as betraying some affective engagement on the part of the ironist.

Ironists are not the only ones, however, who may be drawn in emotionally through irony. If you have ever been the target of irony, you know what I mean. You might have been the butt of many an irony, of course, without ever knowing it: you might have been a less than "good" or "sensitive" (Booth 1974: 1) interpreter and simply not have understood that you were being targeted. You might have "misinterpreted" an irony – that is, read it as non-ironic or assumed it was ironic, when it was not intended as such. Among the "consequences of going astray" (Booth 1974: 23) (or even of just being accused of such a hermeneutic failing) could have been feelings of embarrassment, irritation, annoyance, even anger on your part. Irony can also make you edgy, nervous about how to fix meaning securely and how to determine motivation. Some even say it can undermine certainty in more general, existential terms (Booth 1974: 241; Booth 1975: 339; Glicksberg 1969: 245) and thus create profound unease. Irony, then, would seem to be another example of "ambiguity," at least in the special sense William Empson gave to the word: it too is a form which "gives room for alternative reactions" (1963: 3). But the important word here, for me, is "reactions."

The position I am about to outline, though, runs counter to a strong modern tradition (represented by I.A. Richards and T.S. Eliot, among many others) that equates irony less with provoking emotions than with equilibrating them. In the New Critical usage of the word, irony is usually said to set up an egalitarian, indeed, democratizing tension between emotions and even meanings (cf. Dane 1991: 151; Bové 1980: 111–12). The "ironic mood" in drama, it is argued, creates a paradoxically harmonious contradiction between the true and the untrue, between art and nature: "one is conscious of contradictions but is above being frustrated by them; rather, one includes them in a single perception of living beauty" (Sharpe 1959: viii). But I'd like to suggest that it is in fact *this* view, with its roots in romantic theory, that is running counter to an even longer tradition, for it ignores the critical edge that irony's "active cognition of disparity and incongruity" (Levi 1962: 155) has long been argued to produce. In fact, the dominant view of classical rhetoricians (more recently re-articulated by linguists) has been that irony involves certain judgmental attitudes (beyond simple criticism) on the part of the ironist, attitudes like mockery and derision (Kerbrat-Orecchioni 1980a: 119; Groupe Mu 1978: 428, and 1981: 146; Jankélévitch 1964: 41). If interpreters are faced with such "emotion-charged value judgments" (Booth 1974: 44), it may not be surprising that there is a certain build-up of tension (Heller 1983: 444) involved in the simple (or not so simple) act of attributing irony to an utterance. Whether the irony is felt to signal, on the one hand, derisive disparagement or, on the other, detachment or "the cutting edge of not caring" (Austin-Smith 1990: 51), it would seem to me that emotion is

38

somehow involved here, potentially in the attributing and, of course, in the intention.

Yet, I am also aware that, as with puns and other wordplay, irony might simply signal to some people a desire to amuse or "to preserve but share secrecy" (Redfern 1984: 177). Historically, Western discourses about irony have been divided in their judgments and their explanations of irony's intention and impact; they have been split between models of seduction and aggression, between views of its inclusivity and its exclusivity, between ideas about de-fusion (and diffusion) and about violent detonation of effects and affect. But in all these extreme and opposite formulations, irony remains "axiological" or evaluative (Kerbrat-Orecchioni 1980b: 77) in a way that other tropes never really are. Just as irony oscillates in semantic terms between the simultaneous perception of the said and the unsaid – the topic of the next chapter – so the many descriptions in the critical discourses about it swing between those sets of extremes. But in both cases, as Poe taught, the pendulum can have an edge. This section will provide an introduction to some of the ways irony has been theorized in the Europeanized Western cultures by focusing specifically on the issues raised by one of irony's most distinctive characteristics: that rather pointed edge.

Irony does not simply add complexity or variety or richness (Mizzau 1984: 10) to a discourse; it does much more. As linguists (Grice 1989: 54; Berrendonner 1981: 183–4), psycho-rhetoricians (Kaufer 1981b: 503), literary critics (Abrams 1981: 89), psychologists (Winner 1988: 26) and many others have argued, irony also conveys something else: an attitude or a feeling. It is thereby connected to the Aristotelian rhetorical evaluative genre of the "epideictic" (Kaufer 1981b: 507; Dane 1991: 45–6). Irony is thus an overt case of what has been argued as basic to all discourse, for it foregrounds the "evaluative accent" that context gives any utterance (Vološinov 1973: 81, 103). Both ironist and interpreter likely make judgments about each other's capabilities and emotional positions (Hagen 1992: 19) – detachment or involvement. Irony, from the point of view of both potential participants, might be seen as a version of what Kenneth Burke called a "symbolic act," "the *dancing of an attitude*" (1973: 9). In setting up a differential relationship between the said and the unsaid, irony seems to invite inference, not only of meaning, but of attitude and judgment (Handwerk 1985: 3). In that sense, it is what speech-act theory would call a "perlocutionary" act as well, for it produces "certain consequential effects upon the feelings, thoughts, or actions of the audience, or of the speaker, or of other persons" (Austin 1975: 101). But in what sense does it do so? And, which "consequential effects" get produced? As you will see shortly, the range of these effects is actually very broad, for it runs the gamut from pleasure to pain, from delight to anger.

Part of the determination of effect – and affect – is obviously tied up with

39

the *kind* of evaluative judgment made by the ironist or inferred by the interpreter. Although, in classical rhetoric, irony was felt to allow a two-way evaluation (praise as blame, blame as praise) (N. Knox 1973: 627–8), the positive articulation has come to be much less frequent than the negative. While you might well compliment the brightest student in a class with an ironic "Oh, yes, we know how you 'failed' the examination this time too," you are much more likely to greet your own clumsy fall with "How graceful!" This pejorative norm has made irony into a uni-directional evaluative mode, at least according to many theories (Kerbrat-Orecchioni 1980a: 119; Groupe Mu 1970: 139; Sperber and Wilson 1978: 410). Irony, then, is usually said to involve the expression of an attitude (or inference thereof) that is described as "invariably one of the rejecting or disapproving kind" (Sperber and Wilson 1986: 239). Irony's judgment is seen as "hostile or derogatory"; if a judgment is playful, it cannot be ironical (Grice 1989: 54). This extreme position in terms of negation (Glicksberg 1969: 159) or devaluation (Perelman and Olbrechts-Tyteca 1969: 330) is connected with the view that irony is a weapon used by ironists to judge – and therefore either to break down attitudes of others (Richards 1925: 209) or to put (and to keep) people in their place (Amante 1981: 79). Irony, thus, is always polemical, "belonging to the armoury of controversy, and not fitted to any entirely peaceable occasion" (Thirlwall 1833: 483).

While almost all these commentaries actually contain examples of ironies that seem to me to be as affectionate as they are wounding, as playful as they are derisive, the overwhelming weight of the pejorative and the critical certainly contributes to the sense that irony is often desperately "edged": it has its targets, its perpetrators, and its complicitous audience, though these need not be three separate and distinct entities. This is the case whether irony is theorized from the point of view of the interpreter or the ironist. Since irony involves social interaction, there is no reason for it to be less implicated in questions of hierarchy and power (in terms of either maintenance or subversion) than any other form of discourse. And as soon as power – or lack thereof – enters the picture, affective responses are not usually very far behind, even if they may not be overt. Irony has been said to imply on the part of the ironist "a conviction so deep, as to disdain a direct refutation of the opposite party; ... an emotion so strong, as to be able to command itself, and to suppress its natural tone, in order to vent itself with greater force" (Thirlwall 1833: 484). Obviously, then, irony has to do with what is called the "expressive function" in language (Jakobson 1960: 354), but instead of aiming at a direct expression of the speaker's attitude, it works through indirection. But it seems to me, from experience, that this attitude can range from minimal to maximal in terms of emotional involvement, from cool detachment to engaged hostility. Once in a while, commentators speak of the ironic attitude as one of sympathy and toleration, especially when ironist and interpreter are part of a relatively homogeneous discursive community (Preminger 1974: 408). Irony's indirection is therefore sometimes seen as being "less mean" than direct insult, working to mute any attack (Winner 1988: 156–8). But attack, insult, aggression, derision, even malice are more often seen as the usual emotional conditions at work behind the decision to speak indirectly in this particular way. Indeed, irony is said to be the ironist's "weapon of contempt" (Booth 1974: 43), more powerful precisely because of its indirection.

The tendentiousness and disparagement that are often seen at the base of humor have also been drawn upon to theorize the deployment of irony by satirists throughout the ages in the West. Discussions of *vituperatio* in medieval rhetorical manuals move more strongly in the direction of scorn and disdain (Gaunt 1989: 9–10) as the "felt" emotions to be displayed: this is what is meant by the "emotional tenor" of an utterance, that is, its emphatic expression of anger or indignation (D. Knox 1989: 78). More recently, one particular view of humor – of its disruptive, subversive potential – has been allied with irony in certain feminist theories of laughter and satire as deployed by "the angry woman" (Whitlock 1986: 124–5). But, in each case, the emotional dimension does not go away; indeed, if anything, it appears to get foregrounded.

If anger and hostility mark one negativized extreme of the affective range of irony's deployment, then (as noted in Chapter 1) relatively unemotional detachment would seem to constitute the other. But many argue that ironists only *appear* cool and restrained on the surface as a way to mask actual hostility and emotional involvement (Satterfield 1981: 160; Holman and Harmon 1986: 264). By presenting themselves as in control and distant in their scorn, ironists can appear "unflappable, almost, one might believe, uncommitted" (Satterfield 1981: 160). As this suggests, there would seem to be an element of pretence involved here, of "feigned detachment" and "apparent neutrality" (Gaunt 1989: 31), that again recalls the Greek *eiron* as dissembler (Grice 1989: 54). Often seen as an intellectual mode (Handwerk 1985: 3), as I mentioned earlier, irony also came to be associated in certain European societies with the manner of "superior" address of the educated and upper classes (Swearingen 1991: 5). Indeed, irony has even been said to function as "the intellectual's only sentiment" (C. Newman 1985: 43), replacing commitment and feeling with its cynical knowingness. This, presumably, would be real – not pretended – detachment. Yet not all commentators see such a stand as utterly negative: for the ironist, some argue, it has the potential to moderate and to regulate excess (Mizzau 1984: 83); it can even alleviate tension.

Much of the theorizing of irony's affective component has been from the point of view of ironist *intention*. But what if we turn it around and investigate how emotion gets talked about and how its edge is seen to cut or abrade from the point of view of the *interpreter* of irony? The affective

41

response of this player in the game turns out to be just as complicated (Groupe Mu 1981: 154; Thompson 1948: 3), for it too ranges between extremes: from pleasure to pain, from amusement to wrath. The pleasurable pole was articulated by Freud in terms of the liberation felt with a "contradictory expenditure of energy which is at once recognized as being unnecessary" (1905: 174); others put it in terms of the interpreter's satisfaction that comes with completing or straightening out some kind of lack of fit or incongruity (Hagen 1992: 159). Some claim this is related to the special "intellectual" satisfaction felt from dealing with ambiguity and paradox, contradiction and incongruity (Muecke 1970/1982: 45; Hagen 1992: 159; Safer 1989: 117), including the delight in one's own interpretive virtuosity, of course. From here, the step to feeling a certain pleasure of superiority may not be far behind (Muecke 1970/1982: 47). Certainly the enjoyment that can come from creative participation in meaning-making could well be related to that of sharing in a collaborative process of evaluation (Burke 1969b: 57–8). But if ironists derive pleasure from influencing, from affecting an audience (Kaufer 1977: 93), interpreters' delights need not necessarily derive from sharing the particular evaluative attitude they may infer. Being "initiates" may indeed be part of the satisfaction experienced (Winner 1988: 8), but solidarity is not at all necessarily the direct corollary of understanding.

To see why, we must move from the pleasurable pole to its opposite: Aristotle defined anger as the desire, "accompanied by pain, for revenge" (1991: 142) and offered a long list of what might move people to this emotion, beginning with jeering, scoffing insults and ending with the contemptuousness signalled by irony (ibid.: 146). He also saw fear as an emotion provoked by "those who are mild and ironic and mischievous; for it is unclear when they are near to action, so that it is never obvious that they are remote from it" (ibid.: 154). When irony is used at your expense, you become its target, its butt – whether you comprehend the intended irony or not. Interpreters, however, might conceivably experience anger at the attitudes or values inferred in the ironic utterance, and to do so they would only have to *understand*, not to *share* or appreciate, those attitudes (cf. Winner 1988: 8; Warning 1982: 261).

In a no doubt vain attempt to let certain strong words in English retain their power, I would rather not refer, as so many do, to what are called irony's "victims" (McKee 1974; Almansi 1984: 91; Schoentjes 1993: 135). Like "rape" and "fascist," "victim" seems to me best reserved for other, less metaphoric contexts. I would not even want to argue that all receivers or interpreters of irony are necessarily, if not its "victims," then its targets, though some clearly are (cf. Tittler 1984: 23–4; Winner 1988: 28); often the ironized target is someone or something quite different. Even if the inferring of evaluative intent in an utterance were to work to foster in the interpreter "a certain necessary sense of humility" (McKee 1974: 2), that

42

experience seems hardly worthy of the label of "victimization." Even those excluded – those for whom irony does not happen at all – are not really its "victims" (cf. Richter 1981: 135), even when a deliberate hoax is involved. Somehow the word seems to me simply too inappropriately strong. And yet, at the same time, I do not in any way want to deny the strength of the emotion that exclusion can provoke. Many communicational models of irony are based on the *necessity* of there being an excluded audience that does not understand the ironist's intention (Weinrich 1966: 65; Tanaka 1973: 45n.). Some even assert that to make irony happen interpreters also need to be "aware of some degree of *confident* unawareness or impercipience" (Muecke 1969: 30) in some other audience. In other words, according to such models, no utterance is ironic in itself; it must be possible to imagine some other group taking it quite literally: "Otherwise there is no contrast between apparent and assumed meaning and no space for ironic play" (Culler 1975: 154). But, my point is a simple one: if you have ever "missed" an irony (and who hasn't?), you know that failure to negotiate what, in this modeling, is seen as the "intentional gap" can certainly result in embarrassment and even humiliation (Austin-Smith 1990: 51) when that failure is exposed. This emotional element goes with irony's edge.

Strong images of victimization, common as they are in such models, are perhaps indicative of a certain persistent ethical dimension to critical discourses about irony. From classical antiquity onward, the notion of ironists' duplicity and pretense has sometimes been tied to judgments about "moral indiscretion" (D. Knox 1989: 52) or even weakness of character (Chevalier 1932: 12). Today, this negative ethical evaluation is more likely to be articulated in more political terms, perhaps as "sanctioning skepticism as an explanatory tactic, satire as a mode of emplotment, and either agnosticism or cynicism as a moral posture" (White 1978: 73–4). Are irony and political commitment as incompatible as this suggests? As mentioned in the first chapter, for some critics the answer would seem to be "yes" (Jameson 1979: 56; but see Eagleton 1990: 175); for others – feminist and postcolonial theorists, for example – it might be quite otherwise. Irony may play on the edge, but it can also force people to the edge, and sometimes over it. As I mentioned in the last chapter, other tropes, even those relatively close to irony in semantic terms, never seem to have become embroiled in quite these same sorts of debates. From pleasure to pain, the emotions provoked by irony – as it is both used and attributed, as it is felt as well as deployed – are probably not to be ignored.

II THE "DEVIL'S MARK" OR THE "SNORKEL OF SANITY"?: THE CONTRADICTORY FUNCTIONS AND EFFECTS OF IRONY

The two terms in the title for this section come from the description of the "modern mode" of irony, as defined in *Braithwaite's Dictionary of Accepted Ideas* (itself an ironization of Flaubert's ironic *Dictionnaire des idées reçues*), in Julian Barnes's novel, *Flaubert's Parrot* (1984). The extremes it wittily articulates echo the evaluative and affective polarities provoked by irony's use and/or attribution, at least if many centuries of theorizing are to be believed. If Thomas Mann once praised irony as a moral attitude that woos "even if secretly" (1983: 13), irony's edge has also driven another theorist (though he is not alone) to extreme verbal formulations that reflect a different moral position: "irony by its nature seems to have a power to corrupt the ironist ... by offering him both a refuge from life and a means of subjecting it to his own ego" (Muecke 1969: 242); the "habit of irony" is even seen as a "corrosive and paralysing disease of the spirit" (Muecke 1969: 243). But, a *caveat* is offered too: "There are also dangers in earnestness, in not having a sense of irony" (Muecke 1969: 245). In fact, this sort of flipping from negative to positive is to be found everywhere in the evaluative rhetoric of discourses about irony, and I suspect the reasons have more to do with the nature of the beast itself than with any critical vacillation.

Mikhail Bakhtin once called irony the "equivocal language of modern times," for he saw it everywhere and in every form – "from the minimal and imperceptible, to the loud, which borders on laughter" (1986: 132). Laughter, too, of course, comes in many degrees and kinds, from the aggressive to the teasing (Koestler 1964: 51–63). In other words, the existence of one signifier – "irony" – should never blind us to the plurality of its functions as well as effects. Under that deceptively comprehensive label is included a complex and extensive range of tones, intentions, and effects that forms the topic of the rest of this chapter. However, to complicate the discussion somewhat, in the critical discourses on irony, the various evaluations of its worth and desirability – whatever the tone, intention or effect – encompass the farthest extremes of approval and disapproval.

As I have already suggested, the positive evaluative terms can be found in disciplines ranging from theology (where irony is said to offer amendment as a way to a "vision of truth" [Good 1965: 27]) to literature (where irony can be seen as a sign of the "subtlety and flexibility" of aesthetic expression [Gaunt 1989: 31]). Irony may be approved of as "an inquiring mode" (Furst 1984: 9) or as a way to avoid the single and dogmatic. The terms of disapproval might be in terms of irony as limiting, trivializing, unclear, insincere (Chamberlain 1989: 106), or even as quietistic – "a special kind of substitute for silence" (Bakhtin 1986: 148). These extremes and this

44

range of possibilities have made many others beside myself wonder if all these theorists are, in fact, even talking about the same thing. Or is irony perhaps so protean, so multivalent, that it can indeed evoke such varied responses? One way to investigate this question might be to examine the variety of communicative functions of irony and the impact they are each said to have. While irony certainly does work to reinforce, to ridicule and to refute (Kaufer and Neuwirth 1982: 28), it seems to me that it also does lots of other things.

Too often, in fact, theories inadvertently imply that something called "irony" works in the same way and to the same ends in all possible utterances. Perhaps that is one of the reasons for so much of the disagreement about its workings. In order to fracture that spurious uniformity, I would like to outline some of the many possible functions of irony, but this time from the point of view of the interpreter, not the ironist. In a later chapter on intentionality, the issues of ironist intent and the inferences of the interpreter will be dealt with in more detail, but it is likely clear just from my remarks thus far that my concern here is more with inference than with implication, more with the attribution of irony than with any "original" intent to ironize, however decisively such intent might be proved. It may well be true that the range of irony depends on the ironist's temperament – from oppositional to conciliatory (Morier 1975: 558) – but the temperament of the interpreter of the irony might not be irrelevant either. After all, the final responsibility for deciding whether irony actually happens in an utterance or not (and what the ironic meaning is) rests, in the end, solely with the interpreter.

It is in that frame of reference, then, that I would define function here in the somewhat graceless terms of *attributed or inferred operative motivation*. It is *inferred* because irony is not necessarily a matter of ironist intention (and therefore of implication), though it may be; it is always, however, a matter of interpretation and attribution. I use the term *operative* simply to signal my interest in how irony "works" or happens, and I mean *motivation* in the straightforward sense of a purposeful attitude (though, here, inferred) toward the act of ironizing. My working premise is a simple two-part one: first, that different (projected, inferred) motivations result in different reasons for attributing (or using) irony and, second, that the lack of distinction among the multiple possible functions of irony is one of the reasons for so much of the confusion and disagreement about its appropriateness and value, not to say its meaning.

The history of irony criticism offers many examples of the complexity of the interpreter inferences I am dealing with here. When an eighteenth-century specialist sees Fielding's irony as simply functioning in straightforwardly consolidating and reassuring ways, but infers that Gay's irony in *The Beggar's Opera* is, instead, an important "means of articulating and organizing his knowledge of life" (Preston 1966: 269), he would appear

45

to be making value judgments as much as statements about the functionings of irony in the work of two writers. Similarly, another critic sees Gibbon's irony as one which "habituates and reassures, ministering to a kind of judicial certitude or complacency," but reads Swift's as "essentially a matter of surprise and negation: its function is to defeat habit, to intimidate and to demoralize" (Leavis 1934: 366–7). As these examples suggest, for every way of describing the workings of irony, there are different evaluations, no doubt depending on things like taste, habit, training, politics, temperament, and many other variables. The rhetoric of approval and disapproval takes many forms, however, and can never be reduced to any neat political division between right and left, conservative or revolutionary. This is part of the transideological nature of irony: people of all political persuasions have been known both to endorse and to condemn its use.

Nevertheless, the review of irony's many functions that follows is a provisional attempt to articulate and order some of the ways critics over the years have voiced their approval or disapproval of what is often presented as a single thing – irony – operating in a single way. The functions discussed here are not my inventions: they are all present and easily accounted for in the vast amount of commentary on irony throughout the centuries. It is only the ordering – the schematic, pragmatic organization – for which I am responsible. As the accompanying chart suggests (see Figure 2.1), I have organized them on a kind of sliding scale, from the most benign both in tone and in inferred motivation (on the lower end) to a middle ground where the critical temperature, so to speak, begins to rise, and on to the more contentious zones where irony is generally accepted as a strategy of provocation and polemic. Each of these functions turns out to have both a positive and a negative articulation, for critics have presented each in both approving and disapproving terms. One critic's "emphatic" function is another critic's purely "decorative" one; one's "corrective" function is another's "destructive" one – and so on. Although I have modeled the functions as part of a tonal and emotive *continuum*, they are not intended to be hierarchically organized: despite the obvious difficulties of over-coming the connotations of semiotic representation, the move upwards on the diagram is intended simply to show a move from minimal to maximal affective charge. And, for each function, I have tried to locate in the available critical discourses the most neutral "descriptor" possible.

When I showed a draft of this chapter with this diagram to Peter Hagen, who had just completed a dissertation on the rhetoric of irony, he wrote back to me that he was reminded of the apparatus in a museum exhibit on static electricity:

> two metal rods at an angle to each other with an arc of blue-white
> electricity between them travelling upwards. Sometimes the arc

46

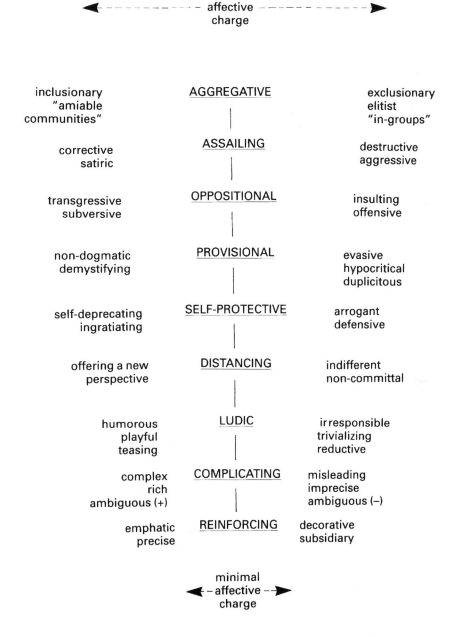

Figure 2.1 The functions of irony.

discharges at the bottom, sometimes halfway up. But when there is a great deal of energy (or when atmospheric conditions are right) the blue arc goes right up to the top in a brilliant display of tension and energy, setting the space between a-crackling with the temporarily unresolved interplay of polarities. What your diagram suggests to me is that neither positive nor negative interpretations are or should be privileged over each other. The tension between them is what counts as well as the point along the scale at which the arc "discharges."

With that assistance, I can only hope that the diagram is even somewhat as suggestive to other readers.

To begin, then, at the bottom: what to most commentators would be irony's most straightforward and basic function, its "<u>REINFORCING</u>" role, already offers the possibility of difference in evaluation, despite relatively little sense of much critical edge. By "<u>REINFORCING</u>," here, I mean the familiar intentional use or interpretation of irony as being used to underline a point in, say, everyday conversation. For some, this has a positive function: it is deemed necessary for **emphasis**, and often for greater **precision** of communication, especially the communication of an attitude, or else ironists wouldn't bother using it at all and interpreters wouldn't be primed to infer that they might. There would seem to exist certain discursive communities (like university literature departments, in my experience) in which the using and attributing of irony seem to play a role in proving communicative competence (Clyne 1974: 344). The disapproving stance on this same function is to say that such reinforcing irony is purely **decorative**, **subsidiary**, non-essential. So, even in its perhaps least problematic form, irony appears to be open to conflicting evaluations as well as interpretations of its functioning. While most discussions of this reinforcing function suggest little or no evaluative force behind such a use or attribution of irony, I think that even approval or disapproval of the assumed cleverness of the ironist might constitute some sort of emotional involvement, or at least response, through evaluation (N. Knox 1961: 76). Because of this, I have left some space, however minimal, at the bottom of the diagram for that arc of ironic affect to "discharge."

Likewise, there must be some, if not much, space for the not terribly sharp edge of irony when it operates as verbally or structurally <u>COMPLI-CATING</u>. In some critics' eyes, irony is typical of the **complexity** or **richness** of all art, a form of controlled and positively valued **ambiguity**, that "*reservoir of irony*" (Barthes 1977b: 147) at the base of all aesthetic discourse. This can include a view of irony as a reflexive modality, issuing a "call to inter-pretation" and its delights (Culler 1974: 211). But negative connotations collect around this function too, concentrating especially in the notion that unnecessary complexity and (what now becomes misleading rather than enriching) **ambiguity** can breed misunderstanding, confusion, or simply **imprecision** and lack of clarity in communication. And such, indeed, is what provokes the irritation of those who feel or are made to feel that they have "missed" ironies.

Another related and also relatively benign function of irony would be the LUDIC. When viewed favorably, this is seen as the affectionate irony of benevolent **teasing**; it may be associated as well with **humor** and wit, of course, and therefore be interpreted as an estimable characteristic of **playfulness** (and so, in language, akin to punning or even metaphor). But, curiously, even critics who assert such positive values often, in the same breath, imply something more negative: irony may be supple and subtle but it is also superficial (Jankélévitch 1964: 35). From there it is a small step to seeing irony as **irresponsible**, empty, even silly: "In an age of few or shifting values irony becomes, very often, a tone of urbane amusement, assuming the right to be amused, but offering no very precise positives behind the right. It can degenerate into a mere gesture of superiority, superficially polished and civilised, but too morally irresponsible to be really so" (Dyson 1965: 1). Even without this familiar moral frame of reference, irony can be seen as **trivializing** the essential seriousness of art. This position was bred in European romanticism, nurtured in later nineteenth-century moralism, and allowed to flourish in certain aspects of twentieth-century modernism; to all appearances, it enjoys a ripe maturity in much academic discourse even today. The "significant" in art (and criticism) is often seen as the highly serious, not to say solemn. In his 1936 essay, "Romanticism and Classicism", T.E. Hulme sought to reinstate classical notions of wit and irony as a means of combating precisely such solemnity, and the impact of this endeavor can be seen in the revaluation of irony by T.S. Eliot and I.A. Richards, as well as by American New Criticism in general.

As you can imagine, the affective charge associated with irony is going to start to increase with the use of words like "trivializing" and maybe even "teasing." When the notion of irony functioning as a DISTANCING mechanism is considered, it increases even more. This is in spite of the fact that, as mentioned earlier, it has for centuries been a commonplace to assert that irony is the trope of the detached (Burke 1973: 419-21; Hutchens 1960: 358) and the witnessing: "the knowledge of irony is usually reserved for observers rather than participants" (Niebuhr 1952: 153; cf. Williams 1984). But, as the first part of this chapter explored, even observers are not exempt from experiencing (if not always revealing) affective responses (cf. Frye 1970: 40–1). Distance can, of course, suggest the **non-committal**, the inferred refusal of engagement and involvement (Worcester 1960: 138), and so its more pejorative associations are with **indifference** (Wilde 1981: 29) or even Olympian disdain and superiority. But distancing reserve can also be interpreted as a means to a **new perspective** from which things can be shown and thus seen differently: "From whatever angle Irony is

49

approached, the habit of making or perceiving incongruities has an impressive tendency to broaden the view, leading to the perception of incongruities on a wider and wider scale" (Chevalier 1932: 44). A related and equally approving reading of the distancing function of the new perspective induced through irony is the one that sees it as refusing the tyranny of explicit judgments, especially at a time when such judgments might not be either appropriate or desirable (Kaufer 1981a: 33). As discussed in Chapter 1, and as Ross Chambers has argued so forcefully, the *"refusal to be pinned down"* (1991: 55) can be a strategic way to be oppositional by exploiting the discourse of power to different ends.

This is clearly trickier terrain, though, and the terms used in discourses about irony to describe both the positive and negative evaluations of the functions are becoming much more "loaded" ones. For instance, to see irony's workings as <u>SELF-PROTECTIVE</u> is to suggest that irony can be interpreted as a kind of defense mechanism (N. Knox 1973: 634). And, in fact, where I come from, this is often seen as a positive function. It has been said that, in the face of a British and French colonial past and a United States-dominated present, Canadians have often resorted to a **self-deprecating** use of irony as a way of signaling their reluctant modesty, their self-positioning (as marginalized and maybe self-marginalizing), their self-doubts, and perhaps even their rejection of the need to presume or to assume superiority – especially against such overwhelming odds. But as Canadian writer Margaret Atwood's novel *The Robber Bride* (1993) suggests, and as Plato's Socrates demonstrated, self-deprecation can be feigned (D. Knox 1989: 110); it can be a form of indirect self-promotion, even **arrogance**, even if Aristotle did argue in the *Ethics* (iv.7.1–17) that the Greek *eiron* was the opposite of the boasting *alazon*. The *eiron*, who gave irony its (bad) name, was indeed a self-deprecating figure, appearing less than he (or, rather less commonly, she) was, but sometimes this was interpreted as a deliberate attempt to render oneself invulnerable. So, self-deprecation can be read as a **defensive** move, as well. This is not to say that such a move may not be viewed with approval, for self-deprecating irony can then be seen to replace the aggressive with the **ingratiating**: "it acknowledges the opinion of the dominant culture – even appears to confirm it – and allows the speaker or writer to participate in the humorous process without alienating the members of the majority" (Walker 1988a: 123). Such an attribution of irony could act to attenuate the effect of, say, an order or a question, perhaps even of a boast or a declaration of love (Mizzau 1984: 82): for the ironist, irony means never having to say you're sorry. You can always protect yourself and argue (from an intentionalist perspective) that you were only being ironic. You can even turn an error into a joke with the same statement; you can certainly use it to get out of any number of embarrassing situations. Using or even attributing irony in this way is drawing on its function to act as a "protective garment" (Worcester 1960: 107).

It doesn't take much of a shift of focus to move along the continuum from such a self-protecting function of irony to one that might be called PROVISIONAL, at least in the sense of always offering a proviso, always containing a kind of built-in conditional stipulation that undermines any firm and fixed stand. The disapproving associations here are with the **evasiveness** of equivocation (Decottignies 1988: 25), **hypocrisy, duplicity** and deception. Thomas Mann once described an irony which "glances at both sides, which plays slyly and irresponsibly – yet not without benevolence – among opposites, and is in no great haste to take sides and come to decisions" (1947: 173). To some critics, the roots of this function are, once again, in that dissembling *eiron* figure, this time seen as cynical and even hypocritical (Worcester 1960: 93; N. Knox 1961: 38–42, and 1973: 627). The Greek root of *eironia* does indeed suggest dissumulation or deception, and it has been claimed that the common denominator of all definitions of irony offered in the *Oxford English Dictionary* is a view of irony as "a deliberately deceptive act which suggests a conclusion opposite to the real one" (Hutchens 1960: 353). Intentionalist theories often take an ethical stand on this: "irony amounts to deceiving plain folk who understand in a plain way" (Kenner 1986: 1151). "Simple" readers, as they are sometimes called, are said to mistake verbal irony for insincerity (Richards 1929: 264), but even very adept and complex readers have been known to evaluate irony as a form of evasion of committed speech (B.H. Smith 1968: 254). Irony's edge, in other words, can blur edges too.

Irony can also hedge: it can allow "a speaker to address remarks to a recipient which the latter will understand quite well, be known to understand, know that he is known to understand; and yet neither participant will be able to hold the other responsible for what has been understood" (Goffman 1974: 515). This is the fence-sitting provisionality of irony as "the attitude of one who, when confronted with the choice of two things that are mutually exclusive, chooses both. Which is but another way of saying that he chooses neither. He cannot bring himself to give up one for the other, and he gives up both. But he reserves the right to derive from each the greatest possible passive enjoyment. And this enjoyment is Irony" (Chevalier 1932: 79). There are many such more or less negatively marked, disapproving statements about the evasive and even potentially paralyzing effects of this conditional function of irony (see Dyson 1965: 1) and of the "deceptive moment" that is seen to be a constitutive element of it (Smyth 1986: 3).

The positively valued version of this function is usually framed by some sense that irony's doubleness can act as a way of counteracting any tendency to assume a categorical or rigid position of "Truth" through precisely some acknowledgement of provisionality and contingency. Its laconic reticence would then be interpreted as an **undogmatic** alternative to authoritative pronouncements (Jankélévitch 1964: 89–91). This is a functioning of irony

51

that "doesn't reject or refute or turn upside-down: not evasiveness or lack of courage or conviction, but an admission that there are times when we cannot be sure, not so much because we don't know enough as because uncertainty is intrinsic, of the essence" (D.J. Enright 1986: 6). When such a provisional position is seen as valuable, it is often called **demystifying**. For some, this provisionality actually becomes the essence of "true" art, over which irony rules as a kind of divine protector (Almansi 1984: 81; cf. Decottignies 1988: 25). But when it is not particularly valued at all, those emotionally charged terms of hypocrisy, duplicity, or equivocation often make an appearance.

The same is the case with the next, the <u>OPPOSITIONAL</u> functioning of irony, for this is where its transideological nature may be most clear, where the critical edge can be seen to cut both ways: "Both conformers and rebels use irony at each other, and both suffer from it" (E. Wright 1978: 524). And, in addition, the same utterance may have opposite pragmatic effects: what is approved of as polemical and **transgressive** to some might simply be **insulting** to others; what is **subversive** to some might be **offensive** to others. In intentional terms, this is how irony can function for the passive aggressive personality, but it also works as the undermining-from-within of the politically repressed (Berrendonner 1981: 239; Almansi 1984: 37) – as the early work of Milan Kundera illustrates so well. This is the function of irony that has specifically been called "counter-discursive" in its ability to contest dominant habits of mind and expression (Terdiman 1985: 12). For those positioned *within* a dominant ideology, such a contesting might be seen as abusive or threatening; for those marginalized and working to undo that dominance, it might be **subversive** or **transgressive** in the newer, positive senses that those words have taken on in recent writing about gender, race, class, and sexuality.

The next function is one that I have rather awkwardly called the <u>ASSAILING</u> one, because I want to be able to draw upon the meaning of its Latin root, *assilire*, to leap upon. Believe it or not, I could find no more neutral descriptor anywhere in the abundant writing on irony. But, in dealing with the sharpest edge or "bite" (Fogelin 1988: 10) of irony, perhaps that is to be expected. The negative charge here is at its maximal when corrosive invective and **destructive** attack become the inferred – and felt – ends of irony. In many discussions of irony, this seems to be the only function considered, especially when it is a question of appropriateness or, especially, of excess in its use. Yet, there does exist what could be interpreted as a positive motivation for "leaping upon" something, however vigorously, and that lies in the **corrective** function of **satiric** irony, where there is a set of values that you are correcting toward. Arguably all irony can have a corrective function (Muecke 1970/1982: 4), but since satire is, by most definitions, ameliorative in intent (Highet 1962: 56), it is satire in particular that frequently turns to irony as a means of ridiculing – and implicitly correcting – the vices and follies of humankind. There is, however, a very wide tonal range possible within this corrective function, from the playfully teasing to the scornful and disdainful.

For some theorists, it is clearly a positive for an ironist or for an interpreter to have a firm perspective from which to correct those vices and follies, to have "real standards" in which to ground moral outrage (Furst 1984: 8–9). But today, others appear to be increasingly suspicious of a stand like this: to presume such a position of Authority and Truth, they argue, might well itself be a folly, if not a vice. What both evaluative stands are responding to here, though, is the "militancy" of irony that is seen to function in a corrective way: "its moral norms are relatively clear, and it assumes standards against which the grotesque and absurd are measured" (Frye 1970: 223) and, of course, found wanting. For perhaps obvious reasons, as mentioned earlier, satire has long been associated with a conservative impulse, but commentators appear to disagree today as to whether, in Europe and North America, for example, the satiric is now as important a function of irony as it was in, say, eighteenth-century England. They argue either that there is certainly a lot around today for irony to correct, or that the very idea of correctable folly or error has given way to a skepticism about the very possibility of change (Wilde 1981: 55). Perhaps both are true. Or, do we need new terms in which to think about this function? As the first chapter explored, the moral categories in which this particular functioning has traditionally been coded might fruitfully be rethought in political terms. The way to such a rethinking was actually prepared by the "neutralizing," so to speak, of irony by American New Criticism – that is, through its removing of the moral implications from the usage of the word by distancing it from precisely this satiric functioning. As Wimsatt and Brooks wrote in the mid-1960s: "One apparently needs to insist nowadays that the term 'irony' need not always be taken with a strongly emotive and moral accent," but could instead be a more neutral, "cognitive principle which shades off through paradox into the general principle of metaphor and metaphoric structure" (1964: 747). But I think it is necessary to insist, none the less, on the continued existence of some emotive accent to irony as well as the continuing presence, even after New Criticism, of some satiric, corrective functioning of irony.

What persists as well is the often disapproving evaluation of this <u>ASSAILING</u> function wherein irony is seen to operate as the **aggressive** put-down that keeps people in their place. In his analysis of humor in *Jokes and Their Relation to the Unconscious*, Freud had argued that ironic modes such as parody, travesty, and caricature are always, despite their seemingly innocent humor, actually "directed against people and objects which lay claim to authority and respect" (1905: 200). So, I might want to interpret Colombian painter Fernando Botero's "bloated" ironic vision of Marie Antoinette as an attack both on a traditionally romanticized figure of history and also on the kind of "inflation" historical reputation brings about. Here that inflation is literalized in the representation of the bloated figure. Prompted by this device, I might also interpret this work as ironizing an entire respected, authoritative tradition of idealized high-art portraiture. In other words, no matter how attenuated it might be because of its seeming playfulness (Groupe Mu 1978: 442), irony can still "leap upon'; it can still be tendentious, even **aggressive** (Freud 1905: 97). The negativized rhetoric of disapproval that circulates around this ASSAILING function of irony is one of cutting, derisive, **destructive** attack or sometimes of a bitterness that may suggest no desire to correct but simply a need to register contempt and scorn.

Somewhat outside this schema, but not unrelated in structural and evaluative terms to this continuum of functions, with their contradictory valuations, is yet another, more general, social functioning of irony that has been touched on already and will be dealt with in much more detail in Chapter 4. I think of this as the AGGREGATIVE function. Irony may create communities, as so many theories argue, but I have also suggested that irony is created *by* communities too. In a negative sense, irony is said to play to **in-groups** that can be **elitist** and **exclusionary**. Irony clearly differentiates and thus potentially excludes: as most theories put it, there are those who "get" it and those who do not. Some theorists have felt that the implied superiority/inferiority dualism is implied in any ironic distancing (de Man 1969: 195), and look to Kierkegaard's famous and much cited statement that irony is not understood by all because it "travels in an exclusive incognito, as it were, and looks down from its exalted station with compassion on ordinary pedestrian speech" (1971: 265). This is why irony has been called an intellectual attitude, an aristocratic and even anti-social one on the part of the ironist (Palante 1906: 158–9). Critics write of the verticality of its "axis of power" and knowledge (Muecke 1983: 402) and of the rhetoric of hierarchy associated with it (Dane 1991: 48–60). Here, the ironist is always figured as on top, and the comprehending (attributing) interpreter not far below, be it in rhetorical or in romantic irony. Images of voyeurism, sadism and, as we have seen, "victimization" proliferate in these discussions of the ironist as a kind of omniscient, omnipotent god-figure, smiling down – with irony – upon the rest of us. This idea of irony functioning in an elitist way obviously involves an inference about both the ironist (as feeling superior) and the interpreter (who "gets" the irony and so is said to feel part of a "small, select, secret society" [Worcester 1960: 77]). As this suggests, however, irony that excludes includes as well, creating those "amiable communities" (Booth 1974: 28) between ironist and interpreter and thus recalling the pleasures of collaboration, even collusion, noted earlier in the chapter. For some, irony is an emblematic interdiscursive act of confrontation with and mediation through another subject (Handwerk 1985). Kenneth Burke has related irony to dialectic and

54

to what he calls the "dramatic," "which aims to give us a representation by the use of mutually related or interacting perspectives" (1969a: 503) which can then result in "[t]rue irony, humble irony ... based upon a sense of fundamental kinship with the enemy, as one *needs* him, is *indebted* to him, is not merely outside him as an observer but contains him *within*, being consubstantial with him" (ibid.: 514), like Flaubert with his Madame Bovary. There are clearly many kinds of community involved when irony functions aggregatively.

In fact, this **inclusionary** view of irony's operations shares with the **exclusionary** view a related perspective on the audience. The latter sees irony as implying an assumption of superiority and sophistication on the part of both the ironist and the intended (that is, comprehending) interpreter – at the expense of some uncomprehending and thus excluded audience. Flattery comes into effect here: Gibbon, for instance, is said to invite his reader to "join him on terms of true equality for the re-enactment of manners, beliefs and customs inferior to our own" (Dyson 1965: 49). This is the function of irony that is argued to play most obviously into arrogance and insensitivity: it "offers special temptations to our weaknesses, especially our pride" (Booth 1974: 44). In its most extreme form, it has been wittily dubbed the "Snotty Sublime" (Booth 1974: 211). Issues of power and authority are clearly going to be involved in this <u>AGGREGATIVE</u> functioning of irony, and it is for this reason that I have positioned it in Figure 2.1 at the top end of the affective scale with the maximal critical and emotive charge: this is where it is *felt*, where it is inferred and sometimes intended. The evaluation inferred through irony's edge need not be shared to be attributed, of course. Though sharing is indeed an "affiliative act" (Kaufer 1977: 98), interpreters do not always agree with the attitudes they infer: irritation and distancing are just as likely affective responses as feelings of intimacy and cohesion.

Yet, a significant recurring theme in all the theorizing about irony is that it creates **in-groups**: "one study has even demonstrated a substantial increase in the use of the definite article in the ironic mode, a use said to be linked with the implicit sense of an initiated group, aware of a real meaning behind an ironically baffled exterior" (Frye 1970: 61). As later chapters will explore in more detail, definite articles are not the only way of bringing about what Erving Goffman has called "collusive communication," wherein there are "those in on it [who] constitute a collusive net and those the net operates against, the excolluded" – to coin a punning term (1974: 84). To see how people react with anger and irritation at being "excolluded," all you need to do is read the newspaper following any ironic political speech or follow the political history of the use of irony in any public forum – as the concluding chapter of this book will do. On the other hand, to know how important the community-enhancing function of irony might be, you need only recall those seductive ironies attributed to rock stars like Madonna and note their "aggregative" effect on the fans.

Irony's edge, then, would seem to ingratiate and to intimidate, to underline and to undermine; it brings people together and drives them apart. Yet, however plural these functions, we still seem to want to call the thing itself by a single name: irony. This pragmatic decision doesn't at all mean that we should forget the complexities of irony's inferred motivations, though: an awareness of the range of operations that irony can be interpreted as carrying out may help resist the temptation to generalize about either the effects of which irony is capable or the affect to which it can most certainly give rise. Retaining this complexity is important because edge is the primary distinguishing feature of irony as a rhetorical and structural strategy, no matter how protean its actual manifestations.

3

MODELING MEANING
The semantics of irony

I IMAGES *EN ROUTE* TO A DEFINITION

You probably didn't need Wittgenstein's later writings to convince you that words evolve their meanings over extended periods of use in different and specific contexts. As Joseph A. Dane's extensive historical review, *The Critical Mythology of Irony* (1991), shows, "irony" is no exception. These days, given the impact of poststructuralist theories of the impossibility of univocal and stable meaning, irony has achieved a somewhat privileged status for some people: its overt production of meaning through deferral and difference has been seen to point to the problematic nature of all language (Fischer 1986: 224; Handwerk 1985: 12; de Man 1969; Mileur 1986: 336): from a purely semantic point of view, the ironic "solution" of plural and separate meanings – the said together with unsaid – held in suspension (like oil and water) might challenge any notion of language as having a direct one-to-one referential relation to any single reality outside itself. To discuss the semantics of irony, however, is inevitably to address a set of complex issues not only centering around the concept of plural meaning, but also involving things like the conditioning role of context and the attitudes and expectations of both ironist and interpreter. In short, the topic of this chapter – how irony "means" – is inescapably related to those that precede and follow it.

Suffice it to say, at this point, that irony illustrates the perhaps self-evident fact that, in practice, we don't make meaning outside of particular situations. Meaning-making is always an activity that goes on in a specific context (Ducrot and Todorov 1972: 326). Because of this, what most linguists call "usage" (see Gibbs 1984: 297–9) – what Saussure called *parole* – has even led some people to argue that all language is ironic: "my meaning is not necessarily the same as the meaning you attribute to me. Nor are either of our meanings necessarily in exact accord with 'things as they are'" (Martin 1983: 415). The next chapter will study in more detail how "semiosis" or the attribution and production of meaning – ironic or otherwise – is a social activity, for it involves the "ways in which systems and codes are used, transformed or transgressed in social practices" (de Lauretis 1984: 167). What I am suggesting is that, in order to deal with the issue of ironic meaning, you have to go beyond traditional concepts of semantics, where meaning is discussed in terms of truth-conditions or the relation of words to things (see Récanati 1981: 11–12), and look as well to pragmatics, to the social and communicative exchange of language (Kerbrat-Orecchioni 1980a: 120; 1980b: 198). There would seem to be no other way to talk about the strange semantic fact that we can use language to convey messages that are different from what we are actually saying (Kempson 1977: 68).

In the last two chapters I have been arguing that ironic meaning, in practice – in a social/communicative context – is something that "happens" rather than something that simply exists. And it happens in discourse, in usage, in the dynamic space of the interaction of text, context, and interpreter (and, sometimes, though not always, intending ironist). As a response to the extensive literature – in many different fields, from linguistics to psychology, from rhetoric to literary criticism – that sees irony as a straightforward semantic inversion (antiphrasis – or saying one thing and meaning its opposite) and thus as a static rhetorical *tool* to be used, this chapter expands on the suggestion made earlier in this book that irony is, instead, a communicative *process*. It is in this framework, then, that I would argue that ironic meaning possesses three major semantic characteristics: it is **relational**, **inclusive** and **differential**.

Irony is a **relational** strategy in the sense that it operates not only between meanings (said, unsaid) but between people (ironists, interpreters, targets). Ironic meaning comes into being as the consequence of a relationship, a dynamic, performative bringing together of different meaning-makers, but also of different meanings, first, in order to create something new and, then, as Chapter 2 explored, to endow it with the critical edge of judgment. As noted, that Greek *eiron*, from whom irony got its name, was a dissembler, a pretender, and that notion of pretense figures frequently in "performative" theories of irony (Koestler 1964: 73–4; and especially Clark and Gerrig 1984: 121), humor (Douglas 1975), and figurative language, in general. In fact, it seems that children have to learn about pretense in order to understand irony (Winner 1988). The social dimension of this **relational** aspect of irony is the subject of the next chapter on discursive communities and their role in the enabling and comprehending of irony. This chapter will concentrate more on the **relational** at the level of meaning–interaction and thus also in terms of the other two aspects of ironic meaning, the **inclusive** (both/and) and the **differential**. The former makes possible a rethinking of the standard semantic notion of irony as a simple antiphrasis which can be understood by a straightforward meaning substitution; the latter offers an explanation of the problematic kinship between irony and other tropes and forms such

RABBIT OR DUCK?

Plate 3.1 "Rabbit or duck?"
Source: From Scheidemann, *Experiments in General Psychology* (Chicago: University of Chicago
Press, 1929); reproduced with the permission of the University of Chicago Press.

as metaphor and allegory. But both these aspects obviously rely upon the
idea of ironic meaning as **relational**, as the result of the bringing – even the
rubbing – together of the said and the unsaid, each of which takes on
meaning only in relation to the other. Admittedly, this (like most) is not a
relation of equals: the power of the unsaid to challenge the said is the
defining semantic condition of irony.

One of the ways I've tried to think about the **inclusivity** of ironic meaning
has been through a number of suggestive images. Like most (by definition,
reductive) attempts to model a complex phenomenon, these analogies are
not perfect. They each need supplementing in different ways, but they may
prove useful none the less. One such image is the well-known example (see
Plate 3.1) – used by Wittgenstein in his *Philosophical Investigations* (taken
from the psychologist Jastrow) and then by E.H. Gombrich in *Art and
Illusion* – of the figure that can be interpreted as either a duck or a rabbit,
depending on whether you see a bird's bill or a long pair of ears in the
extended shape issuing from a central mass. While Gombrich says our eyes

can't experience both readings at the same time (1969: 5), I would suggest that, when it comes to the ducks and rabbits of ironic meaning, our minds almost can. In interpreting irony, we can and do oscillate very rapidly between the said and the unsaid. (On reflexive oscillation in general, see Siegle 1986: 18.) But – and here the visual analogy needs adapting – it is not the two "poles" themselves that are important; it is the idea of a kind of rapid perceptual or hermeneutic *movement between* them that makes this image a possibly suggestive and productive one for thinking about irony.

While it does not permit me to figure the fact that the unsaid is the more weighted or privileged in the mix of semantic meanings that constitute irony, this image (or, rather, the idea of the *perception* of it) does allow a way to think about ironic meaning as something in flux, and not fixed. It also implies a kind of simultaneous perception of more than one meaning (Kerbrat-Orecchioni 1980a: 111; Groupe Mu 1978: 427; de Man 1969; Tittler 1984: 25) in order to create a third composite (ironic) one. To invoke yet another image, this may be a version of what in music is called triple-voicing: "two notes played together produce a third note which is at once both notes and neither" (McCracken 1991: 7). Irony would thus share with puns a simultaneity (Stewart 1978/79: 146–70) and a superimposition of meanings (Redfern 1984: 26; N.V. Smith 1989: 84). While, in reality, of course, one of the "notes" of irony is literally silent, unsaid, to think in terms of a playing together of two or more semantic notes to produce a third (ironic) one has at least one advantage over the related image of irony as a photographic double exposure (Rodway 1962: 113): it suggests more than simply the overdetermined space of superimposition by implying a notion of action and interaction in the creation of a third – the actual ironic – meaning. What both images lack, of course, is any sense of that critical edge or evaluative investment that I have argued to be part of the definition of irony.

All these images – solution, double exposure, triple-voicing, and the duck/rabbit oscillation – do imply, however, that ironic meaning is *simultaneously* double (or multiple), and that therefore you don't actually have to reject a "literal" meaning in order to get at what is usually called the "ironic" or "real" meaning of the utterance. I have used such analogies here, despite their individual inadequacies, because they all imply in one way or another that both the said and the unsaid together make up that third meaning, and I want to argue that *this* is what should more accurately be called the "ironic" meaning. Some theorists claim that we cannot consistently embrace both the literal and ironic meanings (Kaufer 1977: 97), but I would suggest not only that we can but that, if we do not, then we are not interpreting the utterance *as ironic* at all. Others claim that psychological tests show that people often don't "compute" the literal meanings of ironic utterances (Gibbs 1984: 290), and so they draw the conclusion that the literal may not even be obligatory to comprehension.

60

Maybe, but would it still be irony? Would we still be dealing with irony if the multiple components of its said and unsaid meanings were simplified and made single? Just where would the irony happen? Irony needs *both* the stated *and* the unstated, for it is a form of what has been called "polysemia" – "this unsaid that is nevertheless said" (Foucault 1972: 110).

This **inclusive** model need not have built into it the restrictions of the standard semantic notion of irony as direct inversion – that is, as the simple opposite or contrary to be substituted for the literal meaning. Ducks are not the opposite of rabbits; they are simply other, different. We can certainly talk of irony, as many have in relating it to the comic (Niebuhr 1952: viii; Muecke 1969: 53), in terms of an incongruity between what is usual and what is unexpected, between what is said and what is unsaid. But, for one thing, incongruity is not contrariety, and, for another, both terms would still have to be perceived together (with some resultant abrasive edge) for the incongruous comparison to be considered ironic (Paulos 1980: 9). This active process is another way to think about the idea of *agency* and thus to begin to explain both the suspicion of irony's politics and also – paradoxically – the oppositional power it is also seen to have (Chambers 1991: 238–9).

The unnecessary reduction of irony to the *either/or* model of inversion has led to radically simplified notions of how ironic meaning comes into being and therefore of its possible politics. The most common and authoritative of these notions is the theory I have been addressing here: the view that irony involves a conscious rejection of the literal meaning and the substitution of an "ironic" (often opposite) meaning (Fish 1983). Consequently, theories have been developed outlining the steps taken from setting aside the literal meaning to the choice of a new one (Booth 1974: 10–12). These argue that the said is cancelled or withdrawn (Beardsley 1958: 138) and replaced by a "true" meaning (Culler 1975: 157). But this *either/or* theory does not account for the **inclusive** and simultaneous nature of ironic meaning as that third semantic note, or as the dynamic and rapid oscillation between both the duck and the rabbit. The rejection/substitution theory limits the scope and impact of irony (see Barthes 1974: 44–5) by reducing it to a single disparity between said and unsaid, between sign and meaning (C.D. Lang 1988: 194), usually articulated in terms of incompatibility (Beardsley 1958: 256; Muecke 1969: 53; Koestler 1964: 35).

This description of irony's interpretation is based upon the definition of irony as antiphrasis or semantic inversion. This pervasive view can be found everywhere, in treatises of classical and medieval rhetoric (see Karstetter 1964: 165–7; Cuddon 1979: 336; Gaunt 1989: 7–8; Haidu 1968: 14–22; Campbell 1979; D. Knox 1989: 12, 158–69; Monson 1988: 539–40) and in more recent structural theories of figures (Cohen 1970). Downplaying the existence of what I've been calling irony's defining edge, among many

61

other things, this view usually conflates irony, which is said to offer "a meaning opposite to its literal meaning" (Lanham 1991: 93) and antiphrasis, the "use of a word or phrase to convey an idea exactly opposite to its real significance" (Holman and Harmon 1986: 29). This view of irony as the simple "bringing in of the opposite" is shared by theorists as diverse as I.A. Richards (1925: 250) and John Searle, who writes:

> Stated very crudely, the mechanism by which irony works is that the utterance, if taken literally, is obviously inappropriate to the situation. Since it is grossly inappropriate, the hearer is compelled to reinterpret it in such a way as to render it appropriate, and the most natural way to interpret it is meaning the opposite of its literal form.
>
> (Searle 1979b: 113)

From speech act theorists (Grice 1989: 34 and 53) to structural linguists (Kerbrat-Orecchioni 1980a: 118–19; Groupe Mu 1978: 428, and 1981: 146), there is considerable agreement that, taken in semantic terms, irony is simply antiphrastic inversion on the level of the word. My argument is that, of course, *some* ironies can be defined in this way, but what exactly would a general definition of *all* irony solely in terms of opposites and contraries actually entail?

Would it mean that what most people call the "ironic" meaning (but which, as I argue above, should be called, more accurately, simply the unsaid) must necessarily be in a relation of logical contradiction to the said or "literal" meaning? Hegel implied as much when he claimed that "irony contradicts and annihilates itself" (1920: 92). The idea of negation or logical contradiction might actually appear to work on the level of individual word or phrase: "Nice day!" when it is pouring rain translates into its opposite easily enough ... unless, of course, you happen to love rainy weather. And, as the second section of this chapter suggests, it is harder to see how all the parts of a more complex ironic utterance could be logically contradictory (without becoming paradoxical rather than ironic [see Watzlawick, Beavin and Jackson 1967]). And what would you do with even the straightforward-seeming example of "I love people who signal" when uttered by a driver in city traffic who has just been cut off by a driver who did *not* signal (Meyers 1974: 172). In context, this is irony; but the statement is also literally true. So too is its total opposite: "I hate people who do not signal," but such a decoding would, in fact, involve inverting *both* parts (and not simply one) of a relatively simple sentence. Unfortunately, no theory of irony as simply logical contradiction on the level of the word would be able to explain how you would know the difference and choose between "I love people who do not signal" or "I hate people who signal," on the one hand, and "I hate people who do not signal," on the other.

An even more obvious example would be Mark Antony's famous line in *Julius Caesar* (a line all the "ironologists" in the world seem to agree is

62

ironic) – "Brutus is an honourable man." But could it not mean, by the terms of the logical contradiction theory, "all who are *not* Brutus *are* honourable men," as well as, more obviously, "Brutus is *not* an honourable man"? Could it even mean: "Brutus is an honourable *woman*"? I risk silliness here, perhaps, but the problem is a real one, given the restrictive definition and the inability *of the theory* to locate the irony in any particular one word of that sentence in order to guide us in inverting or negating it. *In practice,* of course, as I'll discuss in detail in a later chapter, it is the context of Shakespeare's play that directs our interpretation easily enough, but the ironic meaning happens not simply through a binary (either honorable or dishonorable) choice, but through an **inclusive** one bound up in a complex set of psychological motivations of characters (Mark Antony, Brutus, the other conspirators) as well as responses of various listeners (the Roman crowd, the conspirators, the theater audience or reader). In addition, antiphrastic theories of irony often ignore this kind of contextual conditioning of meaning-making, especially in longer utterances (see Hutcheon and Butler 1981: 245; Iser 1978: 130); they also tend to downplay that important evaluative edge that forms part of the power of Mark Antony's ironic indictment (Jorgensen, Miller and Sperber 1984: 112), an indictment born less of logical contradiction alone than of recontextualized repetition of that one line. Even a brief consideration of the most common rhetorical devices deployed in ironic texts will show that antiphrasis explains only some of them, such as litotes and contradiction; whereas, on the contrary, hyperbole works by excess, not opposition, and meiosis operates by playing down more than by playing against. As is the case with Mark Antony's speech, repetition often qualifies context, but not necessarily in consistent or only opposite terms.

My extended discussion of this one semantic model of irony as simple logical contradiction (and meaning substitution) is only warranted because of its dominant historical position in so many different fields and because of the general restrictive effect I think it has had on thinking about irony differently. This is why I want to consider here what might occur if ironic meaning were seen to be constituted not necessarily only by an *either/or* substitution of opposites but by *both* the said *and* the unsaid working together to create something new. The semantic "solution" of irony would then hold in suspension the said plus something *other than* and *in addition to* it that remained unsaid. My hope is that such a model might open up new and more productive ways to think and talk about irony. For example, the **inclusive** pleasure of irony – similar to that claimed for jokes and puns (Greimas 1986: 71) – might then be seen to reside precisely in the discovery of two or more different "isotopies" or principles of coherence in an utterance thought to be single and homogeneous. Roland Barthes (1977b: 66) once recycled a traditional term for ambiguous discourse – amphibology (or amphiboly) – to describe those doubled terms which keep

63

both their meanings, which allow us to hear "*something else*" at one and the same time as they are uttered (ibid.: 72–3). Some theorists have used the model of the dialectic to understand the tension between the said and the unsaid (Brown 1983: 544; Bloom 1975: 95), especially the dynamic interaction of the two, each upon the other (Burke 1969a: 512). Others have used Bakhtin's (1984) idea of double-voicing or the dialogic (Chamberlain 1989: 104; Mizzau 1984: ch. 2). The related linguistic idea of "disemia" or "diglossia" used to describe language with double registers (Herzfeld 1982) might also help, if the definition of ironic meaning were opened up. Each of these models is **inclusive** (in semantic terms) rather than exclusive or restrictive. Each is also premised upon a notion, not of direct contrariety or opposition, but simply of difference.

One influential and much cited definition suggests that irony operates where "the sign points to something that differs from its literal meaning and has for its function the thematization of this difference" (de Man 1969: 192). This would be the third, the **differential** aspect of ironic meaning that follows upon its **relational** and **inclusive** aspects. Ironic meaning forms when two or more different concepts are brought together: ducks and rabbits. The unsaid is other than, different from, the said. There is a long (but often ignored) tradition of this less restrictive definition of irony, going back to Quintilian (1977: 6.3.89) and Cicero (1979: 2.67.269). Put in structuralist terms, the ironic sign would thus be made up of one signifier but two different, but not necessarily opposite, signifieds. In *A Theory of Parody* (1985), I argued that irony always marks difference but, there, I did so in order to argue for a specific definition of parody as a structure of ironic repetition. Here, my primary interest is, rather, in irony's specific semantic identity and thus in trying to sort out the differences between it and other tropes, other forms of indirection, for often they have all been lumped together in critical discussions.

For example, if metaphor reveals "hitherto unsuspected connectives" (Burke 1984: 90), then irony cannot be "a kind of metaphor" (White 1978: 73). The two tropes may indeed belong to the same general family of semantic deviations (Moore 1982: 1), but metaphor's defining relation of similarity is not the same (in either tone or structure) as irony's defining relation of difference. The notion of irony as metaphor to which is added the idea of contradiction (Sapir 1977: 5n.) fails to take into account both the edge that irony gets from its **differential** semantic structure and the necessarily dynamic, performative and social dimensions of ironic happenings. Metaphor is "rooted in the naming function of language," while irony is "based on the communicative function" (Scholes 1982: 76). Of course, both tropes are obviously semantically plural, bringing together more than one meaning to create a composite, different, interdependent one. As well as being "additive" (cf. Booth 1974: 22–4 on irony as "subtractive") in this way, both are also equally context-dependent (as the famous arguments about metaphor by both Max Black [1962] and Paul Ricoeur [1975] show). Nevertheless, the most significant point for my argument here is one of contrast, not likeness: the basic semantic identity of irony is mostly in terms of difference and that of metaphor is mainly in terms of similarity (see D. Knox 1989: 4–6).

From a semantic point of view, the other form that is often confused or combined with irony is allegory, and again for obvious reasons. Both involve saying one thing and meaning another (Honig 1959: 129; Fletcher 1964: 2; Todorov 1973: 63; Abrams 1981: 4). As is the case with irony, the said of allegory could be seen as inseparable from the unsaid (Honig 1959: 104), and together these two might constitute what would be called the "allegorical" meaning. Interestingly, this view runs counter to prevailing orthodoxy in the study of both forms: it is the unsaid that is usually referred to as the "ironic" or the "allegorical" meaning, thereby implying that the said and the unsaid are indeed separable. Some views of allegory bear a great resemblance to those substitution theories of irony just examined: "there is only one real meaning, which the first meaning is frankly a device to convey" (Empson 1963: 128). The fact that, in terms of semantic structure, irony and allegory would seem to share much has led to their frequent conflation. Irony has been called an "instance of allegory's double meaning" (Lanham 1991: 93), on the one hand; on the other, there is a tradition in the Middle Ages that saw allegory as "the supremely ironic mode" (Campbell 1979: 300).

Their "related conceptual resemblance" (Swearingen 1991: 225) is indeed what led Paul de Man, in his famous essay, "The Rhetoric of Temporality" (1969) to consider allegory and irony as "two faces of the same fundamental experience of time" (ibid.: 207), as both divided and producing a divided self. But, like that of the German romantic ironists before him, de Man's interest in the "reflexive disjunction of irony" (Mileur 1986: 331) is not semantic, but is framed in psychological and existential terms of authenticity (de Man 1969: 203); it is also presented, of course, in deconstructive terms of "tropological cognitions." His use of Friedrich Schlegel's idea of "parabasis" as a revelation of discontinuity, however, does offer a way to think through the differences as well as the similarities between allegory and irony. The major distinction to be made, as in the case of metaphor, is that allegory relies on an "aptly suggestive resemblance" (*OED*) between the said and the unsaid, while irony is always structured on a relation of difference. The relation of allegory's said to its unsaid is also usually restricted to a single set of substitutes (Stewart 1978/79: 178), even if its actual scale can be extensive. According to the **inclusive** (rather than exclusive or antiphrastic) definition of how irony "means," irony would be semantically much more open to multiplicity than allegory; it would also be more omnivorous in its compass (Shapiro and Shapiro 1988: 9).

The etymology of the two terms suggests yet another distinction: the relatively benign nature of allegory's "speaking otherwise" contrasts with the more suspect, dissembling intent at the root of irony's *eiron* to point again to that difference in edge or critical evaluation. Of course, edge is also one of the things that differentiates irony from ambiguity (cf. Furst 1984: 12). Both certainly signify more than one thing (Abrams 1981: 8), but the ambiguous lacks the ironic's critical differential impact and, also, according to some, its precision of communication (Booth 1974: 172): "[i]f the text is ironical, then it is no longer ambiguous" (Dane 1991: 66).

However, as I've already noted, saying one thing and meaning something different with a dissimulating intent defines lying as much as it does irony. And so it has been argued one way or another since Plato's Socrates: "The Western aesthetic and ethical scrutiny of irony, and of related notions of linguistic deceit and lying, is as old as rhetoric and literacy" (Swearingen 1991: ix; see, for a detailed history, D. Knox 1989: 39–57). Vico said irony was "fashioned of falsehood by dint of a reflection which wears the mask of truth" (1968: 408). And, once again, psychologists claim that children can only learn irony when they have learned that people can lie or pretend (Winner 1988). Irony too "presupposes awareness of the distinction between truth and falsehood, of the possibility of misrepresenting reality in language, and of the difference between a literal and a figurative representation" (White 1978: 208). There is no doubt, that, taken directly – at face value – an ironic utterance may make perfect sense, but it would (as irony) still somehow be false (or, as I would prefer, different or other) (Fogelin 1988: 7). The difference here is in the intention: lies are not usually intended to be interpreted or decoded *as lies*; on the contrary, ironies are really only ironies when someone makes them happen. Like paradoxes (Sainsbury 1988: 1), lies are permanently intended contradictions; ironic meanings, however, are formed through additive oscillations between different said and unsaid meanings. Irony arises from "the interaction of terms upon one another," all "integrally affecting one another" (Burke 1969a: 512), even if the unsaid is a sort of *primus inter pares*, weighting the evaluative force of irony's edge to what is unstated, even while oscillating with what is stated.

As a possible way out of the conceptual restrictions put in place by the long and powerful tradition of one particular semantic definition of irony, I am suggesting here that we stop thinking of irony only in binary *either/or* terms of the substitution of an "ironic" for a "literal" (and opposite) meaning, and see what might happen if we found a new way of talking about ironic meaning as, instead, **relational**, **inclusive**, and **differential**. If we considered irony to be formed through a relation both between people and also between meanings – said and unsaid – then, like the duck/rabbit image, it would involve an oscillating yet simultaneous perception of plural and different meanings.

66

II THEATER GOES TO THE MOVIES: *HENRY V*

I have chosen the 1989 film of Shakespeare's play *Henry V* by the young British actor and director, Kenneth Branagh, as my case-study for such a rethinking of the semantics of irony. While a simple antiphrastic model might well work for straightforward, easily contextualized examples ("What splendid weather" uttered during a blizzard), I have been suggesting that longer and more complex examples are not easily explained in terms of opposition alone. My major focus here will be on Branagh's film in its relations with both the original play and the famous 1944 wartime film of it by Laurence Olivier. (In both film versions, the director was also the star actor.) While there have been many movie and video versions (see Rothwell and Melzer 1990: 93–100), this particular pairing of films has been especially suggestive for *me* in the exploring of the shape and definition of ironic meaning. *You* might well find that you have still other, different sets of interplaying texts – other productions of the play (see Tatspaugh 1992), other films, other Shakespearean plays – as did I too, of course. But here I want to try to limit my analysis, however artificially.

A number of important *caveats* are still in order, though. I should stress from the start that I will be working here from the two films themselves, and not from the screenplays. I've always felt that the latter are separate texts – both intentionally and semiotically – and are obviously not identical to the films as actually achieved and, more importantly, as experienced in the visual medium. I mention this because, in fact, most of the recent commentary (especially by literary scholars) on Branagh's film, in particular, is based primarily on the screenplay (Branagh 1989) for its remarks about the film itself. In this chapter I want to try to conduct a kind of admittedly artificial experiment to sort out irony's semantics: in order to do so, I will try to bracket the intentions of the director (as displayed in the screenplay or in other comments). I have been arguing, I know, that intention – the ironist's *and* the interpreter's – is not ignorable in dealing with irony; here, though, in order to keep the focus as much as possible on the **relational**, **inclusive** and **differential** nature of irony *in semantic terms*, I want to analyze the actual text of the film and (because it is unavoidable) how I as spectator interpret or "perform" the interplay of that film, its predecessor, and its source text. In other words, I want to foreground the fact that *I* am attributing irony to the textual interaction of the two films as I "read" them together with the play.

Few critics have denied that Branagh appears to intend viewers to see some sort of connection with Olivier's film. My interpretation of that connection as ironic, however, will be partial and truncated, limited to structural and hermeneutic dimensions, because I am deliberately bracketing Branagh's later autobiography, the interviews he gave and the comments he made during and after filming. All of these have subsequently provoked very different responses to the film itself than are evident in the first reviews and articles which do not refer to anything but the actual film. The change in interpretive context that occurs with the addition of the screenplay and these other intentional documents has been decisive in altering critics' (and even my own) evaluation of the work as a whole. What many see as the pretentious and even pompous tone of many of Branagh's remarks about his film, its alleged inspiration drawn from Prince Charles (as ideal princely monarch), and its perceived general complicity with the ideology of Thatcherite politics and economics, have led many critics (especially British leftist ones) to condemn both the film and its director. It is not that I would necessarily quarrel with such an interpretation of Branagh's personality or ideological position, but here I nevertheless want to limit my focus – for purely heuristic reasons – to the film as visual/verbal text and how I, as spectator, see ironic meaning happening, specifically in its intertextual relationship to the unsaid of the earlier film. I will present the interpretations of others in order to offer both a corrective to and a commentary upon my own limited point of view.

Branagh's *Henry V* has been called a "detailed reply" (Klawans 1989: 725) to Olivier's. And so it is – but, from my artifically restricted (semantic) point of view, it seems to be so in a particularly complex and ironic way. Its differential but structurally inclusive relation to its cinematic intertext (as well as, obviously, in a different way to its dramatic text) is what suggests to me the possibility of multiple-voiced ironic meanings happening, not only at a formal level but also at a thematic one, with the result that my attention was focused on things like the radical changes that have come about over time in the cultural meaning of things like war, nationalism, and leadership. Truisms these may be, but the fact remains that, in 1989, not one of these things meant the same as it did in 1944, or in 1599 when Shakespeare wrote the play, or for that matter, in 1415, when the historical action took place.

It is not that Branagh's film updates Shakespeare's play in the way post-1960 theatrical productions often do – that is, in protest against nineteenth-century "operatic" stage productions that generalized, universalized and moralized. It has not put into action Jan Kott's thesis in *Shakespeare Our Contemporary* by setting the play in modern times; nor does it overtly make the drama topical through parallels with political leaders of our own day, as various Royal Shakespeare Company productions have done (see Sinfield 1985). Yet, Branagh's version is also not offered in ignorance of these newer readings. Indeed, one critic has even stated that, "[d]eeply cognizant of 'political' and 'alternative' Shakespeares, Branagh plumbs more of the play's ironies, more fully engages the dissonance beneath the surface of Shakespeare's epic history than Olivier does" (P.S. Donaldson 1991: 71). Both films basically keep with period costume; yet, in a sense, it could be said that both *have* made Shakespeare into their contemporaries in more subtle ways. Olivier's film offers an inspiring

Henry for a war-weary England; Branagh's film presents a war-weary Henry for a very different England – now "an eclipsed world power" (Holderness 1991: 75) – that might see itself not only through this new film's vision but also through eyes of the past, eyes which have seen Olivier's film.

In order to trace how the ironies in Branagh's *Henry V* happen for me, a certain amount of background context might be helpful, for I suspect that it was my response to what many have seen as the ironies of the *play* that likely sensitized me to other ironic possibilities in the film made of it. I knew, from having taught the play, that *Henry V* seemed to be one of the most thematically, politically, and formally complex of Shakespeare's plays – at least if you go by the amount of controversy and disagreement it has generated. For a number of reasons, it sits on a "site of ideological contestation" (Holderness, Potter and Turner 1987: 62). First of all, themes such as patriotism, foreign wars, national unity, while perhaps unfortunate constants in human history, have specific meanings that are historically and culturally contingent; thus critics through the ages, not surprisingly, have rarely agreed on their interpretation or evaluation. Second, the play itself (like so many of Shakespeare's plays) formally draws upon a variety of genres that are not going to coexist without some tension: epic, history, legend, hagiography, comedy, romance. Third, there are many ironies and internal contradictions – both within the plot and within Henry's character – that have busied commentators for centuries.

One result of this formal and political complexity that turned out to be relevant to my own reading of the film is that the critics have taken a number of opposing positions *vis-à-vis* both the hero and the play. Simply put, there are those who see Henry as the ideal Christian English monarch and those for whom he is the scheming, militaristic Machiavellian prince par excellence. Another position that has been more frequent lately is that which attempts to reconcile the text's contradictions – through balancing or synthesizing them in some sort of dialectic. One version of this is the reading of the play as deftly registering "every nuance of royal hypocrisy, ruthlessness, and bad faith, but it does so in the context of a celebration, a collective panegyric to 'This star of England', the charismatic leader who purges the commonwealth of its incorrigibles and forges the martial nation State" (Greenblatt 1985: 42). In this interpretation, the play's subtle subversion of Henry's glory is bitterly ironic or radically ambiguous, but either way it serves "paradoxically to intensify the power of the king and his war" (Greenblatt 1985: 43). Given what so many see as the play's inherent doubleness or ambiguity, it may not be at all surprising that another critic (Rabkin 1988: 36) should turn to the same rabbit-as-duck-as-rabbit image as I have been using in this chapter to describe the effect of this paradoxical characterization of Henry. For me, it is less paradox than irony at work here: because of the simultaneous inclusiveness of Shakespeare's complex presentation of the king, I find myself flipping back and forth, from seeing

69

the heroic duck to seeing the Machiavellian rabbit (or would it be vice versa?) throughout the play, but at such a rate that I constantly perceive *both* the duck *and* the rabbit. And, while this image has also been used to characterize the "ambiguity" of Branagh's particular portrayal of Henry's character (Deats 1992: 285), my interest here – in semantic terms – is in irony, not ambiguity. Ambiguity does not depend on the simultaneous and edgy playing off of one meaning against another in a **relational, inclusive,** and **differential** way like this; irony does.

Many critics have pointed out the obvious verbal and dramatic ironies of certain scenes of the play itself. One has even claimed that this is the most "persistently and thoroughly misunderstood" of Shakespeare's works precisely because it is ironic (Gould 1969: 81), and therefore its contradictions, far from being a sign of Shakespeare's failing powers (see Van Doren 1939), should be read as a "satire on monarchical government, on imperialism, on the baser kinds of 'patriotism', and on war" (Gould 1969: 83). This particular critic's mode of argument is to cite lines from the play (such as, something from Henry's speech before the gates of Harfleur) and then ask a rhetorical question of the type: "Is it seriously maintained that Shakespeare means us to admire Henry *here*?" (ibid.: 92). Unfortunately, the history of criticism of the play suggests that many have indeed maintained precisely that. (See, for instance, E.E. Stoll's denial of irony in the Harfleur passage in Quinn 1969: 99 – "The words thrill us . . .") Nevertheless, there are still contradictions in the play, contradictions such as the Chorus's "celebration of Henry and his war in France" and "the complicated, ambiguous, and sometimes flatly contradictory scenes which these speeches are made to introduce" (Barton 1988: 13), and these *do* produce a constant kind of double and differential focus that is at least structurally conducive to being interpreted as ironic.

The play's contradictions, tensions, juxtapositions and doublings, as well as its abundant self-deflatings, then, might leave considerable room for a director – or a reader – to set in motion the oscillations of ironic meaning. If, as has been argued, "[p]atriotism, heroism, chivalry, the romance of war, can induce admiration and delight only when detached from their actual historical context and safely recreated in the security of the theatre purely as ideological entities" (Holderness 1992: 109), then it is not only the play's potential structural ironies, but perhaps its insistent meta-theatrical reflexivity that would suggest the possibilities of a distancing, detached irony. Given the conventions of the bare Elizabethan stage, one might argue that all Shakespeare's plays depend mightily upon the audience's powers of imagination. But not all of them are as insistent as this one is upon the limitations of that stage or upon the gap between the visible and the imagined. These constant reminders have the effect, says one critic, of making us "invest in the illusion of magnificence," dazzled by our own "imaginary identification with the conqueror" (Greenblatt 1985: 43).

Intellectual distance need not interfere with imaginative (and even emotional) participation (Pilkington 1991: 120). Dr Johnson, by contrast, simply saw these reflexive reminders as proof that Shakespeare "was fully sensible of the absurdity of showing battles [and the like] in the theatre" (in Woudhuysen 1989: 206), though later critics have chastised the playwright for having to tell rather than show the action. Whatever the historical relativity of the effect and interpretation of the Chorus's role, directors today – working in a general cultural context where reflexivity is almost the norm – have at their disposal a ready turf for ironic oscillation in the Chorus's treatment of what even Shakespeare's sources (Hall's 1548 *Union of the Two Noble Houses of Lancaster and York* and Holinshed's 1587 *Chronicles*) presented as contradictory and unresolved.

In fact, both Olivier's and Branagh's films are very reflexive and self-consciously "historical," though in different ways. Olivier's presents a fictional performance of the play by the Lord Chamberlain's Men, on the first of May 1600 in the newly opened Globe Theatre in London. From a printed handbill blown by the wind in front of the camera, a crane-shot over a deliberately and "patently artificial" (Holderness 1992: 186) model of London (based on Visscher's famous view) comes to rest on the playhouse, with its flag flying. The camera follows the line of the flagpole downward into the building, where the flag raiser is seen finishing his job as the audience gets seated and an orchestra plays Renaissance-style music – composed by Olivier's contemporary, William Walton. (At the end of the film, the camera exits with the exact same series of shots in reverse.) Unlike Branagh's, this is a "stage-centred treatment" (Willson 1991: 28): to start the production, a boy enters with a placard announcing the play's title, a trumpet sounds, the Chorus (Leslie Banks) pulls a painted curtain at the rear of the bare stage and begins the first of his reflexive addresses to the audience. The opening scenes are played broadly, often for comic effect, as actors play to the Globe's pit and get the desired responses from the "Elizabethan" crowd. In the self-reflexive space between scenes i and ii, the camera follows the exiting actors backstage, where Olivier (the actor) is seen to cough, clear his throat somewhat nervously, and then walk onstage (this time as Henry) to rapturous applause. His virtuoso style of acting is very grand and "theatrical"; he projects his voice – and the camera moves back as he does, while the royal oratory remains equally loud and powerful, even at a distance in a long shot (see Manvell 1979: 38). The camera also shows the happy audience responding generously.

This meta-theatrical frame and its action continue on this reconstructed Elizabethan stage until the court also moves – to Southampton in Act II, scene ii – when the set changes and the bareness is replaced by different, that is, painted backdrop, scenery, and the fictional audience disappears. The Chorus, who has been appearing each time the text demanded, pulling a curtain on the back of the Elizabethan stage to signal his different

71

position and status in the story (as well as acting as a reminder of stage conventions), this time appears in utter darkness, as if floating in air on a black screen. His injunction to the audience to "Grapple your minds to sternage of this navy,/And leave your England" (moved here from the Chorus's section in III, 18–19) accompanies miniature model ships on water, presumably crossing the sea to France. The mind-grappling challenge in this version, I remember musing, is perhaps to imagine the real thing from these patent simulacra.

There is then a change to historically different, though equally theatrical conventions in terms of acting styles and also sets (in the French court, then at the walls of Harfleur, and so on). These never look "real" – or I should say, movie-realistic; though some critics have felt that they invoke "painterly, spectacular codes of representation used in the silent cinema before World War I" (Collick 1989: 47), they remain for me more semiotically coded as "pictorial, anti-realistic" (Manvell 1979: 39) and, more importantly, as "stage." The particular art-historical period suggested by these stage-y sets is medieval (with non-naturalistic scale and lack of perspective). In one critic's view, "Olivier's camera and Walton's music prettied up the atmosphere, transporting their war-weary audience to the fairy-tale world of the Duc de Berry" (Rabkin 1988: 44) – who is actually shown examining one such picture from his famous book of hours painted by the Limbourg brothers. In fact, this book, *Les très riches heures du Jean, Duc de Berri*, is what seems to have inspired the idealized artifice of the costumes and sets in the French scenes.

These stage conventions generally prevail until the one major scene that is done outdoors on location and in totally cinematic terms: the battle scene at Agincourt. This is most appropriate, for Shakespeare does *not*, of course, represent this on stage at all. The reflexivity of the (stage) Chorus here disappears:

> *Action* replaces *acting*; the serious business of fighting suppresses the freedom of theatrical play; the world of the film becomes more like the Britain of 1940. The critical exigencies of the contemporary situation pull the film back, away from its aesthetic experiments, into complicity with the ideologies of patriotism, war enthusiasm and national unity.
>
> (Holderness 1992: 190; see too P.S. Donaldson 1991: 62;
> cf. Pilkington 1991: 111)

Horses, men in armour and on foot, do a crowded but relatively stylized and sedate dance of battle that is almost a kind of chivalric tournament, choreographed with the visual aid of an Uccello painting. There are shots of people on horses falling into the mud, of course, and the ironic echoes for me are of Eisenstein's *Alexander Nevsky* (1930) and the battle in the snow. In other scenes, it is Michael Curtiz's *The Adventures of Robin Hood* (1938) that might be recalled for some spectators. In this 1940s-style "romanticized realism" (Deats 1992: 285), there is a lot of human noise and some metallic sounds, but little blood or pain (P.S. Donaldson 1990: 15). The march of the victorious English army into the distance at the end of Act IV marks the move out of the conventions of film again and back to a stage set, for the column of men moves toward what is an obviously painted backdrop with "the shallow, stylized perspective" of those French medieval miniatures (Manvell 1979: 39). The action remains in this particular mode until its final moments when, seamlessly, a transition is made and the camera pulls back to show a theatrically made-up Olivier and a boy actor playing Katharine. The applauding audience turns out to be the one sitting in the Globe Theatre, whence the camera exits as it entered, with shots of the Globe's boys' choir, the flag (descending, this time), an aerial view of the theater and then of all London, with the wind blowing a playbill (with the film's credits inscribed on it) in front of the camera.

The symbolic historical process of moving from the Elizabethan to later, painted (though pictorially medievalized) stage conventions, and finally to film, and then back in a palindromic reverse to the Globe again, is all taking place, of course, within a movie. It is this particular film/play paradox – of which Olivier's film was cleverly and reflexively aware – that I saw Branagh's film ironizing in a cumulative way, right from the start. Its Chorus's voice, opening with the "O for a Muse of fire," accompanies a single match being lit on an otherwise dark screen – a literalizing relational joke that worked as a very early signal for me to watch out for verbal and visual interplay here. This reduction of epic fire to a solitary, uninspiring match also provoked a slight, differential ironic play, to which was added the fact that the "brightest heaven of invention" to which the Muse might ascend here was given inclusive and plural recontextualizing: "invention" here was not only Shakespeare's rhetorical term for poetic creation; it also became the electric power and lighting (a later "invention") that the Chorus was in the process of ostentatiously switching on. (By extension, perhaps, it could also be the camera which is filming all of this.) Metaphorically, this "invention" points to the relation of theater and film to power – political as well as electrical.

Branagh's Chorus walks through an empty set as he speaks of the need for the audience to use its imagination: "let us.../On your imaginary forces work./Suppose within the girdle of these walls/Are now confin'd two mighty monarchies" (Prologue, 17–20). For me, the earlier accumulation of those literalizing and reductive meanings in the verbal/visual interplay suggested potential ironic meaning could be made to happen between these words and the fact that, in film, the audience can be *shown* everything and need not rely on its "imaginary forces" in quite the same way. The "walls" still exist (and we see them clearly on camera) but the illusionary possibility of escape from their restrictions is accepted as a cinematic norm.

The less obvious irony that slipped into place for me – and not without a real edge – was that, in the years from 1599 to 1989 (or even from 1944 to 1989), film has become perhaps the dominant form of staged narrative, though it may still lack the prestige that has accrued to "serious" theater as high art, especially in Britain. The Branagh film's use of the Chorus's opening gambit worked to ironize for me the difference in medium, but also to capitalize on that high art status of theater, as it presents a film of a play, but uses all the devices that only a camera can make possible: everything from rapid changes of scene to showing actual places, from flashbacks (of the times from the *Henry IV* plays with Falstaff and others) to the use of close-up shots – a device this version deploys to what I found myself reading as considerably ironic effect, largely because of the cutting edge of the play/film medium difference.

Of course, Shakespeare's own possible reasons for having the Chorus appear whenever there was a change of scene or the need for an explanation or description are complex and hotly debated; but, on a very simple level, it is in part a matter of what representation is possible, given the conventions and restrictions of the Elizabethan stage (or any stage): "There is the playhouse now, there must you sit;/And thence to France shall we convey you safe," as the Chorus says in the Prologue to Act II. Films can obviously do things that cannot be done on stage: meta-theater becomes meta-cinema. The Chorus may enjoin the audience to "[t]hink, when we talk of horses, that you see them/Printing their proud hoofs i' the receiving earth" (Prologue, 26–7), but no one has to "think" very much at all when you can *see* them actually doing so on the screen. Instead of authorizing the spectator's imagination (P.S. Donaldson 1990: 2), filmic representation may actually in some ways limit it through visualization (and thus the tyranny of the director's imagination).

The use of the Chorus in Branagh's film underlines this shift in medium by outfitting the Chorus, the (Shakespearean) actor, Derek Jacobi, in contemporary dress (to make a visual connection to the audience), and by placing him right in the middle of the action – like an authoritative television news reporter – thereby making his comments increasingly less imagination-provoking and, instead, more descriptive of what is actually shown on screen. His redundancy in terms of information-providing rubbed against his multiple authority invocations with enough edge for irony to start to happen for me: the increasingly unnecessary presence of the Chorus served as an ironic reminder that this is a film *of a play*. In other words, it both calls attention to Shakespeare's own reminder to his audience that they were watching a play and also establishes an ironic difference from at least one of the original purposes of the Chorus's descriptions in that play: to encourage us to imagine and thus transcend the limits of a staged production. Like the Chorus in Olivier's film (see Pilkington 1991: 124), then, this one reminds spectators that they are watching a *performance* after all. If Olivier's reading of the play is close to E.M.W. Tillyard's (Manheim 1983), Branagh's interpretation is in line with at least one aspect of that of a contemporary critic like Graham Holderness: "The relationship between the 'heroic' and 'ironical' dimensions of the play is not in any balance or synthesis of incongruous truths; but in the play's definition of the heroic dimension as a purely *theatrical* reality, an ideology which can be impressive and exciting only in the theatre" (Holderness 1992: 107). Times change; so do critics . . . and films.

Sometimes Branagh's cinematic version of the play invokes another kind of meta-dramatic reminder by having the visual image actually precede the verbal description of it. The Chorus's line at the start of Act III – "Work, work your thoughts, and therein see a siege" (25) – actually *follows* the seeing (and hearing) of the noisy siege of Harfleur. The Chorus is thus reduced to a kind of excited and frightened war correspondent. The most obvious reading would be that Branagh's film is simply showing the enormous power of the visual cinematic medium in contrast to the limits of language and of stage drama's conventions which must rely more on the imagination. But I wonder if the relation of play text to film text here might also be read ironically so as to suggest the *different* use of imagination, the very different (and often naturalized and ignored) work demanded of viewers of film.

The ironic meaning that might happen here, in other words, might not be single or simply contradictory. Nor might it operate to raise only issues of aesthetic form or only problems of spectator response: it might do both. Furthermore, while irony, in this example, can be seen happening in the difference between what can be represented on stage (and in words) and what can be shown to a film audience, the specific thematic content of the discussion – war and patriotism – is itself inevitably implicated in the ironic meaning-making as well. Holderness's reading, stressing the meta-theatricality of the play, making it a "self-mocking dramatic illusion, which inscribes a clear boundary between public morality and the ideological nature of its own 'celebration'" (1992: 111), has not historically been the most common one; until recently, the play had been read as a patriotic play, representing the heightened national self-consciousness of the latter years of Elizabeth's reign. After all, it was written eleven years after the Armada, and the Earl of Essex had just left for Ireland to deal with Tyrone's rebellion. As Sir Edmund Chambers wrote in the early years of our century, the play is "a paean . . . in glorification of the dauntless spirit and invincible endurance of Englishmen, of the folk at unity with itself, among whom king and nobles, yeomen and peasants, vie with each other to show the mettle of their pasture" (1904–1908; in 1925: 111). In the 1990s – in a world politically divided between some sort of "New World Order" and multinational power, on the one hand, and anti-imperial, postcolonial resistance, on the other – this unproblematic enthusiasm might read rather

75

differently. But, this very optimism is also what made the play so attractive
to Olivier in the early 1940s, in the middle of World War II: it made a good
vehicle for exhorting the British to stand firm in the face of uneven odds,
to fight on for England, even to invade Nazi-occupied France, perhaps.

While both films made extensive cuts in the play text, Olivier's choices
are interesting in the light of the film's wartime production and its overt
ideological function: any discussion of internal dissent and treason is
removed (the danger of the Scots in I, ii; the three traitors in II, ii; William's
challenge to Henry-in-disguise in IV, vii and viii), as is any suggestion that
the lower-class characters are anything but benign, indeed, almost innocent
in their comic roguery and thieving (gone are the scenes of Bardolph's
hanging in III, v and Pistol as thief in IV, iv). British theater director,
Michael Bogdanov claims that the cutting of 1,500 lines in Olivier's version
took out "all the disturbing elements, the things that make you wonder
whether *Henry V* really is a hymn to the glory of England" (in Elsom 1989:
19). But it is easier to say that today than it might have been in 1944.
"Shakespeare used for propaganda purposes" (Toby Robertson, in Elsom
1989: 84) is perhaps too facile and ahistorical a judgment to make about a
film made in the dark days of World War II (though it was released after
D-Day). It is a fact, though, that Olivier's film does appear to cut most
scenes that might reflect badly on the warrior king, perhaps in order to
justify its dedication to the "Commandos and Airborne Troops of Great
Britain, the spirit of whose ancestors it has been humbly attempted to
recapture in some ensuing scenes" (cited in Holderness 1992: 184).
Sponsored by the Ministry of Information (see Geduld 1973: 14), Olivier's
film does present Henry's war as a glorious, even stately one: everyone is
healthy, clean, well-armed in fine shining armour, encamped in pristine
white tents. There is strangely little violence, verbal or physical (see
Pilkington 1991, 103–5). The only things that distinguish the French and
English camps are the colour of the flags and the military garb. Despite –
or, more likely, because of – the grim material reality of the conflict in
Europe in 1944, British audiences got to watch what might now seem a
sanitized and uplifting version of war, with their most romantic actor
playing the king most romantically. (North American audiences, when it
was released there in 1946, would have seen it in a somewhat different
context, of course.)

How very different for me (and perhaps for you) was the war of
Branagh's 1989 film – after that World War and the one before it, after
Korea, after Vietnam, and, especially, after all the *movies* made about them.
The film was based on the 1984 RSC stage version (directed by Adrian
Noble and starring Branagh as Henry) that was dubbed by the critics the
"post-Falklands" *Henry V*, and, indeed, Branagh's cinematic version of it also
seems to have provoked the paradoxical doubleness of both patriotic pride
and revulsion against militarism that characterized much of the popular

British response to the Falklands campaign. But there is yet another ideological issue at stake here: how to present war today to a generation of spectators over-accustomed to television and movie depictions of violence – real as well as fictional? In Branagh's film, the siege of Harfleur is not the off-stage, silent event described in the play by the Chorus: that now redundant reporter-figure is placed right in the middle of the action, and the action is loud, violent, brutal. The city explodes behind him as – excited and even frightened – he shouts that "the nimble gunner/With linstock now the devilish cannon touches,/And down goes all before them" (Prologue to III, 32–4). The Irish/Welsh confrontation between Macmorris and Fluellen (in III, ii) does not occur in the peaceful, clean stage surroundings of Olivier's film; instead the men squat in the dirt and mud and noise of the battle. Their squabbling is thus made to echo the larger conflict audible around them; the violence of nationalism is not only an international phenomenon, the more recent film suggests. These men are not neatly decked out in the Olivier film's picturesque stage versions of military dress either. They are dirty and wet; their clothes are dark and drab. Seeing in my mind's eye the dry rabbit as well as the wet duck, irony was set in oscillating motion, with an evaluative edge that, by extension, pointed to the unexpurgated horrors of *real* war, even worse than what could be depicted on film.

In Branagh's film, the march through France of the troops is an on-location trudge through mud and pouring rain, with scenes strongly reminiscent of filmic images of the trench warfare of World War I – which, of course, took place in precisely the same area. The English camps are open, as men sleep around what campfires will still burn in the wet. The French leaders, in their tents, are dry, clean, and smugly comfortable. But they are *not* silly, fractious, and weak, as Olivier's version makes them out to be. In fact, in Branagh's, much of the play's dialogue of bickering and offensive bragging is actually cut (from Act III, vi and IV, ii). Likewise, while the King of France in Olivier's movie (as, it must be said, in historical accounts) is a weak old man who faints when he hears of Henry's threats, in Branagh's he is strong and as respectful of his enemy as Henry is of him. War is serious – and frightening – business here.

The battle itself, between the sick, tense, tired, and bedraggled English and the confident and comfortable French who outnumber them 5:1 is actually a strangely personal battle in Branagh's film: thanks to the power of cinematic close-up, familiar faces (on both sides) are shown as they register the terror, pain and struggle of the fighting. The "choreography" of the battle is one I read as both an echo of Olivier's version (especially in the camera's series of crosscuts between English and French troops) and an ironic reworking of it: in both, the French horses and knights gallop *en masse* down on the English from higher ground; the tense English archers wait and wait (even longer than they do in Olivier's film), and finally let

77

loose their cloud of deadly arrows when the French get within range. Both films could be said to democratize – though for different reasons – Shakespeare's play, returning to the archers the important role the historical sources and recent re-evaluations both claim they had in the victory at Agincourt. But in Branagh's version, those arrows are shown actually hitting their mark: animals and people fall; their screams can be heard, just as can the whistling noise of the arrows in flight . . . six flights, in fact, to the single one in Olivier's film. The recall here can certainly be read as a homage to the scene in Olivier's version (Willson 1991: 28), but it is also possible to interpret it, as I did, as an ironizing "echoic mention" (Sperber and Wilson 1978 and 1981) in its seemingly conscious one-upmanship.

The battle in Branagh's film is a very noisy battle: metal clangs against metal; men and animals scream in both pain and triumph. As I mentioned earlier, unlike Olivier's chivalric dance – but always keeping this unsaid in both mind and eye – this battle is a very messy (and brutal) one, with hand-to-hand fighting in the mud, animals falling into water, mud, and blood, people getting their throats slit, their bodies thrown back by the violence of spears and knives. Human agency, not royal charisma, wins this fight. At one point (echoing the battle scene in Orson Welles's *Chimes at Midnight*), the film goes into slow motion (and sound) to reveal in detail how Henry and all the others fight, fall, rise. The possible aestheticizing of death suggested by the convention of slow motion (via Welles or Penn's 1967 *Bonnie and Clyde*) is partially counteracted by what it allows to be seen more clearly: blood, gore, violence, pain. The connotations of the music playing during all this were not, for me, either martial or glorious, as in the earlier film, but tragic, punctuated with the percussion of metal on metal. This is not the "ageless, romantic storybook notion of the Battle of Agincourt" (Crowther 1972: 61) of Olivier's film. If it is timeless at all, it is because wars still rage today. But, like you, I have seen much graphic violence in other filmic representations of war; the conventions and thus the expectations of the 1990s are different from those of the 1940s.

The ironized contrasts continue for me, as the camera itself works to superimpose the duck on the rabbit, Branagh's on Olivier's vision in a relational, inclusive, but clearly differential and pointed manner. Olivier's Henry hears of the many French killed, compared to the very few English, while he is drinking and celebrating with his happy men; Branagh's Henry – dirty, exhausted, unshaven – learns of these numbers while standing by the bodies of the massacred young boys who guarded the troops' luggage. He picks up the body of Falstaff's murdered pageboy and begins to walk with his men across the bloodied battlefield. This long tracking shot begins in silence; then a single soldier's voice begins singing the "Non nobis" that Henry has just ordered for both victory and the dead. More voices are added to the singing of (Pat Doyle's setting of) the psalm of human humility in the face of God's glory: "Non nobis, Domine, non nobis, sed nomini tuo ad gloriam." At the same time, the carnage of war passes before the camera as Henry and his men walk slowly across the field and view the dead (both French and English). The cart upon which Henry deposits the boy's body is, as I shall discuss shortly, also associated with the death of Bardolph, as well as with Henry's rousing "St Crispin's day" speech just before this very battle. The additive and complex nature of these visual associations allows for the structural juxtaposition and thus the edge of irony in the linking of the "honor" of war, not with some single oppositional notion of peace, but instead with a plurality of things like personal betrayal (for both Henry and Bardolph), human frailty, and tragic loss. Henry kisses the dead boy's head, and then closes his own exhausted eyes on the hymn's final (now bitterly ironic) word "gloriam": the only glory here could be God's; there is no concept of human glory that would even make any sense in such a field of death. Here, physical materiality replaces kingly transcendence (P.S. Donaldson 1991: 64); elegy and loss, not joy and victory, dominate. Branagh's film has not questioned at all the legitimacy of nationalism or of Henry's particular war with France, of course; but it has at least exposed the tragic consequences of human aggression (including Henry's own), then and, by implication, now. Things have *not* changed. Foreign wars, nationalism, internal strife were as terrifying in the reign of Elizabeth I, the film may suggest to some, as they are today in the reign of Elizabeth II. Alongside careful historicizing stands this judgment on continuing tragedy – a judgment I felt to be delivered not with nostalgia but with an ironic edge.

In its consistent and, for me, ironic relation to Olivier's film, Branagh's version *can* be read (though, as many other critics have demonstrated, *need* not be read) as an attempt to turn the earlier film's simple patriotic exhortation into something different and more complex. For some, it might suggest a kind of generalized anti-war statement; for others, it might be seen as an attempt to redefine the meaning of patriotism for a very different England. In the process, no matter how it is read politically, the film can also be seen to heighten other ironies already in the text in the presentation of the character at the center of this history play, where "blood, lineage and breeding" (Dollimore and Sinfield 1988: 98) are the Shakespearean markers of heroism and where it often seems as if Henry has been made into an icon in "appropriately stylized postures" (Siemon 1988: 82) within a series of static tableaux. But Branagh's Henry is not the standard heroic leader that Olivier portrays – strong and valiant, regal and brave (see Deats 1992: 285); this one is actually plain (if sensitive) and quite ordinary (if resolute). His first entrance is not in royal red robes to great audience applause (as in Olivier's Globe) but in drab dark colors. Though his first sighting is in back-lit silhouette, reminiscent of Darth Vader, the very small and boyish king does not declaim, but rather speaks in a very

79

quiet voice, almost whispering, thus suggesting, as one critic remarks, "the intimate, tangible character of his authority" (P.S. Donaldson 1991: 63).

Such whispering, of course, is another of the things that film can do in a way that the stage never can. Olivier's entrance (in I, ii) is one shown from the wings, as I mentioned; it is staged and stagey. And so, when he begins to speak in those grand, round tones, certain (stage) acting conventions are being invoked. Branagh as actor indirectly calls attention to (and gently ironizes, through difference) exactly these conventions in his whispering, which, as he continues, gives way to a louder and more menacing voice – lest the audience too, like the French Dauphin, underestimate his present power. This entire scene involving the Archbishop of Canterbury's justification of Henry's claim to the French throne and the king's decision to go to war is played deadly seriously in Branagh's film, in stark contrast to all the comic fun of Olivier's version which plays to the Globe's pit. By having the new film's duck always in an oscillating relation to the older one's rabbit, I found myself attributing to the manifest differences between them an ironic meaning among whose multiple implications are that war is serious, even solemn, business and that this king is neither the dupe nor the manipulator of his sinister self-serving churchman. Where Branagh's film *alludes* to Olivier's, it was I who kept making irony happen, as I oscillated between the said and the unsaid, the seen and the remembered.

Occasionally, however, it was not this one earlier film but the generic conventions of cinema in general that I found held in suspension with the play in this film's ironic "solution." An example: although Olivier's film had cut it completely, Branagh's leaves in the scene of the arrest of the three traitors, Scroop, Cambridge and Grey, and engages the cinematic apparatus in such a way that a complex kind of inclusive and differential ironic relationship on the level of medium came into being for me. Olivier's film version of this play has been called "epic in scale, oratorical in utterance, and long in shot," while Branagh's is said to be "personal, introspective, and in close and medium shot" (Rothwell and Melzer 1990: 100). In the play itself, of course, this is an episode (II, ii) entirely structured on verbal and situational irony: Henry knows of the three men's treason, but they do not know that he knows. He therefore toys with them, commenting on their "too much love and care" for him (II, ii, 52). As a spectator, you are able to share what the plotters interpret as the irony of his remarks, but you can also add a second level, since you know Henry is not, in fact, being naive, but is himself ironic. When Branagh as Henry accuses the three of their crime to their faces, he physically attacks Scroop and throws him onto a table, pinning him down. Critics of the play text have noted that Scroop's betrayal "evokes a long and suddenly emotional remonstrance in which Henry effectively bids farewell to the possibility of personal relationship" (Barton 1988: 17; cf. Rose A. Zimbardo in Quinn 1969: 166). After all, they point out, the scene is placed between the two London episodes of Falstaff's death. Tillyard found Henry's entire reproof, however, "alien in tone to the norm of the play," more tragic than historical, more personal than public in theme (in Quinn 1969: 72). I found that my ironic reading of Branagh's film kept wanting to take this notion of the personal betrayal one step further, however.

In a full-screen close-up that parodies the visual conventions of a traditional erotic love scene – thus giving (through literalizing) a new ironic edge to Exeter's description of Scroop as Henry's "bedfellow" (II, ii, 8) – the two men's faces (Henry's on top, as he may feel befits his position) are shown. The king moves from royal "we" to personal and painful "I" to berate his erstwhile friend: "But O,/What shall I say to thee, Lord Scroop? thou cruel,/Ingrateful, savage, and inhuman creature!" (II, ii, 93–5). Branagh's film then makes a number of changes to the play's text. When a weeping Henry caresses his friend's face, reminding the traitor that he had shared with him "the very bottom of [his] soul" (97), the film replaces the play's line – "Such and so finely bolted didst thou seem" – with a new one that continues the sexual subtext: "[s]o constant and unspotted didst thou seem" that this treason is like "[a]nother fall of man." The ironic echoing of the seduction of Adam and the casting out of Paradise foregrounds both the implied erotic dimension in this male bonding and also its relation to power. The close-up here may indeed register "the psychological costs of authority" (Holderness 1991: 83), but for me the ironic inclusive doubleness of the cinematic love-scene palimpsest over the play's text does not go away.

Most of the time, however, as I've been suggesting, the ironic oscillation for me was less with the play itself or with cinematic conventions in general but more specifically with Olivier's film. There are many times when Branagh-as-king seemed to me to ironize by exaggeration, out-Olivier-ing Olivier as the dashing hero. Here ironic meaning was constituted for me, with the camera's assistance, by what became my almost unavoidable perception of *both* actors playing the same role, saying the same words, doing the same deeds – but with a difference. Branagh's "Once more unto the breach, dear friends" speech (III, i, 1–34) at the gates of Harfleur is even more declamatory and fierce than Olivier's, and the camera shows the men's faces (in close-up) as his exhortation works. This is certainly "the Word as adrenalin" (Calderwood 1988: 28). What makes irony happen for me here is that Branagh's version deliberately echoes the famous shot in Olivier's film of the king's white horse rearing up on cue at "God for Harry! England! and Saint George!" – but it then accompanies the line with cannon blasts and flames. Branagh's excessive variation-on-the-theme seems paradoxically to mock excess but, at the same time, to milk the scene for the power of both the Shakespearean text and the Olivier film. But the full ironic impact of this scene comes for me a few moments later when – after watching with frustration as his men run away – Henry defiantly confronts the Governor of Harfleur and demands that he give up before even more damage is done. This is played as a *grand bluff* in the film. No wonder, then, that Branagh's Henry looks relieved and exhausted, more than triumphant, when the town surrenders – and so he should, not only because of his army's likely incapacity but also because Harfleur must, in fact, surrender (the text informs us) for it has learned that the French reinforcement troops will not arrive soon enough for it to continue to resist. Both films retain this stated reason, but only Branagh's presents it in such a way that it is believable. There is no glory in this English "conquest"; the bluff simply coincided with the news of the delay. The triumphant victory march into Harfleur in Olivier's version is thus played off – in visual contrast – against the tired trudge of Branagh's exhausted (and somewhat sheepish) men who do not look in the least capable of any of the dreadful deeds with which Henry had threatened the town. This Henry finally gets off his (high?) horse, his defiant voice now reduced to a whisper, and at one point almost collapses, wincing with pain.

Branagh's film also leaves in (and so I was indirectly reminded that Olivier's had cut) the scene of the hanging for theft of Henry's (or more appropriately, Prince Hal's) old drinking companion, Bardolph (III, v). Here, the king must presumably act against any personal feelings of affection because he has given an order that no soldier of his be allowed to steal or to abuse the French people as they march through the land. Branagh's Henry actually makes eye-contact with the disbelieving Bardolph and there is a flashback to an earlier encounter with him that is made to prefigure this scene, with the borrowing of Falstaff's words from *Henry IV, Part I* (I.ii) – "Do not thou, when thou art king, hang a thief" – and Henry's reply – "No, thou shalt." In a deviation from the play's text, the signal for the execution to be carried out is given by Henry himself, who then watches Bardolph die, and almost weeps. This is a sensitive, vulnerable, but also rather "wet" Henry, in more ways than one. He is frequently seen weeping in a way that the valiant character played by Olivier certainly never would; he is also often seen in the rain, with water streaming down his face, as at the end of this scene when he orders his men on to camp beyond the river. The brave defiance, in the 1944 version, of the leader who has just refused the French offer of ransom instead of battle is recalled – but with ironic difference – in the grim endurance of the 1989 one: not surprisingly, perhaps, "We are in God's hand" (III, v, 175) is a line which only the wartime Olivier film cut.

Other ironies suggested to me by Branagh's film come, less from its echoic mention of character portrayal, than from its altering of the particular possibilities of cinematic technology explored in such an innovative way in Olivier's film. For example, Henry's "Upon the king" soliloquy the night before the battle (IV, i, 246–90), a meditation on the responsibilities and burdens of kingship compared to the supposedly

82

carefree life of the common man, is presented in Olivier's version totally in filmic conventions, that is, in voice-over: Olivier's lips do not move as he sits by the fire, but his "thoughts" can be heard. Branagh's film, using similar camera angles, has its Henry speak aloud – though his men are seen sleeping undisturbed around him – as a reminder, through what for me was this ironic difference, of the fact that this is still a play, even if it is a movie of it. There was hardly a moment here when I, as a spectator who knew Oliver's film, did not find myself oscillating between the duck and the rabbit to make this thing called irony happen. For example, Olivier's king ends this scene with a stirring prayer to God to make his men strong; Branagh's, however, falls to his knees in tears and offers an anguished confession of his father's sin in deposing Richard II, offering his own attempts to expiate it as penance – all of which is cut in Olivier's refocusing and silencing of guilt.

The famous "St Crispin's day" speech (IV, iii, 19–67) before the battle begins was another site of oscillation for me. It is equally rousing (if shortened) in both films, with Branagh's again in subtle ways exaggerating and outdoing Olivier's. It does so, not only by putting its Henry up on a cart much higher than his men (and significantly higher than Olivier's cart), but also by having the camera shoot upward so that the king is literally seen from the adulatory viewpoint of the men: low angle shots traditionally produce towering figures of authority and power. But there are important and, for me, ironic differences between the two scenes. That cart upon which Branagh's Henry stands is the one just used in the hanging of Bardolph: human weakness, military discipline, personal pain and betrayal are not separable from the "honor" of war for me here. (When Henry later places the dead boy's body on a similar cart, as I mentioned earlier, I found myself jolted into remembering that – now ironic – promise of glory in this very speech.) The men in Branagh's film are not Olivier's handsome and dashing soldiers in clean military uniforms; they are dirty, dishevelled, and in visible need of any encouragement that their king can offer. Only in Branagh's film does Henry's later description of his soldiers make sense: "Our gayness and our gilt are all besmirch'd/With rainy marching in the painful field" (IV, iii, 110–11). As the camera pulls back from Olivier's king, a vast (and appropriately perhaps – for a wartime audience – comforting) crowd of neat, well-armed men appears; as it zooms out from Branagh's, there are only a dirty few. After all, though, that *was* the point of the victory, as the English were outnumbered something like five to one.

As already discussed, the battle scene in Branagh's film is longer and (given the technical advances over forty-five years and the sheer number of violent films made and seen in that time) inevitably more cinematically proficient and intertextually suggestive. Again, because of close-up shots, Henry can be seen fighting, weeping over his cousin York's death (a scene only described by a weeping Exeter in the play in IV, vi), and finally

83

arousing himself to fury when he sees the massacre of the boys: "I was not angry since I came to France/Until this instant" (IV, vii, 57–8). At these words Olivier's Henry furiously returns to battle and then re-enters to greet the French herald, Montjoy. In Branagh's film, the unfortunate (because sympathetically portrayed) Montjoy enters as Henry speaks this line and gets roughly torn from his saddle, thrown into the mud, and leapt upon by the irate king. Where Olivier's version cut out the next part, Branagh positively revels in it. This vulnerable Henry does not even know if he has won the battle or not, and he admits it: "I tell thee truly, herald,/I know not if the day be ours or no" (85–6). When Montjoy says: "The day is yours," Branagh's Henry closes his eyes and begins to weep, saying: "Praised be God, and not our strength, for it!" (89). He then falls down, flat on his face, in the mud.

On one level, this ironizing of the victorious hero is a simple demystification; but, on another, it ended up suggesting to me that such an unheroic hero may be an even more powerful image of a leader *today* than Olivier's dignified, noble king. The inclusivity and complex relational nature of irony, when not thought of in only antiphrastic terms, can be seen through the structural irony that a king who can fall, exhausted by battle, on his face, who can weep and even snort and sniff his tears in a very non-heroic way, who can laugh at and hug the pedantic but loyal Fluellen in affection and joy – as he cries – can perhaps be more moving and more convincingly human *today* than the stylized victor of Olivier's earlier film. While it is certainly possible to read Branagh's "demonstrative parading of open grief," not as "subversive of the values of tough masculinity" but as "closer to those rituals of mourning ... which are rather a liturgical collusion with the ideology of patriotic war than an emotional interrogation of its values" (Holderness 1991: 89), this Henry can also be interpreted – at least when read through the ironizing, haunting presence of Olivier's – as simply responding more appropriately to the grim realities of war, realities that are brought home to the spectator here, in all their gritty (or rather, muddy) materiality, courtesy of the illusionist technology of film. The ironic juxtaposition of that *materiality* with the *conventions* both of the stage and also of wartime patriotic discourse is what structured this scene for me right to the end, when Henry's words about the troops returning to England "[w]here ne'er from France arriv'd more happy men" (IV, viii, 128) are here played off against the sorrow and pain on the faces of the bedraggled soldiers in such a way that, for some spectators, at least, there might be some edge, some "interrogation" of the consequences of patriotic values, if not – in the end – of patriotic war or heroism themselves.

The final act presents yet another side of Henry as he woos the French princess, Katharine. Both films cut the sexual joking scene between Henry and Burgundy (in V, ii), perhaps in implicit agreement with Dr Johnson that this is "a mean dialogue for princes; the merriment is very gross and the sentiments are very worthless" (in Woudhuysen 1989: 210). But Olivier's Henry is very much the swashbuckling, romantic lead, at ease in his charmingly self-deprecating urging of himself and his cause, joking gallantly in Kate's presence – much as might be expected of the Prince Hal of the *Henry IV* plays. This is Olivier playing the "English hero, great conqueror, master manipulator, and effective lover" (Manheim 1983: 183) in a scene he used to play on RAF Benevolent Fund tours to air bases during the war (Geduld 1973: 14). But I read Branagh's Henry as an ironized playing *against* that model, as a more modest, awkward and unaccomplished (if still charming) lover – but, significantly, as very different from the passionate man who earlier had wept and stroked the face of Scroop, his "bedfellow"-turned-traitor. Unlike the calm, confident and collected king in Olivier's film, Branagh's Henry paces uneasily; he makes faces at Kate; his plainspeaking sounds a bit too much like bravado at times. Tellingly, this version leaves in place the long passage which the Olivier film cut about "the poor and untempering effect" of Henry's "visage" (V, ii, 235–6): "my father," he grimly jokes, was "thinking of civil wars when he got me." No conventionally handsome matinee idol, maybe Branagh is willing to play on his relative plainness in order to ironize, not the Shakespearean text (where all this appears), but more specifically, Olivier as romantic and handsome star. While it can be argued that it is central to the play's reflexivity (and its exploration of feudal politics) that "the king be characterized as an *actor* rather than a monarch" (Holderness 1992: 188), "the ostentatious virtuosity of a famous screen actor" (ibid.: 187) in Olivier's film could be argued to function not in the least reflexively, radically, or in any way that is critical of feudal ideology; it could be seen to be simply supportive of the ideology necessary to the war effort of England in the 1940s. This is less a criticism than an acknowledgement of context and particularity of historical situation. And it is not meant to deny that Branagh's king is equally – though differently – attractive and thus, perhaps, equally uncritically presented (in the context of the values of the 1980s).

The historical union of England and France, achieved through the marriage of Henry and Kate, is visualized in both cinematic versions as an act of balancing, of restoring order: in both, the camera consistently centres the couple on the screen. Branagh's once again ironically outdoes Olivier's, with a close-up of the two lovers kissing, one on each side of the screen in perfect formal symmetry, following it by another shot of them standing on each side of the King of France, and then by yet another of the two in front of everyone – in each case, always relentlessly symmetrically balanced (presumably as equals) on the screen. The visual irony in this formal composition – itself perhaps a microcosmic echo of the palindromic, balanced, macrocosmic structure of Olivier's film – happened for me because there had been an earlier, equally symmetrically filmed scene at the start in which the Archbishop of Canterbury and the Bishop of Ely had framed Henry's head (in I, ii), counselling him to go to war and offering him money to do so, while looking for all the world like two demonic whisperers from traditional iconography. In other words, the irony came about for me here in the visual underlining of the fact that the book-end bishops' self-protective and self-serving plotting is what made possible this marriage – but also its disastrous consequences. As the film continues to its end, of course, I also felt an ironic tension between these ordered, balanced visual images and the lack of lasting political order that the Chorus's words go on to relate.

Olivier's camera returns to the Globe Theatre in this scene, but in Branagh's film, the Chorus appears in the foreground of this fiercely symmetrical scene of marriage. The choice of generic structure (and thus of a romantic comic ending) in Olivier's film may have been what necessitated cutting much of the Chorus's final speech, entirely leaving out the story of the future, of the disastrous historical results of this union. Instead, it puts the focus on the heroic and successful Henry alone. Branagh's film leaves in the tragic history of the coming dissolution of the peace and the unity of the two countries. The last lines of the play and of the Chorus's address to the audience are: "and, for their sake,/In your fair minds let this acceptance take". In Branagh's version, as in Shakespeare's, the "their" refers to all those engaged in this complex and unfortunate history; Olivier's film not only cut all the negative discussion of the future of England but changed this line to "and, for *his* sake . . ." – not "their." This Henry remains the titular hero and the dashing romantic star to the end. In what I read as a palimpsestic ironic contrast, the Chorus of Branagh's film returns the spectators to their world, just as he had drawn them out of it, by quietly closing those framing doors he had once loudly opened, closing them now on the play's visually balanced characters, as he finishes his lines – lines that underline the unstable and momentary nature of the peace and order just achieved. In the dark and silence that follow, the post-battle music of the "Non nobis, Domine" starts up again, in sharp and ironic contrast (at least if you remember the rabbit that goes with this duck) to the boys' choir and orchestra in Olivier's Globe Theatre, playing Walton's triumphant and uplifting music.

Despite what I read as the consistent ironic edge to the Branagh film's recalling of Olivier's version of Henry and the very real differences between the two portrayals, there is at least one way in which, as I have already suggested, they are similar: both Henrys, however different, are most admirable and both encourage "empathetic identification with the psychology of power" (Holderness 1991: 85). I mentioned earlier the view that Olivier's version offers a sort of "E.M.W. Tillyard" or maybe "J. Dover Wilson" Henry as epic hero: the ideal king not only of wartime England but of the classical and Christian tradition of Erasmus, Elyot and Chelidonius,

86

a king attractive as well to an audience in nostalgic need of a "mythical idea of a wholly integrated British literary culture" (Collick 1989: 47). Read positively, then, Olivier's rendition is of the grand "solid and flawless" "Statesman-King" described by Una Ellis-Fermor (1945, in Quinn 1969: 128); read less sympathetically, he is closer to George Bernard Shaw's "Jingo hero" (in Quinn 1969: 55). But Branagh's portrayal is of a very different Henry – a more "modern," vulnerable, emotional, accessible, human, and humane man who happens to be also a king. He is perhaps even more positively presented, in some people's eyes, or at least more in tune with the sensibilities of today's audience which, as one critic argues, might well understand differently things like personal growth and the need to accept the "necessary evils of politics, war, and courtship" (P.S. Donaldson 1991: 61). In neither film, though, is there much of the contradiction that the critics have for years discussed as central to the play. Neither cinematic version of Henry could possess what W.B. Yeats called "the gross vices, the coarse nerves, of one who is to rule among violent people" (in Quinn 1969: 55). Nor is either of them very hypocritical, bloodthirsty, brutal, or ruthless. Both eliminate Henry's orders to cut the throats of the French prisoners taken at Agincourt, for instance. In framing Henry in positive (if different) terms, both films (for perhaps different reasons [see Holderness 1991: 85–6]) may deprive the play and its hero of some of the ambiguity and heterogeneity (Erickson 1988: 133) that have exercised the critics for centuries.

This similarity does not, however, necessarily undo the other ironic meanings at the level of theme and structure that happen for me in the newer film's inclusive but differential relation to that famous actor's famous version of the play. By keeping Olivier's work always firmly in my memory (and before my eyes), through similar camera angles or through echoing variations in character portrayal, Branagh's film set up for me a duck/rabbit relationship; or, to use another image, it sounded a third semantic note that constructed another version of the historical meaning and visual shape of war, nationalism, and heroism. That there should be disagreement among viewers about the value of this construct is not surprising. Some have seen Branagh's film as espousing an unpleasant contemporary form of patriotism, "anchored in the past, and besieged, embattled in the present" (Holderness 1991: 76). Other critics have seen Branagh's version as "conducive" to Thatcherism (Breight 1991: 96; Fortier 1992: 69n.) in its implicit support of conservative themes of royal responsibility and militaristic brotherhood. No matter how it is interpreted, of course, Branagh's film is obviously as ideologically driven as Olivier's, even if you don't see it as "profoundly antirevolutionary" (Fortier 1992: 60). What I read as its ironizing of the Olivier war-inspired representation of conflict and leadership might be seen as offering a redefinition of nationalism and military "glory," but I would agree that it does so in an equally powerful (and,

87

therefore, some would say, dangerous) way – a feat it accomplishes, at least for me, as much through the constant palimpsestic, ironic presence of Olivier's film as through its positive and perhaps even nostalgic presentation of the king. For an audience that knows Olivier's film, the public leader of the 1944 version can consistently be re-interpreted through and against the private man of the 1989 one (see Rothwell and Melzer 1990: 99; P.S. Donaldson 1991: 68) – and vice versa. What, for me, were ironic echoes of scenes and even shots in Branagh's film kept that 1944 version in my mind's eye, and so it was the continuities as well as the differences in the meaning and consequences of patriotism and war that were simultaneously made present through the formal structures and hermeneutic strategies of irony. I felt that the "performative kingship" of Olivier's Henry (P.S. Donaldson 1991: 65) coexisted with and lay behind the intimate one of Branagh in such a way that they commented, ironically, upon each other.

However, no matter what diverse political interpretations this film might provoke, what interests me particularly here is that, for none of these complex ironies is the standard semantic explanation of irony as logical contradiction or antiphrastic inversion adequate. It is not only that Branagh's film is *different* from Olivier's, but that for me irony happened when Branagh's said echoed in some way Olivier's different unsaid (in my memory), and the resulting edgy oscillation between the two created a new meaning – the one I think is the real "ironic" meaning.

4

DISCURSIVE COMMUNITIES

How irony "happens"

I THE MIRACLE OF IRONIC COMMUNICATION

The title of this section is not meant in the least ironically: given the manifest difficulties, it does seem to me to be some kind of miracle that people ever really understand each other at all, much less when they are communicating in an ironic mode. What is true of irony is true of all communication, in other words: comprehension is a complex process (even if most people take that complexity for granted the greater part of the time), a process fraught with difficulties. People lie; people misunderstand one another. Yet they also share meaning, even if they are always having to (re)learn from experience that meaning is not something fixed and firm that is transmitted through some sort of transparent medium. They also have to remind themselves of the need to acknowledge that, in what sociolinguists call a "communicative event," there is a great diversity of speech within even a single speech community (Hymes 1974: 29): "different people live in 'different worlds of discourse'. The whole communicative process is altered and distorted by these different worlds" (Martin 1983: 432).

This chapter expands on my earlier contention that, in ironic discourse, the whole communicative process is not only "altered and distorted" but also *made possible by* those different worlds to which each of us differently belongs and which form the basis of the expectations, assumptions, and preconceptions that we bring to the complex processing of discourse, of language *in use*. Irony rarely involves a simple decoding of a single inverted message; as the last chapter argued, it is more often a semantically complex process of relating, differentiating, and combining said and unsaid meanings – and doing so with some evaluative edge. It is also, however, a culturally shaped process. No theorist of irony would dispute the existence of a special relationship in ironic discourse between the ironist and the interpreter; but for most, it is irony itself that is said to *create* that relationship. I want to turn that around here, and argue instead that it is the community that comes first and that, in fact, *enables* the irony to happen.

The importance of community or social context is, of course, a given in many general theories of how we communicate: "language is always perceived, from the very first, within a structure of norms. That structure, however, is not abstract and independent but social" (Fish 1980: 318). The same is true for other means of communication: gestures, visual iconography or even music (McClary 1991: 27). Discourses are forms of social practice, of interaction between participants in particular situations, whether this be in face-to-face conversation or in interpreting artistic texts, where the "circumstances of utterance" (Eco 1979: 14) which the interpreter infers from a text are what every reader has to take into account. In John Fowles's 1985 historical novel *A Maggot*, to take a fictional illustration, a woman tries to explain what she has seen in a cave using only her eighteenth-century language and conceptual frame of reference. The twentieth-century reader might well interpret what this fictional character calls a "maggot" as a spaceship, reading the wall of gleaming stones as a control panel and the unbreakable window as either a video screen or an observation hatch. This dramatic irony – and collusion – set up between modern reader and modern author, however, has to be reread in the context of the specific circumstances of this woman's (fictive) utterance: we are told that what we are reading is actually the written transcription of her oral account, which was taken down by a scribe who has admitted that he invents what he fails to recall or record, and which was prompted by a patronizing male lawyer whose antagonistic and leading questions have directed her responses in particular ways. The enunciative complexity of the narration here is, in a way, analogous to the kind of complex situation irony always offers its interpreters.

That the entire multidimensional "enunciation" (see Todorov 1970) has to be taken into account in interpreting all utterances – not only ironic ones – has been the premise of many communication theories, from pragmatics to speech-act theory, from polysystem theory (Evan-Zohar 1979 and 1986) to cultural systematics (Pagnini 1987). Michel Foucault's work on discursive formations marked an important extension of this focus into an even broader context of *institutional* networks. Foucault argued that "the production of discourse is at once controlled, selected, organised and redistributed according to a certain number of procedures" (1972: 216): rules of exclusion, classification, ordering, and distribution, as well as rules determining who may speak, when, how, where, and on what topic. This is obviously where the political dimension reveals its inescapable presence within the social (Pêcheux 1982: 111).

As suggested in preceding chapters, irony is one discursive strategy that both cannot be understood apart from its embodiment in context and also has trouble escaping the power relations evoked by its evaluative edge. The (paradoxically) enabling constraints that are operative in all discourses obviously function here as well, but it is not only a question of who may *use* irony (and where, when, how) but who may (or can) *interpret* it. Whether viewed as an isolated trope (Culler 1975: 155) or as the articulation of the human situation (Wilde 1981: 13), irony involves the particularities of time and place, of immediate social situation and of general culture. For example, Peter Partner, in a review of Samir al-Khalil's 1991 book, *The Monument: Art, Vulgarity and Responsibility in Iraq* in the *New York Review of Books*, recalled the book's claim that irony "is a concept virtually unknown to Arabic thought, and indeed it is a word hardly possible to translate into Arabic" (1991: 8). In such a culture (if this is, in fact, the case), the shared context necessary to understand irony would be the most basic one: that is, the very possibility of conceiving of a mode of discourse in which one can say one thing but convey something else (and do so with some evaluative edge), and yet not be lying. Interpreter expectations – at even this fundamental level – are not simply a matter of the "subjective" attitudes (Kaufer 1981b: 505) of either interpreter or ironist, but are a function of the culture, language, and social context in which both participants interact with each other and with the text itself.

Critics of many theoretical persuasions argue, therefore, that irony works in a dialogic or intersubjective way (Chamberlain 1989: 104; Handwerk 1985: viii), invoking or even establishing community or consensus (Handwerk 1985: 4). But others point out, though often simply in passing, that irony is more easily understood in a well-defined or even closed group whose members share a "social environment" (Perelman and Olbrechts-Tyteca 1969: 208) which allows irony to become almost a "dialect" (Hymes 1987: 300) in use among them. It is upon this insight that I want to expand here, for it seems to me that it is precisely the mutual contexts that an *existing community* creates that set the scene for the very use and comprehension of irony. Just as Thomas Kuhn defined scientific communities by a sharing of a "constellation of beliefs, values, techniques" (1970: 175), so I want to define these "discursive communities" in general by the complex configuration of shared knowledge, beliefs, values, and communicative strategies. The issue of multiplicity and diversity – the fact that there are as many discursive communities as there are groupings of any two people – is, for me, less a problem than the very issue at the heart of the complexity of ironic communication.

Before entering into a discussion of this diversity, however, I feel the need to open a short parenthesis on my use of the word "community" here. I know that it is an overburdened word today, used to frame everything from a concept of nationalism as "imagined community" (B. Anderson 1983) to the notion of resistance and power in the "inoperative community" (Nancy 1991). It has been pointed out that "community is now expected to bring the succour previously sought in the pronouncements of universal reason and their earthly translations" (Bauman 1992: xix). But I am also aware that many theorists – feminists, New Historians, and others – have fruitfully turned to the concept of an extended community with shared customs and habits that form and are formed by cultural discourses. It is this general frame of reference that I want to invoke in this chapter: like irony's complex semantics, communities too are relationally defined, just as are people within them. There have been forceful attacks on those uses of the word "community" that ignore "the mobility, multiple forms of contact, and numerous levels and modes of interconnectedness of contemporary life" and thus forget "that contemporary communities are not only internally complex and highly differentiated but also continuously and rapidly reconfigured" (B.H. Smith 1988: 168). Sharing this notion of community as something dynamic and subtly differentiated, I close this parenthesis, then, moving back to the possible tension that might exist between a communitarian idea of shared beliefs and assumptions and an awareness of the diversity and mobility that will inevitably characterize that sharing.

There already exist concepts of community that might at first glance seem to serve the purposes of a theory of irony. Bloomfield's idea of a "speech-community," as a group of people who use the same system of "speech-signals" and share a system of habits or rules of conduct of speech and interpretation or response, provides a very general model that many have indeed adopted in different ways (see van Dijk 1977: 191; Hymes 1972: 54). Specifications have been brought to this idea, such as the notion of "rhetorical communities" created by, say, a television or radio broadcast which unites groups "by sensory perceptions rather than by contiguity in physical space" (Narváez 1991: 192). My particular sense of the term "*discursive* community" here is not quite the same as that of "*discourse* community" which has been defined as "a sociorhetorical construct, neutral in terms of medium and unconstrained by space and time" (Swales 1988: 211). Instead, the notion of discursive community (as signaled, I hope, by the Foucaultian echo of "discursive formations") is not unconstrained at all but acknowledges those strangely enabling constraints of discursive contexts and foregrounds the particularities not only of space and time but of class, race, gender, ethnicity, sexual choice – not to mention nationality, religion, age, profession, and all the other micropolitical groupings in which we place ourselves or are placed by our society. But what this idea shares with that of a socio-rhetorical "discourse community" is a sense that we all belong to many overlapping (and sometimes even conflicting) communities or collectives (Swales 1988: 213; Lefevre 1987: 93). This overlapping is the condition that makes irony possible, even though the sharing will inevitably always be partial, incomplete, fragmentary; nevertheless, something does manage to get shared – enough, that is, to make irony happen.

My move to invert the more customary view that irony is what brings communities into being is also an attempt to think past the usual binary evaluation of this seeming act of consensus-making through irony: it is normally seen, on the one hand, as an elitist act of simultaneous inclusion and exclusion (Frye 1970: 63) or, on the other, as a utopian generation of "reflective community" (Handwerk 1985: vii – via Schlegel). These two extremes of response are both based on the notion that irony creates cozy groupings through complicity (Hutchinson 1983) or collusion (Furst 1984: 95). The somewhat negative connotations of these two terms, however, risk masking the very strongly positive evaluation granted in some circles to any discourse that might serve to generate consensus in a post-industrial world of anarchistic fragmentation and dissent: Habermas's notions of the public sphere and of the ideal speech community are only perhaps the best known examples of what is a relatively common utopian yearning for rational consensus (cf. Wood 1985: 153; Eagleton 1988: 14). The complexity and seeming rarity of such a consensus in general social discourses have not prevented theorists of irony from arguing that irony – though one of the most indirect ways of expressing meaning – is a means of creating precisely that kind of agreement among participants. In his *The Rhetoric of Fiction* in 1961, Wayne C. Booth addressed the "secret communion" – based on the pleasures of deciphering and collaborating – between author and reader (300–3). In his *A Rhetoric of Irony*, over a decade later, he affirmed his belief that irony, in particular, builds "amiable communities" between ironist and interpreter who experience the pleasure of "joining, of finding and communing with kindred spirits" (1974: 28). Irony then becomes a "communal achievement" (ibid.: 13), in a way that is reminiscent of the theory that laughter and humor can both build emotional bridges and make intellectual connections between people. While there are other, differently utopian claims made for irony (such as the view that irony's doubleness can fight totalizing narratives [Scholes 1982: 77; Hutcheon 1991]), many of these claims center around some version of irony such as that which Kierkegaard called "telegraphic communication" which assumes "infinite sympathy" and "captivates with indissoluble bonds" (1971: 85). But because of both the transideological nature of irony and its many and complex functions and effects, this idea of the creation of intimacy through irony has also been read as the more suspect grounds for the possible exploitation of the common knowledge of participants (Kaufer 1977: 96). This would mean that irony does not so much create "amiable communities" as itself come into being in "contact zones" as the "social spaces where cultures meet, clash, grapple with each other, often in contexts of highly asymmetrical relations of power" (Pratt 1991: 34).

Chapter 2 outlined how the discourse *about* irony has a long history in which the positive and negative evaluations of the trope's social dimension have always jockeyed for position. The negative extreme, however, is often seen as being inherent within the positive: irony "inevitably builds a community of believers even as it excludes" (Booth 1974: 28), uniting even as it marginalizes (Mizzau 1984: 95). Expanding now on that earlier

93

discussion, what is of particular interest here is that the exclusionary potential of irony has been articulated in terms that range from the relatively benign – "a game of hidden meanings" (Pagnini 1987: 14) – to the more sadistically suspect (Berrendonner 1981: 222). As a result, the relationship between the ironist and the interpreter has been read as being more akin to one of mastery than of mutual comprehension (Dane 1991: 31). This elitist and/or sadistic argument against irony takes a number of forms, most of them directly tied to the consensual theory, however. One version asserts that ironists flatter or compliment interpreters by making them feel clever (Booth 1974: 205–6) or sophisticated. The assumption of superior knowledge shared by ironist and interpreter, in fact, underlies many of the influential metaphors used by theorists to describe the interaction of participants with the ironic text: for instance, there is a depth model where a deeper (ironic) meaning has been placed below the surface, and lies waiting to be perceived by the knowing audience (Booth 1974: 85–6); another is the image of the "building" of irony, of its reconstruction so that the interpreter too can live "at the higher and firmer location" from whence to look down on those who "dwell in error" (Booth 1974: 35–7). What these metaphors share is a sense of hierarchy: deeper and higher = better. Irony may force us into "hierarchical participation" (Booth 1974: 41), but the hierarchy of *meanings* (deep vs. surface) inherited from the German articulation of romantic irony (see Dane 1991: 81) seems to have too easily become a hierarchy of *participants*. There has been a move from a sense of shared (and, only in that sense, superior) knowledge to a sense of superiority (Chatman 1978: 230), often based on a sense of superior intellect (Brooks 1947: 210). It is not hard to see how the view that irony is elitist in function might have developed.

In effect, what happens in these hierarchical theories is that two separate audiences have to be posited: those who "get" the irony and those who do not (Fowler 1950: 305). These are usually constructed as, on the one hand, a "knowing minority" (Abrams 1981: 90) – "de facto promoted to the same rank as the ironist" (Gaunt 1989: 22) – and, on the other, an imagined group (Culler 1975: 154) who only comprehend the "apparent or pretended meaning" (Green 1979: 9). The smug initiate is said to look down upon and patronize the uninitiated, echoing Friedrich Schlegel's infamous theatrical architecture image of the irony "fürs Parterre" and the one "für die Logen." For every ironist and every initiate who understands irony, the argument goes, a "non-initiated victim" (Gaunt 1989: 22; M.A. Rose 1979: 51) must be imagined who will be outside the elitist community created by irony.

But what if the discursive community *precedes* and *makes possible* the comprehension of irony? Then there would still, perhaps, be two potential kinds of audiences, but instead of initiate and uninitiated, they might more accurately be called "addressees" and "hearers" (Clark and Carlson 1982).

Both would be within the irony's "participation framework" (Goffman 1974); that is, they would both be in perceptual range of the ironic utterance, but they would have different kinds and degrees of participation relative to it. Those who do not "get" the irony are not necessarily what most want to call its victims (cf. Clyne 1974: 345): they may not care at all; they may simply "misunderstand" (i.e. interpret differently) because they are operating within a different discursive context. The so-called uninitiated are not always the same as the targets either, for many miss (or get) ironies directed at others as well as at themselves. Those who engage the multiple said and unsaid meanings of irony are certainly interpreting *differently* than those who engage only the said; yet, for most theorists, there does seem to be more at stake here than simple difference, and the language in which the distinctions are regularly made is revealing of both implicit power relations and evaluative judgments: naive vs. sophisticated (Ben Porat 1979: 245); incompetent vs. competent (Dane 1986: 61); masses vs. informed (Dane 1986: 61); ignorant vs. knowing (Swearingen 1991: 127 *re* Aristotle). Given the transideological nature of irony, the negative of these pairs of positions might as easily be inhabited by the totalitarian censor as by the . . . . (fill in the blank with your personal favourite). In the economy of exchange that we call irony, there is always a power imbalance that does not seem to come into play in the same way in a trope like metaphor, in part because irony is simultaneously disguise and communication.

Great importance has been granted to this notion of a double audience in both exclusionary and inclusionary theories of how irony creates "solidarity" (Stempel 1976; Warning 1982: 259), and frequently there are moral or political overtones. But most often the terms of discussion have been those of "competence." Developing Noam Chomsky's notion of linguistic competence, Jonathan Culler has pointed out that the understanding of any utterance (including an ironic one) demands "an amazing repertoire of conscious and unconscious knowledge" (1975: 113). Extending this notion, he has also posited a specifically literary competence: the tacit knowledge of the conventions by which we read literary texts (cf. Dane 1986: 56–60). Theorists of irony have added other kinds of interpreter competence to the list: paralinguistic (Kerbrat-Orecchioni 1980b: 17); metalinguistic (Mizzau 1984: 36); rhetorical (Kerbrat-Orecchioni 1980a: 116); ideological (Plett 1982: 84–5); social (Berg 1978: 11). Many also invoke a sort of general cultural competence to cover the presuppositions, background information, assumptions, beliefs, knowledge and values that are shared by ironist and interpreter. But, to come back to my original hypothesis, if they are indeed shared, then irony might not so much create communities as come into being because the communal values and beliefs already exist. It might, therefore, be less a matter of interpreter "competence" than of shared assumptions on many different levels. For even the most simple of verbal

95

ironies, for example, there would have to be mutual agreement on the part of both participants about the following basic things: that words have literal meanings; that words can, however, have more than one meaning, especially in certain contexts; that there is such a thing as irony (as distinct from deception) where a spoken meaning is played off against implied but unspoken meanings – with some evaluative edge; that this irony can be deliberate, but need not be; that there will likely be some sort of culturally agreed upon markers in the utterance and/or in the enunciative context to signal both that irony is in play and how it is to be interpreted.

These seem to me less competences than shared assumptions, and indeed there are even a few theorists who go so far as to say that irony in fact requires no special competences or procedures at all (Sperber and Wilson 1986: 238). If that were the case, then the cultural competence that *interpreters* are said to need might be more a matter of overlapping discursive communities between *both* participants. In a sense, then, it would be less a matter of the *competence of one* than of what Dan Sperber and Dierdre Wilson have called the relevance of the context *to both* (1986: 158; see also Sperber 1984: 132). Their theory is careful not to minimize the difficulties of assuring (or even defining) mutual common knowledge or probabilistic assumptions that would guarantee any communication, never mind an ironic one (Sperber and Wilson 1986: 18–20). The theory of "cognitive environment" (ibid.: 41) they propose is related to that broader category of discursive community posited here for it can include everything from a group of any two people to, say, the Freemasons, because in each case there are sets of assumptions operative, and some of these are very basic ones. For instance, in certain discursive communities (certain families, certain professions), there is a positive valuing of irony; in others, there is not. If you are a member of the first, you are more likely to develop an "ear" for irony or a "sense" of irony – though I suspect no one would want to rule out the role of temperament completely in this.

Some have argued, however, that educational institutions have a responsibility to instruct their students in irony in order to empower them (instead of reserving the powers of irony for those in power): "Teaching irony is more than teaching a trope; it means teaching critical thinking, reading, and writing" (Chamberlain 1989: 110). But children appear to learn irony at a relatively early age, though not as early as they learn simple analogy or metaphor (see Winner 1988). Casual eavesdropping on young people would show any teacher that students of all ages are more than capable of deploying irony within their *own* discursive communities. The fact that they do not always understand irony in the classroom is not necessarily because of a lack of ability to master or marshal the trope itself. As I suggested in Chapter 1, I think in this case it is more a matter of different discursive communities. I do not see it as a matter of the students' lacking interpretive competence – that is, "practice at the sorts of critical

96

reading and thinking skills that irony often requires" (Chamberlain 1989: 102) – because in their own communities of discourse they do practice precisely those skills. They may indeed lack contextual information to interpret an ironic literary text presented to them in the classroom, but the teacher might well lack similar contextual information needed to interpret an ironic reference overheard in the schoolyard. In other words, *it is discursive communities that are simultaneously inclusive and exclusive – not ironies.* The closer the cultural or discursive overlapping of contexts, the more likely both the comprehension of specific ironies and also the acceptance of the appropriateness of irony in certain circumstances. It may be quite beside the point, then, to warn students, as Frederick Crews and Ann Jessie Van Sant do (not without irony), in *The Random House Handbook*, not to use irony or other figurative language in their writing ("it is better to make plain assertions than to litter your verbal landscape with those strangled hulks" [1984: 233]).

To argue, as I have been, that the reason why irony is not "universally accessible" (Rosler 1981: 81) might have less to do with interpreter competence than with the need for shared discursive context, is to shift the terms of the discussion away from notions of elitism toward an acceptance of the fact that *everyone* has different knowledges and belongs to (many) different discursive communities. I personally find this a healthy corrective to the loud lamentations of the late 1980s that young people were losing what was claimed to be some sort of homogeneous, general cultural knowledge (see Hirsch 1987, 1988, 1989). My own sense, right or wrong, is that they simply have *different* cultural knowledge, and that their communities' ironies are as often incomprehensible to me as mine (or Swift's) are to them. But, the positive part of this is that we *can* learn – and be taught – enough of each other's communal contexts to enable some comprehension, without the (often dubiously pleasurable, perhaps) privacy of those secret ironic in-jokes being totally lost. Ironists have always played with this inclusionary/exclusionary potential, of course: Burton's *Anatomy of Melancholy* (1621) targeted its adult, male, educated audience by putting its sexual innuendoes into Latin. This could, of course, be read as elitism or implied sophistication (Goffman 1974: 496), but it might also be interpreted as the separating out of different discursive communities for whom not all topics were considered equally appropriate at a given time. Cultures and epochs have differing senses of the "appropriateness" conditions (Keenan 1971) of irony, of the judgment call as to what is common ground to whom (Clark and Gerrig 1984: 124): "where, when, by and to whom is irony permitted? expected? disapproved? Is it common? rare? pervasive? startling?" (Hymes 1987: 297).

Perhaps, then, no irony is ever really "stable" (Booth 1974: 3), even if such communitarian contexts serve at least to frame (Iser 1978: 62) the parameters of the ironic play between the said and the unsaid. There have been many explanations offered for why people "misunderstand" ironies, and they almost all partake of the competence model I have been calling into question here, from I.A. Richards's list of "*ignorance,* lack of acquaintance with the sense of unfamiliar words, the absence of the necessary intellectual contexts, defective scholarship" (1929: 184–5) to Booth's related notions of ignorance, inability to pay attention, prejudice, lack of practice, and emotional inadequacy (1974: 222–7). But perhaps what is called ignorance (and even lack of practice or context) is simply a question of the ironist and the interpreter belonging to different discursive communities which do not intersect or overlap sufficiently for the comprehension of an utterance as ironic to occur. In other words, we are back to the problem of the complexity of the intersubjective activity of setting irony in motion. There is no "failsafe algorithm" (Sperber and Wilson 1986: 44) that will guarantee irony's comprehension. This is in part because of the fact that there are *two* participants in this act called irony (even – though in a different way – if the irony is unintended). As the next chapter will explore in detail, while some stress the role of the interpreter in irony, arguing that irony is not a property of texts but a way of reading (Fish 1983: 189), most other theorists have focused on the role of the encoding ironist (e.g. Kaufer and Neuwirth 1982: 29; Tindale and Gough 1987: 9). In contrast to both, the model I want to suggest here is more of an interactional or relational (Watzlawick, Beavin and Jackson 1967: 21) one between "conditions of production" (Pêcheux 1969: 12) and conditions of interpretation within the context of overlapping discursive communities. This model would take into account, then, not only the ironist's intentions (if present and available) but the "complex and contradictory relations of power that intersect and organize an audience's relation to particular cultural texts" (Grossberg 1988: 169).

Irony, therefore, is like all other communication acts in that it is always culture-specific (Kuiper 1984: 461), relying on the presence of a common memory shared by addresser and addressee (Lotman 1982: 81). While this means that an ironist may presuppose in the interpreter "a determined type of cultural formation" that will permit "particular allusions, particular ellipses" (Pagnini 1987: 46) without endangering comprehension (Kierkegaard 1971: 265), so too might an interpreter infer the same from the text of the ironist, as the next chapter will suggest. And Chapter 6 will study further how the signals or markers that are encoded or decoded in order to establish irony are equally culturally specific (Hymes 1987: 297) but must be shared by both participants who come to some sort of agreement on "how the counters of thought or discourse are to be constituted" (Tyler 1978: 59), for this is the precondition of intersubjective communication. As an indirect speech act, irony relies heavily on mutually shared factual background information (Searle 1975: 61; Meyers 1974: 178; Gibbs 1984: 286; Perri 1978: 300) to set up what has suggestively (if in another context) been called the "interindividual territory of recognition" (Bryson 1983: 131). While acknowledging the evident methodological difficulties inherent in trying to identify what might constitute this territory, I nevertheless want to outline at least some of the kinds of complexities involved in the process of how irony does happen – despite the multiplicity and diversity both within and among discursive communities.

Obviously ironists and interpreters of irony can meet on any number of different terrains: rhetorical, linguistic, aesthetic, social, ethical, cultural, ideological, professional, and so on, but at the most basic and general level, discursive communities are constituted by shared concepts of the norms of communication: "a set of rules prescribing the conditions for production and reception of meanings; which specify who can claim to initiate (produce, communicate) or know (receive, understand) meanings, about what topics under what circumstances and with what modalities (how, when, why)" (Hodge and Kress 1988: 4). For example, even in simple conversations, as Paul Grice (1975) has argued, there are certain "co-operative principles" at work (of Quantity, Quality, Relation and Manner) which, if flouted (as is the case with irony [Meyers 1974: 178–9]), demand on the part of the interlocutors the invoking of "conversational implicature." The success of irony depends upon a lack of disparity or, perhaps more accurately, some degree of coincidence between interpreters' and ironists' senses of "the rules determining when to speak and when to be silent, and when and where and by what means and in what form, tone, and code who may say what to whom" (Muecke 1973: 39). Indirect speech-acts like irony likely require even more of this sense of shared communicative assumptions (Ducrot 1984) than ordinary discourse would (Tyler 1978: 391–6 and 425).

Members of a discursive community share not only these presuppositions about how communication works in general terms, but also how it comes into being in terms of the identity, position and relative social status of the participants. Knowledge of the principles governing conversation, for instance, inevitably involves shared background about operative social and ideological norms (Amante 1981: 79–80; Bally 1965: 44; Hernadi 1988: 749). As suggested by Mary Douglas's work (1975) on the social requirements and controls that function in deciding the conditions for a joke to be both perceived and permitted, the complexity of the "awareness context" (Glaser and Strauss 1964: 670) created by the social system in the intending and attributing of irony should perhaps not be underestimated. Charles Dickens might have been able to use irony because "certain standards of normality common to author and reader are assumed" in a relatively popular mode (Frye 1970: 49). But times have changed, and such communitarian norms appear even more difficult to locate today: despite both leftist and rightist theories of the homogenization and standardization of commodified late capitalist culture, others have convincingly argued,

99

instead, for the multiplicity and fragmentation of publics and of discourses today (Collins 1989: 7).

Time, of course, is a factor in other ways as well. Cultural as well as social norms are often period-restricted: Renaissance audiences may well have recognized the iconographic conventions that Tudor morality plays could invert to ironic effect (Diehl 1982: 206–7), but will contemporary audiences viewing such plays necessarily do so? Might they not perceive other, different ironies? Discursive communities can certainly exist across time periods, but they might then rely on a knowledge of visual conventions that perhaps, in this example, only specialists will have. Because irony is a matter of interpretation as much as of intention, there have been long debates about the existence and appropriateness of irony in certain domains: such as the one in medieval circles about whether one should expect to find irony in courtly romance (Batts 1968 vs. Green 1979) or the one about whether irony, as a shift from apparent to contextual meaning, is part of or alien to philosophical argumentation (H.S. Lang 1985). Michael Fischer has written on the "previously unnoticed or misunderstood ironies (either intended or unintentionally revealing) in past ethnographic writing" (1986: 229), thereby suggesting that, even within a discursive community constituted by a single profession, there might be disagreements about the presence as well as meaning of irony.

What is more important than sharing something like a profession, some claim, is sharing an ideology. "Irony is a matter of unspoken understandings," it has been argued (Chambers 1990: 19); it is a matter of "ideological complicity – an agreement based on shared understandings of 'how the world is'" (Chambers 1990: 19) – which can obviously cut across professional lines. In today's world, such understandings are perhaps more likely to align themselves along axes of race, ethnicity, gender, sexual choice, class, or religion, but even those large categories do not necessarily define or guarantee the formation of a discursive community: there are major differences of ideology within each of the groupings – which are themselves contestable, hence changeable (Hebdige 1988: 206). In other words, you might, but need not, share gender or ethnicity with someone with whom you also share a discursive community based on, say, profession. Obviously things like nationality (Said 1984: 162) and education (Lippard 1984: 38) are also factors, as is geographic location. And the list could go on and on.

The important thing to realize is that we all live in many discursive communities at one and the same time: simultaneously I am Italian Canadian, a teacher, a lapsed Catholic, white, female, middle-class, a spouse but not a parent, an inept but enthusiastic pianist, an avid cyclist, an opera lover. Any one of these could be the basis for a discursive community that would allow me to share with someone else enough background and information to decide on the *appropriateness* as well as the *existence* and

100

interpretation of irony. That these different communities might offer conflicting decisions (especially about appropriateness) is part of the complexity of the reception of irony. The general principle I am invoking here is that "at any given time, as well as over the course of anyone's life history, *each of us* is a member of many, shifting communities, each of which establishes, for *each* of its members, multiple social identities, multiple principles of identification with other people, and, accordingly, a collage or grab-bag of allegiances, beliefs, and sets of motives" (B.H. Smith 1988: 168).

One book on irony begins with a musing about "whether people are more likely or less likely to be ironical, more alert or less alert to irony, according to social class and status, degree of urbanization, strength of religious or political convictions, occupation, sex, education, IQ rating or personality type" (Muecke 1970/1982: 1). A theory of discursive communities as that which enables irony would obviously support the notion that these factors will indeed make some difference. But it is necessary to keep in mind that these communities are not necessarily large monolithic groupings determined by, say, gender or language. Even within "an abstractly unitary national language" there is in fact "a multitude of concrete worlds, a multitude of bounded verbal ideological and social belief systems" (Bakhtin 1981: 288). That we manage to communicate at all is, to return to the title of this section, a miracle. The next chapters will investigate in closer detail how discursive communities come into play in the intentional and interpretive acts that constitute irony, in the kinds of textual contexts and shared markers that trigger the construction of ironic relations between meanings and in the evaluative edge that is implied in and by those relations. But before entering into these other theoretical areas, I would like to draw briefly on my first-hand experience of how a demonstrable change in discursive community (quite literally) made ironies happen for me in unexpected ways.

II PROVOCATION AND CONTROVERSY: THE WORK OF ANSELM KIEFER

The example here is my own response to the paintings and photographs of Anselm Kiefer, a contemporary German artist whose work has been adulated and despised both at home and abroad (though for different reasons) (see Flam 1992: 36). His large-scale paintings on Germanic themes have been called both brilliant and bad, revolutionary and "polit-kitsch" (Buchloh 1989: 100n.). Over time, I came to have *both* these contradictory responses, and that experience is, in fact, what initially sparked my interest in the role of discursive communities in the comprehension of irony. I learned from experience, in other words, that "[e]very utterance must be regarded primarily as a *response* to preceding utterances of the given sphere.

101

Each utterance refutes, affirms, supplements, and relies on the others, presupposes them to be known, and somehow takes them into account" (Bakhtin 1986: 91). My own dual evaluation and interpretation of Kiefer's work are certainly no exceptions.

It turns out that others, German critics in particular, have also had considerable trouble dealing with Kiefer's Teutonic "image worlds" and, at least until his 1991 Berlin exhibition, seemed relatively content to write him off as "an irrationalist and a reactionary, if not a protofascist" (Huyssen 1992: 85). In the light of the positive reception of his work by American Jewish collectors, however, the possibility of different discursive communities at work is raised, for there can be little doubt that Kiefer's Germanness is likely to function differently in the United States and in Germany (Huyssen 1992: 85). As a non-Jewish Canadian who knew embarrassingly little of modern German culture when I first saw Kiefer's work in 1988, I initially found it very disturbing. In trying to sort out the complex of reasons why this was so, I realized that it was in part a question of the paintings' overpowering, monumental size and oppressively dark palette. But it was also, in part, a matter of their subject matter – in two different ways. On the one hand, the references to places like Nürnberg and to historical figures like Richard Wagner had, at that time, only negative associations for someone like me, born shortly after World War II; on the other, my knowledge of these and other contexts from Teutonic history and myth was so limited at this point that, with wounded academic pride, I had to rely on the museum handout to tell me who Brünnhilde was or what the word "Nothung" meant. The combination of bad historical vibrations and what to me were then obscure references meant that I could not really follow the subsequent debates in the press and among friends over whether Kiefer was ironic or not in his dealings with his Germanic heritage.

A few years later, I again had occasion to see many of the same paintings and, this time, my response was utterly different. What had happened in the interim was that I had spent considerable time in Germany, doing research specifically on German opera, and thus an entire, large area of reference in Kiefer's work had been opened up to me. With it, came a view of complex ironies I now felt to be at work. In this case, it was largely but not only the limits of my factual knowledge (Perelman and Olbrechts-Tyteca 1969: 208) (originally connected in part to my age) that had prevented me from seeing what some would call the paintings' "intellectual" ironies (Muecke 1970/1982: 5). What I want to do here is briefly give a sense of what opened up to me when I could interpret more within Kiefer's own frame of reference – that is, when I belonged to a discursive community formed in part by the shared context of the music of Richard Wagner.

Had I known something about Wagner earlier, it would have come as no surprise to me or anyone else who had seen Kiefer's work that those grand nineteenth-century music dramas might have played some role in Kiefer's painterly investigations into his nation's history and its cultural legacy. In fact, in a piece called "Autobiography, 1976" (cited in M. Rosenthal 1987: 11) – a list of important places, people, and events in his life up to that point – Kiefer himself included not only Wagner, but *Nibelung* (Wagner's major work is *Der Ring des Nibelungen*), *Parsifal* (Wagner's final opera), *1976 Siegfried Forgets Brünhilde* (a painting by Kiefer on a theme from the *Ring* operas), and two settings important to Wagnerian plots – the Rhine and the Oden Forest (where the action of one of the *Ring*'s source texts, the *Nibelungenlied*, takes place). In other words, I would not have had to look far beyond this statement or even the titles of paintings to find direct references to Wagner in Kiefer's work. But without more information, more factual knowledge of what those references might mean, I had no way of interpreting them at all – much less ironically. Since learning more about Wagner, though, I have found that the way in which his name, reputation, and work are all recalled by Kiefer's paintings constitutes for me a highly ironic commentary on an entire range of things associated with the composer – from the Nazi appropriation of his work to his faith in the socially redemptive powers of art. In my reading, however, this is an irony that cuts both ways, for it reflects as much on Kiefer himself as a German artist (born after the war) as on Wagner (who died a half-century before it began).

I want to offer this reading as a counterbalance to my own earlier incomprehension, but also to the view of Kiefer's work as nostalgic, conservative resistance (Mays 1988: 61) or, worse, as "a sustained visual lament for a shattered *Vaterland*" (Danto 1989: 27). This last phrase belongs to Arthur C. Danto, in a review from *The Nation* of the 1988 exhibit of Kiefer's works at the Museum of Modern Art in New York. Where I (at least, now) would want to see the existence of multiple meanings rubbing against each other with considerable critical friction, Danto saw only single meaning, and he was not alone in this. (I should explain that I use Danto's response here only because it was so powerfully articulated and so widely cited and discussed.) Drawing from the experience of my own reactions, I would want to argue that a difference in discursive communities (over time as well as between interpreters) might well be at least part of the reason for these opposite interpretations and evaluations. Danto too linked Wagner's operas and what he called Kiefer's "sludged and operatic fabrications" (Danto 1989: 27), finding the painting "dense, dark, prophetic, heroic, mythic, runic, arcane, dangerous, reassuring, accusatory, reinforcing, grandiloquent, too compelling for mere reason to deal with, fraught, fearful, bearing signs that the artist is in touch with powers that will make us whole, and it is spiritual, oceanic, urgent, romantic and vast" (ibid.: 26–7). The very weight of descriptive terms here suggests Danto's unease, but that unease may have come less from Kiefer's work by itself than from

Danto's sense of history and from his view that Germany is, in his terms, "a scary country" (ibid.: 27), even today. He inferred that Kiefer's mission was "to reconnect Germany and its heroic past and prod it in the direction of its true heroic future" (ibid.: 27), and so he castigated Jewish patrons of Kiefer for seeing the work differently – that is, as evidence of a German's contrition over the Holocaust. He then made an important remark that may explain the possibility of that very different interpretation: the work is, he says, "willfully obscure enough that it can be interpreted that way" too (ibid.: 27).

Danto's reading of Kiefer would seem to have been conditioned by what he claimed was the "overall perniciousness of Kiefer's crack-pot message" (Danto 1989: 27), so that, when confronted with what he saw as "cagey obscurantism" that masked as profundity – in other words, when (like me) confronted with symbols and references from areas which either may not have had strong purchase on or, more likely, may have had only strong negative associations in any of his own immediate discursive communities – he was perhaps understandably primed to react. And react he did, with anger, both against Kiefer and against the "curatorial priest class" (ibid.: 27) which was needed, he argued, to "translate" the work for the rest of us. This might suggest that he too didn't like to rely on the museum's handout. But there might also be other factors involved here, such as the position from which Danto was writing. Even knowing nothing other than what the review itself told me about its author, I might infer that, as someone living and working in the United States today, Danto is not (at present) part of the very particular *German* cultural and political community for which many argue Kiefer is explicitly painting (see Huyssen 1989: 26; Flam 1992: 36). The references to Wagner, to Nazi architecture, and to Teutonic history might be anything but obscure (even if repressed) for an older German audience today, though I admit that they might be contaminated by anti-Nazi taboo (or even lost) for some younger German viewers. Either way, however, there is likely going to be a difference in the kind of "obscurity" a North American like myself or Danto might sense and the response of a German.

Ironies that depend on specific German allusions, as Kiefer's often do, when read outside that specific discursive community or even in an antagonistic light do indeed risk being read as "the usual Wagnerian war music, tooted and thumped by the oompah brass of the marching bands of German nationalism, a heavy-handed compost of shallow ideas and foggy beliefs" (Danto 1989: 28). Yet, against my own earlier reading even more than Danto's, I would now want to argue that this itself risks being a dehistoricized interpretation of both Wagner and Kiefer, a reading that fixates (and in only a finger-pointing way) on the recent Nazi past without problematizing and historicizing both that past and its use (and enjoyment) of some German art – such as Wagner's. From the perspective of my new discursive community, in other words, I think Kiefer does problematize and historicize. Yes, he uses Wagnerian allusions and even Nazi images in his work, but perhaps not, as some have argued, in order to reveal himself as a proud fascist. Read without irony, the provocative work *can* be and has been interpreted in this way. This has always been the risk of using irony. My argument here will be that, interpreted *through* irony, Kiefer's engagement with Nazi-related iconography is a way to confront the inescapable fact that, as a German artist today, Kiefer cannot avoid dealing with the Nazi aestheticization of politics. What he can do, and what I now feel he has done, is turn that aestheticization against itself through irony, and thereby also accept responsibility for the past. By this reading, he refuses to pretend that, while National Socialism obviously happened, it had nothing to do with him. Kiefer's Jewish patrons, therefore, are perhaps not the masochists they have been made out to be (Brooks 1991: 120–1); rather, alert to the power of the unsaid, they might see self-implication on Kiefer's part as essential to his critique.

My obvious premise in arguing for the presence of a strong critical irony in Kiefer's work is that, in visual art, as in verbal, it is possible to think of irony not as saying one thing and meaning another – that standard semantic definition examined in the last chapter – but, instead, as a process of communication that entails two or more meanings being played off, one against the other. The irony is in the difference; irony makes the difference. It plays between meanings, in a space that is always affectively charged, that always has a critical edge. This is the kind of irony I see (now) as possible to read in Kiefer's overt play with things Wagnerian. But it wasn't irony that created our overlapping discursive communities. It was my new knowledge that enabled the overlap that in turn set the scene for irony to happen.

The scope and ambition of Kiefer's work, freely intermingling "real and mythic times, spatial depictions, philosophical outlooks, and media in order to create grand, encompassing statements" (M. Rosenthal 1987: 10), set up a kind of analogue to Wagner's equally vast scope and ambition in creating his *Gesamtkunstwerk* or total art form – the music drama. Their sense of scale is equally grand, and both artists are incredibly demanding of their audiences, expecting them to know Germanic history, myth, and legend in considerable detail in order to understand the allusions in their work (B. Rose 1988: 242). Here, obviously, begin the problems with discursive communities. Both artists also share a belief in the transforming potential of art – and specifically of *their* art – within society. The differences may lie in the degree of critical detachment possessed by Kiefer, towards both the Germanic past and the possibilities of the present, a detachment I infer from the manner of his echoing mentions of Wagnerian themes. In the space between the echo and its context functions Kiefer's irony, but for me it is always a double-edged irony. In the words of Andreas Huyssen, a German of Kiefer's generation, this is a space "informed by a gesture of

105

self-questioning, by an awareness of the questionable nature of his undertaking, and by a pictorial self-consciousness that belies such mystifications" (1989: 26).

Critics have pointed to the impact on Kiefer's early work of the biting irony of the satiric paintings of Sigmar Polke and Gerhard Richter (M. Rosenthal 1987: 12) as well as the work of Joseph Beuys (Gohr 1982: 40, 45), and certainly from the late 1960s onward, Kiefer's parodic probing into his nation's and his own relation to history and identity could be seen to show such an influence. But Kiefer has deliberately chosen politically difficult (not to say incorrect) topics not only to explore technically and intellectually, but to relate to his own position, especially topics that involve the work of artists and thinkers approved of by the Nazis and whose reputations have subsequently been damaged by that association: Heidegger, Clausewitz, Wagner. By turning this historical investigation back upon himself and his own art, however, Kiefer turns the ironies so created against more than the obvious.

In the conservative, normalizing climate of the mid-1980s, German historians again debated openly the issues of "German responsibility for the holocaust, the alleged need to 'historicize' the fascist past, and the problem of a German national identity" (Huyssen 1989: 27); but over a decade earlier than that Kiefer had already begun to embarrass and worry Germans by confronting that nationalism/fascism historical linkage directly in his work. In 1969 he deliberately violated a taboo of (then West) German culture – a taboo against the representation of what was called "Nazi-kitsch" – in a series of photographs called *Besetzungen* (*Occupations*). He was instantly denounced as a neo-Nazi for even wanting to engage in a dialogue with forbidden images. These admittedly provocative photos featured Kiefer himself in various European locations, wearing military jodhpurs and performing the (for me) historically menacing Hitlerian salute. Assuming the identity of the conquering Nazi occupying (hence the title) Europe, Kiefer both *confronted* (that is, did not normalize) the past – though not his own personal past, for he was born after the war – and ironized it: the heroicizing image of self as Nazi is always oddly small in scale, ironically dwarfed by the so-called "occupied" site. In one set of photographs, he stands in a bathtub: there are, in other words, no waving flags, no shouting masses, no signs of imperialism beyond the salute – except that he *is* standing, in messianic manner, *on* the water (actually on a slightly visible stool placed in the water). In another photograph, he takes Caspar David Friedrich's *Traveler Looking Over a Sea of Fog* (1818) and self-consciously inserts the National Socialist and the self into the romantic heritage of Germany – while still perhaps distancing himself by posing as the traveler in foreign lands. But, arguably, all this was not really that different *politically* from the dominant ethos of left-liberal German intellectual life over the last 30 years – the *Vergangenheitsbewältigung* or coming to terms with the past. What *was* different was his choice of iconography. In Huyssen's reading, Kiefer was not aiming so much at Germany's perhaps unconscious repression of war guilt, but at the "deliberate and conscious repression of fascist themes and icons," insisting that "Nazi culture's exploitation and abuse of traditional German image worlds had to be worked through as well" (1992: 86).

Therefore, the purpose for a young artist of so flamboyantly breaking the Nazi representational taboo was not only to *live through* the past, to enact, to perform it in one's own body, in order to understand it (see Herzogenrath 1991: 96), but also to confront through irony the post-Auschwitz German refusal to come to terms with the aesthetic dimensions of the political past. Yet, the important question that remains for me is not "is Kiefer a fascist?" but "is irony the appropriate way to deal with fascist terror?" It interests me that Huyssen's response is a sort of qualified "yes": the "Sieg Heil" salute in those early photographs, he argues, is to be read as a

> conceptual gesture reminding us that indeed Nazi culture had most effectively occupied, exploited, and abused the power of the visual, especially the power of massive monumentalism and of a confining, even disciplining, central-point perspective. Fascism had furthermore perverted, abused, and sucked up whole territories of a German image-world, turning national iconic and literary traditions into mere ornaments of power and thereby leaving post-1945 culture with a tabula rasa that was bound to cause a smoldering crisis of identity.
> (Huyssen 1989: 31–4)

It was into precisely this world that Kiefer was born.

Wagner was therefore a likely subject for him, given the paradox of the composer's well-known aesthetic/ideological appeal to Hitler and the National Socialists and yet his own revolutionary associations during his lifetime – both political and musical. Kiefer himself has noted the parallel between his own and Wagner's belief in the power of the artist and art to perform redemptive acts (in M. Rosenthal 1987: 26), but for me such a parallel cannot be viewed outside the context of the *history* of Wagner's *reception* in Germany. Discursive community is crucial here in why and how Kiefer can recall Wagner. While it is true that both artists use the Icelandic *Edda* as source material and that their works share a certain monumental scale and theatricality (M. Rosenthal 1987: 26), to stop there is to ignore what I see as the ironic differences that are in play in any of Kiefer's Wagnerian echoes.

In *Deutschlands Geisteshelden* (1973), for example, Kiefer presents a curious image of the titular "Spiritual Heroes" of Germany: a cavernous wooden room with flaming dishes set into the sides of the walls. These dishes may well recall the torches of Nazi rallies (Flam 1992: 32), but they

Plate 4.1 "Notung" (1973) by Anselm Kiefer. Oil and charcoal on burlap, with oil and charcoal on cardboard; reproduced with the permission of the Museum Boymans-van Beuningen, Rotterdam.

also have names written beneath them. The first and largest of these names on the left of the painting is "Richard Wagner." The bottom of the work is dark, as if singed by flames. Most critics have noted the likely reference to Valhalla, the home of the god Wotan (in *Der Ring des Nibelungen*) that was set alight when Brünnhilde sacrificed herself on her beloved Siegfried's funeral pyre. The ensuing apocalypse – the *Götterdämmerung* – brings about the fall of the gods and the restoration of moral order (with the Rhinemaidens reclaiming the golden ring that had caused all the trouble in the first place). But there is an interesting contextual detail about this painting that acts for me as a marker of irony in this pointing to Wagner by Kiefer: from other paintings of this period, it would seem that the wooden room that is the setting for the naming of these heroic figures is also Kiefer's own studio. In the discursive space between Valhalla and that studio is set up, for me now, an irony that makes the artist into a god-like figure – but one who is awaiting his own demise, and literally playing with fire. This connection between destruction and redemption is directly related to the ideas of both fire and art in many of Kiefer's as well as Wagner's works.

Starting in 1973, Kiefer did a series of works overtly on themes from *Der Ring*. An oil and charcoal called *Notung* (see Plate 4.1) is seen by one critic as a formal study in woodgrain (M. Rosenthal 1987: 22), and it is that . . . but it is also so much more. The setting is once again that wooden attic room – that is, Kiefer's own studio. Stuck in the floor is a sword, with Wagner's line "Ein Schwert verhiess mir der Vater" – "my father promised me a sword" – (from *Die Walküre*, Act 1, Scene 3, opening line) inscribed in the upper middle of the painting. Written directly over the sword is the word which once baffled me but now made sense: "Nothung" – necessity – the name of the sword promised to Siegmund by his father, Wotan, and embedded in a tree awaiting his notice. This is the sword that will enable Siegmund's son, Siegfried, to break Wotan's spear and eventually bring about the fall of the gods through those flames of Brünnhilde's redemptive human love. To have this sword stuck into, not a tree, but the wooden floor of an artist's studio, is both a play on the shared wooden nature of the receptacles and also another of those ironized, double-edged pointings to the role of the artist as potential redeemer – though not without the possibility of self-immolation *en route*. The connection between the saving sword and the artist's "weapon" is made explicit in *Baum mit Palette* (1978) in which the Wagnerian tree has impaled in it, not a sword, but an artist's palette – but a palette made out of metal (lead) and affixed to the oil-painted tree. Swords, like fire, are potentially ways to destroy, and their association with the artist's studio in so many of Kiefer's paintings sets up – again, for me, *now* – an ironic tension between the forces of creation and destruction, transformation and ruination. But I would want to argue that none of this self-implication through location necessarily makes Kiefer himself (or Wagner, for that matter) into a fascist artist or a military aggressor (cf. Brooks 1991: 106).

Other paintings also recall scenes from the *Ring* cycle of operas, some in terms of representational details (such as *Brünhilde-Grane*, 1978, *Grane*, 1980, and *Brünhilde schläft*, 1980), and others in more symbolic terms, such as the barren, snowy, ploughed field with the title, *Siegfried vergisst Brünhilde* (1975) – Siegfried forgets Brünnhilde – painted up the centre, or the relatively small bonfire (that ironically brings on the grand fall of the gods) portrayed in *Brünhildes Tod* (1976). Wagner's opera, *Parsifal* also inspired Kiefer's deployment of similar ironic spaces. In 1973, the same year as *Deutschlands Geisteshelden*, Kiefer produced a work entitled *Parsifal II*, in which that large empty wooden room is the setting for a large, red, chalice-like bowl. John Gilmour reads this as "evoking memories of blood sacrifice and other archaic forms of human expression" (1990: 62). In the context of the title, this bowl is the Holy Grail, however, and the specific sacrifice is that of both Christ and Amfortas, the legend's wounded Fisher King who is the Keeper of the Grail. The final words of Wagner's opera – "Höchsten Heiles Wunder! Erlösung dem Erlöser!" – appear written above Kiefer's grail. These words ("Highest Holy Wonder! Redemption for the Redeemer!") are to be sung in the opera as a white dove hovers over the redeeming Parsifal's head and Amfortas is healed. Gilmour sees these words in the painting as creating "a symbolic conflict that we are left to resolve, raising the question of whether the Parsifal ideal [which is not defined here], the music-drama that celebrated it, and the culture that supported them both has played a positive or negative role within history" (ibid.: 62). Later in his discussion, Gilmour explains the Parisifal "ideal" as being that of "bourgeois humanity, making the quest for the holy grail a journey of piety and heroic grandeur" (ibid.: 66) – which Kiefer relocates in an empty attic room and thus "appears both to revere the myth and to debunk its pretentiousness" (ibid.: 66). What is missing now for me here, however, is any sense of the difference it might make if this empty room were a specific empty room – that is, the artist's own studio (as indeed it is). To relocate Wagner's "consecration" drama of salvation and redemption within that particular personalized setting is to set up ironic tensions not only with Wagner's opera but also within Kiefer's own art. The ironies that happen for me in this attic space between the worlds and works of Wagner and Kiefer suggest that it is art, more than religion, that might now seek to redeem humankind – but that such a redemption is not likely to be without its own spilling of blood, its own destruction and pain. When Kiefer's painting of Parsifal's abandoned mother, *Herzeleide* (1979) shows a woman contemplating a skull-shaped palette, the idea of *art* as all that is left of such complex narratives of sacrifice and salvation combines with the notion of art as itself constituting that salvation.

In the early 1980s, Kiefer explored another Wagnerian opera, *Die Meistersinger von Nürnberg*, which, unlike the *Ring* and *Parsifal*, was indeed one of Hitler's favourites. There are a number of paintings entitled *Die*

Meistersinger, each of which numbers the thirteen figures it presents in order to point directly to the actual history of the thirteen singers allowed to participate in the traditional, early German singing contest that was Wagner's subject matter. In one, the figures are painted strokes of colour; in the others, they are made of straw, a material Kiefer has used to symbolize things Germanic. (The potential ironies of that material, as many have noted, lie in their suggestion of Aryan blondness in conjunction with fragility – that is, with a substance easily rotted or burned.) The fact that this singing contest took place in Nürnberg, the site of not only Nazi rallies and spectacles but of the war crimes trials, makes Kiefer's context a potentially rich one for engaging irony. Indeed, I would read the reflexivity of Wagner's opera-about-singing as here transcoded into Kiefer's equally reflexive painting-about-painting's-responsibility-in-history. While this is also an opera about love and redemption, for me that fact would be less important a connection to Wagner this time than is the well-known association with National Socialism.

At the same time as he painted this *Meistersinger* series, Kiefer was also producing works which take as their settings various examples of Nazi memorial architecture. Unlike the outraged German critics, an American one felt that "Kiefer 'saved' neoclassical architecture from the Nazis" (M. Rosenthal 1987: 133), showing "that architectural conventions are but hollow containers, little more than superficial stylizations by which a culture celebrates its heroes" (ibid.: 106). But the particular way in which these architectural appropriations are used – the play of complex *differences* evoked in an inclusive and relational way – now suggests to me other possible readings. Where another commentator sees Kiefer rescuing "cliched imagery by recasting it in a contradictory setting" (Flam 1992: 33) and thereby moving "beyond mere irony" – which he himself admits to associating only with naughtiness and snickering – I would now want to argue that, for me at least, this space of contradiction is the very terrain of a much more serious kind of irony. For instance, in *Innenraum* (1981) (see Plate 4.2), Kiefer copies Albert Speer's plans for the Mosaic Room in the Reich Chancellery, Berlin, 1939 but his copy is blackened and stained. These are the actual "ruins of fascism" (Huyssen 1989: 38) that Kiefer and his generation literally grew up amidst. There is a fire in the foreground center, recalling for me, and perhaps for you, everything from a memorial flame to the Nazi book-burning fires and the Holocaust – not to mention Valhalla, once again (at least for some discursive communities).

This is part of a series of monumental paintings on the theme of "To the Unknown Painter" and often, where the eternal memorial flame might be expected to burn, a palette is seen to rise. If the place of the glorified Nazi soldier is now taken by the German painter, the ironies set up by this substitution suggest that, given the Nazi view of much modern art as "degenerate," Kiefer's particular fate might well have been more as

111

Plate 4.2 "Innenraum" (1981) by Anselm Kiefer. Oil, acrylic, emulsion, straw, and shellac on canvas, with woodcut; reproduced with permission of the Stedelijk Museum, Amsterdam.

ridiculed victim than as treasured hero. Not surprisingly, perhaps, critics have seen this series either as a critique or as a reinforcement of the myth of artistic genius. Both the soldier and painter may well be seen as men of action who fight for their ideals (M. Rosenthal 1987: 115) or who exhibit aggressive, warlike propensities (Brooks 1991: 106); but to see only the positive or the negative like this is not to see the potential ironic tension created by the charred Nazi setting, a tension which I now read as a suggestion that contemporary German art must face not only its Nationalist Socialist past (for, as noted, that has been part of at least West German ideology for a while now), but must confront the aesthetic as well as moral implications of that past for the *present.*

Kiefer's 1983 work, *Der Rhein* uses Wilhelm Kreis's design for a Nazi memorial Hall of Soldiers (1939) set in contrast with nature – the Rhine and the trees along its banks. The bonfire figured in the centre of the lower

112

part of the work recalls Wagner's funeral pyre for Siegfried along the banks of the Rhine river – the fire whose flames brought about the *Götterdämmerung*. Just as Wagner had linked destruction and cleansing – the Rhine overflowed as Valhalla burned – Kiefer engages the Nazi past and its military values directly in his creation, but always suggesting, through what I see as his ironies' sharp edge, the possibility of further destruction. For instance, another kind of ironic play with Wagner's Valhalla occurs for me in *Sulamith* (1983), where still other of Kreis's plans, this time for the Funeral Hall for the Great German Soldiers, in the Hall of Soldiers (1939), became the ironized site of the interplay of complex meanings formerly unseen. For Wagner, Valhalla was the home not only of the gods but of the great warriors fallen in battle, whom Wotan gathered around him for protection. Of course, in the end, the dead Nazi soldiers were no more able to protect Hitler than Wagner's heroes were able to save Wotan – but the ironic comparison does not stop there. The title of this painting is from "Todesfuge," a poem by Paul Celan written in 1945 when he was in a concentration camp. Sulamith is the ash-haired Jewish woman of the poem, contrasted with Margarete, the blonde German (see A. Benjamin 1991: 118). In Kiefer's work, the memorial grandeur of the Nazi funeral hall is transformed into the ominous horror of a charred stone oven, a sign of the Holocaust and its named victim. Between these two meanings, for me, plays the tragic irony of history, as well as, of course, that of Wagner's own well-documented anti-semitism. Kreis's fascist architectural space, intended for celebrating the death cult of the Nazis, becomes a memorial space for the Nazis' victims, creating an almost Brechtian irony, "an effect that reveals fascism's genocidal telos in its own celebratory memorial spaces" (Huyssen 1989: 43).

And there are still other ironies at work – now – for me here. Kiefer has painted a number of these different furnace images, which his critics have related to his interest in alchemy (perhaps inspired by Joseph Beuys [Flam 1992: 33]), and specifically to the theme of fire as a tool of transformation through purifying destruction. The use of such an alchemical concept in relation to the Nazi book burning and gas ovens – particularly through the use of Speer's Chancellery architecture as the setting for a work called *Athanor* (1983–84) – has become for many besides myself an ironic commentary on the idea of "purifying" the race. But once again, Kiefer complicates the situation by self-implication: the same connection of fire and oven ("athanor" is an alchemical oven) is made in *Des Malers Atelier* (1980), but this time the link is with the artist's studio once again, not with Nazi monuments. For me, the ironies "work" the space not only between destruction and creation, but also between National Socialism and Anselm Kiefer, politics and art, the past and the present. In *Malen = Verbrennen* (1974), Kiefer links the painting and burning equated in the title by figuring a palette hovering over a torched, charred landscape. Kiefer may

113

be echoing the Nazi idea that aggressive destruction was needed to create a better world (M. Rosenthal 1987: 60), but the irony to be explored further might be Kiefer's deliberate identification of his *own* aesthetic beliefs with those of a past many Germans would rather forget. Art, he suggests, is like fire: it can destroy but it can also transform.

But, how different is that from what the Nazis believed? Under what conditions can one believe that art always transforms for the better? These are among the questions Kiefer's paintings still raise for me and others through their provocative and deliberate self-inscription. In *Nero malt* (1974) (*Nero paints*), the artist's palette and brushes set fire to houses. In another complex alchemical reference that has long historical echoes, Kiefer has also worked with lead as an artistic material, physically attaching it to the surface of his paintings. In alchemy, lead is the way to gold; in Wagner's *Ring*, gold is the cause of evil and pain ... but also of the entire cycle of operas. The artist as metalworker recalls the Wagnerian Nibelung, but only ironically – for they were once happy trinket-makers until they were made slaves to the power of the gold. The multiple and complex echoes of Wagner's work in Kiefer's paintings do more now than simply suggest to me a shared theatricality and obsession with the inseparability of Germanic history and myth, for those echoes – in context – set up an ironic space whereby I read Kiefer as commenting both on Wagner's ideals (and failures) and on his own role as an artist in Germany today, openly dealing with a history that extends back through National Socialism to the myths of the *Nibelungenlied*. Wagner is not his only point of reference, to be sure, but for me lately it has come to be an important one, one that I consistently ironize through what I infer to be a tension between identification and critical distance. While Wagner rather grandiosely (even dangerously) appeared to feel that he had managed to find all the answers – aesthetic and ethical – to the world's problems, Kiefer seems to me to suggest that he cannot do any such thing. His winged-palette-as-Icarus in *Icarus-Markischer Sand* (1981) crashes: "redemption through painting is no longer possible, mythic vision itself is fundamentally contaminated, polluted, violated by history," as Huyssen remarks (1989: 45). It may be the case that Kiefer's "recall of a particular incident or subject is meant to introduce a spiritual outlook or moral lesson that is almost always ambiguous or paradoxical, since Kiefer's view of experience is that there are no truths, only interpretations" (M. Rosenthal 1987: 10), but that lesson is almost always, for me, also ironic and historically situated.

In what sense is that really the case, though? Or, as my own double-take suggests, does it depend on your discursive community and thus on the context in which you view his work? My initial response was hardly likely to be sympathetic, thanks to the deadly combination of my own historically negative associations (themselves generationally conditioned) with things Teutonic, the oppressiveness of the works' size and palette, and – to be

114

honest – my academic's irritation at not knowing enough to understand the subject matter. The power of this latter point should not, I think, be ignored: "The spectator's guilt about lack of knowledge, which reappears as resentment in the critics' complaint about Kiefer's reliance on distant bodies of knowledge, may say more about contemporary culture than about his paintings, which, in their fragmentation and allegorical procedure, also participate in the forgetting they are meant to counteract" (Huyssen 1992: 90). Such guilt also says a lot about the importance of discursive communities to the comprehension of all, not only ironic texts. And it is not always a question of exclusionary elitism – or even utopian, amiable communities. Different discursive communities may certainly exist in different countries, for different generations, but also at different times in one person's life. Huyssen too has documented his own move from fascination to suspicion ("Is this fascist painting at one remove?") and then to an understanding of the therapeutic effect of using irony to face the "aesthetic lure of fascism" (1989: 38–9), both in the past and in the present. He acknowledges the risk involved here ("it may strengthen the static and melancholic disposition toward fascism rather than overcome it" [ibid.: 39]), but this has always been the risk of irony. The questions of *who* may use – and interpret – irony *when, where,* and *how* are probably never going to go away.

Anselm Kiefer has been called everything from a politically brave hero to a neo-Nazi opportunist, and one commentator suggests that it is the pictorial and ideological "impurity" of his art that is at fault (Flam 1992: 32). Perhaps. But I think it is more the impurity of irony that is at work here. As a political strategy and as a means of meaning-making, irony has always carried with it considerable risk in our culture. One of the reasons for this is the inevitability of differences in discursive communites and thus the danger of "misunderstanding," as you will see once again in Chapter 7. But there are other contributing factors too, ones that are implicit in my own change of interpretation and evaluation of Kiefer's work, and these the next chapter will address. Is irony in the eye of the beholder? Or, must it always be a matter of intention?

5

INTENTION AND
INTERPRETATION
Irony and the eye of the beholder

I THE UNBEARABLE SLIPPERINESS OF IRONY

In the past, much of the theorizing of irony has been done from the point
of view of the ironist, and has therefore been implicitly or explicitly
"intentionalist." Indeed, the understandable urge to anchor the
slipperiness of meaning in the intention of the encoder is evident in most
studies of figurative language or indirect expression (see Nathan 1982:
254), particularly in historical studies (Green 1979; Gaunt 1989;
Swearingen 1991: 209–10). There, the problems of comprehension that
face all interpreters of irony, as discussed in the last chapter, are even more
evident. As one literary scholar put it: "The only way to be sure that a
statement was intended ironically is to have a detailed knowledge of the
personal, linguistic, cultural and social references of the speaker *and* his
audience" (Gaunt 1989: 25). The complexity of discursive communities,
however, might cast some doubt on the ability of any historical research to
"reconstruct" such references – except in the most general and basic of
terms. Nevertheless, as I have mentioned before, the most influential
theories of irony have asserted that there exist "stable" ironies that are
intended, overt, and capable of being reconstructed by the interpreter
(Booth 1974: 6). These are usually called "intentional" ironies (Muecke
1969: 42).

But there are other kinds too: most obviously, those that are not intended
but are interpreted as ironic. These include (but are not restricted to) those
situational ironies "of events" that are "observable" (Muecke 1969: 42) or
"accidental" (Tittler 1984: 17) or "incidental" (Booth 1961: 159). The
distinction here is said to be the difference between "being ironic" and "it
is ironic that" (Muecke 1970/1982: 22). But what about all those verbal
utterances and structural orderings we also interpret as ironic, but might
find no evidence for their being intended as such? (Indeed, a lack of such
evidence is often part of the pleasure derived from attributing this kind of
irony.) A theory of irony that is totally intentionalist, that believes "being
ironical means deliberately being ironical" (Muecke 1969: 57), would not

seem to be able to deal with one of irony's most common manifestations: as a strategy of interpretation. But perhaps seeing and hearing irony is itself an intentional act that makes irony happen? In that case, as this chapter will explore, it is the concept of intentionality (as much as irony) that needs broadening.

Intention has traditionally entered into discussions of both interpretation and evaluation of meaning (see Newton-de Molina 1976), either to contest its accessibility (and desirability) (Wimsatt and Beardsley 1967) or to assert its centrality. It is not that anyone has ever denied that intentions exist, in other words; the disagreements have been over how they are deployed in the interpretive process. Paul Grice's (1975) complex linking of meaning and intention produced an intention-based semantics that, in turn, spawned an "expressivist semantics" (Altieri 1981). Speech-act theory (Austin 1975; Searle 1983) and pragmatics both contributed to the reconsideration of intentionality. (In another form, more closely related to concepts of reference, intention has been central to phenomenology as well.) In fact, despite the attacks of Anglo-American New Criticism, some ordinary language philosophy, structuralism, and some forms of poststructuralism, intentionalism has never really disappeared. With its roots in idealism and romanticism, it raises epistemological and ontological issues that have persisted, even leading some to assert that it is intentions that provide the very "categorial framework for understanding" (Dutton 1987: 199).

Yet many cogent reasons for abandoning intentionality as the guarantee of meaning have been advanced over the years. Some have said that a Lacanian concept of the subject would invalidate a concern for intention because it would accord the subject "no anteriority or priority over its discourse" (C.D. Lang 1988: 60). A related argument is the one that denies that discourse can or should be viewed as "the majestic unfolding manifestation of a thinking, knowing, speaking subject" (Foucault 1972: 55) who "intends." For others, it is the rather complex and fragmented nature of our public sphere today that invalidates intentions, for they are multiple and thus cannot work uniformly (Collins 1989: 17). Deconstruction too has challenged theories that seek to define meaning in any univocal way, including through intention (Culler 1982: 131).

Yet none of these positions would necessarily deny that intentions exist, that each of us at some time or another has intended to be ironic. The question is: what status should that intention have in theorizing ironic meaning? Is it, as has been claimed, a "false sophistication that thinks to bypass the question of authorial intention as naive" (Smyth 1986: 333)? In some cases, might intention have a privileged but not pre-emptive position (Sparshott 1976: 110) in determining whether an utterance is ironic? Might it be "a necessary but not sufficient condition for the presence of irony" (Muecke 1973: 35)? What I want to suggest in this chapter is that these are

117

not the only (or maybe even the best) questions to ask. To call something ironic is to frame or contextualize it in such a way that, in fact, an intentionalist statement has already been made – either by the ironist *or* by the interpreter (or by both).

In other words, intentional/non-intentional may be a false distinction: all irony happens intentionally, whether the attribution be made by the encoder or the decoder. Interpretation is, in a sense, an intentional act on the part of the interpreter. The recourse to the "invisible anonymity" (Said 1983: 188) of Foucaultian discursive power does not always answer the issues raised by irony, where human agency reasserts itself in complex ways and at many stages: in the intention, execution, interpretation, affective response, and consequences of irony. It is precisely this reassertion of human agency that has attracted oppositional politics to the power of irony. Interpreters, too, are not passive consumers or "receivers" of irony: they make irony happen by what I want to call this intentional act, different from but not unrelated to the ironist's intention to be ironic. This view would then likely work to collapse the distinction (D. Bennett 1985: 30) between "intentionalist" ironies (marked by the complicity of ironist and interpreter) and "voluntarist" ones (where only the interpreter is held accountable). All would be, in the end, voluntarist in some way.

One of my reasons for extending further rather than tossing out the notion of intention is that intention is one of the few ways we have of distinguishing lying from irony. You may recall Swift's Gulliver trying to explain the concept of lying to his Houyhnhnm master to whom it is incomprehensible because "the Use of Speech was to make us understand one another, and to receive Information of Facts." Therefore, "if anyone *said the Thing which was not*," such an aim would be defeated (Swift 1958: 195). Saying "*the Thing which was not*" is a definition of (Yahoo) irony, too, of course, and from Quintilian on, irony has been related by many to *dissimulatio* (D. Knox 1989: 42) and pretense – hence, its suspect moral character. The difference is in lying's intention to deceive (Levin 1988: 127), to withhold information, and irony's temporary or restricted intention to dissimulate (to an evaluative end). Semantically, some have argued, there is no way to distinguish irony and lying (see Kerbrat-Orecchioni 1980a: 114; 1980b: 181) (though irony's edge marks its difference on the pragmatic level). The interpreter has to formulate the hypothesis that the speaker intends either to be ironic or to lie. This act is also, to put it in the terms suggested in Chapter 3, an act of semantic inference of irony's additional, relational and inclusive meaning rather than of lying's contrary or other meaning. But this formulation of the issue does not do away with intention, as I have defined it, because that act of inference is itself an intentional act, based (as the next chapter will explore) on the information provided by immediate context and by textual markers.

An example: the media around the world reported that a certain Father

118

Joseph, a Dominican priest from California, had turned up at the 1992 National Democratic Convention in New York City with an eight-foot confessional (labelled "Portofess") attached to his bicycle and a handout claiming "Religion on the Move for People on the Go! . . . The church must go where the sinners are." While this was widely reported in the media because of its (transgressive) humor, it took reporters a few days to discover that there was no Father Joseph in any Dominican order in California. Was this hoax by New York-based conceptual and performance artist, Joey Skaggs, therefore, a lie? Skaggs has often used the media in this way as his "canvas" – hooking them (always with irony) and then using their gullibility to call attention to serious issues about media responsibility. The meaning of his ironies is always in the intention or, more accurately, in what is revealed about both the media and society when people are let in on the ironic intention.

Rather than use the traditional distinction between ironies that are intended and ironies that are unintended, then, I want to expand the sense of what intention might mean in this context. Because the "*intentional production of meaning*" (Said 1975: 5, his italics) describes the activity of both ironists and interpreters, such an expansion will allow me to bring together three different and usually distinct strands within irony theory: what is usually called the intentionalist position (ironist only); the reverse position that all irony is a function of reading (interpreter only); and the position that there is a shared responsibility (for both) in the use and attribution of irony.

The many intentionalist theories of irony can be distinguished one from the other by their stand on the question of the function of intention: **psycho-aesthetic**, **semantic**, or **ethical**. My awkward term, **psycho-aesthetic**, is meant to refer to the view that intention acts as the guarantee of conscious control – either in terms of psychology or artistry. Textual effects deemed to be ironic (in semantic or evaluative terms) are, therefore, no accident; they are conscious and deliberate (Green 1979: 6; Stern 1980: 124; Richards 1929: 176), part of a "controlled design" (McKee 1974: 107). From this position, intentions (and thus the purposive activity of the ironist) become the "pragmatic conditions of intelligibility necessary for any communicative act" (Altieri 1990: 15). The second, related function granted to intentions in irony theory is thus as the **semantic** guarantee of meaning. Their role here is to make irony "stable" through the invocation of "the real man or woman" who stands behind "each ironic stroke as warrantors of the continuing validity of what we are about" (Booth 1974: 176). Without intentions to anchor meaning, it is argued, anything could be ironic and, of course, nothing could be ironic for certain (Mizzau 1984: 20). A more radical position here would be that there is no need to ground meaning in intention because what is intended is identical with what is meant (Knapp and Michaels 1982: 729), but the long debates in literary

119

studies over the statement by E. D. Hirsch, Jr. that meaning "is, and can be, nothing other than the author's meaning" (1967: 216) would suggest that the issue of semantic anchoring is not resolved quite so simply. It is one thing to assert that interpreters always posit "a speaker who very likely means something" (Hirsch 1967: 225) and quite another to be able to posit a speaker who most definitely is being ironic in this particular case, to this particular end, and with this particular semantic and evaluative effect. Hirsch argues that an author's original purpose or intention is "an historical event" which can be reconstructed by the reader (or scholar, perhaps) (1982: 238), and even asserts that there is a moral obligation on the part of the interpreter to do that reconstructing.

The flip side of this, a basically **ethical** position, is the one that says that the responsibility to guarantee the comprehension of irony (and the avoidance of misunderstanding) lies with the encoding ironist who must coordinate assumptions about codes and contextual information that decoders will have accessible to them and be likely to use (Sperber and Wilson 1986: 43). As the last chapter investigated, however, discursive communities also play an important role in making such a coordinating function even possible. The ethical dimension enters the intentionalist debate around irony in yet another way, though, for without the accountability that could come with intentionality, irony might well mean never having to say you really mean it. The potential for evasion through only tacit affirmation (White 1973: 37) can obviously be viewed as a negative. In Julian Barnes's novel, *Flaubert's Parrot*, the narrator writes of Flaubert's "booby-trapped" ironies: "That is the attraction, and also the danger, of irony: the way it permits a writer to be seemingly absent from his work, yet in fact hintingly present. You *can* have your cake and eat it; the only trouble is, you get fat" (1985: 87). Roland Barthes, of course, had seen Flaubert's irony as causing a "salutory discomfort" because "*one never knows if he is responsible for what he writes*" (1974: 140, italics his). Ironists are said to wear masks – even if only momentarily (Karstetter 1964: 175) – and there exist multiple "levels" of masked intention in ironic utterances, from absent to ambiguous to (paradoxically) clear (Mizzau 1984: 27–35). As Chapter 2 investigated, though, every time the intention to ironize is discussed, this same kind of double evaluative coding (both negative and positive) can be found: ironic intent can be seen as either morally suspect evasion or as healthy suspension of certainty. The ironist's perspective is therefore either "shifting" (Burke 1968: 102) and perhaps shifty, *or* a sign of "mental alertness and agility" (Muecke 1969: 247). The merging of the intellectual and the moral in these discussions of intention is also doubly coded. Irony is seen as either the mode of the detached and witnessing (Barthes 1977b: 86), the dispassionate and distanced (Frye 1970: 40–1) or the mark of the uncaring and the insouciant, the indifferent and the superior (Muecke 1969: 216, 13). Either way, there is a moral dimension implied.

These **ethical**, **semantic**, and **psycho-aesthetic** functions ascribed to intention in irony all – in practice, if not theory – come up against the difficulty of actually, pragmatically, being able to access and to assess the intention of the ironist (Tanaka 1973: 48). Whether intention is something derived from markers in the text in question or from extratextual evidence such as statements by the ironist, the empirical difficulties in establishing intention never go away. Sometimes, people even give contradictory interpretations of their own intentions. After seeing the possible (material) consequences for himself of the literal interpretation of his *Shortest Way with the Dissenters* (1702), Daniel Defoe appended to the second edition a note claiming that he intended no sedition; by 1705, feeling somewhat safer, he could assert that the pamphlet had had the desired effect because his targets had missed his ironies (see Downie 1986: 122). These kinds of reversals can work to undermine the semantic anchoring function of intention, to challenge the ethical function, and to call into question the firmness of the psycho-aesthetic demand for purposiveness.

For these and other reasons, many theorists have gone to the other extreme to argue that irony is not at all a matter of ironist intent, but the result of a particular mode of interpreting that infers or "logically implies" a claim about what the "ironist" intended (Juhl 1980: 148), even if involuntarily (Thomson 1926: 112–13; Eco 1976: 18). A specific version of what has been asserted for all manifestations of "authorial voice" as "an interpretive construct built by the reader" (Siegle 1986: 184), ironic intent might therefore be seen solely as the product of the inference of the interpreter (Eco 1976: 156). In order to put the unsaid into play with the said, the interpreter (at the very least) infers that the sayer understands the overt meaning of her or his own utterance and, as one critic put it, is in possession of her/his faculties (Todorov 1978: 59); in addition, the assumption is that the said/unsaid relationship is consciously and purposively intended to be discerned (through textual and contextual markers) by the interpreter. In some senses, we are back to the psycho-aesthetic function of intention, but this time from the point of view of the interpreter's inference: "the structure of communication is not one of intention → recognition but one of intention → inference" (Adams 1985: 45).

But it is not only intention that is attributed by the interpreter: specific semantic meaning itself and the evaluative edge of irony are also inferred, in a way. And these inferences too are intentional acts. In addition, to see irony anywhere (or everywhere) is the result of interpretive labor performed through learned skills. As I've mentioned before, Ellen Winner has argued that children learn to understand and perform metaphor earlier than irony because metaphor "serves to illuminate the attributes of things in the world, irony to reveal the ironist's attitude about the world" (1988: vii). As also discussed earlier, while both are modes of indirection, metaphor relies on perception of similarity within difference, whereas irony necessitates the discrimination of differences between said and unsaid. Irony therefore involves certain "inferential skills" (ibid.: 160) that operate on several different levels. First, on a semantic level, the child has to be able to detect incongruity and to differentiate falsehood from truth; second, on a pragmatic level, the child has to be able to infer another's beliefs and intentions or "communicative purpose" (ibid.: 174). This involves "social cognitive development": that is, the ability to infer both the knowledge shared by speaker and addressee (ibid.: 13) and the attitude of the speaker toward what is being discussed. While this is an issue in all ironic comprehension, for children the inference of this attitudinal aspect of irony is a learned skill (ibid.: 14), a "metacognitive ability" (ibid.: 188) – one, you may be tempted to add, some people never learn very well at all.

Perhaps, then, it is really the interpreter who "ironizes" (Ducrot *et al.* 1980: 200; Finlay 1978: 37). Rather than saying that "[u]ntil an ironic message is interpreted as intended it has only the sound of one hand clapping" (Muecke 1970/1982: 39), perhaps it is a case of there being no hand clapping at all until an ironic message is interpreted (period) as such. Perhaps the ironic intentional function is one activated and put into play by the interpreter. Irony would then be a function of reading (Chambers 1991: 47), in the broad sense of the word, or, at the very least, irony would "complete itself in the reading" (Said 1983: 87). It would not be something intrinsic to a text, but rather something that results from the act of construing carried out by the interpreter who works within a context of interpretive assumptions (Fish 1980: 277; 1983: 177, 191). This position is always argued to account for situational ironies (Kaufer 1983: 452–3), but it could be seen to apply equally well to verbal or structural ones, since all indirect speech acts involve "an ability on the part of the hearer to make inferences" (Searle 1975: 61). Interpreters are active agents in making all irony happen (Amante 1981: 92), but ironists as intentional actants are necessary and functional only in *certain* ironies (cf. Altieri 1981: 251; Harshaw 1984: 234). Irony is always (whatever else it might be) a modality of perception – or, better, of attribution – of both meaning and evaluative attitude. This is perhaps one way to reinsert more explicitly the agency of the interpreter into Derrida's theory of intention as a textual effect rather as than something prior to the text that determines its meaning (see Culler 1982: 218, 127–8). It is also another way (in addition to the notion of discursive community) to make sense of the empirical observation that interpreters don't always "get" (that is, make) the same message from the same text (see Monson 1988: 539 for one of many possible examples). With the agency that makes irony so politically useful, however, comes the unpredictability of difference: "our physiological, psychological and sociological conditioning, our knowledge, capacities, interests and goals do vary," as one theorist pointedly observes (Prince 1983: 531). In addition, the type and number of ironic utterances one has been exposed to, "personal attitudes toward irony, physical and emotional states up to and including the time of the given utterance" (Hagen 1992: 156) – all these affect the interpretation of irony too. Some even assert that what is required for irony to be inferred is a "doubting mind" and a certain degree of leisure, ease and security (Tittler 1984: 200).

It is for reasons like these that I think the complexity of the potential interaction of interpreter, ironist and text in making irony happen *has* to be part of any consideration of irony as the "performative" happening it is. Theorists have discussed this in terms of what must be "mutually recognized" (Fogelin 1988: 87) or "shared" (Abrams 1981: 90) between the agents through the text. The participatory nature of irony involves "culturally-shared knowledge of the rules, conventions, expectations" (Pratt 1977: 86) in play in a particular context. A discursive community must therefore exist and, as the next chapter will investigate, the immediate context and the text itself must signal or provoke some thought that irony might be possible. If intentions are forms of "conventional behavior that are to be conventionally 'read'" (Fish 1982: 213), then they are "read" within interpretive communities (Fish 1980: 14; Beardsley 1958: 26), but the *meanings* thus produced are as much the product of intentional acts as those *intentions* being "read": both ironist and interpreter create intentionally (Tyler 1978: 459), in other words. It is not a matter of the interpreter "reconstructing" the exact meaning the ironist intended (Booth 1974: 33; cf. Suleiman 1976: 16–19). The regression to the ironist as sole semantic guarantor does not seem necessary, from this perspective. That does not mean that it will not occur: in many cases interpreters will infer not only meaning but intention (rightly or wrongly) as the result simply of the fact that they exist in a social relationship with the ironist and are operating within a communicative situation (Sparshott 1986: 162–3). The ironist is not the only performer or participant and, therefore, the responsibility for ironic communication (or its failure) is a shared one (cf. Bauman 1986: 3; Hermerén 1975: 73). Irony happens – or does not – in complex and numerous ways (Karstetter 1964: 174; Hagen 1992: 152; Eco 1976: 16–18). The intended audience, for instance, may not end up being the actual one; it may reject the ironic meaning, or find it inappropriate or objectionable in some way (Hodge and Kress 1988: 4); it may simply choose not to see irony in a given utterance.

These are among the reasons why I have been emphasizing my own attribution of irony in the analyses in this study: given my interests and tastes, I admit that I may be prone to seeing irony in places where not everyone might. This is not something either to be lamented or to be proud of: it is merely to be lived with. But it also conditions how I think about irony and its workings. As the reader of a novel or the viewer of a painting, I have to accept responsibility for my attribution of irony, even as I explain what led me to that inference. But what happens with more "public" forms of experience in which I am part of an audience that itself, through demonstrable behavior, can exert a collective influence upon my interpretive act? And what happens if (as was suggested in the discussion of the *Henry V* films) more than one intentional ironist is potentially involved – a writer, a director, a designer, a performer, and so on? In order to investigate the complex interrelations among ironist intention, interpreter inference and the text, therefore, I have chosen to look at one novel and one production of an opera, that is, one private and one more public experience of an ironic happening.

II ECO'S ECHOES AND WAGNER'S VICISSITUDES

The two examples will be my reading of Umberto Eco's reflexive and recursive novel, *Foucault's Pendulum* and my interpretation of a production of Richard Wagner's *Der Ring des Nibelungen* that I saw in Brussels in the fall of 1991 at the Théâtre de la Monnaie, a production that directly confronted the Nazi appropriation of Wagner's work that I mentioned in the last chapter. This second example complicates the discussion of intentionality in several ways already suggested above. On the one hand, I saw the four music dramas as part of an audience not afraid to show its collective response on the traditional operatic boo–bravo scale. (Opera audiences, in my experience, tend to be even more vocally and overtly responsive than other theater audiences.) On the other hand, the production of a *Ring* cycle – or of any single opera – involves the complex interaction of a series of agents besides the spectator, any or all of whom could intend (or not intend) ironies: the director, the designer, the singing actors, the conductor (and musicians), and of course Wagner himself as both librettist and composer.

The reading of a novel looks relatively simple in comparison: the inferring interpreter and the intending writer "meet," so to speak, in the relative simplicity and stability of the printed text – unless that text happens to be *Foucault's Pendulum*, with its complicated set of textually inscribed intentional actors, all interpreting and creating *ad absurdum* what they call their parody of hermetic thinking, the "Plan." The kind of fiction Eco has written in this and in his first novel, *The Name of the Rose*, assumes a certain kind of discursive community simply by its length, verbal and structural complexity, and learned subject matter. Hollywood movies not-withstanding, Eco's readership is likely what might be termed an academic or at least an educated one. And when one critical theorist publishes a book which contains in its title the name of another theorist, this particular academic reader, at any rate, was unable to resist looking for the kind of "in-group" ironies that many saw at play in the first novel. But Eco is a theorist who has rarely even mentioned Michel Foucault by name. Perhaps, then, I should only have been thinking of Jean Bernard Léon Foucault, the nineteenth-century physicist whose famous pendulum hangs even today in the Conservatoire des Arts et Métiers in Paris? But I soon discovered that I could not stop myself from making the link to Michel Foucault, and I could not stop myself from making ironies happen when I did.

As both theorist and novelist, Eco has made it difficult for people like me to ignore irony in general when reading his work, but he has also made it equally hard to know how to discuss it, for he has consistently and self-reflexively ironized the position not only of author but also of interpreter. And he has done this not only in his theoretical and critical writings but also within the novels themselves, which seem equally to provoke and to subvert all attempts either to construct or to deconstruct firm meaning. In *Foucault's Pendulum*, pages of contradictions get welded together into a totalized vision of cabalistic order, and the narrative structure – while seemingly loose and baggy – is in fact obsessively ordered around the form of the occult Tree of the Sefirot. The ultra-plotted plot about plots puts into motion and simultaneously calls into question the self-confirming, circular mode of including mutually contradictory elements that is characteristic of hermetic thought. For the mystic adept, according to Eco, every word becomes the sign of something else, the truth of what is not said. Therefore one has to learn to read with suspicion, lest something be missed. But irony too is a sign of something else, something unsaid, and to read ironically is also to read with suspicion. *Foucault's Pendulum* shows what happens to hermetic thought when it confronts the irony that is structurally and hermeneutically its twin.

In 1986 Eco gave a course on hermetic semiosis at the University of Bologna's Istituto di Discipline della Communicazione, in which he investigated the interpretive practice of seeing both the world and texts in terms of relations of sympathy and resemblance. His time-frame ranged from prehistoric times to the present. When I learned – purely by chance – about this course, I began to see better what the novel's narrative might have to do with Michel Foucault. In *The Order of Things* (the English title being more suggestive to me here than the original, *Les Mots et les choses*), Foucault had argued that this particular kind of ordering thought was historically limited: a Renaissance paradigm which gave way over time to a modern scientific one. The epistemological space up to the end of the sixteenth century was one Foucault saw as governed by a rich "semantic web of resemblance" (1970: 17). In the structure of his course, Eco clearly wanted to challenge this temporal periodization, to argue that this kind of thought never really disappeared, that there was no final epistemic break. In his view (later published in Eco 1989a: 9–10), the hermetic semiosis discernible in documents from the early centuries of the Christian era (e.g. *Corpus Hermeticum*) developed clandestinely in the medieval period, triumphed in the humanistic rediscovery of hermetic writings in the

125

Renaissance and Baroque periods, but has continued to exist in parallel to the quantitative science that then developed – often crossing it, more often opposing it. Newton, for example, is known to have combined modern science and cabalistic speculation. More recently, Eco has pointed out, Gilbert Durand (in his *Science de l'homme et la tradition*) has linked contemporary structuralist and poststructuralist thought with the same logic that accepts the plurivocal nature of both interpretation and texts. Think of Derrida's "[b]etween rationalism and mysticism there is ... a certain complicity" (1976: 80). In other words, the pendulum has continued to swing between the extremes of some form of reason and some form of mysticism. This is perhaps one of the many meanings of the title's pendulum.

My interest here in this chapter is not in the numerous and complex ironies that could be inferred from the novel in general (for that, see Hutcheon 1992), but rather in the way in which I would infer – interpret – Eco's text as intending (from the marker embedded in its title onward) to ironize the theories of Foucault in particular. My guiding premise is that, although this is a novel about connections and resemblances that is structured (obsessively so) on connections and resemblances, it is irony – the canker beneath overt resemblance – that makes Eco's plot different from the planning characters' Plan in such a way that a critical commentary on the work of Foucault can be inferred.

Foucault's Pendulum is narrated by a young Italian scholar named Casaubon. The complex intertextual echoings around this name range from George Eliot's *Middlemarch* to Renaissance philology and occultism. He recounts the tale in the hours following the climax of the Plan's plotting, as he awaits what he imagines may be his death. It is in this light – knowing the end of the story, so to speak – that he fills in the background. He tells how, while writing a dissertation on the medieval Knights Templar, he had become an unofficial consultant to Jacopo Belbo and Diotallevi, editors for a small, serious press, when a certain right-wing Colonel Ardenti had approached the press about publishing a rather problematic book. According to its author, this book would act as a call to all the world to pool knowledge and solve at last the mystery of the Templar plan to conquer the world, a plan that involved a secret about some immense power source. When Ardenti disappears under mysterious circumstances, possibly murdered, the book remains unpublished, but its contents lie dormant in the minds of the editors, their consultant, and Eco's reader.

Casaubon completes his dissertation on the Templars, goes to Brazil, and meets a singular Signor Agliè (who would seem to be the Comte de Saint-Germain *redivivus*). It is in Brazil that Casaubon begins to be lulled, as he puts it, by the notion of resemblance, by the feeling that everything might be related to everything else. When he returns to Italy, we are told, he converts this "metaphysics" into "mechanics' – with the aid of Belbo and

Diotallevi, who employ him to do research for their publishing house's vanity press division. Casaubon finds that magic and science seem to go hand in hand, that he has one foot in the cabala and the other in the laboratory. The pendulum begins to swing.

The two divisions of the publishing company decide to publish together a new series of hermetic texts, and Signor Agliè is brought in as a consultant to help the editors deal with the vast number of manuscripts submitted by what they call their "Diabolicals." A trip to Portugal and a chance encounter with the police inspector in charge of the earlier Ardenti case remind Casaubon of the theory of the Templar plot to rule the world. Out of this comes what Belbo, Diotallevi and Casaubon call their Plan, born of a "desire to give shape to shapelessness, to transform into fantasized reality that fantasy that others wanted to be real" (Eco 1989b: 337). Out of data and desire, with the aid of a computer program to randomize information, they set out deliberately and ironically to deploy – rather than to decode – hermetic semiosis. Feeding occult data into the computer, along with connectives and neutral information, they randomize the order and then create connections: "Any fact becomes important when it's connected to another. The connection changes the perspective; it leads you to think that every detail of the world, every voice, every word written or spoken has more than its literal meaning, that it tells us of a Secret. The rule is simple: Suspect, only suspect" (ibid.: 378). The play in English here on E.M. Forster's "Connect, only connect" from *Howards End* marks for me its ironic exaggeration, rather than its negation. Starting with Ardenti's notion of the Templar plot, the planners "narrativize" isolated data, making connections – causal, temporal, spatial. They start with verifiable facts; the fictionalizing is in the "order of things", so to speak. Soon, everything from the cabala to Bacon to Shakespeare to the Templars to the Masons to the Jesuits to Hitler is linked in a plot whose climax should – by the Plan's reasoning – take place in Paris at the Conservatoire des Arts et Métiers where hangs Foucault's pendulum, the laboratory proof of the earth's diurnal rotation. Nothing they discuss or consider remains innocent; all is interconnected, once this hermetic thinking is set in motion. In tandem and in contrast with this male creation of artifice, Casaubon's child is gestating in the womb of Lia, his partner, who is said to be endowed with the "wisdom of life and birth" (ibid.: 365). The pendulum swings.

The Planners have to keep reminding themselves that the idea is to *create* not to discover the Templars' secret, in other words, that their Plan is a fake (Eco 1989b: 387, 391): "We consoled ourselves with the realization – unspoken, now, respecting the etiquette of irony – that we were parodying the logic of our Diabolicals" (ibid.: 467). But the problem is that their "brains grew accustomed to connecting, connecting, connecting every-thing with everything else, until [they] did it automatically, out of habit" (ibid.: 467). Gradually, they lose the ability to tell the similar from the identical, the metaphoric from the real (ibid.: 468). They come to decide that their "story was plausible, rational, because it was backed by facts, it was true" (ibid.: 493). Unfortunately, others also decide likewise: Agliè believes them and, when they refuse to reveal the Secret they claim to know, he disappears.

At this point Belbo too falls into the trap of belief. Given the importance the Plan had granted to the pendulum in Paris, Belbo leaves to fulfil his destiny. Casaubon follows and hides in the periscope in the Conservatoire awaiting the solstice midnight. The TRES or the Templi Resurgentes Equites Synarchici – an invention of the Planners (or so they thought) – appear on time and almost the entire cast of characters of the novel is to be found among these reborn Templars. As Casaubon realizes: "if you invent a plan and others carry it out, it's as if the Plan exists. At that point it does exist" (Eco 1989b: 619). Belbo and the pendulum are at the centre of the bizarre ceremony that Casaubon witnesses, as the TRES try to wrest from Belbo the Secret. Since there is no Secret, he dies, refusing to "bow to unmeaning" (ibid.: 623), hanging by and from the pendulum. Casaubon flees and, as he awaits his own possible death in peace, he offers a reflexive warning to the reader (earlier referred to, in a parody of Baudelaire via T.S. Eliot, as "apocryphe lecteur, mon semblable, mon frère" [ibid.: 200]): "I would like to write down everything I thought today. But if They were to read it, They would only derive another dark theory and spend another eternity trying to decipher the secret message hidden behind my words. It's impossible, They would say; he can't only have been making fun of us. No" (ibid.: 641). Then he adds: "It makes no difference whether I write or not. They will look for other meanings, even in my silence" (ibid.: 641).

And so They will. Or so did I, at any rate, as I read for the secret messages hidden behind words that made irony happen. The kind of thinking represented by the adepts of the occult, as overtly ironized and literalized by the Planners, turns on resemblances and connections like the ones I found myself making throughout the novel with the work of Foucault. As Casaubon puts it: "There are always connections; you only have to want to find them" (Eco 1989b: 225). The ones I found made *Foucault's Pendulum* into an ironic literalizing of Foucault's description of sixteenth-century thought: "The heritage of Antiquity, like nature herself, is a vast space requiring interpretation; in both cases there are signs to be discovered and then, little by little, made to speak" (Foucault 1970: 33–4) by using either *divinatio* (magic, maybe fiction) or *eruditio* (learning, history). Both are part of the same hermeneutic, however. According to Foucault, the esotericism of the sixteenth century is a phenomenon of the written word. The spoken is seen as the "female part of language" (ibid.: 39), the sign of the passive intellect. In what I read as Eco's ironized version, the pregnant Lia's commonsensical speech to Casaubon about the "mysteries" of the human body provides the antidote to the fantastical male-generated Plan. Yet, the

128

irony for me was that it is Lia who is literally creative and (re)productive, and not the males, even if the "male principle" of language – that is, writing – is said to harbour "the truth" (ibid.: 139). But I saw another ironic twist here: because of what Foucault calls a "non-distinction between what is seen and what is read" (ibid.: 39), both the Planners and their occult enemies make this writing into their own "truth".

The computer, the means by which the Planners randomize their data, takes on allegorical – and, for me, ironic – functions in Eco's novel. It comes to stand for the sign of the real Secret of world power: it is not telluric currents (as the Planners speculate) but information technology that is the actual source of power today. An ironized Grail, information becomes that which "nourishes, heals, wounds, blinds, strikes down" (Eco 1989b: 141). In *The Order of Things*, Foucault suggested, in a now infamous formulation, that "man is only a recent invention, a figure not yet two centuries old, a new wrinkle in our knowledge, and . . . he will disappear again as soon as that knowledge has discovered a new form" (1970: xxiii). In the electronic age, many have wanted to see the computer as precisely that new form of knowledge. But, as it is presented in the novel, the computer can never replace "man" (decidedly gendered male here), for it cannot create knowledge; it can only combine and randomize information that is given to it. This limitation, however, echoes precisely the limitation Foucault ascribed to the mechanisms of resemblance in pre-seventeenth-century hermetic thought. The "plethoric yet absolutely poverty-stricken character of this knowledge" means that it always works with the same things: "Hence those immense columns of compilation, hence their monotony" (ibid.: 30). While some unkind reviewers said similar things about *Foucault's Pendulum*, what I saw the novel doing was enacting, through literalizing irony, Eco's premise (from that course given in Bologna) that hermetic thought did not die, but lives on . . . and in a form more familiar and in a manner more ubiquitous than we might expect. Foucault argued that knowledge in the Renaissance "consisted in relating one form of language to another form of language. . . . Language contains its own inner principle of proliferation" (ibid.: 40), leading to commentaries, interpretations of interpretations. One way to read Eco's novel and its Plan is as a literalizing and as an ironizing of precisely such an historical limiting of this view of knowledge. Has this mode of thought really disappeared?

As interpreter, I was the one whose intentional act made irony happen here. Of course, I was emboldened, even lured to attribute ironic intent to Eco from both the novel's title and from the fact that I knew Eco had written many an academic parody himself. (My personal favorite is his ironizing of both reviewing and literary criticism in "My Exagmination Round his Factification for Incamination to Reduplication with Ridecolation of a Portrait of the Artist as Manzoni" [in Almansi and Fink 1976: 125].) I read *Foucault's Pendulum*, with its images of inversion, of upside-down worlds, of mirrored reversals, as being full of allegories of the hermeneutics of irony. One of the simpler examples: Casaubon describes two Rosicrucian manifestoes that tell us to interpret, not literally, but ironically. "Taken literally," he remarks, "these two texts were a pile of absurdities, riddles, contradictions. Therefore they could not be saying what they seemed to be saying. . . . They were a coded message. . . . I had to read with mistrust" (Eco 1989b: 394). If *The Name of the Rose* is, by Eco's own admission, "ironclad" in its obvious scaffolding (in Rosso 1983: 7), then I kept reading *Foucault's Pendulum* as "irony-clad" right to the end. Quite literally to the end.

The description of the Conservatoire death scene, as narrated by Casaubon, is one I again saw as literalizing Foucault's description of that Renaissance semiosis of resemblance – specifically as presented in the chapter on "The Prose of the World" in *The Order of Things*. In this section, Foucault analyzes the four principal figures that determine knowledge by resemblance. The first – spatial adjacency or resemblance by contact – is called "convenientia" and is represented by the image of an "immense, taut, and vibrating chain" (1970: 19). In Eco's novel, I saw this literalized in the pendulum's very physical form. The second figure of hermetic knowledge, according to Foucault, is "aemulatio" or mirroring across distances, polarized into imbalanced weak and strong forces: "Similitude then becomes the combat of one form against another – or rather of one and the same form separated from itself by the weight of matter or distance in space" (ibid.: 20). The importance of the "one and the same form" for the novel comes into focus in conjunction with Foucault's third epistemological figure: analogy. Here the principles of resemblance include reversibility and polyvalency in a universal field of application which is drawn together through a "privileged point" saturated with analogies: man's body, "the fulcrum upon which all these relations turn" (ibid.: 22). Belbo dies by being hanged from the pendulum by the neck. The effect this has on the movement of the pendulum is that it starts to move from Belbo's body downward. His body thus becomes the point of suspension, "the Fixed Pin, the Place from which the vault of the world is hung" (Eco 1989b: 597). As the scientific epigraph of the next chapter explains, a body hanging from a pendulum becomes the fulcrum, thus literalizing in a horrific image Foucault's idea of man's body as the "privileged point."

The fourth and final figure of resemblance ascribed in *The Order of Things* is called "sympathies," the powerful play of the "Same" in a free state throughout the universe: "It is a principle of mobility: it attracts what is heavy to the heaviness of earth" (Foucault 1970: 23) – not unlike the other Foucault's eternally moving pendulum. But this is a dangerous figure: it has the power to assimilate, to make all things the same, destroying individuality – unless it is counterbalanced by "antipathy" (ibid.: 23). The "pendular thought" (Berardinelli 1988) of the entire novel offers countless examples of this antipathy/sympathy binary figure at work (science/magic; male/female, and so on), just as the plot structure opposes the Planners' totalizing assmilation of everything into their Plan to the factionalism and divisiveness of the various credulous occult groups. There is more than one Foucault's pendulum, in other words.

Michel Foucault himself can be read as turning ironic when discussing the need for visible markers or "signatures" of these various kinds of (often secret) resemblances that operate in hermetic thinking. Such a need, not accidently, is also shared by irony, of course. Foucault wrote: "Now there is a possibility that we might make our way through all this marvellous teeming abundance of resemblances without even suspecting that it has long been prepared by the order of the world, for our greater benefit" (1970: 26). In what I read as Eco's ironic literalizing of (what I read here as) Foucault's irony, the Plan is not "prepared by the order of the world" at all, but very much by the order of "man." And resemblance, as Foucault described it, becomes the inversion of irony: both "require signatures" to be interpreted, so that the "space inhabited" by both becomes "like a vast open book; it bristles with written signs.... All that remains is to decipher them" (ibid.: 27). And that is what I have been doing here. This image of the "signature" is one that Eco too has chosen to describe the interpretive habit of hermeticism – though with no direct reference to Foucault: "It is through similitudes that the otherwise occult parenthood between things is manifested and every sublunar body bears the traces of that parenthood impressed on it as a *signature*" (Eco 1990: 24). As the next chapter will theorize in more detail, what I have been doing is attributing meaning to those "signatures" of intentionality, those markers of ironic meaning in Eco's novel where I interpreted irony as a kind of inverted extension (or perverse variant) of hermetic similitude, as exploiting the inevitable if "slight degree of non-coincidence between the resemblances" of which Foucault wrote (1970: 30). This slight degree of non-coincidence provided the space for irony to happen for me. What Foucault asserted about the process of deciphering similitude also defines what I see as the intentionality of ironic reading: "to find a way from the visible mark to that which is being said by it and which, without that mark, would lie like unspoken speech, dormant" (ibid.: 32).

Eco has been called "an author who has irony in his soul" (Vita-Finzi 1989a: 225); this novel has been dubbed a work of irreverence and irony (Toscani 1988: 618). But just as, in Eco's own words, "[i]f Lacan is interesting it's because he resumes Parmenides" (Eco 1986: 127), so Eco was interesting for me because I think that he resumes Foucault – with irony. What I have been describing here, however, is one reader ironizing: attributing intention and meaning to a text written by someone with whom I might be seen to share a certain number of discursive communities constituted by a shared familial and intellectual interest in Italian culture, semiotics, irony (if not hermeticism) ... and the work of Michel Foucault. The consequences of such an inference of irony are minimal, except for me and (perhaps) any students with whom I might study the novel. But if I turn now to my other example, you will see that the stakes are potentially much higher. The last chapter outlined some of the negative responses in Germany and elsewhere to what I chose to interpret as Anselm Kiefer's ironic evocations of both Richard Wagner's works and the Nazi history of appropriation of them and other art forms, including architectural ones. When Wagner's music dramas are themselves put on stage today, that history does not go away for most spectators but is, unavoidably, one of the many filters through which they see and hear the works. To intend or to infer irony in any of these productions is going to be tricky business, for much more is at stake both if the irony happens and if it does not. Let me give a bit of background to explain why.

Adolf Hitler was evidently fond of saying that "[w]hoever wants to understand National Socialist Germany must know Wagner" (Gutman 1990: 426), and that's hard for any composer to live down – whether you believe the version that claims Hitler was inspired at age 12 by seeing Wagner's *Lohengrin*, with its fierce German nationalism and call for a Reich to be established (ibid.: 426), or the one that puts the conversion at age 17 after seeing an early Wagner opera called *Rienzi* in which a "popular upstart" avenges a private wrong by creating his own republic (Lindenberger 1984: 282). Thanks to history (see Large and Weber 1984), Wagner's work seems destined to be the exemplary case of Walter Benjamin's "document of civilization" that is "at the same time a document of barbarism" (1969: 256). For some, Wagner was a "proto-Nazi" anyway (Gutman 1990: 426); for others, the Nazi appropriation was a "perversion" of Wagner's work (Lindenberger 1984: 283).

Was it only thanks to history, however, that this state of affairs came about? Wagner's detractors have never tired of arguing comparisons between him and Hitler as men whose anti-semitism was personal in origin and festered in a time of neglect and poverty: "both were megalomaniac, and in both of them the experience of being brought to the edge of starvation by society's total disregard of them seems to have activated a sense of persecution that bordered on paranoia, cast 'the Jews' as the villains, and became a mad hatred that never died" (Magee 1988: 26). Even Thomas Mann once admitted that "there's a good deal of 'Hitler' in Wagner" (1985: 210). For many people, it is simply poetic justice that no one has been damaged as much by that association as Wagner himself: *Grove's Dictionary of Music* documents how prejudice "affects judgements of Wagner more than that of almost any other composer" (cited in Magee 1988: 34). It has been argued that Wagner's name is so contaminated by the Nazi use of it that he cannot be easily excused by the fact that he had no control over that use after his death (Said 1991: 41). Certainly in Israel and perhaps even in the United States, Wagner has become what one critic called "a conveniently available whipping boy for the past sins of the Germans" (Rather 1979: 168). The horror of the Holocaust has led to a blurring of the very distinctions between a Wagner and a Hitler for some people (Rather 1979: 171). Nevertheless, there is a difference. Context is important to understand, if not to excuse, the anti-semitism Wagner shared with Hitler. Theodor Adorno has written at length about the anti-semitic views Wagner shared "with other representatives of what Marx called the German Socialism of 1848" (1991: 23), and others have noted the officially sanctioned and legally enabled racism of both Europe and North America at that time (Rather 1979: 4), a racism that has been used to describe the thinking of everyone from assimilationists like Disraeli to Marx himself. That none of these could have foreseen the Third Reich does not excuse their racism, but it does put it into a necessary context in a particular time and place.

It has been argued that in "cultivated bourgeois circles in mid-19th-century Germany, anti-semitism was a personal matter, not one that was aired in public, and it did not prevent friendships with individual Jews" (Deathridge and Dahlhaus 1984: 80). But, in 1850, when Wagner published his paper, "Das Judentum in der Musik" ("Jewishness in Music"), he broke this tacit rule of private discourse. Bryan Magee's response to this, over a hundred years later, in an essay called "Jews – Not Least in Music" lists a startling number of Jews active as composers, performers, and conductors of music *since* 1850, but he does so in order to point out the fact that Wagner had noticed something others had not: the lack of important Jewish figures before that date (with the exception of Mendelssohn and Meyerbeer – both of whom Wagner disliked because of their success). Wagner also offered a historical explanation for this relative lack of numbers: the impossibility for Jewish artists to be able to have the same kind of deep cultural roots needed to compose works that would be accepted and popular in that particular German social context. Unfortunately, mixed in with this plausible theory, was a lot of what has been called repellent, unreasoning, and even diseased, as Wagner pitted the scapegoated Jew against the innate virtues and noble instincts of the German *Volk* (see Gilbert 1978: 23). We know of protests at the time by his later patron, King Ludwig II of Bavaria, by Nietzsche, and even by Wagner's own first wife, Minna (see Gutman 1990: 135, 358, 413–14); unfortunately, the anti-semitism of his second wife, Cosima, seems only to have reinforced this bigotry. Wagner's racism was what one commentator has called "pragmatic" (Sabor 1989: 310): he hated Meyerbeer for being a popular composer and thus appearing to bar the way to his own success (Gray 1990: 42), but he allowed a rabbi's son, Hermann Levi, to conduct the first production of his most Christian "consecration" drama, *Parsifal.* Those who want to excuse Wagner point to his many Jewish admirers, financial backers, and friends

133

(Sabor 1989: 213–16); those who prefer to condemn him, like Adorno, point to how sadistic or sentimental or even demonic he could be in his treatment of them all (Adorno 1991: 18–19).

By the 1870s, twenty years after his first essay on the topic, anti-semitism had become part of the public, political ideology of German nationalism. Even while Wagner could write pro-Aryan, anti-Jewish articles, he could also at the same time refuse to sign an anti-Jewish petition to the Reichstag, saying "I have nothing at all to do with the present anti-semitic movement" (cited in Gray 1990: 131). After his death, his son Siegfried (who had taken over the Wagner festival in Bayreuth) refused to bar Jews as either patrons or artists when asked to do so in 1921, and he did so on grounds of human, Christian, and German values – as well as because he knew his father's writings had once caused offence (Sabor 1989: 217). His English-born wife, Winifred, had no such scruples and, after her husband's death, often invited Hitler to the Bayreuth festival which she was then directing. After the war, she was tried and sentenced as a Nazi collaborator and her theater – the one Wagner built especially for his music dramas – was used to stage variety shows for American servicemen.

Nietzsche is said to have started the rumor that Wagner himself had Jewish blood (see Eger 1990: 2–3; Gutman 1990: 6–7); his anti-semitism would then be read as a virulent form of what has been called "Jewish self-hatred" (Rather 1979: 95; Gilman 1986). Certainly racist thinkers like Otto Weininger saw in Wagner's music "an accretion of Jewishness" (Gilman 1991a: 134; Rather 1979: 94), and you can imagine how embarrassing this might have been for Hitler. Perhaps for this reason he was pleased to see the establishment of the Wagner archives and research institute (housed in Wahnfried, Wagner's home) in Bayreuth, which might work to enable proof to the contrary. In the 1980s, that same institute hosted an exhibit on Wagner and the Jews, admitting but attempting to contextualize the composer's often venomous remarks. (Today, of course, Jewish conductors such as James Levine and Daniel Barenboim are often in the Bayreuth pit, though I believe the state of Israel still does not want Wagner's music performed on home soil.) After the war, Wagner's grandsons, Wieland and Wolfgang, asked to assume control of the Bayreuth festival; a German and American court agreed, as long as Winifred kept out of it. In an attempt to de-Germanize and de-Nazify Wagner's name and work, Wieland Wagner moved to experimental, abstract, non-representational productions whereby Wagner's operas were reread as timeless psycho-dramas (reread, that is, against the so-called Master's own explicit directions) (see Carnegy 1992: 61). This transgression established Bayreuth as the perhaps surprising site of the most innovative Wagnerian productions in the 1950s and 1960s. In 1973, however, then "East" German director Götz Friedrich brought the new political climate of post-1968 Europe to his Bayreuth production of *Tannhäuser*: the brown shirts were back, but this time on stage, not in the audience. The politicization of opera in general and of Wagner's in particular is relatively commonly undertaken by directors today – and much lamented by "purists" who argue that the intention of the composer/librettist (fixed, irremediably, in the last century, by definition) not the director should be respected (Magee 1988: 85; Conrad 1987: 278).

This is the context in which I'd like to present the work of Wagner's that interests me in this chapter, one that became increasingly *un*popular with the Nazis to the extent that it was not performed at all in Bayreuth for most of the Second World War. *Der Ring des Nibelungen*, they perhaps noticed, is about lovelessness, power, domination, and conquest; and it all ends in destruction and defeat. (It was that reflexive opera about a truly Germanic art aimed at the *Volk* – *Die Meistersinger von Nürnberg* – that was adopted by Hitler as the festival opera for patriotic occasions.) I am interested in one particular production of the *Ring* cycle where I was part of the live audience openly responding to what is, after all, the very nature of all performance: its heightened, occasional experience and its public setting (see Said 1991). Among my reasons for considering such a performance here is to remind you that opera too takes place in social, cultural and historical contexts. Perhaps because opera is such a mixed art form or perhaps because of its particular institutional context as well as its subject matter, it has escaped to some extent the formalist, asocial readings that have dominated much musicology. As one critic reminds us: "opera gives voice to the historical forces in which it is caught up" (Lindenberger 1984: 285). And particular productions of the *Ring* have given voice to the particular historical forces in which Wagner's operas have inevitably been caught up.

The Théâtre de la Monnaie's *Ring* (1991) was one such production. Directed and designed by Herbert Wernicke and produced by Gérard Mortier, this version foregrounded the Nazi past from which Wagner's work has never been able to escape. This was not the *Der Ring des Nibelungen* that George Bernard Shaw called "the great fourfold drama of which Wotan is the hero" (1967: 62); instead, it became the story of the more general decline of civilization, and the metaphor used for this decline was a politically pointed one. In what I read as an ironization of Wagner's own (as well as Hitler's) anti-semitism, it was not the Jews who were to mark the decline of humankind in this production: it was the Aryan, Teutonic Volsung race whose story is told in the *Ring* cycle. This became for me an ironized reference to the interpretation of Wagner's influential acquaintance, Joseph Arthur, Conte de Gobineau, author of the *Essay on the Inequality of Races*, who saw the *Ring* as the allegory of degradation facing the German people if they did not take heed of the Jewish threat (Gutman 1990: 419).

The director/designer in Brussels chose to set off the operas' textual glorification of the Volsung race against the context of a place and time (Europe before World War II) that is inseparable in most people's minds from the Nazi plans for Aryan racial supremacy. This interpretation took several operas to put in place. The handsome, slim Siegmund (Gary Bachlund), leaping on stage in Bavarian *Lederhosen* in the second opera, was ironically echoed in the figure of his son in the next opera – played by a much heavier, older, coarser-looking (and -acting) Siegfried (William Cochran) – who lumbered on stage in the same costume, but to utterly different effect. What some members of the audience took for simply bad casting was read by others, like myself, as an ironizing of the goal of racial supremacy. We were directed to such an interpretation by the program which interspersed the libretto text with often well-known images (photographs, paintings, drawings) that had acted as the director/designer's intertextual inspirations. Siegfried's entry was accompanied not only by a drawing of a rather plump, older Wagner but by an illustration for an article called "Hoch- und Minderrassige" ("On Superior and Inferior Races") in which the representation of the inferior race featured the fatter of the two male bodies. The physical decline of the Volsung race, in this production, was matched by the moral decline of Siegfried, who turned out to be a violent, boorish anti-hero. Wagner's last written essay ("Über das Weibliche in Menschlichen") might have argued that sexual love shapes noble races, but the offspring of the sexual passion of Siegmund and Sieglinde somehow failed: perhaps the gene pool of twins, even passionate ones, presents problems.

Against this racial decline, Wernicke (as director and designer) set the gods, represented as inert, stiff, convention-bound images of European royalty (also in decline), worried about social form more than about power. Wotan's wife was recognizably dressed in the official gown and tiara of the present Queen Mother, then Queen of England. Lest the audience miss the allusion, the program-libretto offered guiding familiar photographs. According to this same source – this textualization of intentionality through intertextual markers – the giants who built Valhalla had declined here to ape-size (as signaled by the program photo of two small-scale models for King Kong) and actually had to stand on rocks in order even to fake a certain height. The Nibelung villains in the piece all had the bald head of the fascist Mussolini (also represented in the program, in a famous photo of him swimming in the Adriatic, if not the Rhine). Through ironically recalling the likes of Mussolini and King Kong, this production further suggested the self-destructive potential built into theories of power and grandeur, as into plans for supremacy.

In addition, in a radical departure from staging convention, as characters died, their bodies (or models of them) remained on stage for anywhere from one to four operas, acting as visible reminders of the carnage resulting from power struggles over the ring of the Nibelung. By the end, there were ten bodies lying in a heap and, as the last chords of the finale were played, one corner of the stage fell or, rather, was smashed in by an antiquated-looking bulldozer. Men in hard hats appeared, looking in horror and amazement at what they had found: by this time, the scene they entered looked for all the world like a mass grave. For those who knew Brussels' history, this brought to mind the mass grave of the citizens of that city who lost their lives expelling the Dutch in 1830, for it lies only a few hundred yards from the theater; for others, like myself, the incident recalled the mass graves of victims of Nazi persecution that have been found in recent years around Europe.

With the help of the visual intertexts in the program-libretti, then, members of the audience might well attribute an ironizing intention to the director/designer. The set for the cycle of four operas – and there was only one single set – was a large, dilapidated room with an immense picture window looking out over forest and mountains. For a certain, likely European, discursive community (and for the rest of us who joined it, in a way, by purchasing the illustrated programs), this set suggested, in its dimensions and view, the famous and oft-photographed workroom in Hitler's retreat, Berghof, at Berchtesgaden in Bavaria, overlooking the Untersberg. To play a *Ring* in Europe about the degeneration of the race in a setting like this seemed to me pointedly ironic and potently political. Making a virtue out of necessity, the production used its limited stage space in imaginative ways, which included putting into (what became for me) ironic play those visual intertexts interleaved in the program's libretti. The room itself, for example, suggested more than Berghof when the sword, Nothung, was found embedded not in any tree trunk, as the text calls for, but in the wooden floor. For the reader of the last chapter of this study (as well as the program), this might recall Anselm Kiefer's *Notung* painting (Plate 4.1) or, more generally, his comparable ironic play on things Wagnerian in association with National Socialism.

Though this was a Belgian *Ring* – with René Magritte's paintings echoed in everything from the shape of the mountains outside the window to the hats worn by the Nibelungs – the director/designer was German. The Valhalla built by the giants looked to some members of the audience like a replica of the Parthenon; however, for a German discursive community (or, again, one that included the reader of the program or perhaps even someone who had traveled in Germany), it was that and more – an image of the memorial called "Valhalla" built by Ludwig I in 1842 (pre-*Ring*, therefore) near Regensburg to house tributes to Teutonic art and achievement, including in time that to Wagner himself. To have this go up in smoke as *Götterdämmerung* ended, therefore, had ironic echoes not unrelated to the theme of the decline of the Aryan race that the production was built upon, a theme constantly brought to the foreground by a complex series of intertexts that function as visual versions of Wagnerian leitmotivic musical echoes. Wagner's famous structural *Motiven* work musically to "say" the unsaid and thereby to set up many a dramatic irony, as the music "says" more (and other) than do the actual words sung: for instance, Siegfried wonders where his father, Wälse has gone, and the music tells the listener, if not the son, that he is in Valhalla and, what's more, that Wälse is really the god Wotan in disguise. In Wagner's work, the *Motiven* connect "what is seen and spoken with what is not seen and spoken" (Deathridge and Dahlhaus 1984: 146), thereby frequently making them echoic markers of irony. Their visual equivalents in Wernicke's production were often objects, that is, props used on stage. For example, a grand piano, constantly present and used in a variety of ways, recalled Wagner's own, pictured in the program being toyed with by an American soldier after the war. The connection to the United States is also made through images of Liberace, including those made through the presence of a candelabrum on the piano. This ironizing "motif of reminiscence" (to use Deathridge and Dahlhaus's term for the musical version [1984: 146]) took on related (and inclusive) semantic weight for me in many different ways: Liberace, the gay pianist, died of AIDS; the Nazis sent many homosexuals to the gas chamber; the candelabrum is linked to the Jewish menorah, present among the items in the Nibelung treasure-hoard, thus keeping the theme of Aryan suprem- acy and its consequences in the audience's eye and mind. Sitting at the now battered piano (everything on stage was battered and worn, as befits a world in decline) was a black-veiled woman, recalling the mourning Cosima Wagner (pictured in the program) who presided over a world in decline in another sense of the word, jealously guarding all the Master's intentions against change – change like that offered in this production, no doubt. Since this veiled figure sings the role of the earth goddess, Erda, who prophesies the end of it all – "Alles, was ist, endet" – I found myself making further ironies about the inevitable fate of Cosima's (and Wagner's) attempts at control.

Even if you were not part of the perhaps particularly obsessive discursive community constituted by *Ring*-fans, there were reflexive signals in the production you might well have recognized as possible markers of ironic intent, especially in the underlining of how the conventions of operatic artifice can, in fact, be used paradoxically to suggest actual political and historical contexts. The most obvious of these devices was a dark screen that descended between scenes and upon which were projected (in a grainy texture imitating, significantly, early newsreel headlines) Wagner's direc- tions, in German, for scene changes. Sometimes the ironies were created by the fact that a detailed description of a set *change* was followed by the screen rising to reveal exactly the *same* set as before. At another time, the directions informed the audience that the set would look exactly as it did in the last scene of *Die Walküre*, but the screen lifted to show a totally different configuration of the piano, rocks and the few other constants, including those accumulating bodies of dead characters. Nevertheless, here, as always, the printed instructions projected were in fact accurately transcribed from Wagner's text – thereby ironizing for me the demand of those who complain that directors don't pay attention to Wagner's intentions. The point often was, however, that the instructions were totally superfluous: "Es ist Nacht" introduced a dark, night-time set.

This production used other obvious reflexive devices, including those Brechtian defamiliarizing spotlights shining into the eyes of the audience. The end of one scene, with two not terribly happily engaged couples (Siegfried and Gutrune, Gunther and Brünnhilde), is made into an ironized photo-opportunity: the curtain goes down to flashbulbs flashing at a frozen, posing foursome. According to the text, in the final opera, the three Norns (Fate-like) are to sing about and handle a rope from which they "read" a memory-refreshing plot-outline of the earlier three music dramas. Though a large, bright red rope had been present almost constantly on stage in various forms in each opera, and here appeared stretched into a large X-shape across the set from ceiling to floor, the Norns read that story from a large book – the book of life, perhaps, but also the libretto. After all, when they have to sum up the complex plot of three preceding operas, they might need a little prompting to get the details right. This is art, not life. But it is art that has a long life-history that includes the Nazi appropriation of its creator's work and reputation that this production sought to foreground.

The question to be posed is, perhaps, the one asked in the last chapter in the discussion of Kiefer's work as well: is irony an appropriate rhetorical strategy for dealing with the terrible history of National Socialism? In Kiefer's problematic case, I share Andreas Huyssen's qualified "yes," but not without some reservation. In this case, I found myself engaged and enlightened by the deconstructive and historicizing potential of the ironies that happened for me in the space between Hitlerian setting and Wagnerian action, between the director/designer's visual intertexts and my own historical knowledge of the Nazi use of Wagner's music, between the echoing *Motiven* of props and the politics of memory. If I had not purchased the programs and had not entered the discursive community that included the conceivers and executors of the "concept," I might well never have inferred ironic intent (see, for example, Ashman 1992: 45), even if I did make the (perhaps hard-to-ignore) connection to the Nazi context. These intentional program documents provided the necessary context and often the precise intertextual markers necessary to attribute irony to the creations of the director/designer and to the actions of the performers.

From reviews and anecdotal evidence, it would seem clear that not every member of the same audience felt there was irony at play here or that it might be appropriate, even if it were. Unlike the act of reading a novel like *Foucault's Pendulum*, the act of witnessing a *Ring* performance is a collective (as well as public) act – both in the sense that more than one person is involved in its production and also because you are part of a group of spectators and form your response in part in conjunction with others. The mixed boos and bravos that greeted Wernicke and his production signaled more than the complexities of discursive communities in this case; they perhaps also suggested the effect of inferring (or not inferring) an intent to invert through irony the Nazi mission of racial superiority through setting Wagner's Teutonic *Ring* in precisely that context. That the work of the man whom the National Socialists used to inspire their anti-semitism (Gilbert 1978: 23) should itself provide the ground for such ironic deconstruction is utterly appropriate, especially if we recall Wagner's own "Young Hegelian" conviction of the inevitability of historical change (Millington and Spencer 1992b: ix). The next chapter will investigate further this complicated process of moving from textual markers and contextual evidence to inferring (that is, to interpreting) that slippery thing called irony – as intention, as meaning, and as evaluative attitude.

6

FRAME-UPS AND THEIR MARKS

The recognition or attribution of irony

I THE SIGN(S) OF THE BEAST – IN CONTEXT

Trying to write about the ironies that can happen in opera performances is obviously tricky enough, as the last chapter illustrated, but at least there exist narrative texts – libretti, programs – to provide an expanded context. In the case of instrumental music, the difficulties in attributing irony would seem even more problematic: there are often no words (beyond the title) or other handy hermeneutic helpers within the piece, though there may be program notes to read before listening. Take, for instance, Walter Boudreau's *Berliner Momente, Zweiter Teil,* a work recently commissioned by the Toronto Symphony Orchestra. Boudreau is a Canadian, but has written a number of compositions "about" Berlin. According to his own account – and now we enter the realm of intention – the first, *Berliner Momente, Erster Teil* (1988) was a musical response to 33 key events in Berlin's thousand-year history. The second part addressed the things that had occurred since 1988: the tearing down of the Berlin Wall, the fall of communism in East Germany, and the subsequent reunification of the country. Music cannot say this directly, of course; Boudreau must rely (as Kiefer does) upon his audience's ability to recognize certain things – here, at the very least, both the German national anthem (Haydn's Austrian imperial hymn) and Wagner's theme from the death of Siegfried in *Götterdämmerung* – and then begin to make meaning out of his compositional play with them. One might argue that this music is well known to certain audiences, but it is significant that, when the work premiered in the fall of 1991, Boudreau chose to speak to his Toronto audience before the performance, explaining the historical events that had inspired him and the musical allusions upon which he had constructed his composition.

The first part of *Berliner Momente,* he announced, had ended on an unresolved chord, symbolizing the Cold War; the new piece ended in a similar way, because the future of Germany was as yet unknown. However, in structurally opposing the music of the national anthem to that of Siegfried's funeral march – both in citation and in reworked, modulated forms – Boudreau was setting up for me the musical equivalent of what I've been calling "semantic" associations (that is, relational, differential and inclusive), and this is something that he may or may not have actually intended. In Wagner's music drama, the death of Siegfried is both tragic and necessary to the fated unfolding of the plot; it marks both the destruction of the pure, if deluded, war-like hero and the beginning of the fall of the gods, the end of one world and the birth of another, through the redemptive power of human love. But what happens when this gets associated with – either merged with or juxtaposed to – the German national anthem, in a piece whose name points to the city of Berlin, the incarnation of the Cold War (and its thaw, as well)? Boudreau's music connects Siegfried with things war-like by accompanying a citation of the death music with a militaristic drum roll. Is the fall of communism a victory for peace? Is the fall of the Berlin Wall the necessary destruction that precedes a new utopian dream of a unified Germany? My own temptation was to read a certain irony in the often harsh clashes and dissonant interminglings of the two motifs, but such an attribution depends on, among other things, your knowledge and evaluation of German history and your sense of its future. In other words, in order to interpret the repeated citations at all (and certainly to interpret them as ironic), I would have to move out of the immediate textual frame and into broader contexts (social, historical, ideological, political, geographical) that are in part a function of my own discursive-communal knowledge and in part, in this case, created by authorial statements of intent.

Not all art forms or utterances are this stingy with their textual hints, though the aural shares with the visual a number of limitations in how what we call "meaning" can be generated. As the last chapter has already suggested, there are often both contextual signals and specific textual markers that work to lead the interpreter to recognize or to attribute (but either way, to intend) irony. As is always the case when discussing the particular situation of ironic meaning, what is involved here is, in fact, a general problem in all communication: the issue of the role of context in determining meaning. When I.A. Richards wrote of "the interanimation of words" or "the interplay of the interpretive possibilities of the whole utterance" (1936: 55), he was referring to all verbal utterances, not only ironic ones. Speech-act theory, likewise, looks to the total situation or context in which the utterance is issued (Austin 1975: 52). So, whether "context" be thought of as primarily textual (Richards) or as including the circumstances of uttering (Austin), it plays a significant role in the generating of meaning at any time, though perhaps even more so when what is called "wordplay" is involved (Goffman 1974: 442–3). Given that we are dealing, in the case of irony, with a kind of verbal (or aural or pictorial) play in which the said and the unsaid come together in a certain way in order to become "irony," then one and the same utterance could obviously be either ironic or unironic in different contexts.

"Context," however, is a very inclusive term, suggesting as it does the entire "background body of assumptions against which you interpret some utterance" (N.V. Smith 1989: 73). Defined in this way, it overlaps considerably with what, in Chapter 4, was called discursive community: the norms and beliefs that constitute the prior understanding we bring to the utterance. In addition to this, however, there is also what could more narrowly be defined as "context": the more specific **circumstantial**, **textual**, and **intertextual** environment of the passage in question. Somewhat broader than the speech-act notion of "contextual information" (Searle 1979a), context in this sense revises and adds to discursive-communal understanding; it gives "contextual overtones" (Bakhtin 1981: 293) that enable the unsaid to enter into ironic relation with the said. While theorists have devised much more complex inclusive (Groupe Mu 1981; Chiaro 1992; D. Knox 1989) and exclusive (Eco 1976; Kerbrat-Orecchioni 1980a) models of what context should involve, my own sense is that practical experience in the interpreting of irony suggests at least three elements that must be considered: the circumstances or situation of uttering/ interpreting; the text of the utterance as a whole; other relevant intertexts.

The first, the **"circumstantial"** (Groupe Mu 1978: 428) context, would be related to what has variously been labeled the "material ambiance" (Bally 1965: 44), the "communicative context" (Adams 1985: 40), or the operational "enunciative field" (Foucault 1972: 99) that makes statements deployed within it possible and meaningful as irony. It would involve that social and physical context which Roman Jakobson (1960) added to Karl Bühler's 1934 communication triad of sender/message/addressee. The "situation of enunciation" (Monson 1988: 543) of the said, then, provides the circumstantial context for the activating of the unsaid: who is attributing what to whom, when, how, why, where? To offer an example: I once found myself staring at an authentic-looking "life-size" skeletal figure that was part human and part fish. Here, the process of inferring meaning, and then ironic meaning, was as dependent upon the circumstances of my viewing as upon what I was actually seeing. First, this figure was positioned in the lobby of a water filtration plant (so I was tempted to see ironies in the odd meeting of human and marine life in this figure from the start), but the occasion of my being in this unlikely place was an art exhibit entitled *WaterWorks* that was using the major water filtration plant for the city of Toronto (itself a baronial Art Deco construction) as the location for a series of site-specific art installations. The placement of this skeleton, at the entrance of the building, and the style of its presentation suggested, however, the context of a natural history museum. But the label read: "*Triton's Remains*." Rummaging through my memory-store of mythological creatures, I recalled that Triton was the son of Poseidon and was graced with the trunk of a man and the tail of a fish. In this context, the label was

143

accurate. But mythological creatures do not usually appear in natural history museums, much less water filtration plants. The identification card also identified two names – Komar and Melamid – a pair of Russian artists, whose other works, with their ironic distortions of canonical works of Western art, were already familiar to me. This uncanny human/fish form set up for me, in this complex "enunciative" situation (which included an institutional site, a physical environment, and a set of expectations), a series of ironic interactions between the cultural and the natural, the new and the old, the historical and the mythical. So, while speech situations (van Dijk 1977: 191) would provide the most obvious examples of circumstantial contexts, they are not the only ones to be considered.

In Neil Jordan's 1992 film, *The Crying Game*, it is less the communicative sitation of viewing than the actual formal or **textual** context of the work as a whole that provides the frame for attributing irony to the music used in the soundtrack. As the film opens, with Jody (male) being seduced by Judy (female), we hear the song, "When a Man Loves a Woman" – music which takes on ironic significance only when we learn (much later) that the person Jody really loved turns out to be Dil, a man. But Dil is a transvestite, and so when the film ends with her/his visiting in prison the man who took the blame for the (self-defense/revenge) murder of Judy, our knowledge of that fact renders the final song (sung by a woman) ironic in context: "Stand by Your Man." Both the immediate texual environment and the work as a whole are what provide this second, textual kind of context that makes irony happen through a developing "sense of the habitual procedures of the text" (Culler 1975: 157).

The third sort of context is an **intertextual** one made up of all the other relevant utterances brought to bear on the interpretation of the utterance in question. Intertexts are modalities of *perception* (Riffaterre 1980: 625): it is as if the interpreter takes "inferential walks" (Eco 1979: 214) – as I did in those *Ring* programs in Brussels – through various intertextual frames to pick up any useful intertextual information. Critics only read James Joyce's character, Stephen Dedalus in *Portrait of the Artist as a Young Man* as ironized after the 1922 publication of *Ulysses* (Booth 1961: 333), and especially after the appearance in 1944 of *Stephen Hero*. The context of interpretation had changed, as other discourses were made to traverse the one being interpreted. This "inferential process" of interpretation takes place when an utterance is considered in (and works with) a context to yield "contextual effects" or "conclusions which would follow neither from the utterance alone nor from the context alone" (Sperber and Wilson 1986: 9).

American New Critics, of course, also defined irony as that generalized term for the qualification of meaning by context. In a well-known article written over forty years ago, "Irony as a Principle of Structure," Cleanth Brooks used the word "irony" to mean "the *obvious* warping of a statement by the context" (1971: 1042). At times, however, he seemed to suggest that "irony" might not be quite the right word to describe the indirection he saw as characteristic of all poetry, for he lamented that it seemed to him to be "the only term available by which to point to a general and important aspect of poetry" (ibid.: 1043). This kind of vague and generalized usage of the word "context" (as well as "irony") may well be what led Jonathan Culler, in his book *Framing the Sign*, to issue the following warning:

> the notion of context frequently oversimplifies rather than enriches discussion, since the opposition between an act and its context seems to presume that the context is given and determines the meaning of the act. We know, of course, that things are not so simple: context is not fundamentally different from what it contextualizes; context is not given but produced; what belongs to a context is determined by interpretive strategies; contexts are just as much in need of elucidation as events; and the meaning of a context is determined by events. Yet when we use the term *context* we slip back into the simple model it proposes. Since the phenomena criticism deals with are signs, forms with socially-constituted meanings, one might try to think not of context but of the framing of signs: how are signs constituted (framed) by various discursive practices, institutional arrangements, systems of value, semiotic mechanisms?
>
> (Culler 1988: ix)

Signs read as ironic are obviously framed ones – often literally framed, by quotation marks. But, in fact, frames change contexts, so the notion of context is not so much supplanted by as supplemented by the theory of framing. If, as has been suggested (Juhl 1980: 121–4), "Auszug der Schmarotzer" ("Exodus of the Parasites"), a 1934 Nazi poem about Jews, were framed and then read as a poem written by Bertolt Brecht and published in a collection of poems about the rise of National Socialism, new textual and intertextual contexts would come into being which both surround the poem and give it a different meaning. This is context as "the total set of conditions that has in fact determined [a text's] occurrence and form" (B.H. Smith 1979: 16).

In the case of ironies, it may well be that it is "something in their surroundings, and it is usually something merely implicit in their 'place', that gives them away" (Booth 1974: 39). But contexts – **circumstantial, textual,** or **intertextual** – can usually be discerned more precisely than this would suggest by taking into account the frames that bring contexts into being. By changing reading frames, as Guido Almansi (1984: 75) once had fun suggesting, Benedetto Croce's idealist philosophical *Estetica* could be read as a new novel by Umberto Eco. That frames like these are formed by interpretive expectations can be seen in the debates over whether irony might be found in medieval courtly romances (see Green 1979): it seems to depend on your expectations regarding things like courtly romance,

145

medieval categories of rhetoric, and even medieval concepts of humor. Erving Goffman has explored, in *Frame Analysis* (1974), how framing makes possible discrete and different fields of interpretation of experience that allow meaning (ironic or other) to be organized.

To go back to Culler's warning, though, context is not some positivistic entity existing outside the utterance, but rather is itself constructed through interpretive procedures. And these procedures, in turn, have been formed through our prior experience with interpreting other texts and contexts (Stewart 1978/79: 10). It is in this sense that context alters the functioning of the said by making possible its rubbing together with the unsaid. But how does the interpreter know when (and how) to frame an utterance in this way? One of the most common examples used in discussions of this issue (and of irony in general) is one I mentioned earlier, Mark Antony's funeral oration for Caesar ("Friends, Romans, countrymen, lend me your ears") from Act III, scene ii of Shakespeare's *Julius Caesar*. From the **textual** context, we know that Cassius has already warned Brutus of the dangers of letting Mark Antony address the crowd: "Know you how much the people may be mov'd/By that which he will utter?" In this same scene, immediately preceding the one in question, we have watched Antony, though seemingly sworn to friendship with Caesar's murderers, react with revealing anger to seeing the actual dead body. Brutus grants him permission to speak at the funeral, providing he agrees not to blame the killers and to "speak all good you can devise of Caesar." That double injunction sets up the frame for reading Antony's solution as being a decision to use irony; it may also dictate the particular rhetorical form his irony appears to take. His soliloquy – "O, pardon me, thou bleeding piece of earth,/That I am meek and gentle with these butchers!" – makes clear where he stands to the theater audience or reader (but, of course, *not* to the crowd he is about to address). In the next scene, it is Brutus who speaks first to that crowd of Roman citizens, proclaiming his love for Caesar, despite his act ("not that I loved Caesar less, but that I loved Rome more"). He introduces Mark Antony, who arrives with Caesar's body, and asks the crowd to listen to the speech about to be given "by our permission."

There then occurs what may appear a strange and phatic exchange among some of the citizens. When Antony says, acknowledging their seconding of Brutus's wish that he be heard, "For Brutus' sake, I am beholden to you," a citizen asks: "What does he say of Brutus?" The reply is: "He says, for Brutus' sake,/He finds himself beholden to us all." Ignoring any possible irony in the echo here, the enquiring citizen then responds with: "'Twere best he speak no harm of Brutus here" and another adds: "This Caesar was a tyrant." What this seemingly information-less exchange does, however, is signal to the theater audience the need to "listen up," so to speak. Its echoing repetition and insistence set the context for the speech we are about to hear and offer what an interpreter might well see as a

146

second reason (self-protection) for Antony's choice of irony, an indirect rhetorical strategy. When he first speaks of "noble Brutus" who accuses Caesar of having been ambitious, the crowd has no reason to suspect him of the irony or hypocrisy the informed reader or theater audience might infer. So too with the first, indeed functionally (and in some editions literally) parenthetical, use of what will soon become a refrain: "For Brutus is an honourable man;/So are they all; all honourable men." He then does what Brutus asked him to do: he praises his friend Caesar as "faithful and just to me." His next words set up a contrast with the conjunction "but": "But Brutus says, he was ambitious,/and Brutus is an honourable man." On repetition and framed by the contrast, this last assertion begins to take on somewhat different meaning, especially when Antony proceeds to give examples of how Caesar was not at all ambitious, in fact, but on the contrary generous, charitable, sympathetic. It is in this context that we hear the third repetition, prefaced by "yet," another contrastive conjunction (Jakobson 1960: 375): "Yet Brutus says, he was ambitious;/And Brutus is an honourable man." This is followed by a recalling of Caesar's rejection of "a kingly crown": "Was this ambition?/Yet Brutus says, he was ambitious;/and sure, he is an honourable man." The slight alteration in this, the fourth repetition, calls attention to both the form and content; the emphatic "sure" might alert us to the strain Antony could be argued to manifest in continuing to call Caesar's murderer "honourable" in the face of his growing grief in mourning: "Bear with me;/My heart is in the coffin there with Caesar." The response of the citizens is to start to doubt that Caesar was ambitious and to empathize with Antony's grief to the point that they assert: "there's not a nobler man in Rome, than Antony."

In the face of their manifest sympathy, Antony appears to recall his promise to Brutus, and assert: "if I were dispos'd to stir/Your hearts and minds to mutiny and rage,/I should do Brutus wrong, and Cassius wrong,/Who, you all know, are honourable men." They "all know," of course, because he has told them so – in a context that has increasingly called that very designation into question. The result is that when Antony finally puts the perpetrators and the crime verbally together, the presence of the word "honourable" triggers in the crowd devastating, retrospective irony: "I fear, I wrong the honourable men,/Whose daggers have stabb'd Caesar; I do fear it." The repetition of his fear is what provokes one of the citizens to cry out and directly literalize all this ironic indirection: "They were traitors: Honourable men!" In this, the sixth iteration of that adjective and noun combination, the crowd finally echoes and therefore hears what the theater audience likely heard much earlier. That final "Honourable men!" acts as the underlining, the summing up, and (if you missed the irony) the repetition of the paradigm of the irony's form, preceded as it is by the antiphrastic "traitors."

Kenneth Burke once tried to imagine Antony here addressing the theater

147

audience instead of the Roman crowd, and commenting on his role in this scene: "to contrive a *peripety* for my audience, reversing the arrows of your expectations" (1973: 336), turning praise to blame. He points out the "little clue" he gave us – which most of the citizens missed (ibid.: 337). But the reason they missed the hint is that they did not have the circumstantial and textual context in which to interpret it. They lacked the frame provided by the preceding scene's soliloquy, in particular. As the play's readers or spectators, we did not. However, in addition, each repetition itself creates an immediate textual context that accumulates more and more meaning; each repetition is an echoic "mention" (Sperber and Wilson 1981: 315) of its first "use," so that the said and the unsaid come together to make irony happen even for the citizens, in the end. Repetition, in this case, acts as a marker, a clue to an ironic framing. Yet, clearly, not all repetitions are ironic. What would make an interpreter attribute irony in certain contexts?

* * *

> "Truly this is the sweetest of theologies," William said, with perfect humility, and I thought he was using that insidious figure of speech that rhetors call irony, which must always be prefaced by the pronunciatio, representing its signal and its justification – something William never did. For which reason the abbot, more inclined to the use of figures of speech, took William literally and added . . .
>
> (Eco 1983a: 145)

Here, in Umberto Eco's *The Name of the Rose*, the narrating Adso both expounds upon and provokes the interpretive act of processing irony's "signal." He is, of course, recounting in writing an oral encounter and, as transcribers as well as novelists and critics have long lamented, it is hard to reproduce on paper those things, like gesture or tone of voice, that might have acted as triggers to the complicated cognitive and aesthetic processing involved in attributing irony to an utterance (Kaufer 1977: 107n.). Despite critics' assertions that there simply exists something called the "high ironic style" that may possess no one single identifiable ironic signal (Allemann 1956: 12–13), there is usually something that suggests a frame and thus a context in which irony can happen. The difficulty is that this something may differ with each interpreter, or may not even exist for others. Part of the problem, as we have already seen, has to do with the need for overlapping discursive communities: the number and frequency of features that are accepted by all participants in the particular communicative situation as conveying or suggesting an ironic attitude (and thus meaning) are variable (see Hymes 1987: 297). The greater the mutual acceptance of conventions of signaling, the more likely an intended irony will be interpreted as ironic and done so with ease (Plett 1982: 85). What general rhetorical treatises, throughout the ages, have usually *not* taken into account in their descriptions of "pronunciatio" – or the unmasking of ironic markers – in oratory is that even commonly agreed upon signals (such as an air of contempt or a gross exaggeration of claims) are still socially and culturally codified. Nuances of tone of voice or gesture are even more so, as classical and medieval diagrams of oratorical gestures and their coded meanings suggest (see D. Knox 1989: 60, 65). Psychologists have also tended to universalize, assuming that a negative facial expression or bodily gesture (smirking, rolling eyes, making a fist) are shared signals of ironic intent that children learn (Winner 1988: 148). Yet, it is not hard to imagine cultures – even situations – in which actions such as these might signal some totally different meaning.

Is there any way for an ironist to assure the understanding – that is, to prevent the misunderstanding – of intended irony? A number of suggestions have been made over the years, including the creation of some sort of "irony mark" of punctuation. The candidate put up by Alcanter de Brahm (pseudonym of Marcel Bernhardt), in *L'Ostensoir des ironies* (1899), was a reversed question mark. The recent film, *Wayne's World* gave me one of my epigraphs to this book: "Not!" – declared following an affirmative statement. E-mail networks have developed "emoticons" such as :-) known as the "smiley" – to be deciphered by looking at it sideways. But, the problem is that, as soon as an irony signal becomes fixed and thus direct, it loses its usefulness as a marker of ironic indirection and often gets ironized itself (Booth 1974: 55; Hagen 1992: 170). Witness % \ v – the Picasso version of the smiley. It would seem to be the case that there is no such thing as a marker that would allow us to determine *with certainty* the presence (or absence) of irony (Chambers 1990: 19).

This doesn't mean, however, that markers don't exist and don't have functions of some kind in signaling the possibility of recognizing or attributing irony. On this, most commentators agree. Intentionalist theories insist that it is the responsibility of the ironist to leave guiding clues for the interpreter (Amante 1981: 77); formalist, text-based theories assert the existence of textual signals (Riffaterre 1970: 211); pragmatic theories claim that something has to invite response, has to trigger interpreters to seek alternate meanings to the said (Hagen 1992: 10). They even agree, as we shall see shortly, on what these signals are – at least in certain specific cultures. Why, then, are the cases of misfired, misunderstood ironies so frequent and so risky? A typical example can be seen in the fury provoked by a letter to the editor of the *Chronicle*, the student newspaper at Duke University in April 1991. This letter addressed the furor instigated by what it called the "now famous PC community at Duke" over the exclusion of homosexuals from the ROTC (Regular Officers Training Corps), and the subsequent move to have the ROTC banned from campus on the grounds that it violated the university's anti-discrimination policy. The letter went on to suggest, instead, that it was the policy that needed abolishing in the name of national security: gays, like blacks, it said, were a threat to the military's strength and discipline. The next day, another student wrote that he was embarrassed by the homophobic and racist statements of this letter, but wondered if it was all a "joke" – since it offended just about everyone on all sides of the issue. This provoked the original letter-writer to respond that his letter was "written entirely tongue in cheek," and to blame the newspaper for giving it a serious headline ("University, not ROTC, should change"). He claimed to have received forty angry calls on the first day from people who took his piece to be either sarcastic or literally offensive. He then apologized that he hadn't made his "sarcasm" even clearer, but was happy that people reacted negatively if they believed it to be a literal statement of belief. The paper then, rather bravely, published a more overtly ironic letter under the heading "A serious reply to a most serious letter": its spelling and grammar errors, its exaggerated slurs and support for "Uncle Hitler and cousin McCarthy" made its ironic intent rather more evident than the first letter's. The problem for me is, that even in rereading that first letter in the context of its writer's claims of "sarcastic" intent, there are precious few signals to offer as evidence of any ironist's intention – much less actually to suggest to an interpreter the specific meaning and evaluation to attribute to irony in this text.

This example poses an intriguing question: are textual or contextual markers meant to signal the *presence* of irony, the *intent* to be ironic, or maybe simply the possibility that the utterance might be *interpreted as* ironic? Are there, perhaps, different functions for or even different kinds of ironic markers: those that trigger an interpreter to think that irony might come into play (through either ironist or interpreter intention), in the first place, and those that then can direct the interpretation of the irony in specific ways? That need (and even responsibility) to signal irony clearly has always been part of intentionalist theorizing (see, for instance, Tyler 1978: 387). In oratory, the reasons were obvious: Cicero gave detailed advice about how, in order to disappoint listener expectation and activate irony, the "disposition and character" of the speaker should be presented in an opposite manner to what was being said (1979: 2.67.272). Similarly, in speech-act theory the emphasis is on "illocutionary force indicating devices" (Searle 1969: 30) that signal intention and prevent unsuccessfully performed acts or "infelicities" such as "misfires" (Austin 1975: 14–17). From the intending ironist's point of view, then, "marking an ironical text means setting up, intuitively or with full consciousness, some form of perceptible contradiction, disparity, incongruity or anomaly" (Muecke 1978b: 365). From this theoretical vantage point, it is the ironist who must put the interpreter on the trail of the connections between the said and the unsaid by clues that foreground certain norms (Kaufer and Neuwirth 1982: 30) and thus offer hints to guide interpretation.

The problem is that interpreters don't always get hints – or else they read them differently than they might have been intended. An example that one

150

theorist (Dutton 1987: 200) offers of a direct, straightforward signal of irony is the title of Richard Strauss's *Berleske* (1885). The piece is a parody of the romantic virtuoso piano concerto, but is it so very hard to imagine an interpreter, who might not know Strauss or the history of music, thinking this was meant as music to accompany a strip show? In other words, irony signals don't signal *irony* until they are interpreted as such. All the intending ironist can do is present a contextualized stimulus (Sperber and Wilson 1986: 150) and hope that its perception will lead the interpreter to infer ironic intent, in the first place, and a specific ironic meaning, in the second. This is why I want to try in this chapter to theorize the issue of framing and markers primarily from the point of view of the interpreter, rather than from the more usual one of the ironist: irony isn't irony until it is "felt" (Muecke 1969: 53) as such. Irony may well involve a tension between communication and concealment (Furst 1984: 14), but if there are no markers, it may well be interpreted as a case of deception rather than irony. Though there can clearly be unconscious tell-tale signals of deceit – shifty eyes, sweaty palms – the signals of irony are of a different order, with a different intent. And, unlike lies, ironies are not usually "unmasked" simply by replacing the "negative particle 'not' omitted from the speaker's literal statement" (D. Knox 1989: 68): the implied definition of irony here, one of simple inversion and negation, is not infrequent and is certainly easy to handle (see Amante 1981: 77), but as Chapter 3 investigated, it does not account for many of the instances of actual irony in utterances beyond the size of the simplest sentence.

Whatever their position on irony's semantics or on the role of intention, theories of irony have long argued over things like the need for, the existence of, and the nature of ironic markers. Early on, Quintilian, in his *Institutio Oratoria* (8.6.54), advised looking to oratorical delivery, the character of the speaker, and the nature of the subject. Were any one of these out of step with the actual words spoken, that would be a clear signal that "the intention of the speaker is other than what he actually says." Wayne Booth's discussion (1974: 53–76) of the "clues" to the "reconstruction" of ironic intention and meaning in written texts outlines five kinds of markers: (1) straightforward hints or warnings presented in the authorial voice (titles, epigraphs, direct statements); (2) violations of shared knowledge (deliberate errors of fact, judgment); (3) contradictions within the work ("internal cancellations"); (4) clashes of style; (5) conflicts of belief (between our own and that which we might suspect the author of holding). This list provides a mixture of the intentionalist, the formalist, and the inferential; it also combines **circumstantial**, **textual** and **intertextual** "context-indicators" (E. Wright 1978: 526).

If the "reconstruction" of ironic intent were even this straightforward, however, why would translators have so much trouble re-coding irony signals from one language and culture to another? If the markers of ironic

151

intent are so easily identifiable, why are they so often missed? One of the possible replies would be that there is also a strong, if implied, injunction in the use of irony to use as few and as subtle signals as possible: "even when the ironist . . . must nudge – and he frequently must – he must not be *thought* to nudge" (Booth 1974: 206). The most efficacious irony is said to be the least overtly signaled, the least explicit – when the risk of incomprehension and misunderstanding is greatest (Mizzau 1984: 25). The fewer the signals, the "better" the irony, in other words. This judgment can be articulated in various ways: as a matter of sophistication (Frye 1970: 41; Lanham 1991: 92), subtlety (Booth 1974: 172), or greater powers of discrimination (Green 1976: 19) on the part of the ironist and the interpreter. Often it is expressed in terms that make it clear that this is a question involving economy of expression (Muecke 1970/1982: 52–3), and often the aesthetic value attached in certain discursive communities to manifestations of what is deemed "wit." The degree of ironic effect is seen to be inversely proportionate to the number of markers necessary to get that effect (Allemann 1978: 393; Kerbrat-Orecchioni 1977: 139): dull or "heavy" irony provides many overt signals; elegant or "skilful" irony provides hardly any (Worcester 1960: 79; Muecke 1973: 40–1).

A related (and extreme) position is the one that claims that ironic meanings, as well as signals, only exist *in absentia*, that they lose their essence unless they remain only implicit (Kerbrat-Orecchioni 1977: 139 and 1980a: 110). While this may be argued for verbal texts (and written ones more than oral), perhaps visual (see Groupe Mu 1978: 430) and musical ones are more reliant on signals (and thus, meanings) that are *in praesentia*, as I will illustrate shortly. Yet, as Eco once emphatically put it: "irony must not be commented upon" (1986: 273); its identifying rhetorical nature lies in its indirection, as well as its edge. This is why not only context but discursive community figures in the comprehension of irony markers: "The greater the mutual familiarity of speaker and hearer with the presuppositions involved in the act of irony, the lower the signal threshold can be held" (Warning 1982: 258).

For those readers who have already made their way through this chapter to this point and may be interested in feminist theory (thus sharing several discursive communities), here is an example. It is from an article on feminist theory written by Teresa de Lauretis and published in her book, *Technologies of Gender* (1987). I have read it – and thus framed it – in the context of a call, by another feminist theorist, for women's use of irony as a weapon and a tool for change: Nancy Miller's article, "Changing the Subject: Authorship, Writing and the Reader," which was published the year before in a collection, *Feminist Studies/Critical Studies*, edited by de Lauretis herself. My feeling was that, in the passage you are about to read, de Lauretis gave Miller what she asked for – an example of irony used as a feminist weapon for change:

152

It is feminism that has, first, articulated the paradox of woman as both object and sign, at once captive and absent on the scene of Western representation; and it is feminism that now proposes – although, it must be said, there is more controversy on this issue than consensus – that what we thought to be a paradox, a seeming contradiction, is in effect a real contradiction, and, I will go so far as to say, an irreconcilable one. What that means is that I may speak, to be sure, but insofar as I speak I don't speak as a woman, but rather as a speaker (and when I do, I naturally take advantage of the podium). I also may read and write, but not as a woman, for men too have written "as woman" – Nietzsche, Artaud, Lautréamont, even Joyce apparently did – and others nowadays, all honorable men, are "reading as a woman."

(de Lauretis 1987: 113)

The ironies – and their markers – come for me at the end, in the last sentence, after the rest of the passage has set the textual and even circumstantial context. The quotation marks around "as woman" and "reading as a woman" mark citations, and thus suggest an intertextual context. For me, as for some of you perhaps, that context includes Jonathan Culler's chapter in *On Deconstruction* on reading "as a woman," Paul Smith and Alice Jardine's book, *Men in Feminism*, and the long debate of the last decade on the role of men in feminist discourse. For de Lauretis, they (as well as the modernist male writers mentioned) are "all honorable men." Within the discursive community created by reading this chapter – or reading Shakespeare's *Julius Caesar* – this cannot be other than an ironic echoic mention of Mark Antony's repeated ironic designation of the traitors . . . with the added emphasis, in this textual context, on the gender: "all honorable *men*." By my reading, the ironic echoing of an intertextual context of treason and betrayal within the larger context of the politics of feminism might have yet other targets, however understated or indirect the attack: those male modernists who "apparently" read and wrote "as a woman," and the French feminist theorists (like Hélène Cixous and Julia Kristeva) who made precisely that claim.

The interaction of discursive community with circumstantial, textual and intertextual context here provides a framing that makes signals such as quotation marks, understatement, and echoic mention into markers of irony. In other contexts, however, none of these would *necessarily* signify irony; here they do. This is what makes problematic those long lists of markers – of "ironic techniques" and strategies, of rhetorical figures and physical gestures (N. Knox 1973: 629), of types of disruptive factors in speech acts (see Groeben and Scheele 1984: 62–78). The fact that markers are pragmatic entities, that they take on the character of ironic signs "only within the framework of an interpretation specific to a particular communication act" (Warning 1982: 258), is what has led some theorists to throw up their hands in despair and say that markers cannot even be localized and that interpreters simply "sense" irony through tone and style (Allemann 1956: 12–13) or some "impression of discord" (Bally 1914: 462).

Indeed, if nothing is intrinsically ironic and anything can become ironic in certain contexts, then what is the sense in providing lists of ironic markers? As speech-act theory has argued, there is no "absolute criterion" (Austin 1975: 67) of grammar or vocabulary that we can rely on to separate the functionings of language; one cannot even argue that a violation of Grice's (1975) "conversational maxims" (of Quantity, Quality, Relation and Manner) will necessarily result in irony rather than confusion (Kaufer 1981b: 501). Therefore, any aspect of speech (lexical, syntactic, phonetic) could be (but would not necessarily be) a marker of irony (Clyne 1974: 346), and perhaps there are as many ironic strategies in any medium as there are strategies of discourse in general (Kaufer 1977: 99). And yet, like everyone else who writes on irony, I cannot resist the list completely. But I would at least like to contextualize my capitulation. My perspective on ironic signals – as on irony's semantics and on the role of intentionality – is a pragmatic one: whatever they are, to be called irony markers, an interpreter has to have decided that they have worked in context to provoke an ironic interpretation. In addition, I suspect that they have to have been, in the first place, what have been called "gestures of noticeability" (Rabinowitz 1987: 53).

Given this framework, however, it seems to me that the distinction to be made is less one between *kinds* of signals than one between *functions* signals can have. There are certain markers that often accompany an utterance (Muecke 1970/1982: 40) and whose function is to act as "warning signals" (Muecke 1978b: 373) to the interpreter to be alert for ironic intent (Mizzau 1984: 22; Muecke 1978a: 492) or, to put it another way, to expect the possibility that irony can be made to happen. These are related to what, in play theory, are called "metacues" (see Paulos 1980: 52) that often mark the beginning and ending of playfulness and thus signal the need to switch in and out of a play code (Goffman 1974: 44–6). By analogy, then, we might be able to speak of a **"meta-ironic"** function, one that sets up a series of expectations that frame the utterance as potentially ironic. Signals that function **meta-ironically**, therefore, do not so much constitute irony in themselves as signal the possibility of ironic attribution (Hermerén 1975: 73) and operate as triggers to suggest that the interpreter should be open to other possible meanings (Karstetter 1964: 175).

A second function of markers is to signal and indeed to structure the more specific context in which the said can brush up against some unsaid in such a way that irony and its edge come into being. Those that function in this **structuring** manner do not directly lead to a "*re*construction" of a latent and opposite or even "true" meaning, as many theories suggest; they simply act to make available, that is, actually to structure a ground in which become possible both the relational, inclusive and differential semantics and also that evaluative edge that characterize ironic meaning. There are, as we shall see, many different discursive entities that can function in this way, many of which can also act meta-ironically – which is another reason why one must speak of functions here rather than types of signals (cf. Booth 1974; Mizzau 1984; Muecke 1978a; Wright 1976). And all markers, of course, are more than likely culture- and situation-specific: what may function ironically in one social context might well gravely offend in another.

This chapter began with a discussion of the difficulties of signaling irony in music. Like the visual (Mayenowa 1981: 134), the aural has different and perhaps more limited abilities to suggest (and means to convey) context than does the verbal, in either oral or written form. This may be why both rely heavily upon citations to mark irony, and why citations therefore function simultaneously meta-ironically and structurally in these media. This limitation may also explain why theoretical discussions of irony have usually centered on the more varied examples possible in language. Another possible reason is that verbal irony is the only rhetorical figure that often has accompanying paralinguistic markers (Mizzau 1984: 22) that function meta-ironically to signal reflexively that irony is either being intended (Weinrich 1966: 60) or can be interpreted as present. Some of these paraverbal markers are **gestural** ones: in North American culture, we recognize a smirk, a wink, a raised eyebrow, even the tongue in cheek (Almansi 1984 and 1979). But not all such markers are single and unambiguous in their associations: for academics giving lectures, the act of holding up both hands in front of them and then curling and wiggling one or two fingers on each hand can function as a marker of either literal *or* ironic citation, depending on tone and context.

Other markers are **phonic**: throat clearing, change of voice register (as Laurie Anderson manages by electronically lowering her voice an octave in *United States*), alterations of speed, or the stressing of certain words. Among the most cited of these phonic signals that function meta-ironically are intonation and tone of voice, but, once again, these are both language- and culture-specific. Studies on ironic tone in the vocal expression of Hungarian speakers (Fónagy 1971a and 1971b), for instance, do not necessarily correlate with English speakers in Britain, Canada, the United States, Australia, India and so on – all of whom speak the same language but appear to have somewhat different "intonational contours" (Bach and Harnish 1979: 67) that function to signal irony. The sheer variety of tones of voice – deadpan, mocking, exaggerated (Winner 1988: 148; D. Knox 1989: 68–9) – that are said to function ironically shows the difficulty and complexity involved in trying to fix for certain the meaning of phonic, paraverbal markers. **Graphic** punctuation signs and typographical markers are not much more straightforward, unfortunately, since all have non-ironic functions as well, and so rely entirely on context for appropriate framing: quotation marks, inverted commas, italics, diacritics, exclamation marks, question marks, dashes, ellipses, parentheses. Overtly metalinguistic remarks are less ambiguous: [*sic*], so-called, so to speak, of course, as they say, to be ironic. These and their ilk function by openly soliciting the inference of irony.

Some markers have the potential to operate *both* meta-ironically, like this, and structurally: these are usually the ones that form part of the actual text itself rather than being present as a phonic, gestural or graphic accompaniment to it. *Only* these, however, can actually function structurally to enable irony to happen in semantic and evaluative terms. While some theorists, when making lists of these kinds of markers, have been meticulous in their discriminations among morphological, syntactical, semantic and other domains (see Meyers 1974: 175; Muecke 1978b: 368–73; Groeben and Scheele 1984: 58–9 and 62–78), I get the sense from reading widely in this area that there is, in fact, a limited number of examples of signals which are repeated often enough in most Western cultures that they get discussed in the abundant commentary on the subject. For ease and economy, these will be articulated here in verbal terms, but will be seen in action – signaling irony (to me, at least) – in the next section of this chapter through performative visual and musical texts.

The five generally agreed-upon categories of signals that function structurally are: (1) various changes of register; (2) exaggeration/ understatement; (3) contradiction/incongruity; (4) literalization/ simplification; (5) repetition/echoic mention.

When, in the context of a "serious" academic volume (*Staging the Renaissance: Reinterpretations of Elizabethan and Jacobean Drama*, edited by D.S. Kastan and Peter Stallybrass), an article appears by someone named "Random Cloud," the sudden change of register might work to set up an ironizing frame, especially when the article is entitled "'The very names of the Persons': Editing and the Invention of Dramatick Character" and when, on the opening page, the following variations on one name appear: Shakespeare, Shakespear, Shakspere, Shakspeare, Shakesper. "Random Cloud" is, in fact, one of the many pseudonyms of my colleague, "Randall McLeod", whose provocative violations of the tonal and stylistic registers of standard academic discourse certainly work to structure my own ironic interpreting of his writing. Other texts may present shifts in sociolects or even dialects (Muecke 1973: 41), but the important thing is that they be noticeable and interpretable in context.

Almost every manual of rhetoric states that hyperbole and litotes or meiosis represent the two common extremes of ironic signaling and, certainly, examples of both exaggeration and understatement are not hard to find. When the *Canadian Medical Association Journal* (146.7 [1 April 1992]: 1191–7) published an article on the "Psychopharmacology of lycanthropy,"

156

even those who might have to look up the meaning of lycanthropy could conceivably catch on to the April Fool's Day spoof through the article's heading ("*Very* Original Research") and the description of its analysis design as not the usual *double*-blind but *quadruple*-blind. These hyperbolic and exaggerated signals are usually relatively easy to spot, at least in comparison with the nuances of understatement which, by definition, perhaps, are going to be less easy to locate with sureness. Kazuo Ishiguro's novelistic *tour de force* of the unsaid and the un(der)stated, *The Remains of the Day* (1989) solicits a reading both between the lines and into the style of the lines of the novel, in order to move beyond the seemingly unrevealing professional "dignity" of the English butler, Mr Stevens. It does so, in part, by foregrounding the character's nervousness about his new American employer's habit of what he calls "bantering." Stevens's remarks about this situation constitute a reflective *mise en abyme* that functioned to trigger and then structure at least this reader's worries about irony:

> It is all very well in these changing times, to adapt one's work to take in duties not traditionally within one's realm; but bantering is of another dimension altogether. For one thing, how would one know for sure that at any given moment a response of the bantering sort is truly what is expected? One need hardly dwell on the catastrophic possibility of uttering a bantering remark only to discover it wholly inappropriate.
>
> (Ishiguro 1989: 16)

It was this kind of early and overt meta-ironic framing that then made the structuring understatement of the rest of the novel work so well for me.

The third category of marker that functions to structure the ground for the inference of irony (and can also, at times, function meta-ironically) is composed of a complex of things clustered around the notions of contradiction, incongruity, contrast, and juxtaposition: in its simplest form, Mark Antony's praise is actually blame. Scottish artist Ian Hamilton Finlay places in his garden statues of truncated aircraft carriers to be used as birdbaths, and so for me multiple ironies start to happen around things like: the incongruous inappropriateness of winged things plunging into water instead of being kept out of them; the contrast between small living birds and large deadly aircraft; the associative parallel with those truncated classical statues of humans placed in formal gardens. Sometimes the juxtaposition that structures irony's happening is between an utterance and its uttering (Berrendonner 1981: 223–4) – as in the familiar narrative device, used, for example, by Margaret Atwood in her novel, *Cat's Eye*, of a "naive" child focalizer and an adult narrator.

In the fourth type of signal, it is less contrast than the uncanny similarity produced by literalizing the figurative that triggers and structures the attribution of irony. A perhaps silly but none the less clear example: in the

157

British television series, *BlackAdder*, the protagonist asks his dupe – who has just missed his joke: "Have you any idea what irony is?" The reply he gets is: "It's like goldy and bronzy, but made with iron." In the visual arts, a more pointed literalization can be seen in Spring Hurlbut's sculptural "Sacrificial Ornaments" series in which the artist plays with the terminology and form of classical Greek architectural moldings: for instance, the "dentil" – a molding formed of tooth-like projections from a horizontal lintel – becomes a molding made of the representation of actual teeth. The literalizing ironies, meta-cued by the series' title, address a possible history of the actual usage of what, many centuries later, we read as innocent architectural sites, but which might well once have served as places of sacrifice and death. Functioning somewhat similarly to this kind of marker is that form of simplification or reduction that works to defamiliarize, as in the unexpected suppression of explanation to ironic ends in those startling dictionary definitions by Flaubert (*Dictionnaire des idées reçues*) or Ambrose Bierce (*The Devil's Dictionary*) or even Samuel Johnson (Ball 1976: 216–20).

I have left one of the most common of categories of markers to the end, because it is the one that is so frequently put into play in non-verbal as well as verbal discourses: repetition, echoic mention, mimicry. The early *Rhetorica ad Alexandrum* recognized the power of "briefly recalling things said before" (1434a), and Dan Sperber and Dierdre Wilson's theory of "echoic mention" (1981) offers a clear articulation of the process by which decoders identify (by inference) echoes of other utterances and the role this can have in creating the expectation of ironic meaning and intention. (For a psychological study of how this might work, see Jorgensen, Miller and Sperber 1984.) The position that this is the *only* way irony works, however, would appear to be unnecessarily limiting. Extending such insights, others have outlined different types of echoic mention: explicit, evoked, self-evoking, indirect, and direct (Berrendonner 1981: 198–212). The presence of quotation marks would obviously potentially be an overt meta-ironic signal to the interpretation of citational ironies (Stewart 1978/79: 123; Compagnon 1979: 40; Récanati 1979: 68). Repetition can be (intra)textual as well as intertextual, though: John Harwood's parodic mimicking of the Bible, "From 'The Annotated Gospel According to Jacques'" (1985) opens with "1. In the beginning was the Word, and the word was *différance*." This last term is duly annotated as: "the ground of all being; that which makes *writing* possible. See note 11 below." Note 11 explains: "'*Writing*'. That activity by which *différance* is manifested. See note 1 above."

In none of these cases – of register alteration, exaggeration or understatement, contradiction or incongruity, literalization or simplification, and repetition or echoic mention – is it a matter of somehow getting past the structural or textual signal to reach the actual irony, or even of being led to some "real" meaning intended by the ironist (Muecke 1978a: 492).

Rather, in each, the marker is part of the very form of the utterance (though each can also function meta-ironically as well). In certain contexts – with circumstantial, textual, or intertextual support – each can work to structure the semantic and evaluative happening called irony. But no matter how familiar any one of these may be in this role, its existence as a successful "marker" will always be dependent upon a discursive community to recognize it, in the first place, and then to activate an ironic inter-pretation in a particular shared context: nothing is an irony signal in and of itself.

II TRICKSTERS AND *ENFANTS TERRIBLES*: PERFORMING IRONIES

If signs become markers of irony through their successful functioning – meta-ironic or structural – within a frame or context, then it should be possible to some extent to retrace the process by which one has made irony happen in a text. Given the inevitable complexities of this process, I have chosen as my test cases two sets of examples that rely for the most part on one basic marker: echoic mention. To facilitate the task of those who read the last chapter, and thus share some discursive-communal background, I have selected as one of these examples two other cycles of Wagner's *Ring* operas. But my second example is from the visual domain: Beauvais Lyons's painstakingly fabricated and documented fictional civilizations that are presented through real-seeming archaeological conventions. Though in different media, both these examples have "performed" irony, for me as for others, and so show the interaction of those things I had to begin in this study by keeping separate for purposes of analysis: affect, semantics, intentionality, discursive-communal frameworks, and now, context and markers.

The two productions of Wagner's *Der Ring des Nibelungen* that interest me in this chapter were both from the Bayreuth Wagner Festival. The first is one that ran from 1976 to 1980 and thus marked an important anniversary: the centenary of the first complete *Ring* cycle. Wolfgang Wagner, grandson of the composer and director of the festival, named Pierre Boulez as conductor and Patrice Chéreau as director. What was so startling about this decision was that the fiercely German composer's negative feelings about the French were probably only exceeded by his feelings about Jews, as noted in Chapter 5. Also startling was Chéreau's youthful age (30) and his relative inexperience in operatic direction. Not surprisingly, perhaps, most of the negative reviews of this production cited the director's youth before issuing the usual laments about the "current usurpation of stage director over composer" (see Schonberg 1976: 13). The second cycle that interests me here is the one that ran from 1988 to 1992, conducted by Daniel Barenboim and directed by (then East German) *enfant terrible*, Harry Kupfer.

My reasons for selecting Bayreuth productions in particular are plural. First, as mentioned earlier, the theater was designed and built by Wagner in a relatively isolated, small North Bavarian town. Aside from a few years after World War II (when it was used for entertaining occupation troops – and *not* with operas), it has been used only to play Wagner's works. The audience attracted to the summer festival is particular in a number of ways. Given how difficult it is to get tickets (the demand is said to be 6–10 times greater than the available number of seats), those who actually succeed in getting them tend to be self-selected – both economically (though tickets are no more expensive than other opera houses anywhere else) and also in terms of their knowledge of the texts, the music, and the history of productions and recordings. For this very reason, directors like Chéreau and Kupfer could play upon this discursive community's knowledge of stage, iconographic, and musical conventions, and often, I felt, did so to ironic ends. What both managed to do was invoke and draw upon the power of any traditional associations the audience might have, and still set up a marked context which, for me, ironized those very associations and their seemingly lasting power.

That power has always relied, to a large extent, upon Wagner's own milking of the power of myth. In the *Ring* operas, Wotan, the Nordic ruler-god, is said to have drunk from the Spring of Wisdom at the base of the World-Ash tree. He lost an eye for his pains, and an eyepatch is used in most productions as the symbol of his wisdom, as of his daring to achieve it. But Wotan then cut off a branch of that tree and fashioned out of it a spear, upon which he wrote the moral treaties by which he proceeded to rule the world. All must obey these treaties – including himself. Much of the plot of the four music dramas revolves around his temptations to break his own laws in his desire to get possession of the powerful golden ring of the Nibelung. The operas tell of how he tries to get around those laws or to go back on them; in the end, however, he has to obey, even at the cost of the lives of those dear to him and, finally, of everything he has stood for.

Most people think of the *Ring* as the story of gods, dwarfs, giants, heroes, and magic rings, all set in magnificent, romantic Germanic forest scenes. Even though, as noted in Chapter 5, Wieland Wagner had stripped the stage bare after the war, many productions – such as the current one at New York's Metropolitan Opera – still offer what are in effect antiquarian reproductions of Wagner's own nineteenth-century stagings. Imagine the response of an audience with these conditioned expectations when faced with an opening scene in which the Rhinedaughters were presented as three prostitutes cavorting around a hydro-electric power dam on the Rhine. When the curtain goes up on Chéreau's *Rheingold*, nature has already been spoiled and corrupted: industry is part of modern myth. What was called a "programmatically controversial and basically foolish production" (Joseph Kerman, cited in Lee 1990: 105), when it opened, was more

160

than just "Euro-trash," though. It can be read as a systematic reconfigura-
tion of the four music dramas as seen through the lenses of subsequent
interpretive history: that is, through Thomas Mann's description of them as
the German contribution to the nineteenth-century bourgeois novel and
through George Bernard Shaw's reading (via Engels) of them as "frightfully
real, frightfully present, frightfully modern" (1967: 11) – a vision of
"unregulated industrial capitalism" (ibid.: xvii). Shaw had argued that
Wagner knew, by 1876, that he was no longer writing an epic about dwarfs
and giants and gods but something that demanded "modern costumes, tall
hats for Tarnhelms, factories for Nibelheims, villas for Valhallas" (ibid.: 80).
And that is more or less what Chéreau gave the Bayreuth audience. Jean-
Jacques Nattiez has argued in great detail in his book on this cycle that the
conception is less Shavian than Adornian or Brechtian (1983: 76), but
either way, the critique of power in relation to class, society at large, and the
state was set mostly in the nineteenth-century industrial world in which it
was first *performed* – not in some German romantic, story-book, mythic
world. Once noble gods and heroes were transformed into brutal and
violent representatives of a brutalizing and violent world – a world Wagner
himself might well have liked to forget (Carnegy 1992: 67). The response
at Bayreuth was scandal, uproar, the loudest boos ever heard in the theater.
Nevertheless, even the most vituperative reviews grudgingly admitted that
no one had ever put such raw drama, such fine and powerful acting, on the
Bayreuth stage. And, by the time this *Ring* was performed for the last time
and released on television (the first televised *Ring* ever), it had actually
become a kind of familiar, accepted norm, a norm that subsequent
productions could and would feel the need to meet – and match.

Chéreau's 1968-inspired, leftist *Ring* was echoed a few years later by
another politicized production: what I think of as Harry Kupfer's "Green"
Ring. Kupfer is a close and almost literal reader of texts, and so the
ecological motivation for the interpretation lies within the plot itself: you
may recall from Chapter 5 that the final opera, *Götterdämmerung*, opens with
the three Norns singing about how the World-Ash tree, from which Wotan
had broken off that branch to make his spear, has died because of this
primal violation, this original sin against nature. The Spring of Wisdom too
has dried up. Despite this negative framing, most interpretations of this
opera (and thus of the entire *Ring*) see the plot as being about "the
downfall of a world of law and force, and the dawn of a utopian age"
(Dahlhaus 1979: 81), usually basing such optimism on Wagner's early
Hegelian beliefs. Kupfer's reading marks itself as a different one from the
start: it opens with a silent tableau of a few lost-looking, trench-coated
people looking at a body lying on the ground, before wandering off to the
back of a very deep stage. The stage darkens and, when the famous,
"primordial," long-held E-flat notes on the double-basses begin, a startling
blue-green laser beam shoots out of the rear of the stage; with the addition

161

of the dominant B-flat on the bassoons in the fifth bar, comes another beam, and so on until the music of the Rhine river takes on striking visual dimensions.

Kupfer's stated premise is that the *Ring* cycle story is really a cycle, a ring in structure as in name, and that everything has already happened before this particular version begins. In his words:

> What we see is our world a million years later, after it has been destroyed by a nuclear bomb. Life was almost wiped out, but the buildings are still standing, rusting away into ruins. . . . We begin this *Ring* with the assumption that the entire story has already taken place, and the ruins you see onstage are the result of a type of *Götterdämmerung*. Then the population of this future world walks down an enormous street, fifty-four meters long, into the beginning of a new story. They are emigrants walking on the long, difficult path of world history.
>
> (Cited in Boutwell 1988: 16)

In this ironized "Green" *Ring*, there is no nature, no forest for a character like Siegfried to sit in and sing about. There are either utterly bare, empty stages (meta-ironically marked by their exaggeration of even Wieland Wagner's bare sets), lit up every 10 metres or so by side lights, or sets that show those ruins, the twisted girders and torn-up concrete of a landscape after a nuclear bomb or meltdown or some chemical disaster. Brünnhilde's cave becomes a mine shaft. The clothing worn cannot be the animal skins of romantic stage tradition or even the nineteenth-century bourgeois finery of Chéreau's production. Here all wear plastic: Wotan's eyepatch is replaced by sunglasses; the gods carry lucite suitcases and spears. But this was also what we used to call an "East" German *Ring*: the gods are presented as capitalist consumers of the first order, as are those who believe in them. The bourgeois Hunding's house, with its shiny Italian-design furniture, is juxtaposed to the bare plane and the blasted tree outside it. Through this contrast, I found myself making a direct connection between capitalist, consumer culture and environmental disaster. Setting the work one step back from Götz Friedrich's mid-1980s Berlin production, which set the operas in a subway tunnel (because there were no more sky gods and no more nature), Kupfer, by my reading, was showing the process by which that very state of affairs came about.

It wasn't only the choice of setting that worked meta-ironically to upset my (and others') expectations, however. Where – much to purist critics' disgust – Boulez had earlier reduced the powerful music of the *Ring* to a kind of aural accompaniment to Chéreau's drama on stage, especially in the first years of the production Barenboim too seemed, occasionally, deliberately to dampen the power of the traditionally "glorious" moments of the music. This suggested to me a musical interpretation totally in keeping with Kupfer's dramatic conception of a world of sordid power struggles, a world without redemption, even (or especially) through aestheticization. What I read as an ironic deconstruction of the music was also prompted and structured for me by the almost frantic action on stage. Both productions distracted (at least my) attention, moving it from the music to the drama. In Kupfer's version of *Die Walküre*, Siegmund runs 54 meters from the back to the front of the stage, then drops 3 meters to the ground (after the set has moved up from under his feet), and then has to sing. The Rhinedaughters were said to have trained for a year in gymnastics so that they could roll, flip, somersault and dive into the "waves" of the river – all while singing what is not the world's easiest music.

Taking Chéreau's lead, Kupfer, I felt, foregrounded another kind of distraction for the audience: this may have been a consumer and a "Green" *Ring* but it was also what my medically trained husband called a "hormonal" one. The brutal god, Wotan, a philandering spouse, was portrayed as convincingly attractive and sexually powerful by bass John Tomlinson. Larger than life, his search for power (and for the ring) became that of all the charismatic leaders of history. The figure who attracts by his energy and drive, who cannot renounce love – or, for that matter, sex – (as he must, in order to attain the ring) but who wants the gold and its power anyway, became in my interpretation a kind of figure for our times. That Wotan is a consumer (he has his palace, Valhalla, built especially for him) and a destroyer of nature came together for me in a politicized reading of his power. I thought of Adorno's remark that "domination over nature and subjugation by nature are one and the same" (1991: 137), and so they were for me too by the end of the cycle.

But, as discussed earlier, spectators and directors are not the only ones who interpret performances: singer-actors, designers, musicians, the conductor, and many others do as well. To direct an opera is very obviously to reinterpret it, of course. And to the director falls the general responsibility to mark the performance "text" in such a way that the audience will be able to make sense of its experience of it. Directors, therefore, are in a position not unlike that of ironists – and some actually are both. Directors also face the same difficulties as ironists in determining available contexts for the different discursive communities that might constitute their audience. The self-selected spectators at Bayreuth might well be expected to be able to interpret reflexive references to generic conventions about opera itself, allusions that can potentially function as ironic echoic mentions. For example, there are only a few totally orchestral passages in the *Ring*, including the one that Mann called one of the "pieces of unspeakable splendour" (1985: 108): Siegfried's funeral march, the one that Boudreau cited in his *Berliner Momente* compositions with which this chapter opened. When the hero, Siegfried is murdered, we are informed by the stage directions that the sorrowing vassals then pick up his body and bear it in solemn procession along the banks of the Rhine accompanied by this impressive music. We have to recall, however, that the convention in opera is that characters are deaf – deaf to the music, that is: they "do not *hear* the music that is the ambient fluid of their music-drowned world" (Abbate 1991: 119). That's why there are so many self-consciously presented *songs* in opera (Cone 1989). My interpretation of what Chéreau's production does is that it ironizes everything about this scene and these conventions. Siegfried dies and the curtain is immediately dropped over half of his body. A crowd of vassals gathers in front of the curtain, around the half-hidden body, gradually obscuring it completely. Everyone then turns to face the audience. No one moves. The funeral *march* is immobilized. This signal functioned for me to activate an ironic contrast between convention and production, between composer intent (known through stage directions) and director intent (known through the performance being watched). In addition, this crowd appears to be lit only from the indirect light of the pit below them: in Bayreuth, the orchestra pit cannot be seen from the auditorium, for it goes under the stage and the musicians and conductor are invisible to the audience. But these "vassals" stare down into the pit, intently listening to the grand music whose various *Motiven* lead them – and us, if we are familiar with the music's associations – through the history of Siegfried's life and death. They are *not* deaf, in other words; they listen with us to the music and its tale of heroism and defeat. Framing this scene reflexively in the context of the conventions of opera, I can make irony happen, but I also read ironic intent into the performance text.

I did likewise when I interpreted certain scenes ironically in Kupfer's production. My framing thoughts went something like this: knowing that the Bayreuth audience not only shares an awareness of this kind of generic convention, but also a knowledge both of the libretto and of the way scenes are usually played, Kupfer could direct his Wotan in *Rheingold* to sing the words he is supposed to sing while looking at his newly built castle, Valhalla – "Vollendet das ewige Werk" ("The eternal work is completed") – while gesturing into the Festspielhaus auditorium where the audience sits. In the reflexive irony which I felt solicited to make happen here, the completed "eternal work" became the theater itself, which Wagner had labored hard to build and complete. In other words: the audience is literally in Valhalla, the home of the gods. Heaven is where you can hear Wagner's operas!

It is not just circumstantial contexts like this one that Kupfer's production activated for me. Intertextual echoes provided me with constant signals that functioned to provoke ironic interpretation. Given the critical notoriety of Chéreau's *Ring* and the fact that it had been televised and thus widely seen, I suspected that Kupfer could to a large extent count on a discursive-communal as well as intertextual memory at work in his audience. Where Chéreau figured his Fafner, the giant-turned-"Wurm", as a statue of an oriental(ized) dragon wheeled about by attendants dressed in black (as in the Japanese Bunraku puppet tradition), Kupfer cast Korean singer Philip Kang as his giant and then dressed him as the West's clichéd oriental(ist) villain, Fu Man Chu. Exaggeration and one-upmanship functioned here for me to signal the potential for a very odd irony. Both productions suggested to me a reflexive awareness of the way in which Western cultures have stereotyped the East as the West's evil "other," and so simultaneously debunked and defamiliarized both nineteenth- and twentieth-century versions of what Edward Said calls European "orientalism." Reflexive intertextual markers, in other words, do not simply point to solipsistic operatic concerns, but to larger social and cultural contexts, as well.

That first televised *Ring* provided other intertextual grounds for ironies, too. Ulrich Melchinger's 1974 Kassel production of *Götterdämmerung* had made the Norns into surreal, futuristic telephone operators, plugged into the past, as they indulge in what Mann called "solemn cosmic gossip" (1985: 100): as you may recall from Chapter 5, they are supposed to be "reading" the rope of life and, at the same time, offering us all a plot refresher. Triggered by the fact that Kupfer dressed his Norns as nuns, I found myself thinking about the possible punning in German on *Norne* and *Nonne* (Norn and nun). Indeed, instead of "singing their rope," as it passed through their hands, these Norns appeared to "say their beads." But they did so, not around the pine trees the libretto describes, but around a forest of TV aerials – perhaps all that is left of a world in which nature has been ravaged (and this is what they are singing *about*, after all). Television became for me here the ironized symbol of how we know (and construct) reality today – the equivalent of the Norn's narrative rope of life, but mediated through technology rather than the gods, this time. Of course, thanks to Chéreau's *Ring* (and then the Met's version), television is also how many people come to know Wagner's operas today.

Even more than Chéreau's, Kupfer's *Ring* world is a technologically driven one, where Wagnerian deities get to Valhalla not by the libretto's "rainbow bridge" but by a rainbow neon elevator; where red laser enclosures replace the flames of the "magic fire" that, according to the libretto, protect the sleeping Brünnhilde. It is a world which comes to its end not with the overflowing of the Rhine as Valhalla burns (the libretto is precise, if demanding, on this count), but with people grouped around a series of television sets. The textual frame that made irony happen for me here is that balancing opening scene of the act with the Norns amid the TV aerials. But what were these people watching on television? Brünnhilde's death on Siegfried's funeral pyre – as distanced spectacle? A replay of the nuclear holocaust and its aftermath with which Kupfer's cycle of operas began? Or, could they have been watching Chéreau's televised version of this final scene? Not everyone was as willing to read multiple ironies – or, for that matter, any ironies – in this scene, of course. One critic declared: "Brünnhilde's sacrifice was cheapened to impotence by being 'quoted' as a spectacle staged for groups watching it on television sets" (Carnegy 1992: 73). And the response of the first audience when the curtain went down in 1988 was what has been called a "boo of horrifying vindictiveness," "the most spectacular display of hostility" (Tanner 1989: 921) ever witnessed at Bayreuth – surpassing even that directed at Chéreau in 1976. It was as if no one in that audience liked the idea of seeing simulacra of themselves as passive spectators to mass destruction: those onstage television viewers in that first year of the production were indeed in evening dress like the audience. Kupfer was called everything from simple-minded to "highly intelligent and persuasive ... with a crushingly circumscribed world-view" (Tanner 1989: 921), one that refused the redemption a long tradition had claimed for Wagner's final message (for the music, if not for the action of the cycle's narrative). The very markers that functioned to solicit an ironic interpretation from me, however, were what made me decide that it was Kupfer who was being, strangely, the more faithful to Wagner's intentions: as a German who lived and worked in what was then East Berlin, Kupfer was known to share Wagner's belief that theater can influence political and social ideas, in part because it offers a collective rather than individual experience. Like Brecht, he might have wanted to disturb his audience, to make us reflexive about our experience. Like Chéreau, Kupfer chose to transcode (often in such a way that irony resulted for me) the "timeless" mythic Wagnerian text and tradition into a politicized parable for an industrial, capitalist, and nuclear age, an age in which power is still as dangerous as ever, perhaps even more so. To frame *Der Ring des Nibelungen* in this way is to offer an entirely new set of contexts in which to interpret the libretto's words, the staged narrative, and even the music. What, as part of the audience, I found myself doing was making irony happen, performing it, in a sense, through the solicitation of the performance's markers of circumstantial, textual and intertextual contexts.

But, as those reviews reveal, not everyone interpreted these productions in this way. What happens when the unsaid does *not* rub productively and seductively against the said, when only the stated is perceived? Recently, I'm told (Lyons 1994), a retired schoolteacher from Oak Ridge, Tennessee went to the Ewing Gallery of Art and Architecture at the University of Tennessee in Knoxville to see a traveling exhibition entitled "Reconstruction of an Aazudian Temple." After a careful and engaged examination of the many items in the show – ceramics, frescoes, a facsimile of a temple wall, photographs, hand-printed lithographic bookplates, excavation drawings – she asked a member of the gallery staff about one of the pieces of pottery, labelled as "Vessel with an Inverted Spout" (see Plate 6.1). She was provided with a photocopy of an article on Aazudian ceramics which speculated that this vessel may have been "a water clock or a meditation device." Not convinced, she asked more questions and was directed to a packing crate near the entrance on which were stencilled the words "Hokes Archives." As

166

Plate 6.1 "Vessel with an inverted spout"
Source: From *Reconstruction of an Aazudian Temple* by Beauvais Lyons. Ceramic. Photograph
provided by the artist.

Beauvais Lyons – the self-appointed Director of the Hokes Archives, and the
artist who had created this entire civilization and all its artifacts – tells the
story: "As she pronounced the word Hokes, she rolled her eyes and
exclaimed 'I should have known that!' She then went through the entire
exhibition again, this time experiencing it as one would a novel." The
connection Lyons makes here between novelistic fiction and his "archaeological" fiction is not accidental, for, while his initial inspiration came from
things as diverse as Sir Thomas More's *Utopia* and Piranesi's hypothetical
architecture, the paradigm is drawn specifically from Jorge Luis Borges'
story, "Tlön, Uqbar, Orbis Tertius" where a secret society of scholars
reconstructs through imagination and speculation an entire culture it only
knows from a few fragments (Lyons 1985: 82). They even fabricate "hrönir,"
described as objects from the past brought into being by expectation.
Norman Daly's 1972 *Civilization of Llhuros* is thought to be the first
multimedia presentation of an archaeological fantasy world, the first
"conceptualization of an entire civilization presented as an archaeological
discovery and installed as an anthropological study" (Daly and Lyons 1991:

167

265). Using the cast-off debris of contemporary culture, Daly constructed sculptural figures out of found objects; he also produced maps, literary texts, music, and illustrations of the social customs of Llhuros. The kind and the noticeability of the markers of his ironies were deliberately varied throughout the exhibition, "offering constant challenge to visitors' innocent assumptions of the reality of the ancient culture and of the reliability of their own senses" (Daly and Lyons 1991: 265). At the start, the objects and their manner of presentation were normalizable within anthropological exhibiting conventions. But the name "Llhuros" does suggest "lure," and the viewer soon had to deal with "innumerable contradictory clues, fragmentary evidence" and other familiar markers of irony that provoked an active process of interpretation and reinterpretation on the part of the visitor.

An "archaelogical fiction" like this will likely have a number of possible audiences: those who catch on right away, or who know in advance that this is a parodic artist's show and not an archaeological exhibition at all; those, like the retired teacher Lyons describes above, who catch on at some point and then have the double experience of an initial and a reconsidered (or a realist and a fictionalist) viewing; and those, presumably, who leave the exhibition without having interpreted anything beyond the said. The possible reasons for missing the fictionality of the exhibit are multiple. If the clues were recurrent and obvious, then it might well be what one reviewer rather fiercely called a question of "mental vacuity" which "allows viewers to be deceived by style and appearance" (Elledge 1988: 6). But, in Lyons's case, there are other possible reasons, for his work has increasingly under-marked or understated its ironies, almost as if it prefers to delight those who are already in the know rather than provoke the uninitiated into awareness of the "hoax." Fewer signals function meta-ironically, in other words, and more work structurally.

In the early 1980s, Lyons used to give lectures on his work at the Arizona State University's Department of Anthropology. He would give these as if they were authentic scholarly accounts, but the day on which he spoke was always April lst. His first project (1977–79) was the invention of the ancient civilization of the "Arenot" from north-central Turkey. The overt contradiction in the name was an overt clue to fictionality that functioned to set up a frame in which ironies potentially abounded for the viewer of what were presented (using the conventions of an ethnographic exhibition) as "authentic" archaeological remains and the documentation thereof: hand-constructed clay ceremonial vessels, lithographed plates, charts and texts, and even tours given by Lyons in the guise of German archaeologist, Heinrich *Dreck*müller.

But with his second project, *The Excavation of the Apasht* (1980–83), the signals appear to me to be considerably less overt. Lyons's elaborate process of imagining and then fabricating and documenting an imaginary culture

168

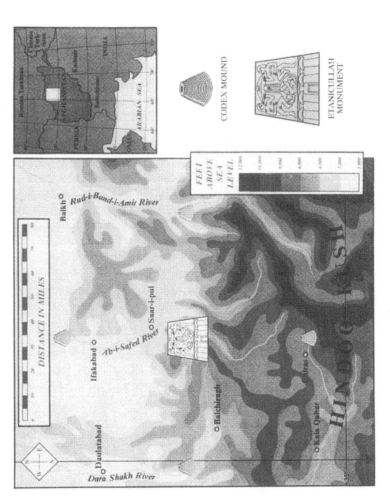

Plate 6.2 "Catalogue of the Apasht Excavations, Volume II, Plate I" by Beauvais Lyons. Lithograph.
Photograph provided by the artist.

in all its complexity through a wide range of media – relief sculpture, lithography, ceramics, rubber stamps, cartography, writing, and performance – relies on echoic mention of real archaeological finds and their display to trigger the attribution of irony. But in order for this to occur, the fictional status of the Apasht must first be recognized by the interpreter. For me, the complication (or subtlety) occurs when precisely what provides the documentation with its look of authenticity is what triggers the attribution of irony – that is, the fictionality of the Apasht is bracketed (or not yet noticed) and so the likelihood of the irony not being attributed is increased. At the start of the show, in accord with convention, there was a map marking where the excavations took place (see Plate 6.2); it was taken directly from a 1934 *National Geographic* map of Persia and Afghanistan, but Lyons added to it only one location – a conditionally named, fake village of "Ifakabad." And this time, when he gave tours and lectures (his performance pieces), it was not in any fictional persona but as "Dr Lyons." (He is currently an Associate Professor of Art at the University of Tennessee.)

There were still, however, some relatively overt meta-ironic markers – if you were alert: the stamp on the plate from the *Catalogue of the Apasht Excavations, Volume II* that reads "Hokes Scholarly Lithography"; the name of the translator, Henri le Truquer (trickster); the very name of the civilization, Apasht, which is said to be an Urdu word for "the unintelligible"; a certain *Catalogus Van Neit Vereenzelvigen Oudheidkundig Kaarblijkelijkheid* (Dutch for *Catalogue of Unidentified Archaeological Evidence*), from which six prints are shown, and which is identified by a plaque citing a scholar's opinion of it as "a Dutch Piltdown" that was "perpetrated by a secret society of renegade bibliomaniacs" – an echo of the Borgesian creation of Tlön. These are, for the most part, meta-ironic signals that function to suggest the possibility of interplay between the historical and the imagined, the real and the hoax. Each object or text in the exhibition also incorporates markers that function to structure the ground of irony: exaggerations (the Apasht are said to have "very archaic origins ... possibly older than all civilization itself"); contradictions and changes of register (glyphic images that are said to be indecipherable but are clearly faces, genitals, hands with crossed fingers); echoic mentions (the performance-lecture tours that parody pedantic, long-winded archaeological discourse). Yet these are all relatively subtle, set as they are in the midst of meticulously constructed and abundantly documented material. By the end of a full experience of this exhibition, when everything is interpreted in the context of the whole, the cumulative impact of the ironies attributed may well be to make seeing into disbelieving. But I still think it would help to be aware of the fictionality before you went to the exhibition.

Lyons's most recent creation, *Reconstruction of an Aazudian Temple*, the one with which I began, has to my eyes even fewer overt markers, fewer meta-ironic signals: witness the progression from a civilization negatively named the "Arenot" to one whose name is said to mean "the unintelligible" to the Aazud, apparently from the Assyriac root *aa-zud* meaning "those who are free, unrestricted." Nevertheless the advertising for the 1990 show at the Cheekwood Fine Art Center did invite you to meet the *artist*, Beauvais Lyons, to take a tour from a certain "Dr. Lyons" and to hear a lecture on artists "who create imaginary cultures." In opposition to these overt clues of the fictionality needed to activate the ironies, press releases for the 1993 Aazud show in Knoxville were sent out and information from them was duly published with no seeming awareness of the hoax: the fact that Lyons has collaborated with Joey Skaggs, the New York trickster discussed earlier, will come as no shock to those of you who read Chapter 5. These press statements were signed by a certain "Vera Octavia," Assistant Director of the Hokes Archives. And, yet another extra for those of you whose discursive community includes the knowledge of Latin, the "ex libris" stamp (see Plate 6.3) reads: "Aazudiis liberi – quae sint vera fabricare."

The signals are certainly there, you might argue, but a booklet from the *Cheekwood Monograph Series* on "Rare Discoveries from the Hokes Archives" mounts a formidable campaign to convince the reader of its authenticity, while paradoxically subverting it with subtle ironic signals. We read of the founding of the Hokes Archives by Everett Ormsby Hokes (1864–1939), of the conditions of its purchase by Beauvais Lyons, and the work commenced on conserving and exhibiting its contents. Going well beyond one single exhibition and into the construction and dissemination of information about the history and material identity of the entire archives, Lyons has increased the scope of his work without sacrificing at all his amazing care for detail and continuity on conceptual, stylistic, and material levels (see, for example, Plate 6.4). At this level, many of the signals of irony are, as Lyons himself has noted, in the formal arrangements of pieces or in the absurdities of the reconstructions (see Plate 6.5).

Increasingly, I find my attributing of irony to his work moving from the scale of the individual object or text (where I actually think the markers are more and more understated) to the context of his show or *oeuvre* as a whole. When I learned about the "deconstructivist" position in archaeology, I read more and different literalizing ironies into Lyons's work: if Michael Shanks and Christopher Tilley (in *Reconstructing Archaeology* and *Social Theory and Archaeology*) were going to argue that "the past did not exist, but is merely a text that we write" (Watson 1990c: 673), then Lyons might well be seen to have created what Borges called "hrönir." The conflation of art and artifact, fiction and fact, in these "archaeological fictions" is one that Lyons has written about at length: in other words, I have intentional statements to guide my interpretation – or what might more accurately be called my recognition than my attribution – of irony. But to "recognize" the ironies – through Lyons's framing and marking – is in itself to engage in an intentional activity; so too would be the act of "missing" his intended ironies.

171

Plate 6.3 "View of the Immudab Temple and the seal of the organization which conducted the excavations" by Beauvais Lyons. Photograph and seal provided by the artist.

Plate 6.4 "Installation view of *Reconstruction of an Aazudian Temple*" (1993) by Beauvais Lyons. Photograph provided by the artist.

Plate 6.5 "Aazudian relief fresco depicting the Goddess Tamoot fighting pestilence"
by Beauvais Lyons. Photograph provided by the artist.

Of course, the consequences are not too terrible if a visitor "misses"
Lyons's irony or if a late-night television viewer doesn't understand that the
Larry Sanders Show is really a fictional talk show on which real guests (actors
who, paradoxically, for once play themselves but within a fiction) chat with
"Larry Sanders" as played by Garry Shandling. That doesn't mean that
there might not be a lot more at stake in other situations, however. The

174

concluding chapter, as a way to draw together all the artificially separated elements of a theory of irony, directly addresses the consequences of the politics of the unsaid.

7

THE END(S) OF IRONY
The politics of appropriateness

Irony is the rhetorical necessity of the age, the critical accessory no one
should leave home without. It has also replaced patriotism as the last refuge
of scoundrels, for it means never having to say you really mean it.
                                B. Austin-Smith, "Into the Heart of Irony"

The suspicion voiced in these remarks – balancing the warnings that
opened Chapter 1 – is perhaps a good place to start to bring to some sort
of conclusion a study of that edgy "problematic of affect" accompanying
irony's "problematic of meaning" (Hebdige 1988: 223). Some of you may
recall the outcry when Randy Newman released his record "Short People
Got No Reason to Live," thinking that by ironizing a benign object of
prejudice he could satirize all prejudice. His good intentions turned out to
be irrelevant to those who were angered by the song: "Some simply declared
that he had lied. Others invoked the familiar distinction between intention
and utterance: he may have intended no slur on short people, but his words
say otherwise. Still others turned to psychology and explained that while
Newman perhaps *thought* he was free of prejudice, his song displayed his
true feelings" (Fish 1983: 175). Irony's edge cuts many ways.

The final example that I have chosen – in order to bring together the
previously separated elements of the theory of irony and its politics offered
in this book – is another one in which the risks of irony were made manifest,
not only through the proliferation of public as well as academic discourse
on the topic but also through real material consequences for the participants. My "text" this time is a cultural text: a museum exhibition that can
be read as a "text" because it is very much the "product of social interaction,
contingent upon social process" (Stewart 1978/79: 14). From 16 November
1989 to 6 August 1990, the Royal Ontario Museum in Toronto presented an
exhibition entitled "Into the Heart of Africa." This was the first complete
(and thus long-awaited) showing of the African collection of the museum,
but what began with good intentions ended with picketing by members of
the African Canadian community, court injunctions against them by the
museum, encounters between demonstrators and police that led to
criminal charges being laid, and the later decision of Jeanne Cannizzo, the

176

curator (a white anthropologist and expert on African art) to leave her part-time university classroom for a complex set of reasons, including continuing harassment by former demonstrators who accused the show of racism. (For details of the events, see Young 1993 and, especially, S.R. Butler 1993.) Throughout this chapter, I will refer to Cannizzo as "the curator" in order to put the emphasis on her institutional role and, implicitly, to remind you that curators do not work alone but in conjunction with both museum administration and technical, design, and educational workers in the institution. I do not wish to downplay her personal role (or the consequences of the controversy for her). I do want to contextualize it all. This is also one of the reasons for the existence of explanatory notes in this chapter: a desire to give you as much context as possible for the complex and contentious issues raised.

What was so surprising about the controversy and the degree of emotional furor unleashed was that this was an exhibition that *attempted* to be the opposite of the kind of thing one might find in an institution like the Royal Museum of Central Africa near Brussels, where a statue of Leopold II dominates a room "celebrating the triumphs of colonialism with the guns and flags of expeditions and the chests carried by native bearers, the plumed hats of the conquerors, models of their railway lines and the honoured names of those who laid down their lives controlling the natives" (Horne 1984: 222). Those guns and flags and plumed hats were present in the (similarly named) Royal Ontario Museum too, but the stated intention of this exhibition was to expose the imperial ideology of the people – Canadian soldiers and missionaries – who had borne them and who had brought back to Canada many African objects which, over time, found their way into the museum. My own engagement with this controversy dates from the weeks in the summer of 1990 – at the height of the public confrontations taking place in front of the museum – when I was teaching a seminar on the politics of irony right across the road: police sirens and chanting demonstrators provided choral commentary on the political perils of irony.

"Into the Heart of Africa" provides a pointed case-study of the transideological complexities of irony – with a particular focus on the question of when and whether irony is deemed appropriate and even ethical (see Swearingen 1991: vii) as a discursive strategy. The responses to the exhibition also offer a commentary on the various aspects of irony that the previous chapters have outlined in more detail. The degree of anger – from, as you will see, all possible sides of the issue – was ample testimony to the affective charge of irony's edge. There were serious disagreements over the identifying and evaluating of the functioning of the irony. Was it elitist or inclusive? Was it evasive or cautiously indirect? The said and the unsaid were held in a semantic suspension so unstable that irony did not always happen for everyone, and, when it did, disagreement about interpretation was rife. Ironic meaning here was relational in several senses:

177

it came into being in the interactions between the said and unsaid, most obviously, but also between intention and interpretation, as well as between verbal and visual sign systems. The ironies in "Into the Heart of Africa" could not be explained by any simple antiphrastic semantic model or any theory of meaning substitution: operating more inclusively and differentially, irony's indirect meanings were born of the rubbing of the edge of the said against the plural edges of the unsaid – in such a way that sparks were certainly created for some viewers. In addition to these semantic and affective complications, the complexity of possible discursive communities involved in the presentation and viewing of an exhibit in a public institution is staggering. Do curators and the "general public" share enough assumptions to make irony safe? Given the nature of this particular show about the role of the British Empire (here represented by colonial Canadians) in Africa, the usual community categories to be taken into account (such as age, education, language, gender, and so on) were greatly expanded. Race and nationality, of course, were primary community-defining factors, but so was timing of viewing and background knowledge: it mattered whether you attended in the first few months, before the controversy erupted, or after; it mattered how much you knew about the conflict and where you had got your information about it. The discursive communities to which viewers belonged determined how they might construct ironic meaning from the exhibition's objects and texts.

The experience of visiting a museum is, as one commentator explains, the result of variable effects of "the original makers' intentions in making the displayed object, the curator's and designer's intentions in displaying it in a certain way, and the observer's own interests and assumptions about all these matters and the museum itself" (Jones 1992: 917). The curator's intentions – which I will address in detail shortly – in deploying irony in the displaying of objects were not necessarily either interpreted as such or appreciated when they were. The intentional acts of a wide variety of interpreters/viewers – those for whom the ironies did happen, those for whom they did not, and those for whom irony was felt to be utterly inappropriate – illustrate the difficulties of relying on intentional theories in discussing irony's politics. Were imperial racist attitudes simply repeated – though in quotation marks – or were they ironized by those very marks? Does any repetition in a different context necessarily change meaning (Mizzau 1984: 43)? Or are only some echoes going to be real examples of ironic echoic mention that involve the implication of a judgmental attitude (Sperber and Wilson 1981: 303)? Who is to decide? What markers are needed to insure that irony happens? Are quotation marks around certain words on explanatory panels sufficient signals of irony's possible presence – especially when they were used in varying ways throughout the exhibition?

On top of all this, the contexts that framed "Into the Heart of Africa" for viewers were complex and multiple, so difficulties in signaling were bound to increase. For some – anthropologists, museum workers – the exhibit might have been viewed as an example of the "new" museology, revealing the changes in the discipline of ethnography over the last decades. For others, the frame of viewing might have been the challenges to the cultural authority of museums as institutions of "modernity." For still others, it was the current postcolonial interest in the material and cultural consequences of Empire that might have been the focus of attention. The general debates over multiculturalism in Canada and the more specific ones over the relations of the Metropolitan Toronto Police and the black community provided still other contexts for Canadians and Torontonians. In addition, the positioning of this exhibition within the museum and the display conventions of the rest of the institution were important framing elements for most viewers. All of these now familiar theoretical points of reference – affect, semantics, discursive communities, intention, markers and con- texts – will be discussed in much more detail in what follows, but this brief overview might already give you a sense of why "Into the Heart of Africa" seemed to me to be such a fitting test case for theorizing irony and its politics.

Few would disagree that, here, irony turned out to be tendentious, and part of the reason was that, as always, irony took interpreters "out of the text and into codes, contexts, and situations" (Scholes 1982: 76). In order to set the scene for the conflict I would like to fill in some of those situations and contexts, beginning with the most general ones that came into play. For me, the broadest context was the relation of museums to what has been generalized and usually demonized into this thing called "modernity." Put in the admittedly reductive (but perhaps heuristically useful) terms of "cultural shorthand": in most accounts these days, the movement from Renaissance humanism to the beginning of the "modern project," to use Jürgen Habermas's term, starts with the Cartesian and Enlightenment shift to what has been described as "a higher, stratospheric plane, in which nature and ethics conform to abstract, timeless, general, and universal theories" (Toulmin 1990: 35). On this plane – or so goes the simplified version of the story – connections between knowledge and objects of knowledge (nature, the self, history, society) are said to be objectively determined, providing a foundation which permits a systematization that works toward what is seen as an inherently progressive grasp of "truth." Knowledge thus accrued is said to be not only culture-neutral, but value- free. Doubt and contingency, however, are just as much a part of this modern heritage, and of course, the debates over the politics of the ordering, legitimizing, system-building power of reason and method are part of the very history of modernity; they are also ongoing, however, with Habermas (1983) arguing that the "project of modernity" has not yet been completed, that its moral imperative to free humanity from injustice and to

179

extend equality to the oppressed through rational communal grounds of consensus has not yet been achieved. Yet, what Habermas sees as liberatory consensus, others have seen as inhibiting conformism, as an "obsessively legislating, defining, structuring, segregating, classifying, recording and universalizing state [which] reflected the splendour of universal and absolute standards of truth" (Bauman 1992: xiv).

As an academic, I know that I work within one of the major cultural institutions of modernity and, whatever my individual evaluation of the modern project and, whatever my personal position (consensual support or oppositional resistance), I participate in what has been called the "exercise of social control through the meting out of learning, mediated and identified with the achievement of worth" (Hooper-Greenhill 1988: 224). But these words were, in fact, written to describe the ideological and historical assumptions of curators of ethnographic museums, not literature teachers like me. Nevertheless, both the museum and the academy in Europe and North America have traditionally shared an institutionalized faith in reason and method, not to mention an unavoidable intersection with governmental agencies; together (and when added to the often imposing architecture of such institutions), these connections have contributed to the "authority effect" (Hooper-Greenhill 1988: 225) they each create. Not surprisingly, both institutions have come under considerable scrutiny from various branches of contemporary theory, intent on deconstructing that effect and its ideological consequences. Both institutions could be said to work toward the acquisition of knowledge (Jordanova 1989: 22) through collecting, ordering, preserving, and displaying – in their different ways – the "objects" of human civilization in all its varieties. If it is the ideology of these processes of constructing meaning and significance that has provoked the recent theoretical critique, it is the nature of those very "objects" that has initially brought the *postcolonial* into the current academic debates – in literary criticism and anthropology especially – and, increasingly, into the discourse of museums, especially ethnographic ones.

An important context for many viewers of "Into the Heart of Africa" was the fact that, over the last few decades, museums have begun to see themselves as cultural texts and have become increasingly self-reflexive about their premises, identity, and mission. Among the questions being asked anew are: Do objects speak for themselves? If so, how? What objects have been collected, and why? What constitutes the so-called authenticity of an object? (See Crew and Sims 1991.) The history and economics of collecting have received much attention lately from many quarters, as have the current legal, ethical and financial constraints on acquisition, custody and disposal of "cultural property" (see Palmer 1989). But the history of most European and North American ethnographic museum collections is one that cannot be separated from the specific history of imperialism (Ames 1992: 3; Thomas 1991; see for bibliography, Arnoldi 1992: 454–5,

180

n.2). Not only were the objects collected often the spoils of colonial conquest – seen at the time as "discovery" and "exploration" – but their acquisition and retention have been legitimated by the institutionalization of an ideal (and an ideology) of apolitical, detached objectivity and a positivist commitment to science (Durrans 1988: 155).

This connection between historical imperialism and what some see as intellectual imperialism (C.S. Smith 1989: 17) might best be understood within the context of the common denominator of what I too have here been calling "modernity." However much they might be called into question in *theory*, the assumptions of neutrality and objectivity and of the value of rationality, empiricism, and technology are modern assumptions that form the *practical* foundations of the post-Enlightenment public museum (MacCannell 1976: 84), even to this day. If museums are still structured on "rigid taxonomies and classification, whereby it was believed that artefacts could be laid out in a consistent, unitary and linear way" (C.S. Smith 1989: 19), it is because they are still in some ways the physical embodiments of what (in those shorthand terms, once again) can be called modernity's desire to make order and therefore meaning. What some see as the universalization inherent in the Enlightenment project (Fisher 1991: 95) works to smooth over gaps and unite fragments into a systematized cultural totality. One of the manifestations of this process is the display of diverse, culturally specific objects in highly aestheticized (C.S. Smith 1989: 17), (architecturally) late modernist galleries that effectively wipe out particularity of context or history. Of course, the very act of technically preserving objects from the ravages of time and decay (not to mention that of "restoring" them to their "original" state) could be seen as universalizing in its denial of change over time. This stewardship model of the museum as the guardian of the human heritage entails a going beyond this conservation function to include a scholarly and educational mandate, both for experts and for the general public.

In the last twenty years or so, however, experts working in the field of ethnography have articulated in a museum context the view of culture as "text," reminding all that texts are interpreted and contextualized by ethnographers themselves. To borrow from the title of one of Clifford Geertz's influential books (1983), the aim of "interpretive anthropology" is "local knowledge" (see also Geertz 1973; Crapanzano 1992). What has been called a "conceptual shift, 'tectonic' in its implications" (Clifford 1986a: 2) in ethnography is, in fact, a response to modernity that has major postcolonial implications. Gone are the days when anthropology (conceived of as apolitical and neutral) could speak "with automatic authority for others defined as unable to speak for themselves" (Clifford 1986a: 10). The acknowledgement – at last – of the "unequal power encounter" (Asad 1973: 16) that marks both the discipline of anthropology and, in a different way, colonialism itself has brought the politics of representation to the fore.

The universalizing urge of modernity then begins to give way to the cultural politics of difference, described as the drive

> to trash the monolithic and homogeneous in the name of diversity, multiplicity and heterogeneity; to reject the abstract, general and universal in light of the concrete, specific and particular; and to historicize, contextualize and pluralize by highlighting the contingent, provisional, variable, tentative, shifting and changing.
>
> (West 1990: 19)

What has been referred to (if not generally accepted) as the "new museology" works in this contentious territory, asking what the different purpose of the museum would be if it gave up its modern claims of neutrality and objectivity, and what the role of the spectator could be in the now acknowledged act of the interpretation of objects, objects which do not independently transmit meaning. Instead, they are open to many possible constructions of meaning, depending on things like the design of the display, the context in the institution, the visual semiotics engaged, the historical background presented. However, not only objects change meaning over time; so too does the museum itself as institution, for it too is a constantly evolving social artifact (Weil 1990: xiv) that exists in a constantly changing social world. The current discourse of museums now includes a discourse of community access and involvement, of two-way interactive communication models, and of empowerment through knowledge (see Gurian 1991). There is talk of a desire to find ways to engage with living cultures rather than only with objects of the past, of a desire not only to inform but to provoke thought.

These are the most general contexts, then, for the particular focus of this chapter: one museum exhibition that certainly did engage with its immediate community and that definitely provoked thought, not to say controversy; as I mentioned at the start, it was an exhibition that intended to put into play irony and reflexivity in order to attempt to deconstruct the ideology of Empire that had determined its particular collection of African objects. It thus ran counter to the more customary (unavoidable, but usually discreet) indirect mention of imperial provenience that could be read as an attempt to "close its history at the end of the colonial era itself" (Durrans 1988: 150).

The intention – according to museum authorities – was to offer a (postcolonial) "critical examination of the Canadian missionary and military experience in turn-of-century Africa";[1] the mode of presentation was what museologists might have recognized as consciously "new" in its foregrounding of how objects changed meaning over time and in different contexts. But the self-evident difficulty of effectively deconstructing a museum *from the inside* became acute when that institution was viewed by at least some members of the African Canadian community as part of

182

European modernity's "attempt to measure, categorize and hierarchize the world with the white male on top. And all at the expense of the African, Asian and aboriginal peoples."[2] In a city like Toronto (and in a country like Canada),[3] where the multicultural and multiracial mix is perhaps as great as anywhere in the world today, what cannot be ignored is the inevitable change in what the social meaning of a museum might entail. If a museum is a means by which a society represents its relationship to its own history and to that of other cultures (Lumley 1988b: 2), then changes in that society should also be reflected in the institution, whose meaning – like that of the objects within it – is a constructed and negotiated one.

A bit of context for non-Canadians: Canadian society has changed radically since World War II. Outside Québec, its once British majority has sometimes found itself, in large urban centers in particular, in a minority position. Such is the case in Toronto, where the influx of immigrants from southern Europe, South Asia, Africa, the West Indies, and the Middle and Far East has made the city multiracial as well as multiethnic. Since many of the new arrivals have come from other Commonwealth countries, there has been an inevitable new awareness of both similarity and difference in the experience of Empire. If colonialism can be defined as a broad form of structural domination (Stam and Spence 1983: 4), there are going to be many varieties of it: "to be one of the colonized is potentially to be a great many different, but inferior, things, in many different places, at many different times" (Said 1989: 207; see also Said 1993). Many working in the field of postcolonial studies today stress the distinctions even within communities, based on gender, class, race (see Spivak 1990; Donaldson 1992). Others have pointed to what are, in this particular case, important differences between kinds of colonies – for example, between so-called settler colonies[4] like Canada and subjugated ones like the many in Africa (see Tiffin 1983; Brydon 1987; Ashcroft, Griffiths and Tiffin 1989). Both may indeed partake of that "specifically anti-colonial counter-discursive energy" (Slemon 1990: 3) that some see as postcolonial, but there are important differences[5] that are crucial to the responses to "Into the Heart of Africa," differences that obviously involve the "unbridgeable [racial] chasm" (Mishra and Hodge 1991: 408) between white and non-white colonies, as well as the related cultural and historical chasms between settler and subjugated colonies. In the latter, cultural imposition took place on "the body and space" of Empire's "Others" (Slemon 1990: 30; see also Tiffin 1983: 31) through military and bureaucratic power.

While I do not in any way want to underestimate either the multiplicity of past and present responses to Britain and Empire from Canadians of other nationalities or the very real trauma of settler colonies like Canada, which have had to deal with the psychic and cultural (as well as economic) dependency of colonization and have struggled to articulate autonomy through constitutional or cultural means,[6] I cannot help thinking that the problems at the Royal Ontario Museum a few years ago stemmed in part, at least, from the difference between Canada's relation to Empire (as a settler colony)[7] and that of Africa's nations, invaded by European (and in this case, Canadian) powers and subjugated to them by military might or missionary evangelism. While Canada may well want to position itself today oppositionally, as either anticolonial or postcolonial, in order to make a "space-clearing gesture" (Appiah 1991: 348) for its New World self-definition, this particular exhibition – with its focus on the Canadian role in the colonizing of Africa – forced an awareness of English Canada's official historical position *within* Empire. Not everyone liked this new self-image: to borrow Albert Memmi's strong but not inappropriate terms, Canada was suddenly "disfigured into an oppressor, a partial, ... treacherous being, worrying only about ... privileges and their defense" (1965: 89). Canadians (or more specifically white English Canadians) were shown that their own history was not separable from the colonizer's struggle to reconcile "the notions of political freedom cherished by [the] home country with the actual political suppression and disfranchisement of the colonized people" (JanMohamed 1983: 4–5).[8] Black Canadians, as you will see, were positioned rather differently. But, as a nation, Canada was represented as having an uncomfortable dual historical identity, as both colony and colonizing force.

What particularly interests me here about this exhibition and about the explosive affective responses to it is that its ironic and allusive nature was identified early on as part of the problem. Yet, as explored in Chapter 1, the postcolonial and the feminist enterprises, among others, have often turned to irony as a "counter-discourse," as the rhetorical figure of the dialogic whose "function is to project an alternative through which any element of the here-and-now may be shown as contingent, and thereby subject the whole configuration of power within which it took its adversative meaning to the erosive, dialectical power of alterity" (Terdiman 1985: 76–7). As the "linguistic repository of difference," irony, when seen as an oppositional strategy, can work to problematize authority, including those modern assumptions about museums' structures and forms of historical authority. But, to recall irony's transideological politics, irony can work in many other ways too.

An important and, here, relevant theme of much writing on the "new museology" is a call to institutions to make themselves and their publics aware of the history of their collections and of the values embodied therein (see C.S. Smith 1989: 20; Jordanova 1989: 40; P. Wright 1989: 1367; Weil 1990: 52). Against the view that it is high time to abandon the concepts of irony and reflexivity (Jameson 1988b: 64), it has been argued that reflexivity about historical role and museum context can have the potential to raise important political, epistemological and aesthetic issues: the idea is that the "metatext" would make visible to the public the ways to read and make sense of a display as "text," as well as offer the history of the choices leading to it (Lumley 1988b: 13). It seems to be assumed that such internal self-awareness would lead to a liberation from the constraints of modernity's concepts of apolitical scientificity and authority (Greenhalgh 1989: 95), and thus free museums to take on what previously might have been considered risky or controversial subjects, because the public would now be made more aware and less complacent about what they expect to find in a museum. If combined with "wider historical experiences such as explorations of colonial relations" (Durrans 1988: 162), it has been argued, new questions might be provoked. "Into the Heart of Africa" certainly provoked many questions – about colonialism and the relationship between the politics of culture and the politics of meaning and representation (Seidel 1989: 230) – but it was reflexivity itself, like irony, that came under fire. (For a full analysis of this see S.R. Butler 1993: 67–73.)

Actually, almost everything about this exhibition came under fire, from its focus to its subject matter – indeed, even its title. Depending on how you interpret Conrad's *Heart of Darkness*, the echoing of the novel's title in "Into the Heart of Africa" is going to suggest either an adventurist/imperialist perspective or a critique thereof (see Torgovnick 1990). From the start, then, this ideologically freighted doubleness encodes in microcosm the terms of the ensuing conflict over the show's interpretation and evaluation of imperialism. According to the curator, writing *after* the fact, the title was intended to signal that the exhibition would deal "with the past, with journeys, interaction and the disjunction between Canadian images and African realities" (Cannizzo 1991: 151–2). The museum later asserted that its intent was "to explore attitudes of the past but not, for a moment, to suggest that the ROM endorsed the biases of those times."[9] That there was considerable confusion about the realization of this intention was evident within a few months of the opening, however.

Prior to this occasion, the museum's small and fragmentary collection of 375 objects from Central and West Africa had remained in its basement for most of the century, available (as a whole) only to researchers, though parts of it had been displayed in some of the ethnographic galleries. It was fragmentary because it lacked, in the curator's words, "chronological depth, geographical concentration or ethnographic focus" (Cannizzo 1991: 150) and the reasons for this lay in the history of its acquisition. It had come into being largely through bequests from the families of Canadian missionaries and soldiers in the British African colonies at the end of the last century and the beginning of this one. This is where the problems with the collection's unrepresentative nature also began: military men often collected weapons (and I suppose it is not hard to imagine how at least some of them might have been obtained) and missionaries tended to bring home things like hair pins or combs or musical instruments that they could display when fund-raising. In other words, this was not a full collection of a range of African objects; there could be little pretense that it would represent the cultural diversity, social complexity, or artistic achievement of the multiple peoples of Central Africa.[10]

For this reason, the decision was made to foreground in the exhibition both the material limitations of the collection and the history and politics of its coming into being in this one, specifically Canadian, cultural institution. The openly articulated intent was a familiar one in current anthropological theory: to focus on the imperial ideology of those who collected the objects (for which rich archival materials did exist), on how those objects came to enter this museum, and thus on the more general cultural assumptions of museums and of the disciplines of museology, anthropology, and history. In short, the focus was not to be on Africa itself. In addition, given this meta-museological conception, it would seem that the primary intended audience was more academic than general – an impression that was borne out by the catalogue. In accord with that "new museology" being articulated during those very years, it emphasized what the curator later called the "transformational power of context" – the importance to the meaning and significance of objects of the circumstances in which they appear and are understood (Cannizzo 1991: 151). The catalogue constantly called the reader's attention to the history of objects, tracing the cultural transformations of each as its context changed (through what have been called "unanticipated appropriations" [Fisher 1991: 96]) from that of use in African society to being collected by Canadian missionaries or soldiers to being exhibited in the Royal Ontario Museum (known as the ROM). But, as I mentioned, there was yet another transformation to come after the exhibition opened: from museum specimen to political symbol. There are times when the failure of discursive communities to overlap can be particularly risky, and this was one of them.

A few months after the opening, an umbrella group known as the "Coalition for the Truth about Africa" began picketing the museum, handing out leaflets which called the show "a clear and concise attempt to mislead the public and to further tarnish the image of Africa and African people." These handouts also stated that "Into the Heart of Africa" "according to the ROM, is a portrayal of African history." And indeed, despite the catalogue and despite later statements of intent, the museum's advertising brochure describing the exhibition does invite you "on an historical journey through the world of sub-Saharan Africa.... The rich cultural heritage of African religious, social and economic life is celebrated through objects brought back by Canadian missionaries and military men over 100 years ago." But this description misrepresented not so much the *material* as the *focalization* of the exhibition: the focus was never intended to be entirely on Africa itself, but on the material remains of the ideology of Empire in Africa. That "historical journey" was a Canadian one.

Why, then, would the brochure appear to mislead? One reason might be

186

that this was the second one printed. At the cost of over $20,000, the first
was scrapped when consultations with members of the African Canadian
community led to complaints against what was called its "tired, stereotypical
language" about Africa, language which "subtly recalled the glory of the
Imperial Age" (da Breo 1989–90: 33). But the fact remained that the second
brochure, however closer it might have been to representing what the
community would have liked the exhibit to be, actually proved seriously
misleading with respect to the reality. In this way, the initial decision as to
the focalization of the show became a primary point of contention for those
in certain discursive communities. The first printed message at the entry to
the exhibition openly stated that *Canadians* (implicitly, white British
Canadians) were to be the focus, that their "experience of Africa, as seen
in this exhibition, was very different from the way Africans perceived
themselves, their own cultures, and these events." The objects presented, it
continued, "remind us of a little-remembered era of Canada's past." Now,
first-person plural pronouns always function to "hail" a discursive community; here, however, that "us" was problematic, not only in its implicit
exclusions (perhaps some African Canadians did indeed remember that
past[11]), but also because not all of those white Canadians so "hailed" wanted
to be reminded of such a past.

Certainly, the initial, almost empty (and, for me, imperial) blue rooms
labeled "For Crown and Empire" set up the historical relation of Canada to
the British Empire in Africa in the last century (see Plate 7.1). A few objects
(both African and imperial) were presented here in a traditional museum
fashion, isolated in their beauty in glass cases, abstracted from their context
and function. Although everyone connected to the museum[12] insisted that
the irony and reflexivity of the show were meant to signal the detachment
of the institution from the imperial perspective being presented, the textual
markers of that intention were less than clear and self-evident from the
start. In these first rooms, for instance, I could find no semiotic signal to
separate the African from the imperial, despite the later claims that the
intent was to show the beauty of the African objects as a way of refuting "the
19th century [*sic*] Canadian supposition of barbarism" (Cannizzo 1991:
152). But was one also to admire the shining, ribboned British-Canadian
officer's helmet similarly placed in a locked glass case? The curator may
have intended a kind of reflexive, ironic "ethnographizing" effect (Cannizzo 1991: 153), but the context of the museum as a whole (where such
glass cases are un-ironized commonplaces) inevitably worked against such
a result for some viewers. The beauty of the objects and the emptiness of
the room made this feel like a kind of holy place where Empire was being
revered, or at the very least, admired.[13]

What jolted the viewer out of this mood, however, was the fact that, visible
from the entrance, was an enormous, wall-sized enlargement of an image
of a mounted British soldier thrusting his sword into the breast of an

Plate 7.1 "For Crown & Empire," installation from "Into the heart of Africa" exhibition, 1989–90, Royal Ontario Museum, Toronto, Canada. Photo courtesy of the Royal Ontario Museum.

African warrior (see Plate 7.2). This was labeled (none too readably) "Lord Beresford's Encounter with a Zulu," and it wouldn't be hard to imagine viewers engaging differently with the named aristocratic soldier than with the generic Zulu victim. The text posted nearby identified this as the cover of the *Illustrated London News* of 1879. As you can imagine, the impact of this kind of image is going to be different on a small catalogue page, where it is also reproduced, than it is on a large wall. As many commentators subsequently noted, the violence of this representation worked not to produce a response against jingoistic Victorian imperialism (as was intended[14]), but to turn the tables against the exhibition itself for perpetuating precisely such representations. In today's culture, where visual images may indeed make more of an impression than printed text, and in an institution visited by schoolchildren of all ages and races who just might not stop to read the contextualizing accompanying texts, the placing and size of this image were, at the very least, signs of semiotic inattention or inexperience. While the relationship of text to image is a general

Plate 7.2 "Lord Beresford's Encounter with a Zulu." Cover of the *Illustrated London News*, No. 2099, Vol. LXXV, Saturday, 6 September 1879. Photo courtesy of the Royal Ontario Museum.

problem for all museum exhibits, here it proved critical because many African Canadian visitors could not bring themselves to go beyond this violent representation of their race's history.

After the contentious "Military Hall" section over which this image loomed, a relatively small area called "The Life History of Objects" constituted the only explicitly meta-museological part of the exhibition itself, though this was a major focus of the catalogue. The reconstituted front hallway of a Canadian house revealed the movement of African objects (such as spears and shields) from being spoils of war to becoming pure (if exotic) decoration – before being donated to the museum. This section indirectly raised questions about appropriation and exploitation, but did not offer any answers or even any extended commentary (Schild-krout 1991: 19). The ambiguities made possible by the general rhetorical strategy of indirection here even allowed one visitor to suggest that, for her, this home setting was a kind of humanizing of the experience of imperialism (Crean 1991: 26).

The next section took the form of a large, bright, white, cross-shaped room, labeled "Civilization, Commerce, and Christianity," and in it were presented the artifacts collected by missionaries (who thought they were bearing "light" to the "dark continent," as accompanying texts explained). There were also photographs of these evangelical Christians with their African converts. The last and largest area of the exhibition was introduced by a reconstruction of an Ovimbundu village compound from Angola, wherein some of the objects seen in cabinets elsewhere were inserted into a simulated context of use. At the entrance of the final large room, containing drums, masks, textiles, head-dresses, weapons, and musical instruments (with headphones to listen to African music), was a reflexive message attesting to the "impossibility actually to reconstruct another cultural reality in a museum. The artifacts you see here are displayed according to their 'function' or 'form' in a way that would be quite familiar to late nineteenth-century museum-goers, but not the people who made them. The things are theirs, the arrangement is not." Such a sign was intended to mark the change in interpretive emphasis at this point in the exhibition, as the theme changed from the history of the collection to the objects themselves which were said to "speak of the varied economies, political or cosmological complexities, and artistry of their African crea-tors" (Cannizzo 1991: 156). Yet the problem with calling attention to the fictional or artificial arrangement of the objects in this particular space became evident when you considered it in the context of the *rest* of this museum, where such traditional arrangements are still the norm for even the twentieth-century museum-goer. Given that, in Western culture, priority is usually signaled by position, there was yet another potential conflict between the intention – to show that "African cultural life and historical experience were not being reduced to a codicil of imperial history"

190

(Cannizzo 1991: 152) – and the fact that this section did come *after* the one that focused on imperial acquisition.

The corridor leading out of the exhibition housed a scattered and miscellaneous collection of small photographs of Africans today, perhaps in an attempt to give a sense that, although the collection may be historical, the realities of urbanization and industrialization have brought many changes to African society. Just outside the doorway was a special African museum-store "boutique" which eased the visitor (who could now become a "collector" too) back into Canadian consumer society, thereby coming full circle, since the initial (conventional) sign thanking corporate sponsors set up (for me, as for others) an unintended ironic frame: if anyone should have been acknowledged as being those without whom this show would not have been possible, it was the Africans who made the objects displayed.

Even my brief description (itself hardly innocent of interpretation) might offer some clues as to why "Into the Heart of Africa" managed to engage so much strong emotion in so many very different people. As one critic remarked:

> What was most amazing was that the exhibition offended audiences from all parts of the political spectrum: missionaries whose colleagues were depicted in the exhibition, the descendants of colonial officers whose collections were shown . . ., and most strongly, Africans and people of African descent who saw the exhibition as racist and insulting. The exhibition was also offensive to some within another, somewhat less vocal group, that is, historians of Africa, art historians, and anthropologists working in universities and museums.
>
> (Schildkrout 1991: 17)

One might add to that list even liberal, white Canadians who thought of themselves as multiculturally tolerant and even postcolonially oppositional. But what specifically enraged and offended people? From all accounts (see, for a summary, Fulford 1991: 24), the anger of many was provoked as much by the visual representation of verbal texts as by any actual objects or pictures. Here it was again irony's edge that cut, but in ways different from those I have explored so far. From the start, explanatory signs presented certain words framed in quotation marks. An interpretive conflict was set up at once: were these citations (and thus historically authenticated and validated) or were they echoic mentions to be read ironically? Words like "the unknown continent," "barbarous," and "primitive" were placed in these quotation marks, but the problem was that so too were metaphors, titles, and some object descriptions. In other words, the proliferation of quotation marks made the visitor wonder whether those placed around words like "Dark Continent" and "primitive" could or should be read as markers intended both to signal ironic distance (see Chung 1990: 7) and also to act as accurate citations – in other words, to represent the colonial

191

perspective that the *post*colonial exhibition wanted to show it did not share (Nazareth 1990: 11). In the museum's own initial news release, there was arguably some awareness that people might not know exactly how to interpret such quotation marks, for it added "*what was then called by some* the 'unknown continent'" (emphasis mine). The curator, in a later article, likewise wrote of "the *alleged* barbarity of 'savage customs'" (Cannizzo 1991: 154, emphasis mine). Of course, inverted commas or quotation marks are a commonplace rhetorical technique (used to disclaim and to distance, while still echoing) in "new" museological theorizing (and even, obviously, in this chapter). But when the context is not academic or museological (and depending on your discursive community), the interpretation of these ironizing quotation marks may differ. For some visitors to "Into the Heart of Africa" they were simply disapproving disclaimers;[15] for others they were a form of devious "sugarcoating."[16] For many, irony was also simply an inappropriate strategy to use. One viewer, whose great-uncle was featured as one of the Canadian military, found that they created too subtle an irony, one "lost on those who can't (or don't) read the explanatory texts." She added: "it is also a pretty limp way to examine a subject as grave as racially motivated genocide" (Crean 1991: 25). The Curriculum Adviser on Race Relations and Multiculturalism for the Toronto Board of Education went even further, stating: "In dealing with issues as sensitive as cultural imperialism and racism, the use of irony is a highly inappropriate luxury."[17] And yet, as explored earlier, postcolonial theorists have argued that irony is one of the most effective ways of dealing with precisely such difficult issues – at least when used oppositionally from within. But there was the transideological rub: this irony was perceived as coming from a colonial source, even if a self-deconstructing one, and even if the irony was largely at the expense of imperialists not Africans.

One instance of ironic citational signaling was mentioned in almost every public response to this exhibition:[18] it was the relation between a missionary photograph of a (named and standing) white woman watching a number of (unnamed and crouching) black women doing washing and its caption – "Taken in Nigeria about 1910, this photograph shows missionary Mrs. Thomas Titcombe giving African women 'a lesson in how to wash clothes'. African labour was the mainstay of mission economies." To the interpretation offered in the Coalition's handout – "Did Africans not know how to wash before the arrival of Europeans?" – one white Canadian reviewer replied: "An observant reader will note that the words 'a lesson in how to wash clothes' are in quotation marks. The description is offered as evidence, not of the actual activity, but of Mrs. Titcombe's intentions and sense of superiority."[19] But I hasten to add the obvious: the comprehension of irony has never been quite that simple. The curator might have intended the labels in this "Civilization, Commerce, and Christianity" section to show "the sense of cultural superiority" inherent in the missionary goals

192

(Cannizzo 1991: 155), but if colonial discourse contains both colonizer and colonized, caught in a problematics of indeterminacy and ambivalence (Bhabha 1984), then does this sort of irony re-enact (even as it critiques) "an ambivalent mode of knowledge and power" (Bhabha 1990: 71)? Does this particular irony embody Manichaean dualisms or subvert them? Or, does it depend on who is doing the interpreting? And, on a more pragmatic level, what about visitor expectations about the conventions of museum labeling? In an institution where the norm is that visual messages and verbal texts convey the *same* meaning, the risks taken through ironic disjunction here are great. And, of course, what if people do not read the labels at all?[20]

Another related and equally problematic part of the exhibition was a small white room where visitors could sit to watch a slide show and listen to a male voice give a 7-minute recreation (from missionary archives) of a magic-lantern illustrated lecture called "In Livingstone's Footsteps." This was presented as what a missionary might have said, in 1919, to his Ontario protestant congregation when fund-raising for his African mission. The fictional context was asserted orally at the outset and again at the end. In addition, outside the room was a notice that read:

> The sense of cultural superiority and paternalism that you will hear in this fictional narrative was characteristic of the missionary worldview at the time. So was the genuine spirit of adventure and the sincere belief that missionaries were bringing "light" to the "dark continent".

But what if you did not read the sign? What if you missed the beginning or end of the long 7-minute tape? Well, you certainly heard the "cultural superiority and paternalism," but without the ironizing, contextualizing frame. And, even more unfortunately, the paternalistic voice could be heard as you walked through this part of the exhibition, aurally framing your viewing, driving one exasperated visitor to exclaim that the "unctuous voice delivering highly derogatory commentary could have been that of the ROM's director on his intercom for all I knew" (Crean 1991: 25).

However didactic or heavy-handed[21] some people might have found the ironies in the exhibition, it was not by any means a matter of their being paradoxically too subtle for the protesters; nor do I think the negative response was the result of willful misreading.[22] One commentator (Schildkrout 1991: 21) felt that the ROM acknowledged the failure of the ironies but implied that it was the fault of an unsophisticated audience. The Coalition for the Truth about Africa argued that the subtleties of irony could not compete with the power of images of subjugation;[23] yet some of the demonstrators themselves used irony in their protests to claim a position. This too was an example of irony that was interpreted in a different way than was intended. For still others, the show's ironies were both scholarly and subtle and therefore elitist (Mackey 1991: 46–7). Irony

193

has always been risky, but in this context the stakes were particularly high for this institution: this was its first major African exhibit; the city was facing racial tensions over police shootings of black youths. Even if irony were deemed appropriate here, the desirability of framing it less ambiguously became increasingly evident.

Framing helps to delimit response, of course; nevertheless, response also depends on the particular audience doing the responding. The very indirection of the ironies here might well presuppose an audience (liberal, white, European Canadian) that can – or is willing to – read between the lines: that is, an audience that positions itself as anticolonial or postcolonial and multicultural, and not as colonial and racist. Is there not a danger, however, that even this audience might be lulled into thinking that the irony has done its critical work for it, and that it need *only* bother to question those words set apart in quotation marks?[24] After all, there are no ironic quotation marks around the description of David Livingstone as a hero – though many Africans (were their point of view offered) might insist upon their appropriateness (Crean 1991: 25). Do the intended ironies implicitly rely too much on an audience that can be affectively and politically detached from the pain represented in the exhibition's visual images (Austin-Smith 1990: 52)?

The issues of the so-called "misreading" of irony and of the appropriateness of its very use on this occasion are issues which engage in complex ways the exclusionary potential of irony – and therefore of the anger it can cause, as seen in Chapter 2. But the affective charge of anger can also extend to the target of the ironies, of course. And, indeed, many did protest the stereotyped portrayal of the Canadian missionaries in the exhibit, arguing the case for their more complex and frequently oppositional relationship with colonial authorities.[25] But this was a muted protest compared to the Coalition's, which argued that African Canadian children came away from "Into the Heart of Africa" with a negative impression of black history, with the idea that Africans did not know how to wash their clothes or comb their hair before the whites arrived.[26] No one, to my knowledge, however, argued that white, British Canadian children came away embarrassed or traumatized to learn that their families had been guilty of everything from paternalism and exploitation to extermination. Yet columnists did note that, if the exhibition was hard on any group, "it was the white missionaries and soldiers; their prejudices and ignorance are documented in some detail";[27] one black reviewer even suggested that the exhibit promoted racism against whites who were made to look ignorant and dangerous.[28] As another viewer summed it up: "old-time Christian missionaries are now almost beyond the range of human sympathy" (Fulford 1991: 19).

As I have been arguing throughout this study, irony is a discursive strategy that depends on context and on the identity and position of both the ironist

194

and the audience. So, a feminist critic, writing in a book about women and comedy, can begin an article entitled "Jane Austen: Irony and Authority" with: "It is a truth universally acknowledged, right now, that language is involved in giving and taking both power and pleasure" (Brownstein 1988: 57), and expect that her readers (themselves self-selected and having at least read her title) will understand both the allusion to the opening of *Pride and Prejudice* and the irony. If it is true that jokes do not travel well because of the need for shared knowledge (Chiaro 1992: 10–12), then this is even more the case with irony. I have suggested that discursive communities do not come into being as the result of sharing irony together; they are what make irony possible in the first place. The many discursive communities to which we each belong in our different ways can, of course, be based on things like language, race, gender, class, and nationality – but they might also encompass all the other elements that constitute (or are made to constitute) our identities. The infinite variations and combinations possible are what make irony both relatively rare and in need of markers or signals. As suggested in Chapter 3, it is almost a miracle that irony is ever understood as an ironist might intend it to be: all ironies, in fact, are probably unstable ironies.

Those intentionally deployed in "Into the Heart of Africa" were received very differently by different discursive communities, as was the show as a whole. To a black lawyer and activist, the effect of seeing Africa through the eyes of those who colonized and killed was chilling;[29] to a self-described "white Canadian liberal," the exhibit was "a recognizable piece of British-Canadian history" – not a show about Africa and not about the present.[30] Research on the complexity of how people experience an exhibit suggests that responses might be idiosyncratic, but that the general public (whatever that might be) is very likely going to respond differently from what professional critics and curators might expect (Durrans 1988: 163). One of the reasons is that they usually belong to different discursive communities: "visitors bring a multiplicity of different attitudes and expectations and experiences to the reading of an artefact, so that their comprehension of it is individualized" (C.S. Smith 1989: 19; see also P. Wright 1989: 133–4). So too is their affective response to it. Where certain white Canadians might find the exhibit a self-searching, ironic examination[31] of historical intolerance, some black Canadians saw the "painful detritus of savage exploitation and attempted genocide" and a perpetuation of racist attitudes of white superiority.[32] Even the use of irony was read by some as belonging to a white culture's model of discourse,[33] and its use (and alleged incomprehension) seen as a replication of the missionaries' attitudes (Austin-Smith 1990: 52). In other words, this kind of objection goes well beyond the issue of whether, in this particular case, irony was used *well* to question its very appropriateness as a discursive strategy.

As a white Canadian visitor of European (though Italian, not British) background, I certainly felt that I was being "hailed" by the references to "Canadians" in the show, in the press releases, and also in the brochure, where the late nineteenth century in Africa was described as a "turbulent but little-known period in history." The point was made well by the visitor who pointed out: "For whom ... was this period merely turbulent, and to whom is the period so little-known?" (Crean 1991: 25). The answer is: white Canadians ... perhaps. The answer is likely *not*: the black protester who said, "All my life I've been looking for my roots, I come here looking for them – and you've shown me nothing" (cited in Fulford 1991: 23).

The exhibition's configuration of the "imagined community" (B. Anderson 1983) called Canada was a limited one, to be sure. But race was not the only issue involved in this complex "lack of fit" of discursive communities. If position in "social space" determines the point of view of each individual agent (Bourdieu 1990: 130), then your perspective on "Into the Heart of Africa" was not going to be separable from things like class and education. If economic power is mobilized through symbolic power – which comes from having and accumulating "cultural capital" (Bourdieu 1984) – then the very question of who it is who regularly goes to a museum becomes a relevant issue. Surveys in North America and Europe suggest that the most frequent adult museum visitors are well educated, middle class,[34] and relatively affluent. They may visit as tourists, volunteers, teachers (with student groups), self-educators, or researchers. The question is whether, despite this relative homogeneity, you should ever assume that visitors will necessarily share the "values, the assumptions and the intellectual pre-occupations that have guided not only the choice and presentation of exhibitions, but also, more fundamentally, the selection and acquisition of objects" (Hooper-Greenhill 1988: 215). When the audience includes African Canadians, from whose ancestors' cultures came the objects displayed in "Into the Heart of Africa," such a question is not a politically neutral one. Many commentators noted that the show seemed to be designed for and aimed at white, educated, liberal-minded people with an interest in museums and anthropology;[35] to assume any broader consensus on an exhibition of African objects was, perhaps, not to take sufficiently into account the growing black population of Toronto and the different discursive communities to which people might well belong[36] (and along with those, the different expectations, different assumptions, different associations with museums in general).

In an explanatory article written after the closing of the exhibition, the curator herself defined museums as social institutions which "cannot be divorced from the historical context in which they developed, and their collections occasionally reflect the violence and disruptive social forces characterizing the European colonization of Africa" (Cannizzo 1991: 154). While that violence was made more than clear in some of the visual images within the exhibition, what was missing from "Into the Heart of Africa" was this very kind of overt statement of judgment. The indirection and obliqueness of its irony worked to render the exhibition's position ambiguous. The use of irony might well have been intended as a way of subverting the ideology of colonialism from within – and thereby also avoiding openly offending the missionary and military families (and their descendants) who had loaned and donated so much to the museum.[37] Yet, the very depiction of racism (in the past) was interpreted by some as – not only Eurocentric – but racist (in the present).[38] The problem of embodying that which one is trying to analyse and the difference between endorsing and examining are pragmatic issues of crucial importance in postcolonial theory today. In this exhibition, Africans tended to be represented as passive, as victims, as physically smaller and positioned lower in pictures: this was because such indeed was the view of the colonizers. But the difficulty was that it was also the *only* view offered in the exhibition; so too was the colonizers' the only authenticated voice. Presumably, the assumption was that the visitors would be able to distinguish between the voice represented on the labels (some in quotation marks) and the voice of the museum. There was much evidence of a certain confusion over this, however. And, after all, why should visitors assume, knowing all that these colonial collectors had given to the museum, that the institution was necessarily (or even likely) going to be ironic about or critical of them?

The ideology of collecting itself has become a major interest of "new" museology, it is true. Theorists have studied issues such as the gendered and historically specific way in which the passion to collect, preserve and display has been articulated, the role of collections in the processes of Western identity formation (Clifford 1990: 144), and the representativeness and presentation of collections. There has been a certain amount of demystification of what I earlier referred to as the "modern" – and unacknowledged – institutional practices that, in the language of the "new" ethnology, might be expressed in such terms as: "The collector discovers, acquires, salvages objects. The objective world is given, not produced, and thus the historical relations of power in the work of acquisition are occulted. The *making* of meaning in museum classifications and display is mystified as adequate *representation*" (Clifford 1990: 144). It was in order to contest precisely this ideological position of modernity that the catalogue of "Into the Heart of Africa" argued:

> A museum collection may be thought of as a cultural text, one that can be read to understand the underlying cultural and ideological assumptions that have influenced its creation, selection, and display. Within such a collection, objects act as an expression not only of the worldviews of those who chose to make and use them, but also of those who chose to collect and exhibit them.
>
> (Cannizzo 1989: 62)

197

The catalogue directly addressed issues such as the museum as cultural "charnel house" (ibid.: 80), full of the remains of dead civilizations; the decontextualized museum display as "cultural vandalism" (ibid.: 84) and aestheticism (ibid.: 88); and the danger of partial collections promoting stereotypes (ibid.: 86). This was a theoretically aware document in that it did indeed work to show how the "relations of power whereby one portion of humanity can select, value, and collect the pure products of others need to be criticized and transformed" (Clifford 1988: 213).

As I understand the term to be invoked today, to be unequivocally *postcolonial*, however, the exhibition would have had to present and then make a judgment about the effects of colonization, not simply outline its intentions and then imply an indirect, oblique evaluative attitude. Let me give you an example of what I see as emblematic of the rhetorical strategy of the show as a whole. This is the curator's later description of the Europeanization of African social structures, dress and habitation: "These changes would transform the women from producers of baskets, garden foods and pottery into consumers of soaps, spoons, forks, while tying them tightly to the developing mission economy" (Cannizzo 1991: 155). Whether you read this as ironic would depend upon your valuing of soaps, spoons, and forks (as well as "consuming"). Likewise, the subsequent statement that such practices "weakened alliances between lineages, discouraged the intergenerational and polygynous family, emphasized the loyalty of the couple to each other at the expense of kindred, and created a different concept of privacy" would not necessarily be read as critical at all within certain discursive communities. Indeed, it would not be hard to read it as a (modern) authoritative-sounding assertion of anthropological or historical "fact." A black writer responded to this strategy by saying that the exhibit "used the propaganda of the period without proper explanation or preamble. [The curator] did not want to manipulate the material, but she ended up implanting racist images because the critique of 'intellectual arrogance' did not come through. People missed it" (Ayanna Black, cited in Crean 1991: 27). Sometimes, they might have "missed" an intended, critical irony because it was not adequately marked, because it thus remained ambiguous in its silence about the effect of such "arrogance" upon the Africans. Because the only perspective offered was that of the colonizers, you were indeed told that the missionary involved in the social transformations described above never understood the effect his changes of custom had on kinship alliances, for example (Cannizzo 1989: 35), but you were not told what those effects actually were. As one anthropologist reviewing the exhibit remarked, it went to great lengths to remind you of the process by which objects arrived in the museum as the result of Canadians' participation in an act of conquest, but:

What about this conquest? Was it brutal, violent and shameful? Or

198

should we, when passing the soldiers' suits and the prizes the soldiers stole from sovereign African kingdoms, swell with pride and admiration for men who braved great distances and terrible dangers to subdue fierce natives? The exhibition is strangely silent here, as if there were no moral or political issues involved.

(Freedman 1990: 40)

For a museum to choose not to take an unequivocal stand might be interpreted as a refusal of any single, modern, "master narrative" of Truth; but from a postcolonial perspective – given the position of authority of the institution – the possible reading was more problematic. What might be read as irony or ambiguity becomes, from a postcolonial perspective, potential evasion.[39] To go one step further, for those, like the Coalition, seeking the "Truth about Africa," ambiguity within an institution associated with cultural and educational authority itself makes a kind of truth-claim. In the face of the Coalition's tactical desire for what might (awkwardly, if aptly) be called an emancipatory meta-narrative articulated from a position of strategic essentialism,[40] the institution (in press releases) fell back on very "modern" assertions of historical accuracy and curatorial expertise, thereby arguably undermining even the exhibition's reflexive and ironic deconstructive intentions.

However, it must also be said that, for *this* visitor, those intentions were not always consistently realized in the exhibition itself. The curator may indeed have believed that museums are fictional in nature, that "the meaning of their collection is generated in the interaction between the curator, the object, and the visitor" (Cannizzo 1991: 151). But both within the structure of the exhibit and in the response to the protests, this particular museum did not live up to its definition as a "negotiated" reality. There was none of the dialogic museum mode that theorists (such as Tchen 1992) have argued should replace the impersonal, objective, distanced observer-model of modernity: there was no answering African voice in "Into the Heart of Africa." While implicitly acknowledging that, in theory, "culture" is indeed relational, "an inscription of communicative processes that exist, historically, *between* subjects in relations of power" (Clifford 1986b: 15), the exhibit none the less never let the other side be heard. One did hear the interaction between the museum officials of 1989 and the collectors of a century before,[41] but none at all with the Africans whose objects are presented. This was ethnography ("in which European metropolitan subjects present to themselves their others" [usually their conquered others]) and not "autoethnography" ("in which people undertake to describe themselves in ways that engage with representations others have made of them") (Pratt 1991: 35; see also hooks 1990: 150–2).

Given the complex public stands taken by both sides on this issue of voice, more communication took place, on this occasion, through the press

199

than face to face. Both the Coalition and the museum implicitly acknowledged, in different ways, that communication always involves political interaction and thus power differences.[42] It is this realization that has led museological theory to advocate more community consultation and dialogue in the mounting of exhibitions.[43] But the specificities of context are relevant and important here, for in 1989 Canadian public institutions were still trying to deal with the implications of the controversy over the boycott by the Lubicon Lake First Nations of the Native art exhibition, "The Spirit Sings," at the Glenbow Gallery during the 1988 Calgary Olympics.[44] There have been generally recognized examples of more successful dialogue, however (see Vogel 1991). For instance, a small gallery, the Valentine Museum in Richmond, Virginia, did consult with its community to discover what people felt they needed to learn about their past. One result, in the same year as "Into the Heart of Africa," was "Jim Crow: Racism and Reaction in the New South." Unlike the ironic Canadian exhibition, this one was frequently confrontational, judgmental, and even unpleasant in its openly anticolonial dealings with racist attitudes.[45]

Museums are finding still other reflexive ways to deal with the postcolonial implications of collecting and exhibiting. Having been given 100 pieces of African art from a private collection, the University of British Columbia Museum of Anthropology in 1991 mounted a show entitled "Fragments," the premise of which was that it is "neither possible nor ethical, in the 1990s, to exhibit Africa; what we can and do exhibit in 'Fragments' are historic African objects valued by a Canadian museum and a Canadian collector" (Halpin 1991: 2). In a challenge to the "modern" anonymous, expert narrative voice of labels and text, this exhibit offered instead a plurality of voices and perspectives on the care, handling, and collecting of African objects, as well as on Africa itself. In a more confrontational postcolonial vein, African American artist Fred Wilson mounted, in "The Other Museum," an overt and bold critique of colonialism, stereotyping and racial misrepresentation. Visitors were given a brochure upon entering the gallery that explained this intention to expose prejudices and even announced how irony would be used to label objects and parody the presentation of a natural history museum. In addition, the brochure's style was a parody of a *National Geographic* magazine, and, at the entrance to the displays, an upside-down map of the world signaled the entry into the realm of ironic inversion. This may indeed be heavy-handed – Dan and Ibo masks were blindfolded and gagged with imperial flags – but there was little chance of mistaking the artist's intent (Schildkrout 1991: 22). It is also the case, however, that this exhibit was considered as *art* and viewed in an art gallery, not *ethnography* presented in a museum: visitors' expectations about politicized art exhibitions are not the same as those about anthropological or historical ones. By mounting this particular show in an art gallery, Wilson also reversed the usual associations with that location: works displayed in galleries are traditionally provided with no cultural background information (as is normal in ethnographic museums), as if "great art" is recognizable by some universal standards (Clifford 1988: 200). Context is crucial for all interpretation, of course, but especially so for risky ironic interpretation. It is not as if television and film have not represented images of imperialist conquest of Africans for years and in ways much more offensive than "Into the Heart of Africa," with its reflexivity and indirection. But part of the heritage of modernity is that museums are places of special authority and respect, and therefore have special cultural responsibilities that come with their institutional positions of cultural and educational power within the communities in which they exist. No single exhibit is going to change this situation overnight, no matter how powerful its critique and deconstruction. However, if museums really are "historical-cultural theaters of memory" (Clifford 1990: 164), more than institutional memory will have to be dramatized on their stages. In deciding not to focus the Royal Ontario Museum exhibit on Africa itself, but on the emissaries of Empire who journeyed "into the heart of Africa," the curator, one might argue, was actually being careful to avoid appropriation and to stay within the boundaries of her unavoidably white Canadian point of view. Yet, in some eyes, she managed to perpetuate the very situation she sought to critique, offering yet another example of the controlling colonizing gaze. Yet, silence about the collection's imperial origins was likely not the answer either. It seems to have been this choice of one single focalization (and its consequences) that provoked much of the controversy. An American African Studies professor, Molefi Asante, is said to have compared the choice here to presenting the Holocaust from the viewpoint of the Nazis.[46] There is no doubt that many felt that those once subjected to the gaze of Empire should have been given a voice. An important line of argument in the "new" museology – one of particular interest to the understanding of irony's workings – is that "[e]xhibitors cannot *represent* cultures. Exhibitors can be tactful but stimulating impresarios, but exhibition is a social occasion involving at least three active terms" – makers of objects, exhibitors of those objects, and interpreting viewers (Baxandall 1991: 41).

The "Epilogue" to the exhibition catalogue makes for sad reading in the aftermath of the initial decision about single focalization:

> By studying the museum as an artifact, reading collections as cultural texts, and discovering the life histories of objects, it has become possible to understand something of the complexities of cross-cultural encounters. In the same process, the intricacies of different cultural configurations are revealed in objects through which various African peoples have expressed not only their individual artistry but also their deepest communal concerns. Finally, by placing in context the relationships, however brief, problematic, and painful, that developed

201

as Canadian soldiers and missionaries travelled into the heart of Africa, it has become clear that the past is part of the present.

(Cannizzo 1989: 92)

When a Canadian reviewer began her analysis with the words, "We consider ourselves a former colony, not a colonizing power,"[47] she put her finger on how difficult it was for some members of the white, English Canadian community to see that past as "part of the present." According to the Coalition, black Canadians had no trouble at all seeing the continuity; nor might Irish, Scots, Native or some other Canadians. The curator intended (white) Canadians to be "horrified by the Canadian participation in this history. Remember that until fairly recently, Canada was a part of the British Empire and participated fully in all aspects of it, including negative ones" (Cannizzo and da Breo 1989–90: 37). The exhibit certainly did place British Canadians and Torontonians right in the middle of Empire, citing James Morris's *Pax Britannica* about Canada at the end of the nineteenth century: "Hundreds of thousands of British Canadians regarded the imperial saga as part of their own national heritage. The excitement of the New Imperialism was almost as intense in Toronto as it was in London" (repeated in Cannizzo 1989: 14). (See Plate 7.3.)

To turn that around, today, the excitement of the new *postcolonial* critique is equally intense in Toronto (or in Canada as a whole) as elsewhere in the once colonized world, and, perhaps for that very reason, there are times when a reflexive, ironic challenge is either not appropriate or simply not strong enough, no matter how demystificatory it might be of modernity's assumptions and even if there had not been those unfortunate internal inconsistencies and difficulties.[48] The question of irony's appropriateness in this situation was one raised often: "Given the difficulty of using irony, the ROM would have been well advised to consider whether there really was a need to couch a critique of colonialism in ironic terms" (Schildkrout 1991: 21). But it is a question that has haunted the history of irony too (see McKee 1974: 91) and one that consistently points to the transideological nature of irony's politics. The many-voiced play of said and unsaid can be used to ironize the single-voicing of authoritative discourse – no matter what the politics of that discourse. And not only those on the receiving end are perhaps going to find this inappropriate. But, are there times when indirection is wise? Or is irony's evasiveness always suspect? To what end can irony work – both in intentions and in attributions? What are the dangers, in the extreme, "of putting the whole world in quotation marks" (Clifford 1986a: 25)? What is at stake when irony happens – and when it does not?

These are among the questions that have interested me in this chapter and in the book as a whole. Irony's transideological politics complicate the theorizing of irony mightily, and part of the reason is irony's edge. The affective responses provoked by "Into the Heart of Africa" show that viewers

202

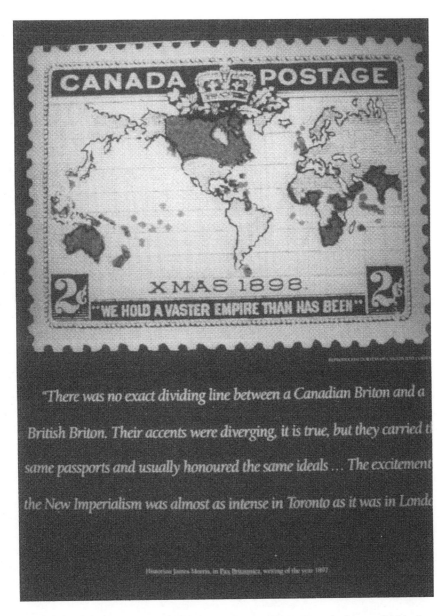

Plate 7.3 Canadian stamp and explanatory panel from "Into the heart of Africa" exhibition, 1989–90, Royal Ontario Museum, Toronto, Canada. Photo courtesy of the Royal Ontario Museum.

203

(like readers and listeners) are not passive receivers; they are interpreting agents, with the emphasis on agency and, thus, on action. Because of this there were real, material consequences for the intending ironist. I raise this issue of the risks of irony most forcefully here at the end of this study primarily because it is too easy to forget the dangers in the face of the valorization of irony's subversive potential by much feminist, gay and lesbian, postcolonial, and poststructuralist[49] theory and practice. While it is likely the case that "[e]very act of saying is a momentary intersection of the 'said' and the 'unsaid'" (Tyler 1978: 459), the particular intersection – in the communicative space set up by both meaning and affect – that makes irony happen is a highly unstable one, sometimes even a dangerous one. Whether it will become too dangerous, too risky is for the future to decide. Will there ever be another – safe – "age of irony"? Did one ever really exist?

NOTES

INTRODUCTION

1 See Furst 1984: 47; Wilde 1981: 178.
2 See Japp 1983: 90–106; D. Knox 1989: 97–138; Thirlwall 1833.
3 See Alford 1984; Allemann 1969: 55–82; Behler 1971 and 1972; Conrad 1978;
   Eagleton 1990: 123, 140–2; Furst 1984; Garber 1988; Haas and Mohrlüder 1973:
   143–80; Japp 1983: 106–67; Mellor 1979 and 1980; Muecke 1969: 159; Prang
   1972; Schlegel 1971; Simpson 1979; Sperry, 1977; Strohschneider-Kohrs 1960;
   Turner 1969; W. Vaughan 1979; Wellek 1955: 14–17, 298–300.
4 See Lukács 1971: 93.
5 See Behler 1990: vii, 73; Handwerk 1985: 5; C.D. Lang 1988.
6 See C. Brooks 1971; Wimsatt and Brooks 1964: 747; Ransom 1941: 96; Bové
   1980: 95–6.
7 See Gellner 1974: 193; Gass 1978: 144–5; Fussell 1975; Hofmannsthal 1923;
   Niebuhr 1952; White 1973: 38.
8 See Booth 1961: 372, and 1974: 12n; Burke 1968: 104–5; Frye 1963: 11;
   Glicksberg 1969; Ortega y Gasset 1956: 13; Siegle 1986; Spanos 1987; Thurley
   1974; Wilde 1981.
9 See Behler 1990: 113–31; Shapiro and Shapiro 1988: 17.
10 See, respectively, Smyth 1986; C.D. Lang 1988; Handwerk 1985 and Wilde 1981;
   Kierkegaard 1971 and Schlegel 1971; Worcester 1960: 90.
11 Monson 1988: 541; see, for instance, N. Knox 1972: 53; Muecke 1969.
12 See Bergson 1971; Birney 1985: 20–35; Büchner 1941; Dane 1991; Gaunt 1989;
   Good 1965; Green 1979; Hagen 1992; D. Knox 1989; N. Knox 1961; Muecke
   1969 and 1970/1982: 14–32; Novak and Davis 1966; Ong 1982a; Rowland 1985;
   Schoentjes 1993; Sedgwick 1948; Sharpe 1959; A.R. Thompson 1948; Thomson
   1926.
13 Dyson 1965: ix; Muecke 1969: 3; Thomson 1926: 171.
14 See Rorty 1990: 639, 636; McCarthy 1990b: 647.
15 For example, Almansi 1984; Dyson 1965.
16 See M. Ross 1986: 23; Frye 1982: 73; Kilbourn 1988: 24–5; Hutcheon 1991 and
   1992.

205

7 THE END(S) OF IRONY: THE POLITICS OF APPROPRIATENESS

1 John McNeill, *Globe and Mail*, 21 September 1990, C9. See also Young 1993: 178.

2 Marlene Nourbese Philip, *Toronto Star*, 14 January 1991, A4.

3 Since 1971, Canada has had an official government policy of what is called "multiculturalism"; in 1988 the "Act for the Preservation and Enhancement of Multiculturalism in Canada" was passed. The term has always been accepted as a description of the demographic realities of Canada, but the policy and law have been seen in different ways. Some view it still as a federal government ploy to divert attention from Québec separatist energies; others accuse it of assimilationist aims. The word and policy certainly gained currency when Canada's unofficial self-image as a northern nation was being challenged from within by the immigration of people from southern European and non-white nations, largely those of the British Commonwealth. The law has been called custodial, paternalistic, anachronistic, reductive, retentive; it has been said to create an enforced inclusiveness and a kind of ethnicity industry. But its defenders argue that, as an ideal of civic tolerance, it has liberal and liberating possibilities. It makes room for diversity and specificity as the defining characteristics of a nation that seems to feel it is in need of self-definition.

4 To generalize, settler colonies are those in which new arrivals (in Canada's case, from Europe) could be motivated by any number of reasons – from enforced exile to adventure; they often marginalized or exterminated the indigenous populations, rather than merging with them; they transplanted and internalized (while deracinating) Old World culture and traditions, including language, of course.

5 Among these is the relation settler colonies have with their aboriginal peoples, of course. In addition, each settler colony, like each forcibly colonized nation, has its own history that cannot be ignored. As the example of the USA and Canada reveals, it matters whether a nation has fought for political independence or has evolved a form of government out of imperial institutions: breaks and ruptures force an articulation of difference and enable the creation of a discourse of identity. This may explain why Canada perpetually lives out its identity crisis.

6 One way to think of the difference here is as between being considered (or considering yourself) "inferior" by metropolitan standards because your "official" culture is generally seen as continuous with and derivative of Empire's, and doing so because your indigenous culture is radically different from that of the imperial power (and thus suppressed). My thanks to Shirley Neuman for this concise and cogent articulation of the distinction.

7 I am bracketing here Canada's problematic and likely neo-colonial relationship with the United States, a nation whose cultural, political and economic hegemony and whose relation to multinational capitalism have rendered it one of the new imperial nations of the world. See Jara and Spadaccini 1989: 10; Hitchens 1990.

8 See too Homi Bhabha's discussion of the double role of the colonizer, "'in double duty bound', at once civilizing mission and a violent subjugating force" (1990: 71).

9 From a public letter of apology for the offence "felt by some," written over six months after the close of the exhibition (issued on 1 March 1991).

10 As Cannizzo explained to the *Toronto Star*, 5 June 1990.

NOTES

11 In the context of the Canadian debates over "appropriation of voice," Cannizzo rightly noted that at least the exhibit did not appropriate the black voice (1991: 152). That it also silenced that voice is not discussed, however.

12 Though the acting director of the museum and, especially, the curator took most of the pressure, it is worth yet another reminder that there was a team involved in creating this (like any other) show: in addition to the curator, there was a graphic designer, an architect, an artist, and an interpretive planner. Since, as you will see shortly, display involves design as much as conceptual framing, many of the problems could not be directly attributed only to the curator.

13 See Jordanova 1989: 32 on how trophies from colonial expansion in museums usually express "victory, ownership, control and dominion" which trigger "fantasies and memories" and elicit admiration.

14 Cannizzo 1991: 157: the intention was to expose "a rather brutal historical reality" and make "clear that the imperial advance was not some sort of adventure story but resulted in death and destruction."

15 Robertson 1990: 4; Charles Roach, *Toronto Star,* 5 June 1990.

16 The word is that of one of the demonstrators, as cited in the *Toronto Star,* 13 June 1990, A3.

17 Cited in "Analyzing Racism at ROM" in *The Varsity* (June 1990), p. 4.

18 Individual visitors saw other ironies which the evidence of the curator's comments and the catalogue would suggest were not actually intentional ones. For instance, see Schildkrout 1991: 21: "In both text and image, the exhibition attempted to use irony in order to present its condemnation of the colonial point of view. In addition to the unfortunate quotations and pseudo-quotations, the exhibition contained section titles that were meant to be read as ironic cues. For example, the ROM assumed (wrongly) that the audience would understand the irony intended in the use of the word 'Commerce' as a title for an exhibit case devoted to artifacts of the slave trade."

19 Christopher Hume, *Toronto Star,* 15 May 1990.

20 See Vergo 1989c: 53 on the persistent museological belief that elucidation can only take the form of words.

21 This term was used quite often in the press: see, for example, the editorial in the *Globe and Mail,* 19 October 1990, A16; Bronwyn Drainie's article in the same newspaper, 24 March 1990.

22 Cf. David Cayley, *Globe and Mail,* 10 August 1990.

23 Oji Adisa and Ras Rao, cited by Isabel Vincent in the *Globe and Mail,* 14 July 1990, pp. D1–D2.

24 This question was raised by Zhao Meichang in 1990 in a thought-provoking graduate course paper (Department of English, University of Toronto) entitled "ROM's Into the Heart of Africa: A Commentary."

25 See the letter to the editor by A.W. Frank Banfield, the son of one of those missionaries, in the *Toronto Star,* 26 May 1990, D3; Isabel Vincent, *Globe and Mail,* 28 July 1990, C12 on William Samarin's defense in *Christian Week;* cf. Colan Mitchell, letter to editor, *Toronto Star,* 5 June 1990, A16. On the nineteenth-century missionary conjunction of the construction of white English ethnicity in relation to "otherness" and the moral power of speaking "God's Word," see Hall 1992.

26 See *Globe and Mail,* 20 June 1990.

27 Christopher Hume, *Toronto Star,* 29 September 1990.

28 Hazel Da Breo, cited in Nazareth 1990: 11; see too Doug Robinson, *Now* (5–11 April 1990).

NOTES

29 Charles Roach, *Now* (22 March–4 April 1990); *Toronto Star*, 5 June 1990.
30 Michael Valpy, *Globe and Mail*, 6 June 1990.
31 Austin-Smith (1990: 52) felt only white audiences could have "access to the luxury of ironic detachment."
32 See Bronwyn Drainie, *Globe and Mail*, 24 March 1990 and 6 April 1991. Part of the reason for such a response, as Marlene Nourbese Philip pointed out, is that, for Africans, museums have been seen as a "significant site of their racial oppression" (*Toronto Star*, 14 January 1991, A4).
33 As explored in Chapter 1, however, the powerful use of irony by black artists such as Robert Colescott or, working within the museum setting, Fred Wilson, would suggest that this view is not shared by all.
34 Indeed Merriman (1989: 170) suggests that people who are better off in the present and who visit museums "because of their cultured connotations, as a way of legitimating their higher status with an appropriate leisure activity," are more likely to have a negative view of the past, "seeing it as something we have progressed from, as a way of legitimating their present status."
35 Eva Mackey has described herself as the "perfect" viewer of the exhibit: a student of anthropology, with a grounding in reflexive anthropological and feminist theory, and therefore interested in how "meaning about 'others' is constructed," she had also done research on the white colonial presence in Africa and was part of the white, anglophone majority of Canada (1991: 7).
36 Unlike the situation in the USA, there was historically no large black former slave population in Canada. In Toronto, there are a variety of black communities from various Caribbean islands and African nations, most recently Somalia.
37 See Gaunt 1989: 32: an ironist "can pander to the tastes and requirements of one section of his public whilst ridiculing its trite and commonplace ideas and use of language for another section of his audience."
38 Cf. Donna Laframboise, *Toronto Star*, 22 October 1990.
39 See Crean 1991: 24: the organizers were "awfully quiet and oblique in their disapproval, never directly condemning or examining its legacy."
40 See Mackey 1991: 61 (via Lyotard) and Fuss 1989: 105–7 especially. See also Clifford 1988: 12: "If authenticity is relational, there can be no essence except as a political, cultural invention, a local tactic." For a detailed discussion of the Coalition and its strategies, see S.R. Butler 1993: 90–132.
41 Cannizzo 1991: 156: "period quotations and historical photographs were used to suggest interaction, the process of collection and the presence of individuals behind the objects."
42 See B.H. Smith 1988: 102: "Communication is ... a political interaction, not only in that its dynamics may operate through differences of power between the agents but also in that the interaction may put those differences at stake, threatening or promising (again it must cut both ways) either to confirm and maintain them or to subvert or otherwise change them." See too Haraway 1991: 163 on the "informatics of domination."
43 In this case, the difficulties with consultation began with the multiple and fragmented African communities in the city of Toronto – of West Indian, African, and American/Canadian origins. The museum did have its promotional, publicity and educational material screened for possible problems by paid experts from the black community; it introduced the show five months before its opening at a reception for that community and, subsequent to a negative response at this stage, set up focus groups and made changes to some of the promotional material – though not, I believe, to the

show itself. An expert in African anthropology vetted the catalogue. Lectures and other events were set up by a black African historian, Dr Kasozi, in conjunction with the exhibition. Some of these were later cancelled because of lack of attendance (after the demonstrations began). See Young 1993 and S.R. Butler 1993.

44 As a possible example of how it might indeed be possible to live "openly with differences in a dialogic community" (Stimpson 1991: 408), this led to a "Task Force on Museums and First Peoples" whose 1992 report was introduced by a letter from Ovide Mercredi, National Chief of the Assembly of First Nations: "Out of controversy can come understanding and an opening for constructive dialogue. The Assembly of First Nations is pleased to have been involved in the Task Force on Museums and First Peoples. The many cultures of the peoples of Canada have so much to share with each other. Out of this sharing can only come a renewed pride in their respective cultures." What the actual result of the task force's recommendations for museum practice will be remains to be seen, of course.

45 Not every anticolonial or postcolonial exhibit has been well received, of course. The Smithsonian's 1991 "West as America" showed how some nineteenth-century artists glorified the European conquest of the Americas, downplaying exploitation, genocide, cultural displacement, and greed, while representing the indigenous peoples as fierce, brutal, and thus worthy of suppression. The museums planning to host the show after the Washington opening backed out in the face of negative response from the American public. This was also the fate of "Into the Heart of Africa": the four American and Canadian museums which had agreed to present the show cancelled after the Toronto protests.

46 Cited by Ahmed Elamin, *Share*, 4 April 1991, 1.

47 Adele Freedman, *Globe and Mail*, 17 November 1989, C11.

48 With the notoriously fine vision of hindsight and admittedly *not* taking into account the difficulties of timing and of institutional constraints, it is (perhaps too) easy to suggest a number of design and framing changes that might have been made to the exhibition even after it opened: reducing the size of certain violent visual images; being more clear and consistent about the function of quotation marks; perhaps choosing to rely less on ironic indirection; reducing the necessity of having to read texts to get meaning; being more aware of the power and semiotic coding of visual images; removing the African "boutique" and its white staff; even inverting the order of the exhibition – introducing the objects in their African context first, then tracing how they came to enter the museum's collection.

49 On Derrida's work as operating under the sign of catachresis, "the *ironic* trope par excellence," see White 1978: 281, and also Ulmer 1982 on Derrida's ironizing of the conventions of criticism. On Foucault's viewing the human sciences in the twentieth century as "projections of the trope of irony," see White 1978: 255. Foucault himself defined his archaeological project in what I see as structurally ironic terms as erecting "the primacy of a contradiction that has its model in the simultaneous affirmation and negation of a single proposition" (1972: 155).

BIBLIOGRAPHY

Abbate, C. (1991) *Unsung Voices: Opera and Musical Narrative in the Nineteenth Century,* Princeton: Princeton University Press.

Abrams, M.H. (1981) *A Glossary of Literary Terms,* 4th edn, New York: Holt, Rinehart & Winston.

Adam, I. and Tiffin, H. (eds) (1990) *Past the Last Post: Theorizing Post-Colonialism and Post-Modernism,* Calgary: University of Calgary Press.

Adams, J.-K. (1985) *Pragmatics and Fiction,* Amsterdam and Philadelphia: John Benjamins.

Adorno, T. (1974) *Minima Moralia: Reflections from Damaged Life,* trans. E.F.N. Jephcott, London: New Left Books.

—— (1991) *In Search of Wagner,* trans. R. Livingstone, London and New York: Verso.

—— and Horkheimer, M. (1972) "The culture industry: enlightenment as mass deception", *Dialectic of Enlightenment,* trans. J. Cumming, New York: Seabury Press.

Agress, L. (1978) *The Feminine Irony: Women on Women in Early Nineteenth-Century English Literature,* Cranbury, N.J.: Associated University Presses.

Alford, S.E. (1984) *Irony and the Logic of the Romantic Imagination,* New York: Peter Lang.

Allemann, B. ([1956] 1969) *Ironie und Dichtung,* Pfullingen: G. Neske.

—— (1978) "De l'ironie en tant que principe littéraire", *Poétique* 36: 385–98.

Almansi, G. (1979) *L'ironie de l'ironie, Documents de Travail,* Centro Internazionale di Semiotica e di Linguistica, Università di Urbino.

—— (1984) *Amica Ironia,* Milano: Garzanti.

—— and Fink, G. (1976) *Quasi Come,* Milano: Bompiani.

Alter, J. (1990) *A Sociosemiotic Theory of Theatre,* Philadelphia: University of Pennsylvania Press.

Altieri, C. (1981) *Act and Quality: A Theory of Literary Meaning and Humanistic Understanding,* Amherst: University of Massachusetts Press.

—— (1990) *Canons and Consequences: Reflecting on the Ethical Force of Imaginative Ideals,* Evanston, Ill.: Northwestern UP.

Amante, D.J. (1981) "The theory of ironic speech acts", *Poetics Today* 2, 2: 77–96.

Ames, M.H. (1992) *Cannibal Tours and Glass Boxes: The Anthropology of Museums,* Vancouver: University of British Columbia Press.

Anderson, B. (1983) *Imagined Communities: Reflections on the Origin and Spread of Nationalism,* London: Verso.

Anderson, D.C. and Sharrock, W.W. (1983) "Irony as a methodological theory: a sketch of four sociological variations", *Poetics Today* 4, 3: 565–79.

Anderson, B. (1983) *United States*, New York: Harper & Row.

Ansen, D. (1990) "Madonna: magnificent maverick", *Cosmopolitan Magazine* (May): 309–11.

Appiah, K.A. (1991) "Is the post- in postmodernism the post- in postcolonial?", *Critical Inquiry* 17, 2: 336–57.

Aristotle (1977) *The Ethics of Aristotle*, trans. J.A.K. Thomson, New York: Penguin.

—— (1991) *The Art of Rhetoric*, trans. H.C. Lawson-Tancred, Harmondsworth: Penguin.

Arnoldi, M.J. (1992) "A distorted mirror: the exhibition of the Herbert Ward Collection of Africana", in I. Karp, C.M. Kreamer and S.D. Lavine (eds) *Museums and Communities: The Politics of Public Culture*, Washington, DC: Smithsonian Institution Press.

Asad, T. (1973) "Introduction" to Asad, T. (ed.) *Anthropology and the Colonial Encounter*, New York: Humanities Press.

Ashcroft, B., Griffiths, G. and Tiffin, H. (1989) *The Empire Writes Back: Theory and Practice in Post-Colonial Literatures*, New York and London: Routledge.

Ashman, M. (1992) "Producing Wagner", in B. Millington and S. Spencer (eds) *Wagner in Performance*, New Haven: Yale University Press.

Atwell, D. (1993) *J.M. Coetzee: South Africa and the Politics of Writing*, Berkeley: University of California Press; Capetown: David Philip.

Atwood, M. (1983) *Bluebeard's Egg*, Toronto: McClelland & Stewart.

—— (1993) *The Robber Bride*, New York: Doubleday.

Auden, W.H. (1949) "The ironic hero", *Horizon* 20, 116 (August): 86–94.

Austin, J.L. (1975) *How to Do Things with Words*, 2nd edn, Oxford: Oxford University Press.

Austin-Smith, B. (1990) "Into the heart of irony", *Canadian Dimension* 27, 7: 51–2.

Ayre, J. (1989) *Northrop Frye: A Biography*, Toronto: Random House.

Bach, K. and Harnish, R.M. (1979) *Linguistic Communication and Speech Acts*, Cambridge, Mass.: Massachusetts Institute of Technology Press.

Baker, H.A., Jr. (1986) "Caliban's triple play", *Critical Inquiry* 13, 1: 182–96.

Bakhtin, M. (1981) "Discourse in the novel", trans. C. Emerson and M. Holquist, in *The Dialogic Imagination*, Austin: University of Texas Press.

—— (1984) *Problems of Dostoevsky's Poetics*, ed. and trans. C. Emerson, Minneapolis: University of Minnesota Press.

—— (1986) *"Speech Genres" and Other Late Essays*, trans. V.W. McGee, C. Emerson and M. Holquist (eds), Austin: University of Texas Press.

Ball, D. (1976) "La définition ironique", *Revue de Littérature Comparée* 199, 3: 213–36.

Bally, C. (1914) "Figures de pensée et formes linguistiques", *Germanisch–Romanisch Monatsschrift* 6: 405–42, 456–70.

—— (1965) *Linguistique générale et linguistique française*, Berne: Francke.

Barnes, J. (1985) *Flaubert's Parrot*, London: Picador.

Barreca, R. (ed.) (1988) *Last Laughs: Perspectives on Women and Comedy*, New York: Gordon & Breach.

—— (1991) *They Used to Call Me Snow White ... but I Drifted: Women's Strategic Use of Humor*, New York: Viking.

—— (ed.) (1992) *New Perspectives on Women and Comedy*, Philadelphia: Gordon & Breach.

Barthes, R. (1966) *Critique et Vérité*, Paris: Seuil.

—— (1974) *S/Z*, trans. R. Miller, New York: Hill & Wang.

—— (1977a) *Image Music Text*, trans. S. Heath, New York: Hill & Wang.

—— (1977b) *Roland Barthes by Roland Barthes*, trans. R. Howard, New York: Hill & Wang.

—— (1987) *Criticism & Truth*, ed. and trans. K.P. Keuneman, London: The Athlone Press.

Barton, A. (1988) "The king disguised: the two bodies of Henry V", in H. Bloom (ed.) *Modern Critical Interpretations: William Shakespeare's Henry V*, New York: Chelsea House.

Basire, B. (1985) "Ironie et métalangage", *DRLAV, Revue de linguistique* 32: 129–50.

Bateson, G. (1972) *Steps to an Ecology of Mind*, San Francisco: Chandler.

Batts, M.S. (1968) "Hartmann's humanitas: a new look at *Iwein*", in F.A. Raven, W.K. Legner and J.C. King (eds) *Germanic Studies in Honor of Edward Henry Sehrt*, Coral Gables, Fla.: University of Miami Press.

Baumann, R. (1986) *Story, Performance and Event: Contextual Studies of Oral Narrative*, Cambridge: Cambridge University Press.

Baumann, Z. (1992) *Intimations of Postmodernity*, London and New York: Routledge.

Baxandall, M. (1991) "Exhibiting intention: some preconditions of the visual display of culturally purposeful objects", in S.D. Lavine and I. Karp (eds) *Exhibiting Cultures: The Poetics and Politics of Museum Display*, Washington, DC: Smithsonian Institution Press.

Beardsley, M.C. (1958) *Aesthetics: Problems in the Philosophy of Criticism*, New York: Harcourt Brace.

Behler, E. (1971) "Techniques of irony in the light of romantic theory", *Rice University Studies* 57, 4: 1–17.

—— (1972) *Klassische Ironie, Romantische Ironie, Tragische Ironie*, Darmstadt: Wissenschaftliche Buchgesellschaft.

—— (1990) *Irony and the Discourse of Modernity*, Seattle: University of Washington Press.

Behrens, R.R. (1982) "Making history: the art of mock-documentation", *The North American Review* (March): 37–40.

Belsey, C. (1980) *Critical Practice*, London: Methuen.

Benjamin, A. (1991) "Painting words: Kiefer and Celan", in A. Papadakis, C. Farrow and N. Hodges (eds) *New Art: An International Survey*, London: Academy Editions.

Benjamin, W. (1969) *Illuminations*, trans. H. Zohn, ed. H. Arendt, New York: Schocken.

Bennett, B. (1993) *Beyond Theory: Eighteenth-Century German Literature and the Poetics of Irony*, Ithaca, N.Y.: Cornell University Press.

Bennett, D. (1985) "Parody, postmodernism and the politics of reading", *Critical Quarterly* 27, 4: 27–43.

Bennett, T. and Woolacott, J. (1987) *Bond and Beyond: The Political Career of a Popular Hero*, London: Macmillan Education.

Ben Porat, Z. (1979) "Method in *Madness*: notes on the structure of parody, based on *MAD* TV satires", *Poetics Today* 1, 1–2: 245–72.

Benton, G. (1988) "The origins of the political joke", in C. Powell and G.E.C. Paton (eds) *Humour in Society: Resistance and Control*, Houndsmills and London: Macmillan.

Benveniste, E. (1970) "L'Appareil formel de l'énonciation", *Langages* 17 (March): 12–18.

Berardinelli, A. (1988) "Eco, o il pensiero pendoiare", *Linea d'ombra* (31 October): 3–6.

Berg, W. (1978) *Uneigentliches Sprechen: Zur Pragmatik und Semantik von Metapher, Metonymie, Ironie, Litotes und rhetorischer Frage*, Tübingen: TBL Verlag Günter Narr.

Bergson, L. (1971) "Eiron und eironeia", *Hermes* 99: 409–22.

Berrendonner, A. (1981) *Eléments de pragmatique linguistique*, Paris: Minuit.

Bérubé, M. and Graff, G. (1993) "Regulations for literary criticism in the 1990s", *Democratic Culture* 2, 2: 2–3.

Bhabha, H.K. (1983) "The other question – the stereotype and colonial discourse", *Screen* 24, 6: 18–36.

—— (1984) "Of mimicry and man: the ambivalence of colonial discourse", *October* 28: 125–33.

—— (1990) "The other question: difference, discrimination and the discourse of colonialism", in R. Ferguson, M. Gever, Trinh T. Minh-ha and C. West (eds) *Out There: Marginalization and Contemporary Culture*, New York: New Museum of Contemporary Art; Cambridge, Mass.: Massachusetts Institute of Technology Press.

Birney, E. (1985) *Essays in Chaucerian Irony*, ed. B. Rowland, Toronto: University of Toronto Press.

Birringer, J. (1991) *Theatre, Theory, Postmodernism*, Bloomington: Indiana University Press.

Black, M. (1962) *Models and Metaphors: Studies in Language and Philosophy*, Ithaca, N.Y.: Cornell University Press.

Bleich, D. (1978) *Subjective Criticism*, Baltimore: Johns Hopkins University Press.

Bloom, H. (1975) *A Map of Misreading*, New York: Oxford University Press.

—— (ed.) (1988) *Modern Critical Interpretations: William Shakespeare's Henry V*, New York: Chelsea House.

Bloomfield, L. (1961) *Language* [1933], New York: Holt, Rinehart & Winston.

Bolen, F.E. (1973) *Irony and Self-Knowledge in the Creation of Tragedy*, Salzburg: Institut für Englische Sprache und Literatur.

Booth, W.C. (1961) *The Rhetoric of Fiction*, Chicago: University of Chicago Press.

—— (1970) "The first full professor of ironology in the world", in his *Now Don't Try to Reason with Me: Essays and Ironies for a Credulous Age*, Chicago: University of Chicago Press.

—— (1974) *A Rhetoric of Irony*, Chicago and London: University of Chicago Press.

—— (1975) "Irony and pity once again: *Thaïs* revisited", *Critical Inquiry* 2, 2: 327–44.

—— (1983) "The empire of irony", *Georgia Review* 37 (Winter): 719–37.

Bourdieu, P. (1984) *Distinction*, trans. R. Nice, London: Routledge.

—— (1990) *In Other Words: Essays Towards a Reflexive Sociology*, trans. M. Adamson, Cambridge: Polity Press.

—— and J.-C. Passeron (1970) *Reproduction in Education, Society and Culture*, trans. R. Nice, London: Sage.

Boutwell, J. (1988) "Complex and dangerous", *Opera News* 53, 2: 14–16.

Bové, P.A. (1980) "Cleanth Brooks and modern irony: a Kierkegaardian critique", in his *Destructive Poetics: Heidegger and Modern American Poetry*, New York: Columbia University Press.

Branagh, K. (1989) *Henry V by William Shakespeare: A Screen Adaptation by Kenneth Branagh*, London: Chatto & Windus.

Brandt, Di. (1987) *Questions i asked my mother* [*sic*], Winnipeg: Turnstone Press.

Breight, C. (1991) "Branagh and the Prince, or a 'royal fellowship of death'", *Critical Quarterly* 33, 4: 95–111.

Brooks, C. (1947) *The Well-Wrought Urn: Studies in the Structure of Poetry*, New York: Harcourt Brace.

—— (1971) "Irony as a principle of structure", in H. Adams (ed.) *Critical Theory since Plato*, New York: Harcourt Brace Jovanovich.

Brooks, L. (1991) "Portrait of the artist as hero: Anselm Kiefer and the modernist semiotics of fascism", in R. Bogue (ed.) *Mimesis in Contemporary Theory: An*

Interdisciplinary Approach, Philadelphia, Amsterdam: John Benjamins.

Brown, R.H. (1983) "Dialectical irony, literary form and sociological theory", *Poetics Today* 4, 3: 543–64.

Brownstein, R.M. (1988) "Jane Austen: irony and authority", in R. Barreca (ed.) *Last Laughs: Perspectives on Women and Comedy*, New York: Gordon & Breach.

Brydon, D. (1987) "The myths that write us: decolonising the mind", *Commonwealth* 10, 1: 1–14.

Bryson, N. (1983) *Vision and Painting: The Logic of the Gaze*, New Haven: Yale University Press.

Buchloh, B.H.D. (1989) "A note on Gerhard Richter's *October 18, 1977*", *October* 48: 88–109.

Büchner, W. (1941) "Über den Begriff der eironeia", *Hermes* 76: 339–58.

Burbridge, P. and Sutton, R. (eds) (1979) *The Wagner Companion*, London: Faber & Faber.

Burke, K. (1966) *Language as Symbolic Action: Essays on Life, Literature and Method*, Berkeley: University of California Press.

—— (1968) *Counter-Statement* [1931, 1953], Berkeley: University of California Press.

—— (1969a) *A Grammar of Motives* [1945], Berkeley: University of California Press.

—— (1969b) *A Rhetoric of Motives*, Berkeley: University of California Press.

—— (1973) *The Philosophy of Literary Form: Studies in Symbolic Action* [1941, 1967], Berkeley: University of California Press.

—— (1984) *Permanence and Change: An Anatomy of Purpose* [1954], Berkeley: University of California Press.

Burks, D.M. (1985) "Dramatic irony, collaboration, and Kenneth Burke's theory of form", *Pre/Text* 6, 3-4: 255–73.

Butler, J. (1990) *Gender Trouble: Feminism and the Subversion of Identity*, London and New York: Routledge.

Butler, S.R. (1993) "Contested representations: revisiting 'Into the heart of Africa' ", MA thesis, York University.

Calderwood, J.L. (1988) "*Henry V*: English, rhetoric, theatre", in H. Bloom (ed.) *Modern Critical Interpretations: William Shakespeare's Henry V*, New York: Chelsea House.

Callinicos, A. (1990) *Against Postmodernism*, New York: St. Martin's Press.

Campbell, K.S. (1979) "Irony medieval and modern and the allegory of rhetoric", *Allegorica* 4, 1-2: 291–300.

Cannizzo, J. (1989) *Into the Heart of Africa*, Toronto: Royal Ontario Museum.

—— (1991) "Exhibiting cultures: 'Into the heart of Africa' ", *Visual Anthropology Review* 7, 1: 150–60.

—— and da Breo, H.A. (1989–90) "Interview", *Fuse* 13 (Winter): 36–7.

Carnap, R. (1942) *Introduction to Semantics and Formalization of Logic*, Cambridge, Mass.: Harvard University Press.

Carnegy, P. (1992) "Designing Wagner: deeds of music made visible?", in B. Millington and S. Spencer (eds) *Wagner in Performance*, New Haven: Yale University Press.

Carter, A. (1979) *The Bloody Chamber*, London: V. Gollancz.

Chamberlain, L. (1989) "Bombs and other exciting devices, or the problem of teaching irony", in P. Donahue and E. Quandahl (eds) *Reclaiming Pedagogy: The Rhetoric of the Classroom*, Carbondale and Edwardsville: Southern Illinois University Press.

Chambers, E.K. (1925) *Shakespeare: A Survey*, Harmondsworth: Penguin.

Chambers, R. (1990) "Irony and the canon", *Profession 90* (MLA): 18–24.

—— (1991) *Room for Maneuver: Reading (the) Oppositional (in) Narrative*, Chicago: University of Chicago Press.

Chatman, S. (1978) *Story and Discourse: Narrative Structure in Fiction and Film*, Ithaca, N.Y. and London: Cornell University Press.

Chevalier, H.M. (1932) *The Ironic Temper: Anatole France and His Time*, New York: Oxford University Press.

Chiaro, D. (1992) *The Language of Jokes: Analysing Verbal Play*, London and New York: Routledge.

Chomsky, N. (1965) *Aspects of the Theory of Syntax*, Cambridge, Mass.: Massachusetts Institute of Technology Press.

Chow, R. (1986–87) "Rereading mandarin ducks and butterflies: a response to the 'postmodern' condition", *Cultural Critique* 5: 69–93.

Chung, S. (1990) "Into the heart of the ROM's racism", *Lexicon* (10 October): 7.

Cicero (1979) *De Oratore*, trans. E.W. Sutton, Cambridge, Mass.: Harvard University Press.

Clark, H.H. and Carlson, T.H. (1982) "Hearers and speech acts", *Language* 58: 332–73.

Clark, H. and Gerrig, R. (1984) "On the pretense theory of irony", *Journal of Experimental Psychology: General* 113, 1: 121–6.

Clifford, J. (1986a) "Introduction: partial truths", in J. Clifford and G.E. Marcus (eds) *Writing Culture: The Poetics and Politics of Ethnography*, Berkeley: University of California Press.

—— (1986b) "On ethnographic allegory", in J. Clifford and G.E. Marcus (eds) *Writing Culture: The Poetics and Politics of Ethnography*, Berkeley: University of California Press.

—— (1988) *The Predicament of Culture: Twentieth-Century Ethnography, Literature and Art*, Cambridge, Mass.: Harvard University Press.

—— (1990) "On collecting art and culture", in M. Ferguson, M. Gever, Trinh T. Minh-ha and C. West (eds) *Out There: Marginalization and Contemporary Culture*, New York: New Museum of Contemporary Art; Cambridge, Mass.: Massachusetts Institute of Technology Press.

—— and Marcus, G.E. (eds) (1986) *Writing Culture: The Poetics and Politics of Ethnography*, Berkeley: University of California Press.

Clyne, M. (1974) "Einige Uberlegungen zu einer Linguistik der Ironie", *Zeitschrift für deutsche Philologie*: 343–55.

Coetzee, J.M. (1985) "Confessions and double thought: Tolstoy, Rousseau, Dostoevsky", *Comparative Literature* 37, 3: 193–232.

—— (1986) *Foe*, Toronto: Stoddart.

Cohen, J. (1970) "Théorie de la figure", *Communications* 16: 3–25.

Cole, P. (ed.) (1981) *Radical Pragmatics*, New York: Academic Press.

Coles, R. (1974) *Irony in the Mind's Life: Essays on Novels by James Agee, Elizabeth Bowen, and George Eliot*, Charlottesville: University Press of Virginia.

Collick, J. (1989) *Shakespeare, Cinema and Society*, Manchester: Manchester University Press.

Collins, J. (1989) *Uncommon Cultures: Popular Culture and Post-Modernism*, New York and London: Routledge.

Compagnon, A. (1979) *La Seconde Main ou le travail de la citation*, Paris: Seuil.

Cone, E. (1989) *Music; A View from Delft: Selected Essays*, ed. Robert P. Morgan, Chicago: University of Chicago Press.

Conrad, P. (1977) *Romantic Opera and Literary Form*, Berkeley: University of California Press.

—— (1978) *Shandyism: The Character of Romantic Irony*, Oxford: Blackwell.

—— (1987) *A Song of Love and Death: The Meaning of Opera*, New York: Poseidon Press.

Conway, D.W. and Seery, J.E. (eds) (1992) *The Politics of Irony: Essays in Self-Betrayal*, New York: St. Martin's Press.

Cooke, D. (1979) "Wagner's musical language", in P. Burbridge and R. Sutton (eds) *The Wagner Companion*, London: Faber & Faber.

Cooke, M.G. (1984) *Afro-American Literature in the Twentieth Century*, New Haven: Yale University Press.

Crapanzano, V. (1992) *Hermes' Dilemma and Hamlet's Desire: On the Epistemology of Interpretation*, Cambridge, Mass.: Harvard University Press.

Crean, S. (1991) "Taking the missionary position", *This Magazine*, 24, 6 (February): 23–8.

Crew, S.R. and Sims, J.E. (1991) "Locating authenticity: fragments of a dialogue", in S.D. Lavine and I. Karp (eds) *Exhibiting Cultures: The Poetics and Politics of Museum Display*, Washington, DC: Smithsonian Institution Press.

Crews, F. and Van Sant, A.J. (1984) *The Random House Handbook*, 4th edn, New York: Random House.

Crowther, B. (1972) "Henry V", in C.W. Eckert (ed.) *Focus on Shakespearean Films*, Englewood Cliffs, N.J.: Prentice-Hall.

Cuddon, J.A. (1979) *A Dictionary of Literary Terms* [1976], Harmondsworth: Penguin.

Culler, J. (1974) *Flaubert: The Uses of Uncertainty*, Ithaca, N.Y.: Cornell University Press.

—— (1975) *Structuralist Poetics: Structuralism, Linguistics and the Study of Literature*, London: Routledge & Kegan Paul.

—— (1980) "Prolegomena to a theory of reading", in S.R. Suleiman and I. Crosman (eds) *The Reader in the Text*, Princeton: Princeton University Press.

—— (1982) *On Deconstruction: Theory and Criticism after Structuralism*, Ithaca, N.Y.: Cornell University Press.

—— (1988) *Framing the Sign: Criticism and its Institutions*, Oxford: Blackwell.

Da Breo, H.A. (1989–90) "Royal spoils: the museum confronts its colonial past", *Fuse* 13 (Winter): 28–36.

Dahlhaus, C. (1979) *Richard Wagner's Music Dramas* [1971], trans. M. Whittall, Cambridge and London: Cambridge University Press.

Daly, N. with Lyons, B. (1991) "*The Civilization of Llhuros*: the first multimedia exhibition in the genre of archaeological fiction", *Leonardo* 24, 3: 265–71.

Dane, J.A. (1986) "The defense of the incompetent reader", *Comparative Literature* 38: 53–72.

—— (1991) *The Critical Mythology of Irony*, Athens: University of Georgia Press.

Danto, A.C. (1989) "Anselm Kiefer", *The Nation* (2 January): 26–8.

David, R. (1979) "Wagner the dramatist", in P. Burbridge and R. Sutton (eds) *The Wagner Companion*, London: Faber & Faber.

Deathridge, J. and Dahlhaus, C. (1984) *The New Grove Wagner*, New York: Norton.

Deats, S.M. (1992) "Rabbits and Ducks: Olivier, Branagh, and *Henry V*", *Literature/Film Quarterly* 20, 4: 284–93.

Decottignies, J. (1988) *Ecritures ironiques*, Lille: Presses Universitaires de Lille.

Defoe, D. (1872) *The Works of Daniel Defoe*, J.S. Keltie (ed.), Edinburgh: Wm. P. Nimmo.

—— (1975) *The Life and Adventures of Robinson Crusoe*, M. Shinagel (ed.), New York: Norton.

de Lauretis, T. (1984) *Alice Doesn't: Feminism Semiotics Cinema*, Bloomington: Indiana University Press.

—— (1987) *Technologies of Gender: Essays on Theory, Film, and Fiction,* Bloomington: Indiana University Press.

Deleuze, G. (1967) *Présentation de Sacher-Masoch: Le froid et le cruel,* Paris: Minuit.

de Man, P. (1969) "The rhetoric of temporality", in C.S. Singleton (ed.) *Interpretation: Theory and Practice,* Baltimore: Johns Hopkins University Press.

—— (1979) *Allegories of Reading,* New Haven: Yale University Press.

—— (1983) *Blindness and Insight: Essays in the Rhetoric of Contemporary Criticism* [1971], Minneapolis: University of Minnesota Press.

Derrida, J. (1974) *Glas,* Paris: Galilée.

—— (1976) *Of Grammatology,* trans. G. Spivak, Baltimore: Johns Hopkins University Press.

Diehl, H. (1982) "Inversion, parody and irony: the visual rhetoric of Renaissance English Tragedy", *Studies in English Literature* 22: 197–209.

Dikkers, S.J.E. (1970) *Ironie als Vorm van Communicatie,* Den Haag: Kruseman.

Dines-Levy, G. and Smith, G.W.H. (1988) "Representations of women and men in *Playboy* sex cartoons", in C. Powell and G.E.C. Patton (eds) *Humour in Society: Resistance and Control,* Houndsmills and London: Macmillan.

Dollimore, J. and Sinfield, A. (eds) (1985) *Political Shakespeare: New Essays in Cultural Materialism,* Manchester: Manchester University Press.

—— and —— (1988) "History and ideology: the instance of *Henry V*", in H. Bloom (ed.) *Modern Critical Interpretations: William Shakespeare's Henry V,* New York: Chelsea House.

Dompierre, L. (1989) *Attila Richard Lukacs,* Catalogue of exhibit at The Power Plant, Toronto, Canada, 29 June–10 September.

Donahue, P. and Quandahl, E. (eds) (1989) *Reclaiming Pedagogy: The Rhetoric of the Classroom,* Carbondale and Edwardsville: Southern Illinois University Press.

Donaldson, L.E. (1988) "The Miranda complex: colonialism and the question of feminist reading", *Diacritics* 18, 3: 65–77.

—— (1992) *Decolonizing Feminisms: Race, Gender and Empire-Building,* Chapel Hill: University of North Carolina Press.

Donaldson, P.S. (1990) *Shakespearean Films/Shakespearean Directors,* Boston: Unwin Hyman.

—— (1991) "Taking on Shakespeare: Kenneth Branagh's *Henry V*", *Shakespeare Quarterly* 42, 1: 60–71.

Douglas, M. (1975) *Implicit Meanings: Essays in Anthropology,* London: Routledge & Kegan Paul.

Dovey, T. (1988) *The Novels of J.M. Coetzee: Lacanian Allegories,* Cape Town: Ad. Donker.

Downie, J.A. (1986) "Defoe's *Shortest Way with the Dissenters*: irony, intention and reader-response", *Prose Studies* 9: 120–39.

Ducrot, O. (1972) *Dire et ne pas dire: Principes de sémantique linguistique,* Paris: Hermann.

—— (1984) *Le Dire et le dit,* Paris: Minuit.

—— and Todorov, T. (1972) *Dictionnaire Encyclopédique des sciences du langage,* Paris: Seuil.

—— *et al.* (1980) *Les Mots du discours,* Paris: Minuit.

Dupriez, B. (1991) *A Dictionary of Literary Devices, Gradus, A–Z,* trans. and adapted A.W. Halsall, Toronto: University of Toronto Press.

Durand, G. (1979) *Science de l'homme et la tradition,* Paris: Berg.

During, S. (1985) "Postmodernism or postcolonialism?", *Landfall* 39, 3: 366–80.

—— (1987) "Postmodernism or post-colonialism today", *Textual Practice* 1, 1: 32–47.

217

Durrans, B. (1988) "The future of the other: changing cultures on display in ethnographic museums", in R. Lumley (ed.) *The Museum Time Machine: Putting Cultures on Display*, London: Routledge.

Dutton, D. (1987) "Why intentionalism won't go away", in A.J. Cascardi, *Literature and the Question of Philosophy*, Baltimore: Johns Hopkins University Press.

Dyson, A.E. (1965) *The Crazy Fabric: Essays in Irony*, London: Macmillan.

Eagleton, T. (1986) *Against the Grain*, London: Verso.

—— (1987) "Estrangement and irony", *Salmagundi* 73: 25–32.

—— (1988) *Nationalism: Irony and Commitment*, Derry: Field Day Theatre Co., Pamphlet No. 13.

—— (1990) *The Ideology of the Aesthetic*, Oxford: Blackwell.

Eco, U. (1976) *A Theory of Semiotics*, Bloomington: Indiana University Press.

—— (1979) *The Role of the Reader: Explorations in the Semiotics of Texts*, Bloomington: Indiana University Press.

—— (1983a) *The Name of the Rose*, trans. W. Weaver, New York: Harcourt Brace Jovanovich.

—— (1983b) *Postscript to The Name of the Rose*, trans. W. Weaver, New York: Harcourt Brace Jovanovich.

—— (1986) *Travels in Hyperreality: Essays* [1967], trans. W. Weaver, New York: Harcourt Brace Jovanovich.

—— (1989a) "Introduzione: la semiosi ermetica e il 'paradigma del velame'", to M.P. Pozzato (ed.) *L'idea deforme: interpretazioni esoteriche di Dante*, Milano: Bompiani.

—— (1989b) *Foucault's Pendulum*, trans. W. Weaver, New York: Harcourt Brace Jovanovich.

—— (1990) *The Limits of Interpretation*, Bloomington: Indiana University Press.

Eger, M. (1990) "Fakten und Fairness: zur Situation der Bayreuther Wagner-Archive", *"Siegfried" Programmheft V*, Bayreuth: 1–9.

Eliot, G. (1956) *Middlemarch*, Boston: Houghton Mifflin.

Elledge, T. (1988) "Skewing perceptions with lies and imaginary culture", *Context* (8 September): 6–7.

Elliott, R.G. (1960) *The Power of Satire*, Princeton: Princeton University Press.

Ellis-Fermor, U. (1945) "Shakespeare's portrait of the statesman-king", reprinted in M. Quinn (ed.) (1969) *Shakespeare: Henry V: A Casebook*, London: Macmillan.

Ellmann, M. (1968) *Thinking About Women*, New York: Harcourt Brace and World.

Elsom, J. (ed.) (1989) *Is Shakespeare Still Our Contemporary?*, London and New York: Routledge.

Empson, W. (1963) *Seven Types of Ambiguity: A Study of its Effects on English Verse* [1930, 1953], London: Chatto & Windus.

Enright, D.J. (1986) *The Alluring Problem: An Essay on Irony*, Oxford: Oxford University Press.

Enright, R. (1992) "Regendering the garden: the very rich painting of Attila Richard Lukacs", *Border Crossings* 11, 3: 14–25.

Erickson, P. (1988) "Fathers, sons and brothers in *Henry V*", in H. Bloom (ed.) *Modern Critical Interpretations: William Shakespeare's Henry V*, New York: Chelsea House.

Even-Zohar, H. (1979) "Polysystem theory", *Poetics Today* 1: 1–2: 287–310.

—— (1986) "Literary Systems", 463–6 in *Encyclopedic Dictionary of Semiotics* vol. 1, T.A. Sebeok (ed.), Berlin, New York, Amsterdam: Mouton de Gruyter.

Felman, S. (1983) *The Literary Speech Act: Don Juan with J.L. Austin, or Seduction in Two Languages*, trans. C. Porter, Ithaca, N.Y.: Cornell University Press.

Felshin, N. (1991) "No Laughing Matter," in *No Laughing Matter*, Catalogue for exhibit, *Dalhousie University Art Gallery* (6 March–19 April): 7–11.

Ferguson, R., Gever, M., Trinh T. Minh-ha and West, C. (eds) *Out There: Marginalization and Contemporary Culture*, New York: New Museum of Contemporary Art; Cambridge, Mass.: Massachusetts Institute of Technology Press.

Ferraz, M. de L.A. (1988) *A Ironia romântica: Estudo de um processo comunicativo*, n.p.: Imprensa Nacional – Casa da Moeda.

Fillmore, C.J. (1981) "Pragmatics and the description of discourse", in P. Cole (ed.) *Radical Pragmatics*, New York: Academic Press.

Finlay, M. (1978) "Perspectives of irony and irony of perspectives: a review", *Canadian Journal of Research in Semiotics* 5, 3 (Spring–Summer): 31–50.

Fischer, M.M.J. (1986) "Ethnicity and the post-modern arts of memory", in J. Clifford and G.E. Marcus (eds) *Writing Culture: The Poetics and Politics of Ethnography*, Berkeley: University of California Press.

Fish, S. (1980) *Is There a Text in This Class? The Authority of Interpretive Communities*, Cambridge, Mass.: Harvard University Press.

—— (1982) "Working on the chain gang: interpretation in the law and in literary criticism", in W.J.T. Mitchell (ed.) *The Politics of Interpretation*, Special issue, *Critical Inquiry* 9, 1 (September): 201–16.

—— (1983) "Short people got no reason to live: reading irony", *Daedalus* 112, 1: 175–91.

—— (1989) *Doing What Comes Naturally*, Durham, N.C.: Duke University Press.

Fisher, P. (1991) *Making and Effacing Art: Modern American Art in a Culture of Museums*, New York: Oxford University Press.

Flam, J. (1992) "The alchemist", *New York Review of Books* (13 February): 31–6.

Flax, J. (1987) "Postmodernism and gender relations in feminist theory", *Signs* 12, 4: 621–43.

Fletcher, A. (1964) *Allegory: The Theory of a Symbolic Mode*, Ithaca, N.Y.: Cornell University Press.

Fogelin, R.J. (1988) *Figuratively Speaking*, New Haven: Yale University Press.

Fónagy, I. (1971a) "Synthèse de l'ironie", *Phonetica* 23: 42–51.

—— (1971b) "The functions of vocal style", in S. Chatman (ed.) *Literary Style: A Symposium*, London and New York: Oxford University Press.

Fortier, M. (1992) "Speculations on *2 Henry IV*, theatre historiography, the strait gate of history, and Kenneth Branagh", *Journal of Dramatic Theory and Criticism* 7, 1: 45–69.

Foucault, M. (1970) *The Order of Things: An Archaeology of the Human Sciences*, London: Tavistock.

—— (1972) *The Archaeology of Knowledge and the Discourse on Language*, New York: Pantheon.

Fowler, H.W. (1950) *A Dictionary of Modern English Usage* [1926], Oxford: Clarendon Press; London: Geoffrey Cumberlege.

Fowles, J. (1985) *A Maggot*, Toronto: Collins; London: Jonathan Cape.

Freedman, A. (1989) "A revealing journey through time and space", *The Globe and Mail* (17 November): C11.

Freedman, J. (1990) "Bringing it all back home: a commentary on *Into the Heart of Africa*", *Museum Quarterly* 18, 1: 39–43.

Freud, S. (1905) "Jokes and their relation to the unconscious", in *The Standard Edition of the Complete Psychological Works of Sigmund Freud*, 1953–74, J. Strachey (ed.), vol. 8, London: Hogarth Press and the Institute of Psycho-Analysis.

Frye, N. (1963) "The road to excess", in B. Slote (ed.) *Myth and Symbol*, Lincoln: University of Nebraska Press.

—— (1970) *Anatomy of Criticism: Four Essays* [1957], New York: Atheneum.

—— (1982) *Divisions on a Ground: Essays on Canadian Culture*, J. Polk (ed.) Toronto: House of Anansi Press.

Fulford, R. (1991) "Into the heart of the matter", *Rotunda* (September): 19–28.

Furst, L.R. (1984) *Fictions of Romantic Irony*, Cambridge, Mass.: Harvard University Press.

Fuss, D. (1989) *Essentially Speaking: Feminism, Nature and Difference*, New York: Routledge.

Fussell, P. (1975) *The Great War and Modern Memory*, New York: Oxford University Press.

Gagnier, R. (1988) "Between women: a cross-class analysis of status and anarchic humor", in R. Barreca (ed.) *Last Laughs: Perspectives on Women and Comedy*, New York: Gordon & Breach.

Gallagher, Susan Van Zanten (1991) *A Story of South Africa: J.M. Coetzee's Fiction in Context*, Cambridge, Mass.: Harvard University Press.

Garber, F. (ed.) (1988) *Romantic Irony*, Budapest: Akademiai Kiado.

Gass, W. (1978) *The World within the Word*, New York: Knopf.

Gates, H.L., Jr. (1984) "Criticism in the Jungle", in H.L. Gates, Jr. (ed.) *Black Literature and Literary Theory*, London and New York: Methuen.

—— (1988) *The Signifying Monkey: A Theory of Afro-American Literary Criticism*, New York: Oxford University Press.

—— (1991) "The master's pieces: on canon formation and the Afro-American tradition", in D. LaCapra (ed.) *The Bounds of Race: Perspectives on Hegemony and Resistance*, Ithaca, N.Y.: Cornell University Press.

Gaunt, S. (1989) *Troubadors and Irony*, New York and London: Cambridge University Press.

Geduld, H.M. (1973) *Filmguide to Henry V*, Bloomington: Indiana University Press.

Geertz, C. (1973) *The Interpretation of Cultures*, New York: Basic.

—— (1983) *Local Knowledge: Further Essays in Interpretive Anthropology*, New York: Basic.

Gellner, E. (1974) *Legitimation of Belief*, Cambridge: Cambridge University Press.

Genette, G. (1982) *Palimpsestes: La Littérature au second degré*, Paris: Seuil.

Gibbs, R.W. (1984) "Literal meaning and psychological theory", *Cognitive Science* 8: 275–304.

Gilbert, F. (1978) *Bismarckian Society's Image of the Jew*, New York: Leo Baeck Institute.

Gilbert, S.M. and Gubar, S. (1979) *The Madwoman in the Attic: The Woman Writer and the Nineteenth-Century Literary Imagination*, New Haven: Yale University Press.

Gilman, S.L. (1985) *Difference and Pathology: Stereotypes of Sexuality, Race, and Madness*, Ithaca, N.Y.: Cornell University Press.

—— (1986) *Jewish Self-Hatred: Anti-Semitism and the Hidden Language of the Jews*, Baltimore: Johns Hopkins University Press.

—— (1991a) *The Jew's Body*, New York and London: Routledge.

—— (1991b) *Inscribing the Other*, Lincoln: University of Nebraska Press.

Gilmour, J.C. (1990) *Fire on the Earth: Anselm Kiefer and the Postmodern World*, Philadelphia: Temple University Press.

Gitlin, T. (1988) "Hip-deep in postmodernism", *New York Times Book Review* (6 November): 1.

—— (1989) "Postmodernism and politics", in I. Angus and S. Jhally (eds), *Cultural Politics in Contemporary America*, New York: Routledge.

Glaser, B.G. and Strauss, A.L. (1964) "Awareness contexts and social interaction", *American Sociological Review* 29: 669–79.

Glicksberg, C.I. (1969) *The Ironic Vision in Modern Literature*, The Hague: Martinus Nijhoff.

Godzich, W. (1986) "Foreword: the further possibilities of knowledge", in M. de Certeau, *Heterologies: Discourse on the Other*, trans. B. Massumi, Minneapolis: University of Minnesota Press.

Goffman, E. (1974) *Frame Analysis: An Essay on the Organization of Experience*, Cambridge, Mass.: Harvard University Press.

—— (1981) *Forms of Talk*, Oxford: Blackwell.

Gohr, S (1982) "The situation and the artists", *Flash Art* 106 (February–March): 30–46.

Gombrich, E.H. (1969) *Art and Illusion: A Study in the Psychology of Pictorial Representation*, Princeton: Princeton University Press.

Good, E.M. (1965) *Irony in the Old Testament*, Philadelphia: Westminster Press.

Gordimer, N. (1984) "The idea of gardening", *New York Review of Books* (2 February): 3–4.

Gould, G. (1969) "Irony and satire in *Henry V*" [1919], in M. Quinn (ed.) *Shakespeare: Henry V: A Casebook*, London: Macmillan.

Gray, H. (1990) *Wagner*, London and New York: Omnibus Press.

Green, D.H. (1976) "On recognising medieval irony", in A.P. Foulkes (ed.) *The Uses of Criticism*, Bern: Herbert Lang.

—— (1979) *Irony in the Medieval Romance*, Cambridge, London, New York: Cambridge University Press.

Greenblatt, S. (1985) "Invisible bullets: Renaissance authority and its subversion, *Henry IV* and *Henry V*", in J. Dollimore and A. Sinfield (eds) *Political Shakespeare: New Essays in Cultural Materialism*, Manchester: Manchester University Press.

Greenhalgh, P. (1989) "Education, entertainment and politics: lessons from the great international exhibitions", in P. Vergo, (ed.) *The New Museology*, London: Reaktion Books.

Greimas, A.J. (1986) *Sémantique structurale* [1966], Paris: PUF.

Grice, H.P. (1975) "Logic and conversation", in P. Cole and J. Morgan (eds) *Syntax and Semantics 3: Speech Acts*, New York: Academic Press.

—— (1978) "Further notes on logic and conversation", in P. Cole (ed.) *Syntax and Semantics – Pragmatics*, New York: Academic Press.

—— (1989) *Studies in the Way of Words*, Cambridge, Mass.: Harvard University Press.

Groeben, N. and Scheele, B. (1984) *Produktion und Rezeption von Ironie*, 2 vols, Tübingen: Gunter Narr Verlag.

Grossberg, L. (1988) "Putting the pop back into postmodernism", in A. Ross (ed.) *Universal Abandon?: The Politics of Postmodernism*, Minneapolis: University of Minnesota Press.

——, Nelson, C. and Treichler, P. (eds) (1992) *Cultural Studies*, London and New York: Routledge.

Groupe Mu (1970) *Rhétorique générale*, Paris: Larousse.

—— (1978) "Ironique et iconique", *Poétique* 36: 427–42.

—— (1981) *A General Rhetoric*, trans. P.B. Burrell and E.M. Slotkin, Baltimore and London: Johns Hopkins University Press.

Gurian, E.H. (1991) "Noodling around with exhibition opportunities", in S.D. Lavine and I. Karp (eds) *Exhibiting Cultures: The Poetics and Politics of Museum Display*, Washington, DC: Smithsonian Institution Press.

Gutman, R.W. (1990) *Richard Wagner: The Man, His Mind and His Music* [1968], New York: Harcourt Brace Jovanovich.

Gutwirth, M. (1993) *Laughing Matter: An Essay on the Comic*, Ithaca, N.Y.: Cornell University Press.

Habermas, J. (1973) *Kultur und Kritik*, Frankfurt: Suhrkamp Verlag.

——— (1983) "Modernity: an incomplete project", in H. Foster (ed.) *The Anti-Aesthetic: Essays on Postmodern Culture*, Port Townsend, Washington: Bay Press.

Hagen, P.L. (1992) "The rhetorical effectiveness of verbal irony", Ph.D. dissertation, Pennsylvania State University.

Haidu, P. (1968) *Aesthetic Distance in Chrétien de Troyes: Irony and Comedy in Cligès and Perceval*, Geneva: Droz.

——— (1978) "Au début du roman, l'ironie", *Poétique* 36: 443–66.

Hall, C. (1992) "Missionary stories: gender and ethnicity in England in the 1830s and 1840s", in L. Grossberg, C. Nelson and P. Treichler (eds) *Cultural Studies*, London and New York: Routledge.

Halliday, M.A.K. (1978) *Language as Social Semiotic: The Social Interpretation of Language and Meaning*, London: Edward Arnold.

Halpin, M. (1991) "Fragments: reflections on collecting", University of British Columbia Museum of Anthropology, Museum Note 31.

Handwerk, G.J. (1985) *Irony and Ethics in Narrative: From Schlegel to Lacan*, New Haven and London: Yale University Press.

Haraway, D. (1990) "A Manifesto for cyborgs: science, technology, and socialist feminism in the 1980s", in L.J. Nicholson (ed.) *Feminism/Postmodernism*, London and New York: Routledge.

——— (1991) *Simians, Cyborgs and Women: The Reinvention of Nature*, New York: Routledge.

Hare, R.M. (1952) *The Language of Morals*, Oxford: Clarendon Press.

Harshaw, B. (1984) "Fictionality and fields of reference: remarks on a theoretical framework", *Poetics Today* 5, 2: 227–51.

Hartman, G. (1981) *Saving the Text: Literature/Derrida/Philosophy*, Baltimore: Johns Hopkins University Press.

Harwood, J. (1985) "From 'The annotated gospel according to Jacques'", *English* 24: 44–50.

Hass, H-E. and Mohrlüder, G-A. (eds) (1973) *Ironie als Literarisches Phänomen*, Köln: Kiepenheuer & Witsch.

Hassan, I. (1980) "Pluralism in postmodern perspective", *Critical Inquiry* 12, 3: 503–20.

Headlam, B. (1993/1994) "Attila up against the wall", *Saturday Night* (December/January): 54–9, 84, 86–8.

Hebdige, D. (1988) *Hiding in the Light: On Images and Things*, London and New York: Methuen.

Hegel, G.W.F. (1920) *The Philosophy of Fine Art*, trans. F.P.B. Osmaston, London: G. Bell & Sons.

Heller, E. (1985) "Introduction" to T. Mann, *Pro and Contra Wagner*, trans. A. Blunden, London: Faber & Faber.

Heller, L.G. (1983) "Puns, ironies (plural) and other type-4 patterns", *Poetics Today* 4, 3: 437–49.

Hermerén, G. (1975) "Intention and interpretation in literary criticism", *New Literary History* 7, 1: 57–82.

Hernadi, P. (1988) "Doing, making, meaning: toward a theory of verbal practice", *PMLA* 103, 5: 749–58.

Herzfeld, M. (1982) "Disemia", in M. Herzfeld and M.D. Lenhart (eds) *Semiotics 1980*, New York and London: Plenum Press.

Herzogenrath, W. (1991) "Bilder entstehen nicht nur aus 'Nach-denken', sondern aus 'Vor-leben'", in *Anselm Kiefer*, Catalogue of exhibition at the Nationalgalerie Berlin, Berlin: Staatliche Museen, Preussischer Kulturbesitz.

Highet, G. (1962) *The Anatomy of Satire*, Princeton: Princeton University Press.

Hirsch, E.D., Jr. (1967) *Validity in Interpretation*, New Haven: Yale University Press.
—— (1971) "Objective interpretation", in H. Adams (ed.) *Critical Theory Since Plato*, New York: Harcourt Brace Jovanovich.
—— (1982) "The politics of theories of interpretation", *Critical Inquiry* 9, 1: 235–47.
—— (1987) *Cultural Literacy: What Every American Needs to Know*, with J. Kett and J. Trefil, Boston: Houghton Mifflin.
—— (ed.) (1988) *The Dictionary of Cultural Literacy*, Boston: Houghton Mifflin.
—— (1989) *A First Dictionary of Cultural Literacy: What Our Children Need to Know*, W.G. Rowland, Jr. and M. Stanford (assoc. eds), Boston: Houghton Mifflin.
Hirst, P.Q. (1976) "Althusser and the theory of ideology", *Economy and Society* 5, 4: 385–412.
Hitchens, C. (1990) *Blood, Class and Nostalgia*, London: Chatto & Windus.
Hodge, R. and Kress, G. (1988) *Social Semiotics*, Ithaca, N.Y.: Cornell University Press.
Hofmannsthal, H. von (1923) "Two essays: I: irony – the irony of things", *London Mercury* 9, 50: 175–7.
Holdcroft, D. (1976) "Forms of indirect communication: an outline", *Philosophy and Rhetoric*, 9: 147–61.
—— (1983) "Irony as a trope, and irony as discourse", *Poetics Today* 4, 3: 493–511.
Holderness, G. (1985) "Radical potentiality and institutional closure: Shakespeare in film and television", in J. Dollimore and A. Sinfield (eds) *Political Shakespeare: New Essays in Cultural Materialism*, Manchester: Manchester University Press.
—— (1991) "'What ish my nation?': Shakespeare and national identities", *Textual Practice* 5, 1: 74–93.
—— (1992) *Shakespeare Recycled: The Making of Historical Drama*, Hemel Hempstead: Harvester Wheatsheaf.
——, Potter, N. and Turner, J. (1987) *Shakespeare: The Play of History*, Iowa City: University of Iowa Press.
Holman, C.H. and Harmon, W. (1986) *A Handbook to Literature*, 5th edn, New York: Macmillan; London: Collier Macmillan.
Holquist, M. (1971) "Whodunit and other questions: metaphysical detective stories in post-war fiction", *New Literary History* 3: 135–56.
Honig, E. (1959) *Dark Conceit: The Making of Allegory*, Evanston: Northwestern University Press.
hooks, b. (1990) *Yearning: Race, Gender and Cultural Politics*, Boston: South End Press.
Hooper-Greenhill, E. (1988) "Counting visitors or visitors who count?", in R. Lumley (ed.) *The Museum Time-machine: Putting Cultures on Display*, London: Routledge.
Horne, D. (1984) *The Great Museum: The Re-presentation of History*, London: Pluto Press.
Hulme, T.E. (1936) "Romanticism and classicism", in *Speculations: Essays on Humanism and the Philosophy of Art*, London: Kegan Paul, Trench, Trubner & Company.
Hutchens, E.N. (1960) "The identification of irony", *English Literary History* 27: 352–63.
Hutcheon, L. (1978) "Ironie et parodie: stratégie et structure", *Poétique* 36: 467–77.
—— (1981) "Ironie, satire, parodie: une approche pragmatique de l'ironie", *Poétique* 46: 140–55.
—— (1985) *A Theory of Parody: The Teachings of Twentieth-Century Art Forms*, London and New York: Methuen.

223

—— (1988a) *A Poetics of Postmodernism: History, Theory, Fiction*, London and New York: Routledge.

—— (1988b) *The Canadian Postmodern*, Toronto: Oxford University Press.

—— (1989) *The Politics of Postmodernism*, London and New York: Routledge.

—— (1991) *Splitting Images: Contemporary Canadian Ironies*, Toronto: Oxford University Press.

—— (1992) "Eco's echoes: ironizing the (post)modern", *Diacritics* 22, 1: 2–16.

—— (forthcoming) "The politics of impossible worlds", in W. Hamarneh and C. Mihailescu (eds) *Fictions and Worlds*, Toronto: University of Toronto Press.

—— and Butler, S.A. (1981) "The literary semiotics of verbal irony: the example of Joyce's 'The Boarding House'", *Recherches Sémiotiques/Semiotic Inquiry* 1, 3: 244–60.

Hutchinson, P. (1983) *Games Authors Play*, London and New York: Methuen.

Huyssen, A. (1989) "Anselm Kiefer: the terror of history, the temptation of myth", *October* 48 (Spring): 25–45.

—— (1992) "Kiefer in Berlin", *October* 62: 84–101.

Hymes, D.H. (1972) "Models of the interactions of language and social life", in J.J. Gumperz and D. Hymes (eds) *Directions in Sociolinguistics*, New York: Holt, Rinehart & Winston.

—— (1974) *Foundations in Sociolinguistics*, Philadelphia: University of Pennsylvania Press.

—— (1987) "A theory of irony and a Chinook pattern of verbal exchange", in J. Verschueren and M. Bertuccelli-Papi (eds) *The Pragmatic Perspective: Selected Papers from the 1985 International Pragmatics Conference*, Amsterdam, Philadelphia: John Benjamins.

Immerwahr, R. (1951) "The subjectivity or objectivity of Friedrich Schlegel's poetic irony", *Germanic Review* 26: 773–91.

Irigaray, L. (1985) *Speculum of the Other Woman*, trans. G.C. Gill, Ithaca, N.Y.: Cornell University Press.

Iser, W. (1978) *The Act of Reading: A Theory of Aesthetic Response*, Baltimore: Johns Hopkins University Press.

Ishiguro, K. (1989) *The Remains of the Day*, Toronto: Lester & Orpen Dennys.

Jakobson, R. (1960) "Linguistics and poetics", in T. Sebeok (ed.) *Style in Language*, Cambridge, Mass.: Massachusetts Institute of Technology Press.

Jameson, F. (1979) *Fables of Aggression: Wyndham Lewis, the Modernist as Fascist*, Berkeley: University of California Press.

—— (1988a) *The Ideologies of Theory – I*, Minneapolis: University of Minnesota Press.

—— (1988b) *Modernism and Imperialism*, Derry: Field Day Theatre Company, Pamphlet No. 14.

—— (1990) "Allegorizing Hitchcock", in *Signatures of the Visible*, London: Routledge.

—— (1991) *Postmodernism, or, The Cultural Logic of Late Capitalism*, Durham, N.C.: Duke University Press.

Jankélévitch, V. (1964) *L'ironie*, Paris: Flammarion.

JanMohamed, A.R. (1983) *Manichean Aesthetics: The Politics of Literature in Colonial Africa*, Amherst: University of Massachusetts Press.

Japp, U. (1983) *Theorie der Ironie*, Frankfurt am Main: Klostermann.

Jara, R. and Spadaccini, N. (1989) "Introduction: allegorizing the New World", in *1492–1992: Re/Discovering Colonial Writing*, Minneapolis: University of Minnesota Press.

Johnson, K. (1989) "Colescott on black and white", *Art in America* (June): 149–53, 197.

Jones, P. (1992) "Museums and the meanings of their contents", *New Literary History*, 23, 4: 911–21.

Jordanova, L. (1989) "Objects of knowledge: a historical perspective on museums", in P. Vergo (ed.) *The New Museology*, London: Reaktion Books.

Jorgensen, J., Miller, G.A. and Sperber, D. (1984) "Test of the mention theory of irony", *Journal of Experimental Psychology: General* 113, 1: 112–20.

Juhl, P.D. (1980) *Interpretation: An Essay in the Philosophy of Literary Criticism*, Princeton: Princeton University Press.

Karp, I., Kreamer, C.M. and Lavine, S.D. (eds) (1992) *Museums and Communities: The Politics of Public Culture*, Washington, DC: Smithsonian Institution Press.

Karstetter, A.B. (1964) "Toward a theory of rhetorical irony", *Speech Monographs* 31 (June): 162–78.

Kaufer, D. (1977) "Irony and rhetorical strategy", *Philosophy and Rhetoric* 10, 2: 90–110.

—— (1981a) "Ironic evaluations", *Communication Monographs* 48, 1: 25–38.

—— (1981b) "Understanding ironic communication", *Journal of Pragmatics* 5: 495–510.

—— (1983) "Irony, interpretive form and the theory of meaning", *Poetics Today* 4, 3: 451–64.

—— and Neuwirth, C.M. (1982) "Foregrounding norms and ironic communication", *Quarterly Journal of Speech* 68: 28–36.

Keenan, E. (1971) "Two types of presupposition in natural language", in C. Filmore and D.T. Langendeon (eds) *Studies in Linguistic Semantics*, New York: Holt, Rinehart & Winston.

Kempson, R. (1977) *Semantic Theory*, Cambridge: Cambridge University Press.

Kenner, H. (1962) "Art in a closed field", *Virginia Quarterly Review* 38: 597–613.

—— (1986) "Irony of ironies", *Times Literary Supplement* (17 October): 1151–2.

Kenshur, O. (1988) "Demystifying the demystifiers: metaphysical snares of ideological criticism", *Critical Inquiry* 14, 2: 335–53.

Kerbrat-Orecchioni, C. (1976) "Problèmes de l'ironie", *Linguistique et sémiologie* 2: 9–46.

—— (1977) *La Connotation*, Lyon: Presses Universitaires Lyon.

—— (1980a) "L'ironie comme trope", *Poétique* 41: 108–27.

—— (1980b) *L'Enonciation: de la subjectivité dans le langage*, Paris: Armand Colin.

Kerman, J. (1988) *Opera as Drama*, rev. edn, Berkeley: University of California Press.

Kierkegaard, S. (1971) *The Concept of Irony with Constant Reference to Socrates*, trans. L.M. Capel, Bloomington: University of Indiana Press.

Kilbourn, W. (1988) "The peaceable kingdom still", *Daedalus* 11, 4: 1–29.

King, T. (1989) *Medicine River*, Toronto: Penguin Books.

Klawans, S. (1989) "Films", *The Nation* 249, 20 (11 December): 725–6.

Knapp, S. and Michaels, W.B. (1982) "Against Theory", *Critical Inquiry* 8, 4: 723–42.

Knox, D. (1989) *Ironia: Medieval and Renaissance Ideas on Irony*, Leiden: E.J. Brill.

Knox, N. (1961) *The Word "Irony" and its Context, 1500–1755*, Durham, N.C.: Duke University Press.

—— (1972) "On the classification of ironies", *Modern Philology* 70: 53–62.

—— (1973) "Irony", in P.P. Wiener (ed.) *Dictionary of the History of Ideas: Studies of Selective Pivotal Ideas*, Vol. 2, New York: Scribner & Sons.

Koestler, A. (1964) *The Act of Creation*, London: Hutchinson.

Kott, J. (1967) *Shakespeare Our Contemporary*, trans. B. Taborski, 2nd rev. edn, London: Methuen.

Kröller, E-M. (1984) "Postmodernism, colony, nation: the Melvillean texts of Bowering and Beaulieu", *University of Ottawa Quarterly* 54, 2: 53–61.

Krysinski, W. (1985) "The dialectical and intertextual function of irony in the modern novel", *Canadian Review of Comparative Literature* 12, 1: 1–11.

Kuhn, T.S. (1970) *The Structure of Scientific Revolutions* [1962], Chicago: University of Chicago Press.

Kuiper, K. (1984) "The nature of satire", *Poetics* 13: 459–73.

Kundera, M. (1986) *The Art of the Novel*, trans. L. Asher, New York: Grove.

LaCapra, D. (1985) *History and Criticism*, Ithaca, N.Y.: Cornell University Press.

——— (1987) *History, Politics and the Novel*, Ithaca, N.Y.: Cornell University Press.

——— (ed.) (1991) *The Bounds of Race: Perspectives on Hegemony and Resistance*, Ithaca, N.Y.: Cornell University Press.

Lalla, H. and Grant, P. (1990) "Analyzing racism at ROM", *The Varsity* (June): 4.

Lamy, S. (1987) "Les enfants uniques nés de père et de mère inconnus", in B. Godard (ed.) *Gynocritics: Feminist Approaches to Canadian and Quebec Women's Writing*, Toronto: ECW Press.

Lang, C.D. (1988) *Irony/Humor: Critical Paradigms*, Baltimore and London: Johns Hopkins University Press.

Lang, H.S. (1985) "Philosophy as text and context", *Philosophy and Rhetoric* 18: 158–70.

Lanham, R.A. (1991) *A Handlist of Rhetorical Terms*, 2nd edn, Berkeley: University of California Press.

Large, D.C. and Weber, W. (eds) (1984) *Wagnerism in European Culture and Politics*, Ithaca, N.Y.: Cornell University Press.

Lavine, S.D. and Karp, I. (eds) (1991) *Exhibiting Cultures: The Poetics and Politics of Museum Display*, Washington, DC: Smithsonian Institution Press.

Lawson, T. (1984) "Last exit: painting", in B. Wallis (ed.) *Art After Modernism: Rethinking Representation*, New York: New Museum of Contemporary Art; Boston: Godene.

Leavis, F.R. (1934) "The irony of Swift", *Scrutiny* 2, 4 (March): 364–78.

Lee, M.O. (1990) *Wagner's Ring: Turning the Sky Round*, New York: Summit Books.

Lefevre, K.B. (1987) *Invention as a Social Act*, Carbondale: Southern Illinois University Press.

Lejeune, P. (1989) *On Autobiography*, trans. K. Leary, Minneapolis: University of Minnesota Press.

Lentricchia, F. (1980) *After the New Criticism*, Chicago: University of Chicago Press.

Levi, A.W. (1962) *Literature, Philosophy and the Imagination*, Bloomington: Indiana University Press.

Levin, S.R. (1988) *Metaphoric Worlds: Conceptions of a Romantic Nature*, New Haven: Yale University Press.

Lewis, P. (1989) *Comic Effects: Interdisciplinary Approaches to Humor in Literature*, Albany: State University of New York Press.

Lieberson, J. (1988) "Bombing in Bayreuth", *New York Review of Books* (10 November): 24–30.

Lindenberger, H. (1984) *Opera: The Extravagant Art*, Ithaca, N.Y.: Cornell University Press.

——— (1989) "From opera to postmodernity: on genre, style, institutions", in M. Perloff (ed.) *Postmodern Genres*, Norman: University of Oklahoma Press.

Lippard, L.R. (1984) "Give and take: ideology in the art of Suzanne Lacy and Jerry Kearns", in *Art and Ideology*, Exhibit catalogue, New York: New Museum of Contemporary Art.

Lotman, Y.M. (1982) "The text and the structure of its audience", *New Literary History* 14, 1: 81–7.

Lukács, G. (1971) *The Theory of the Novel*, trans. A. Bostock, London: Merlin Press.

Lumley, R. (ed.) (1988a) *The Museum Time Machine: Putting Cultures on Display*, London: Routledge.

—— (1988b) "Introduction" to *The Museum Time Machine: Putting Cultures on Display*, London: Routledge.

Luperini, R. (1981) *Il Novecento: apparati ideologici, ceto intellettuale, sistemi formali nella letteratura italiana contemporanea*, Torino: Loescher.

Lyons, B. (1985) "*The Excavation of the Apasht*: artifacts from an imaginary past", *Leonardo* 18, 2: 81–9.

—— (1994) "Art of the Trickster", *Archaeology* 47, 2: 72.

MacCannell, D. (1976) *The Tourist: A New Theory of the Leisure Class*, New York: Schocken.

McCarthy, T. (1990a) "Private irony and public decency: Richard Rorty's new pragmatism", *Critical Inquiry* 16, 2: 355–70.

—— (1990b) "Ironist theory as a vocation: a response to Rorty's reply", *Critical Inquiry* 16, 3: 644–55.

McClary, S. (1989) "The undoing of opera: toward a feminist criticism of music", Introduction to C. Clément, *Opera, or the Undoing of Women*, trans. B. Wang, London: Virago.

—— (1991) *Feminine Endings: Music, Gender, and Sexuality*, Minneapolis: University of Minnesota Press.

McCracken, T. (1991) "Triple-voicing: the multicultural canon", Unpublished typescript.

McHoul, A.W. (1982) *Telling How Texts Talk: Essays in Reading and Ethnomethodology*, London: Routledge & Kegan Paul.

McKee, J.B. (1974) *Literary Irony and the Literary Audience: Studies in the Victimization of the Reader in Augustan Fiction*, Amsterdam: Rodopi.

Mackey, E. (1991) "The politics of race and representation in Toronto, Canada: events and discourses around the Royal Ontario Museum's 'Into the Heart of Africa' exhibit", MA thesis, University of Sussex.

Magee, B. (1988) *Aspects of Wagner*, rev. edn, Oxford: Oxford University Press.

Magidson, D. and Wright, J. (1973) "True patriot love", *Art and Artists* 8, 7 (October): 38–41.

Mahood, M. (1979) *Shakespeare's Wordplay*, London: Methuen.

Manheim, M. (1983) "Olivier's *Henry V* and the Elizabethan world picture", *Literature/Film Quarterly* 11, 3: 179–84.

Mann, T. (1947) "Goethe and Tolstoy", trans. H.T. Lowe-Porter, in *Essays of Three Decades*, New York: Knopf.

—— (1983) *Reflections of a Nonpolitical Man*, trans. W.D. Morris, New York: Ungar.

—— (1985) *Pro and Contra Wagner*, trans. A. Blunden, London: Faber & Faber.

Mannoni, O. (1964) *Prospero and Caliban: The Psychology of Colonization* [1950], New York: Praeger.

Manvell, R. (1979) *Shakespeare and the Film*, South Brunswick and New York: A.S. Barnes & Co.

Marcus, J. (1988) "Daughters of anger/material girls: con/textualizing feminist criticism", in R. Barreca (ed.) *Last Laughs: Perspectives on Women and Comedy*, New York: Gordon & Breach.

Martin, G.D. (1983) "The bridge and the river: or the ironies of communication", *Poetics Today* 4, 3: 415–35.

Mayenowa, M.R. (1981) "Verbal texts and iconic-visual texts", in W. Steiner (ed.) *Image and Code*, Ann Arbor: University of Michigan Press.

Mayer, H. (1990) "Der *Ring* als bürgerlicher Roman", *"Die Walküre" Programmheft IV*, Bayreuth.

Mays, J.B. (1988) "Heroic Life", *C. Magazine* 17 (Spring): 54–63.

Medvedev, P.N./Bakhtin, M.M. (1978) *The Formal Method in Literary Scholarship: A Critical Introduction to Sociological Poetics*, trans. Albert J. Wehrle, Baltimore: Johns Hopkins University Press.

Mellor, A.K. (1979) "On romantic irony, symbolism and allegory", *Criticism* 21 (Summer): 217–29.

—— (1980) *English Romantic Irony*, Cambridge, Mass. and London: Harvard University Press.

Memmi, A. (1965) *The Colonizer and the Colonized*, trans. H. Greenfeld [1954], New York: Orion Press.

Merriman, N. (1989) "Museum visiting as a cultural phenomenon", in P. Vergo (ed.) *The New Museology*, London: Reaktion Books.

Meyers, A.R. (1974) "Toward a definition of irony", in R. Fasold and R. Shuy (eds) *Studies in Language Variation*, Washington, DC: Georgetown University Press.

Mileur, J-P. (1986) "Allegory and irony: 'The rhetoric of temporality' re-examined", *Comparative Literature* 38, 4: 329–36.

Miller, J.H. (1982) *Fiction and Repetition: Seven English Novels*, Cambridge, Mass.: Harvard University Press.

Millington, B. and Spencer, S. (eds) (1992a) *Wagner in Performance*, New Haven: Yale University Press.

—— and —— (1992b) "Introduction" to *Wagner in Performance*, New Haven: Yale University Press.

Mishra, V. and Hodge, B. (1991) "What is post(-)colonialism?", *Textual Practice* 5, 3: 399–414.

Mitchell-Kernan, C. (1973) "Signifying", in A. Dundes (ed.) *Mother Wit from the Laughing Barrel: Readings in the Interpretation of Afro-American Folklore*, Englewood Cliffs, N.J.: Prentice-Hall.

Mizzau, M. (1984) *L'ironia: La contraddizione consentita*, Milan: Feltrinelli.

Moi, T. (1985) *Sexual/Textual Politics*, London and New York: Methuen.

Monk, P. (1983) "Colony, commodity and copyright: reference and self-reference in Canadian art", *Vanguard* 12, 5–6: 14–17.

Monson, D.A. (1988) "Andreas Capellanus and the problem of irony", *Speculum* 63: 539–72.

Moog, C. (1990) *'Are They Selling Her Lips': Advertising and Identity*, New York: William Morrow.

Moore, F.C.T. (1982) "On taking metaphor literally", in D.S. Miall (ed.) *Metaphor: Problems and Perspectives*, Brighton: Harvester Press; Atlantic Heights, N.J.: Humanities Press.

Morier, H. (1975) "Ironie", *Dictionnaire de poétique et de rhétorique*, 2nd edn, Paris: Presses Universitaires de France.

Morris, C. (1938) *Foundations of a Theory of Signs*, Chicago: University of Chicago Press.

Moser, W. (1984) "The factual in fiction: the case of Robert Musil", *Poetics Today* 5, 2: 411–28.

Moynihan, R. (1986) *A Recent Imagining: Interviews with Harold Bloom, Geoffrey Hartman, J. Hillis Miller and Paul de Man*, Hamden, Conn.: Archon Books.

Muecke, D.C. (1969) *The Compass of Irony*, London: Methuen.

—— (1970/1982) *Irony and the Ironic*, London and New York: Methuen.

—— (1973) "The communication of verbal irony", *Journal of Literary Semantics* 2: 35–42.

—— (1978a) "Analyses de l'ironie", *Poétique* 36: 478–94.

—— (1978b) "Irony markers", *Poetics* 7: 363–75.

—— (1983) "Images of irony", *Poetics Today* 4, 3: 399-413.

Mukherjee-Blaise, B. (1983) "Mimicry and reinvention", in U. Parameswaran (ed.) *The Commonwealth in Canada*, Calcutta: Writers Workshop Greybird.

Müller, U. (1992) "Wagner in Literature and Film", in U. Müller and P. Wapnewski (eds) *Wagner Handbook*, J. Deathridge (trans. ed.), Cambridge, Mass. and London: Harvard University Press.

Musil, R. (1972) *Der Mann ohne Eigenschaften*, Hamburg: Rowohlt.

Nadaner, D. (1984) "Intervention and Irony", *Vanguard* 13 (September): 13–14.

Nagler, A.M. (1981) *Misdirection: Opera Production in the Twentieth Century*, Hamden, Conn.: Archon Books.

Naipaul, V.S. (1967) *The Mimic Men*, New York: Macmillan.

Namjoshi, S. (1981) *Feminist Fables*, London: Sheba Feminist Publishers.

Nancy, J-L. (1991) *The Inoperative Community*, P. Connor (ed.), trans. P. Connor, L. Garbus, M. Holland, S. Sawhney, Minneapolis: University of Minnesota Press.

Narváez, P. (1991) "Folk talk and hard facts: the role of Ted Russell's 'Uncle Mose' on CBC's 'Fishermen's Broadcast'", in G. Thomas and J.D.A Widdowson (eds) *Studies in Newfoundland Folklore: Community and Process*, St. John's, Nfld: Breakwater Books.

Nathan, D.O. (1982) "Irony and the artist's intentions", *British Journal of Aesthetics* 22, 3 (Summer): 245–56.

Nattiez, J-J. (1983) *Tétralogies: Wagner, Boulez, Chéreau: Essai sur l'infidélité*, Paris: Christian Bourgeois.

Nazareth, E. (1990) "Royal Ontario Museum showcase showdown", *Now* (March 29–April 4): 10–12.

Newman, C. (1985) *The Post-Modern Aura*, Evanston: Northwestern University Press.

Newman, E. (1988) *Wagner Nights* [1949], London: Bodley Head.

Newman, M. (1982) "Irony and the Amazonians: post-modernism in the media jungle", *Art Monthly* 61: 30–2.

Newton-de Molina, D. (ed.) (1976) *On Literary Intention*, Edinburgh: Edinburgh University Press.

Nichols, B. (1981) *Ideology and the Image: Social Representation in the Cinema and Other Media*, Bloomington: University of Indiana Press.

Nicholson, L.J. (ed.) (1990) *Feminism/Postmodernism*, London and New York: Routledge.

Niebuhr, R. (1952) *The Irony of American History*, New York: Scribner's Sons.

Novak, M.E. and Davis, H.J. (1966) *The Uses of Irony: Papers on Defoe and Swift*, Los Angeles: William Andrews Clark Memorial Library.

O'Brien, C.C., Said, E. and Lukacs, J. (1986) "The intellectual in the post-colonial world: response and discussion", *Salmagundi* 70–1: 65–81.

Ong, W.J. (SJ) (1982a) "From mimesis to irony: the distancing of voice", in P. Hernadi (ed.) *The Horizon of Literature*, Lincoln: University of Nebraska Press.

—— (1982b) *Orality and Literacy: The Technologizing of the Word*, London: Methuen.

Ortega y Gasset, J. (1956) *The Dehumanization of Art*, trans. W.R. Trask, Garden City, N.Y.: Doubleday.

Ostriker, A.S. (1986) *Stealing the Language: The Emergence of Women's Poetry in America*, Boston: Beacon Press.

Paglia, C. (1992) *Sex, Art and American Culture: Essays*, New York: Vintage.

Pagnini, M. (1987) *The Pragmatics of Literature*, trans. N. Jones-Henry, Bloomington: Indiana University Press.

Palante, G. (1906) "L'ironie: étude psychologique", *Revue philosophique de la France et de l'Etranger*, 61: 147–63.

Palmer, N. (1989) "Museums and cultural property", in P. Vergo, (ed.) *The New Museology*, London: Reaktion Books.

Partner, P. (1991) "In Saddam's arms", *New York Review of Books* 38, 8 (25 April): 8–10.

Paulos, J.A. (1980) *Mathematics and Humor*, Chicago: University of Chicago Press.

Pavel, T.G. (1986) *Fictional Worlds*, Cambridge, Mass. and London: Harvard University Press.

Pearce, S.M. (ed.) (1990) *Objects of Knowledge*, London: Athlone Press.

Pêcheux, M. (1969) *Analyse automatique du discours*, Paris: Dunod.

—— (1982) *Language, Semantics and Ideology: Stating the Obvious*, trans. H. Nagpol, London: Macmillan.

Perelman, C. and Olbrechts-Tyteca, L. (1969) *The New Rhetoric: A Treatise on Argumentation*, trans. J. Wilkinson and P. Weaver, Notre Dame: University of Notre Dame Press.

Perri, C. (1978) "On alluding", *Poetics* 7: 289–307.

Peterson, C.A. (1987) *Photographs Beget Photographs*, Minneapolis: Minneapolis Institute of Art.

Pevere, G. (1991) "The battle of the icons", *The Globe and Mail* (5 July): C3.

Pilkington, A.G. (1991) *Screening Shakespeare from Richard II to Henry V*, Newark: University of Delaware Press; London and Toronto: Associated University Presses.

Plett, H.F. (1982) "Ironie als stilrhetorisches paradigma", *Ars Semeiotica* 4/5, 1: 75–89.

Powell, C. and Paton, G.E.C. (eds) (1988) *Humour in Society: Resistance and Control*, Houndmills and London: Macmillan.

Prang, H. (1972) *Die romantische Ironie*, Darmstadt: Wissenschaftliche Buchgesellschaft.

Pratt, M.L. (1977) *Toward a Speech Act Theory of Literary Discourse*, Bloomington: Indiana University Press.

—— (1986) "Ideology and speech-act theory", *Poetics Today* 7, 1: 59–72.

—— (1987) "Linguistic utopias", in N. Fabb *et al.* (eds) *The Linguistics of Writing*, Manchester: Manchester University Press.

—— (1991) "Arts of the contact zone", *Profession 91* (MLA): 33–40.

Preminger, A. (ed.) (1974) *Princeton Encyclopedia of Poetry and Poetics*, enlarged edn, Princeton, N.J.: Princeton University Press.

Preston, J. (1966) "The ironic mode: a comparison of *Jonathan Wild* and *The Beggar's Opera*", *Essays in Criticism* 16, 3: 268–80.

Prince, G. (1983) "Narrative pragmatics, message and point", *Poetics* 12: 527–36.

Pronger, B. (1990) *The Arena of Masculinity: Sports, Homosexuality and the Meaning of Sex*, Toronto: University of Toronto Press.

Purdie, S. (1993) *Comedy: The Mastery of Discourse*, Toronto: University of Toronto Press.

Quinn, M. (ed.) (1969) *Shakespeare: Henry V: A Casebook*, London: Macmillan.

Quintilian (1977) *The Institutio Oratoria* [1921], trans. H.E. Butler, Cambridge, Mass: Harvard University Press.

Rabinowitz, P.J. (1987) *Before Reading: Narrative Conventions and the Politics of Interpretation*, Ithaca, N.Y.: Cornell University Press.

Rabkin, N. (1988) "Either/or: responding to *Henry V*", in H. Bloom (ed.) *Modern Critical Interpretations: William Shakespeare's Henry V*, New York: Chelsea House.

Radway, J. (1991) "Interpretive communities and variable literacies: the functions of romance reading", in C. Mukherji and M. Schudson (eds) *Rethinking Popular Culture: Contemporary Perspectives in Cultural Studies*, Berkeley: University of California Press.

Rafoth, B.A. (1988) "Discourse community: where writers, readers and texts come together", in B.A. Rafoth and I. Rubin (eds) *The Social Construction of Written Communication*, Norwood, N.J.: Ablex.

Ramazani, V.K. (1988) *The Free Indirect Mode: Flaubert and the Poetics of Irony*, Charlottesville: University Press of Virginia.

Randall, M. (1988) "The context of literary communication: convention and presupposition", *Journal of Literary Semantics* 17, 1: 46–53.

Ransom, J.C. (1941) *The New Criticism*, New York: New Directions.

Rather, L.J. (1979) *The Dream of Self-Destruction: Wagner's Ring and the Modern World*, Baton Rouge: Louisiana State University Press.

Récanati, F. (1979) *La Transparence et l'énonciation: pour introduire à la pragmatique*, Paris: Seuil.

—— (1981) *Les énoncés performatifs: contribution à la pragmatique*, Paris: Minuit.

Redfern, W. (1984) *Puns*, Oxford: Blackwell.

Rhetorica ad Alexandrum (1957), trans. H. Rackham, Cambridge, Mass.: Harvard University Press.

Rich, P. (1982) "Tradition and revolt in South African fiction: the novels of André Brink, Nadine Gordimer and J.M. Coetzee", *Journal of Southern African Studies* 9, 1: 54–73.

Richards, I.A. (1925) *Principles of Literary Criticism*, New York: Harcourt Brace and World.

—— (1929) *Practical Criticism: A Study of Literary Judgment*, New York: Harcourt Brace and World.

—— (1936) *The Philosophy of Rhetoric*, New York: Oxford University Press.

Richter, D.H. (1981) "The reader as ironic victim", *Novel* 14: 135–51.

Ricoeur, P. (1975) *La Métaphore Vive*, Paris: Seuil.

Riffaterre, M. (1970) "Describing poetic structures: two approaches to Baudelaire's *Les Chats*", in J. Ehrmann (ed.) *Structuralism* [1966], Garden City, N.Y.: Doubleday, Anchor.

—— (1980) "Syllepsis", *Critical Inquiry* 6, 4: 625–38.

Riley, D. (1988) *"Am I that name?" Feminism and the Category of "Women" in History*, Minneapolis: University of Minnesota Press.

Robertson, H. (1990) "Out of Africa, into the soup", *Canadian Forum* 69, 792 (September): 4.

Rodway, A. (1962) "Terms for Comedy", *Renaissance and Modern Studies*, 6: 102–25.

Rorty, R. (1989) *Contingency, Irony, and Solidarity*, Cambridge: Cambridge University Press.

—— (1990) "Truth and freedom: a reply to Thomas McCarthy", *Critical Inquiry* 16, 3: 633–43.

Rose, B. (1988) Review of Anselm Kiefer's work, *Vogue* (January): 177, 242.

Rose, M.A. (1979) *Parody/Meta-fiction*, London: Croom Helm.

Rosenthal, A.L. (1973) "Feminism without contradictions", *The Monist* 57 (January): 28–42.

Rosenthal, H. (1976) "Bayreuth: A centenary to remember or … ?", *Opera* (Autumn): 18–27.

Rosenthal, M. (1987) *Anselm Kiefer*, Chicago: Art Institute of Chicago; Philadelphia: Philadelphia Museum of Art.

Rosler, M. (1981) "In, around and afterthoughts (on documentary photography)", in *Three Works*, Halifax, N.S.: Press of Nova Scotia College of Art and Design.

Ross, A. (1989) *No Respect: Intellectuals and Popular Culture*, London and New York: Routledge.

Ross, M. (1986) "Our sense of identity" [1954], reprinted in *The Impossible Sum of Our*

Traditions: Reflections on Canadian Literature, Toronto: McClelland & Stewart.

Rosso, S. (1983) "A correspondence with Umberto Eco", trans. C. Springer, *Boundary 2* 12, 1: 1–13.

Rothwell, K.S. and Melzer, A.H. (1990) *Shakespeare on Screen: An International Filmography and Videography*, New York and London: Neal-Schuman.

Rowland, B. (1985) "Seven kinds of irony", in E. Birney, *Essays in Chaucerian Irony*, ed. B. Rowland, Toronto: University of Toronto Press.

Russell, C. (1985) *Poets, Prophets and Revolutionaries: The Literary Avant-garde from Rimbaud through Postmodernism*, New York and Oxford: Oxford University Press.

Sabor, R. (1989) *The Real Wagner*, London: Sphere.

Safer, E.B. (1989) *The Contemporary American Comic Epic: The Novels of Barth, Pynchon, Gaddis and Kesey*, Detroit: Wayne State University Press.

Said, E.W. (1975) *Beginnings: Intention and Method*, New York: Basic Books.

—— (1983) *The World, the Text and the Critic*, Cambridge, Mass.: Harvard University Press.

—— (1984) "Reflections on exile", *Granta* 13: 157–72.

—— (1986) "Intellectuals in the post-colonial world", *Salmagundi* 70–1: 44–64.

—— (1988) *Yeats and Decolonization*, Derry: Field Day Theatre Company Pamphlet No. 15.

—— (1989) "Representing the colonized: anthropology's interlocutors", *Critical Inquiry* 15, 2: 205–25.

—— (1991) *Musical Elaborations*, New York: Columbia University Press.

—— (1993) *Culture and Imperialism*, New York: Knopf.

Sainsbury, R.M. (1988) *Paradoxes*, Cambridge: Cambridge University Press.

Sapir, J.D. (1977) "The anatomy of metaphor", in J.D. Sapir and J.C. Crocker (eds) *The Social Use of Metaphor*, Philadelphia: University of Pennsylvania Press.

Satterfield, L. (1981) "Toward a poetics of the ironic sign", in L. Satterfield and R.T. DeGeorge (eds) *Semiotic Themes*, Laurence: University of Kansas Press.

Schaerer, R. (1941) "Le méchanisme de l'ironie dans ses rapports avec la dialectique", *Revue de métaphysique et de morale* 8: 181–209.

Schildkrout, E. (1991) "Ambiguous menages and ironic twists: *Into the Heart of Africa* and *The Other Museum*", *Museum Anthropology* 15, 2 (May): 16–23.

Schlegel, F. (1958–80) *Kritische Friedrich-Schlegel-Ausgabe*, 22 vols, E. Behler (ed.), Munich: Verlag Ferdinand Schöningh.

—— (1971) *Friedrich Schlegel's Lucinde and the Fragments*, trans. P. Firchow, Minneapolis: University of Minnesota Press.

Schoentjes, P. (1993) *Recherche de l'ironie et ironie de la "Recherche"*, Gent: Rijksuniversiteit te Gent.

Scholes, R. (1977) "Towards a semiotics of literature", *Critical Inquiry* 4, 1: 105–20.

—— (1982) *Semiotics and Interpretation*, New Haven: Yale University Press.

Schonberg, H.C. (1976) "New Bayreuth 'Ring' alarms the old guard", *New York Times* (8 August), Section 2: 1, 13.

Searle, J. (1969) *Speech Acts*, Cambridge: Cambridge University Press.

—— (1975) "Indirect speech acts", in P. Cole and J.L. Morgan (eds) *Syntax and Semantics 3: Speech Acts*, New York: Academic Press.

—— (1979a) *Expression and Meaning*, Cambridge: Cambridge University Press.

—— (1979b) "Metaphor", in A. Ortony (ed.) *Metaphor and Thought*, Cambridge: Cambridge University Press.

—— (1983) *Intentionality: An Essay in the Philosophy of Mind*, Cambridge: Cambridge University Press.

Sedgwick, G.G. (1948) *Of Irony, Especially in Drama* [1935], Toronto: University of Toronto Press.

Seidel, G. (1989) "'We condemn apartheid, BUT . . .' a discursive analysis of the European parliamentary debate on sanctions (July 1986)", in R. Grillo (ed.) *Social Anthropology and the Politics of Language*, London: Routledge.

Shakespeare, W. (1954) *King Henry V*, ed. J.H. Walter, London: Methuen; Cambridge, Mass.: Harvard University Press.

Shapiro, M. and Shapiro, M. (1976) *Hierarchy and the Structure of Tropes*, Bloomington: Indiana University Press.

—— and —— (1988) *Figuration in Verbal Art*, Princeton: Princeton University Press.

Sharpe, R.B. (1959) *Irony in the Drama: An Essay on Impersonation, Shock and Catharsis*, Chapel Hill, N.C.: University of North Carolina Press.

Shaw, G.B. (1967) *The Perfect Wagnerite: A Commentary on the Niblung's Ring* [1898], New York: Dover.

Siegle, R. (1986) *The Politics of Reflexivity: Narrative and the Constitutive Poetics of Culture*, Baltimore and London: Johns Hopkins University Press.

—— (1989) *Suburban Ambush: Downtown Writing and the Fiction of Insurgency*, Baltimore: Johns Hopkins University Press.

Siemon, J.R. (1988) "The 'image bound': icon and iconoclasm in *Henry V*", in H. Bloom, *Modern Critical Interpretations: William Shakespeare's Henry V*, New York: Chelsea House.

Simpson, D. (1979) *Irony and Authority in Romantic Poetry*, London: Macmillan.

Sinfield, A. (1985) "Royal Shakespeare: theatre and the making of ideology", in J. Dollimore and A. Sinfield (eds) *Political Shakespeare: New Essays in Cultural Materialism*, Manchester: Manchester University Press.

Slemon, S. (1987) "Monuments of empire: allegory/counter-discourse/post-colonial writing", *Kunapipi* 9, 3: 1–16.

—— (1988) "Post-colonial allegory and the transformation of history", *Journal of Commonwealth Literature* 23, 1: 157–68.

—— (1990) "Modernism's last post", in I. Adam and H. Tiffin (eds) *Past the Last Post: Theorizing Post-Colonialism and Post-Modernism*, Calgary: University of Calgary Press.

Smith, B.H. (1968) *Poetic Closure: A Study of How Poems End*, Chicago: University of Chicago Press.

—— (1979) *On the Margins of Discourse: The Relations of Literature to Language*, Chicago: University of Chicago Press.

—— (1988) *Contingencies of Value: Alternative Perspectives for Critical Theory*, Cambridge, Mass.: Harvard University Press.

Smith, C.S. (1989) "Museums, artefacts and meanings", in P. Vergo (ed.) *The New Museology*, London: Reaktion Books.

Smith, N.V. (1989) *The Twitter Machine: Reflections on Language*, Oxford: Blackwell.

Smyth, J.V. (1986) *A Question of Eros: Irony in Sterne, Kierkegaard and Barthes*, Tallahassee: Florida State University Press.

Sollors, W. (1986) *Beyond Ethnicity: Consent and Descent in American Culture*, Oxford and New York: Oxford University Press.

Sontag, S. (1982) *A Susan Sontag Reader*, New York: Farrar, Strauss, Giroux.

Spacks, P.M. (1976) *The Female Imagination: A Literary and Psychological Investigation of Women's Writings*, London: Allen & Unwin.

Spanos, W.V. (1972) "The detective and the boundary: some notes on the postmodern literary imagination", *Boundary 2* 1: 147–68.

—— (1987) *Repetitions: The Postmodern Occasion in Literature and Culture*, Baton Rouge: Louisiana State University Press.

Sparshott, F.E. (1976) "Criticism and performance", in D. Newton-de Molina (ed.)

On Literary Intention, Edinburgh: Edinburgh University Press.

—— (1986) "The case of the unreliable author", *Philosophy and Literature* 10, 2: 145–67.

Sperber, D. (1984) "Verbal irony: pretence or echoic mention", *Journal of Experimental Psychology: General* 113, 1: 130–6.

—— and Wilson, D. (1978) "Les ironies comme mentions", *Poétique* 36: 399–412.

—— and —— (1981) "Irony and the use-mention distinction", in P. Cole (ed.) *Radical Pragmatics*, New York: Academic Press.

—— and —— (1986) *Relevance: Communication and Cognition*, Oxford: Blackwell.

Sperry, S. (1977) "Toward a definition of Romantic irony in English literature", in G. Bornstein (ed.) *Romantic and Modern: Revaluations of a Literary Tradition*, Pittsburgh: University of Pittsburgh Press.

Spivak, G.C. (1990) *The Postcolonial Critic: Interview, Strategies, Dialogues*, ed. S. Harasym, New York and London: Routledge.

Stallybrass, P. and White, A. (1986) *The Politics and Poetics of Transgression*, London and New York: Methuen.

Stam, R. and Spence, L. (1983) "Colonialism, racism and representation", *Screen* 24, 2: 2–20.

States, B.O. (1971) *Irony and Drama: A Poetics*, Ithaca, N.Y. and London: Cornell University Press.

Steig, M. (1989) *Stories of Reading: Subjectivity and Literary Understanding*, Baltimore: Johns Hopkins University Press.

Steiner, G. (1975) *After Babel: Aspects of Language and Translation*, New York and London: Oxford University Press.

Stempel, W.-D. (1976) "Ironie als Sprechhandlung", in W. Preisendanz and R. Warning (eds) *Das Komische*, Münich: Wilhelm Fink.

Stephanson, A. (1987) "Regarding postmodernism – a conversation with Fredric Jameson", *Social Text* 17: 29–54.

Stern, L. (1980) "On Interpreting", *Journal of Aesthetics and Art Criticism* 39, 2: 119–30.

Stevens, M. (1992) "After Sex", *The New Republic* (9 November): 20–1.

Stewart, S. (1978/79) *Nonsense: Aspects of Intertextuality in Folklore and Literature*, Baltimore: Johns Hopkins University Press.

Stimpson, C.R. (1988) "Nancy Reagan wears a hat: feminism and its cultural consensus", *Critical Inquiry* 14, 2: 223–43.

—— (1991) "On differences" (MLA Presidential Address 1990), *PMLA* 106, 3: 402–11.

Strohschneider-Kohrs, I. (1960) *Die romantische Ironie in Theorie und Gestaltung*, Tübingen: Max Niemeyer Verlag.

Subotnik, R.R. (1991) *Developing Variations: Style and Ideology in Western Music*, Minneapolis: University of Minnesota Press.

Suleiman, S. (1976) "Interpreting Ironies", *Diacritics* 6, 2: 15–21.

Swales, J. (1988) "Discourse communities, genres and English as an international language", *World Englishes* 7, 2: 211–20.

Swearingen, C.J. (1991) *Rhetoric and Irony: Western Literacy and Western Lies*, New York: Oxford University Press.

Swift, J. (1958) "A Modest Proposal", in *Gulliver's Travels and Other Writings*, ed. R. Quintana, New York: The Modern Library, Random House.

Tamburri, A. (1992) "The Madonna complex: the justification of a prayer", *International Semiotic Spectrum* 17 (April): 1–2.

Tanaka, R. (1973) "The concept of irony: theory and practice", *Journal of Literary Semantics* 2: 43–56.

Tani, S. (1984) *The Doomed Detective: The Contribution of the Detective Novel to Postmodern American and Italian Fiction*, Carbondale and Edwardsville: Southern Illinois University Press.

Tanner, M. (1979) "The total work of art", in P. Burbridge and R. Sutton (eds) *The Wagner Companion*, London: Faber & Faber.

—— (1989) "Ideals and sacrifices", *Times Literary Supplement* (August 25–31): 921.

Tatspaugh, P.E. (1992) "Theatrical influences on Kenneth Branagh's film of *Henry V*", *Literature/Film Quarterly* 20, 4: 276–83.

Tchen, J.K.W. (1992) "Creating a dialogic museum: the Chinatown History Museum experiment", in I. Karp, C.M. Kreamer and S.D. Lavine (eds) *Museums and Communities: The Politics of Public Culture*, Washington, DC: Smithsonian Institution Press.

Tennenhouse, L. (1985) "Strategies of state and political plays: *A Midsummer Night's Dream, Henry IV, Henry V, Henry VIII*", in J. Dollimore and A. Sinfield (eds) *Political Shakespeare: New Essays in Cultural Materialism*, Manchester: Manchester University Press.

Terdiman, R. (1985) *Discourse/Counter-Discourse: The Theory and Practice of Symbolic Resistance in Nineteenth-Century France*, Ithaca, N.Y. and London: Cornell University Press.

Thirlwall, C. (1833) "On the irony of Sophocles", *The Philological Museum* 2: 483–537.

Thomas, N. (1991) *Entangled Objects: Exchange, Material Culture and Colonialism in the Pacific*, Cambridge, Mass.: Harvard University Press.

Thompson, A.R. (1948) *The Dry Mock: A Study of Irony in Drama*, Berkeley and Los Angeles: University of California Press.

Thompson, M.R. (SSMN) (1989) *The Role of Disbelief in Mark: A New Approach to the Second Gospel*, New York: Paulist Press.

Thomson, J.A.K. (1926) *Irony: An Historical Introduction*, London: Allen & Unwin.

Thurley, G. (1974) *The Ironic Harvest: English Poetry in the Twentieth Century*, London: Edward Arnold.

Tiffin, H. (1983) "Commonwealth literature: comparison and judgement", in D. Riemenschneider (ed.) *The History and Historiography of Comparative Literature*, Tübingen: Gunter Narr Verlag.

—— (1987) "Post-colonial literatures and counter-discourse", *Kunapipi* 9, 3: 17–34.

—— (1988) "Post-colonialism, post-modernism and the rehabilitation of post-colonial history", *Journal of Commonwealth Literature* 23, 1: 169–81.

Tindale, C.W. and Gough, J. (1987) "The use of irony in argumentation", *Philosophy and Rhetoric* 20, 1: 1–17.

Tittler, J. (1984) *Narrative Irony in the Contemporary Spanish-American Novel*, Ithaca, N.Y.: Cornell University Press.

Todorov, T. (1970) "Problèmes de l'énonciation", *Langages* 17: 3–11.

—— (1973) *The Fantastic: A Structural Approach to a Literary Genre*, trans. R. Howard, Cleveland: Press of Case Western Reserve University.

—— (1978) *Symbolisme et interprétation*, Paris: Seuil.

Torgovnick, M. (1990) "Travelling with Conrad", in M. Torgovnick, *Gone Primitive: Savage Intellects, Modern Lives*, Chicago: University of Chicago Press.

Toscani, C. (1988) "Review of *Il pendolo di Foucault*", *Critica letteraria* 16: 617–20.

Toulmin, S. (1990) *Cosmopolis: The Hidden Agenda of Modernity*, New York: Free Press.

Trilling, L. (1972) *Sincerity and Authenticity*, Cambridge, Mass.: Harvard University Press.

Turner, F. McD.C. (1969) *The Element of Irony in English Literature* [1926], Folcroft, Pa.: Folcroft Press.

Tyler, S.A. (1978) *The Said and the Unsaid*, New York: Academic Press.

Ulmer, G. (1982) "Of a parodic tone recently adopted in criticism", *New Literary History* 13: 543–60.

Valdés, M.J. (1992) *World-Making: The Literary Truth-Claim and the Interpretation of Texts*, Toronto: University of Toronto Press.

Van Dijk, T.A. (1976) "Preface" to T.A. Van Dijk (ed.) *Pragmatics of Language and Literature*, Amsterdam and Oxford: North Holland Publishing Company.

—— (1977) *Text and Context: Explorations in the Semantics and Pragmatics of Discourse*, London and New York: Longman.

Van Doren, M. (1939) "The fragmentation of the heroic idea in *Henry V*", in M. Quinn (ed.) (1969) *Shakespeare: Henry V: A Casebook*, London: Macmillan.

Vattimo, G. (1992) *The Transparent Society*, trans. D. Webb, Baltimore: Johns Hopkins University Press.

Vaughan, M. (1982) "Literature and politics: currents in South African writing in the seventies", *Journal of Southern African Studies* 9, 1: 118–38.

Vaughan, W. (1979) "Landscape and the 'Irony of Nature'", *Art History* 2, 4: 457–73.

Venturi, R. (1977) *Complexity and Contradiction in Architecture*, New York: Museum of Modern Art.

Vergo, P. (ed.) (1989a) *The New Museology*, London: Reaktion Books.

—— (1989b) "Introduction" to *The New Museology*, London: Reaktion Books.

—— (1989c) "The reticent object", in *The New Museology*, London: Reaktion Books.

Vico, G. (1968) *The New Science of Giambattista Vico*, trans. T.G. Bergin and M.H. Fisch, Ithaca, N.Y.: Cornell University Press.

—— (1982) *Selected Writings*, ed. and trans. L. Pompa, Cambridge: Cambridge University Press.

Vita-Finzi, C. (1989a) "Omnivorous fantasy", Review of *Il Pendolo di Foucault*, *Times Literary Supplement* (3 March): 225.

—— (1989b) "Tales told by a savant, signifying . . .", Review of *Foucault's Pendulum*, *Times Literary Supplement*, (November): 1272.

Vivas, E. (1936) "The esthetic judgment", *Journal of Philosophy* 33: 57–69.

Vogel, S. (1991) "Always true to the object", in S.D. Lavine and I. Karp (eds) *Exhibiting Cultures: The Poetics and Politics of Museum Display*, Washington, DC: Smithsonian Institution Press.

Vološinov, V.N. (1973) *Marxism and the Philosophy of Language*, trans. Ladislav Matejka and I.R. Titunik, New York and London: Seminar Press.

Vossius (1978) "Rhétorique de l'ironie", *Poétique* 36: 495–508.

Walker, N. (1988a) *A Very Serious Thing: Women's Humor and American Culture*, Minneapolis: University of Minnesota Press.

—— (1988b) "Ironic autobiography: from *The Waterfall* to *The Handmaid's Tale*", in R. Barreca (ed.) *Last Laughs: Perspectives on Women and Comedy*, New York: Gordon & Breach.

—— (1990) *Feminist Alternatives: Irony and Fantasy in the Contemporary Novel by Women*, Jackson and London: University Press of Mississippi.

Warning, R. (1982) "Irony and the 'Order of Discourse' in Flaubert", trans. M. Morton, *New Literary History* 13, 2: 253–86.

Watson, R. (1990a) "Studies on nuclear waste disposal leave one alternative: bury it!", *St. Louis Journalism Review* 20, 128 (August): 12–13.

—— (1990b) "Irony is not for the deadly serious", *St. Louis Journalism Review* 20, 128 (August): 14.

—— (1990c) "Ozymandias, king of kings: postprocessual radical archaeology as critique", *American Antiquity* 55, 4: 673–89.

Watzlawick, P., Beavin, J.H. and Jackson, D.D. (1967) *Pragmatics of Human Communication: A Study of Interactional Patterns, Pathologies, and Paradoxes*, New York: Norton.

Waugh, P. (1984) *Metafiction: The Theory and Practice of Self-Conscious Fiction*, London and New York: Methuen.

Weil, S.E. (1990) *Rethinking the Museum and Other Meditations*, Washington, DC and London: Smithsonian Institution Press.

Weinrich, H. (1966) *Linguistik der Lüge*, Heidelberg: Verlag Lambert Schneider.

Wellek, R. (1955) *A History of Modern Criticism: II: The Romantic Age, 1750–1900*, New Haven: Yale University Press.

—— and Warren, A. (1949) *Theory of Literature*, New York: Harcourt Brace.

Wertenbaker, T. ([1988]1989) *Our Country's Good*, London: Methuen.

West, C. (1990) "The new cultural politics of difference", in R. Ferguson, M. Gever, Trinh T. Minh-ha and C. West (eds) *Out There: Marginalization and Contemporary Culture*, New York: New Museum of Contemporary Art; Cambridge, Mass.: Massachusetts Institute of Technology Press.

White, H. (1973) *Metahistory: The Historical Imagination in Nineteenth-Century Europe*, Baltimore: Johns Hopkins University Press.

—— (1978) *Tropics of Discourse: Essays in Cultural Criticism*, Baltimore: Johns Hopkins University Press.

—— (1987) *The Content of the Form: Narrative Discourse and Historical Representation*, Baltimore and London: Johns Hopkins University Press.

Whitlock, G. (1986) "Have you read the one about the angry women who laughed?", in K.H. Petersen and A. Rutherford (eds) *A Double Colonization: Colonial and Post-Colonial Women's Writing*, Mundelstrup, Denmark: Dangaroo Press.

Wilde, A. (1975) Review of Wayne Booth, *A Rhetoric of Irony*, *Journal of Modern Literature* 4, 5, supplement: 942–3.

—— (1981) *Horizons of Assent: Modernism, Postmodernism, and the Ironic Imagination*, Baltimore and London: Johns Hopkins University Press.

Williams, J.P. (1984) "Does mention (or pretence) exhaust the concept of irony?", *Journal of Experimental Psychology: General* 113, 1: 127–9.

Willson, R.F., Jr. (1991) "War and reflection on war: the Olivier and Branagh films of *Henry V*", *Shakespeare Bulletin* 9, 3: 27–9.

Wilson, A. (1990) "The English Stage Company visits the Canadian Stage Company", *Queen's Quarterly* 97, 1: 140–53.

Wilson, G.M. (1992) "Again, theory: on speaker's meaning, linguistic meaning and the meaning of a text", *Critical Inquiry* 19, 1: 164–85.

Wimsatt, W.K., Jr. and Brooks, C. (1964) *Literary Criticism: A Short History*, New York: Knopf.

—— and Beardsley, M.C. (1967) "The Intentional Fallacy", in W.K. Wimsatt, Jr., *The Verbal Icon*, Lexington, Ky.: University of Kentucky Press.

Winner, E. (1988) *The Point of Words: Children's Understanding of Metaphor and Irony*, Cambridge, Mass.: Harvard University Press.

Wolfe, T. (1989) "Stalking the billion-footed beast: a literary manifesto for the new social novel", *Harper's Magazine* (November): 45–56.

Wood, A.W. (1985) "Habermas's defense of rationalism", *New German Critique* 35: 145–64.

Worcester, D. (1960) *The Art of Satire* [1940], New York: Russell & Russell.

Woudhuysen, H.R. (1989) *Samuel Johnson on Shakespeare*, Harmondsworth: Penguin.

Wright, E. (1976) "Arbitrariness and motivation: a new theory", *Foundations of Language* 14: 505–23.

—— (1977) "Words and intentions", *Philosophy* 52: 45–62.

—— (1978) "Sociology and the irony model", *Sociology* 12: 523–43.

Wright, P. (1989) "The quality of visitors' experiences in art museums", in P. Vergo (ed.) *The New Museology*, London: Reaktion Books.

Young, T.C., Jr. (1993) "*Into the heart of Africa*: the director's perspective", *Curator* 36, 3: 174–88.

Zeitlin, F.L. (1985) "Playing the other: theatre, theatricality and the feminine in Greek drama", *Representations* 11: 63–94.

NAME INDEX

Butler, S.R. 177, 185, 208*n*, 209*n*

Campbell, K.S. 61, 65
Cannizzo, Jeanne 176–7, 178, 185–202, 205*n*, 207*n*, 208*n*
Caravaggio, Michelangelo Merisi 14
Carnegy, P. 134, 161, 166
Carter, Angela 32
Celan, Paul 113
Cézanne, Paul 6
Chamberlain, Lori 17, 36, 44, 64, 91, 96, 97
Chambers, Sir Edmund 75
Chambers, R. (Ross) 14, 16–17, 18, 30, 50, 100, 122, 149
Chatman, S. 94
Chéreau, Patrice 159–66
Chevalier, H.M. 43, 50, 51
Chiaro, D. 26, 143, 195
Chomsky, Noam 95
Cicero 64, 150
Cixous, Hélène 153
Clarkson, David 36
Clausewitz, Karl von 106
Clifford, J. 181, 197, 198, 199, 201, 202, 208*n*
Clyne, M. 48, 154
Coetzee, J.M. 30–1
Colescott, Robert 20, 26, 208*n*
Collins, J. 12, 100, 117
Compagnon, A. 158
Conrad, Joseph 185
Conrad, P. 8, 135
Coppola, Francis Ford 19
Crean, S. 190, 192, 193, 194, 196, 198, 208*n*
Crews, Frederick 97
Croce, Benedetto 145
Culler, Jonathan 28, 43, 48, 91, 94, 95, 117, 122, 144, 145, 146, 153
Curtiz, Michael 72

Da Breo, Hazel 207*n*
Dahlhaus, C. 132, 138, 161
Dali, Salvador 6
Daly, Norman 167–8
Dane, Joseph A. 9, 38, 39, 57, 66, 94, 95
Danto, Arthur C. 102–3
Deathridge, J. 138
Decottignies, J. 51, 52
Defoe, Daniel 30, 121
de Lauretis, Teresa 58, 152–3

de Man, Paul 16, 54, 57, 60, 64, 65
Derrida, Jacques 9, 11, 28, 32, 122, 126, 209*n*
Descartes, René 179
Dickens, Charles 99
Disraeli, Benjamin 133
Dollimore, J. 79
Donaldson, L.E. 183
Douglas, Mary 99
Doyle, Pat 78
Drainie, Bronwyn 207*n*, 208*n*
DuBois, W.E.B. 31
Ducrot, O. 57, 99, 122
Durand, Gilbert 126
Durrans, B. 181, 182, 185, 195
Dyson, A.E. 51, 55

Eagleton, Terry 15, 29, 43
Eco, Umberto 13, 90, 121, 123, 124–31, 139, 143, 144, 145, 148, 152
Eisenstein, Sergei 72
Elamin, Ahmed 209*n*
Eliot, George 126
Eliot, T.S. 38, 49, 128
Elizabeth I, Queen 75, 79
Elizabeth II, Queen 79
Elliott, R.G. 29
Ellis-Fermor, Una 87
Ellmann, M. 32
Elyot, Sir Thomas 86
Empson, William 38, 65
Engels, Friedrich 161
Enright, D.J. 10, 29, 52
Erasmus, Desiderius 86
Essex, Earl of 75
Evergon 14

Fantin-Latour, Henri 6
Farquhar, George 22–5
Fielding, Henry 45
Fink, G. 129
Finlay, Ian Hamilton 157
Fischer, Michael 100
Fish, Stanley 12, 18, 61, 90, 98, 122, 123, 176
Flaubert, Gustave 55, 120, 158
Fletcher, A. 65
Fogelin, R.J. 52, 66, 123
Forster, E.M. 127
Foucault, Jean Bernard Léon 125, 127, 131
Foucault, Michel 11, 61, 90, 92, 117,

SUBJECT INDEX

245

operative motivation, attributed or
    inferred 45
The Order of Things (Foucault) 125, 129,
    130
orientalism 166
Our Country's Good (Wertenbaker) 22–5

painting *see* visual art
parabasis 65
paradox 42, 53, 62, 69, 90, 153
parody 3–4, 53, 64
Parsifal (Wagner) 103, 110, 133
photography 6, 19–20, 101, 106–7 *see
    also* visual art
playfulness 49, 154
plays 22–5, 38, 67–88, 100, 124
play theory 154
poetry 145
polemics 52
politics 43; *see also* irony
postcolonialism 5, 27, 30, 32, 43, 75,
    179, 180, 182, 183, 184, 192, 194,
    198, 199, 204, 209n
postmodernism 3
poststructuralism 4, 57, 117, 126, 204
power 93, 95
pragmatics 90, 117, 119, 122, 149, 154
precision 48
punning 49, 60

quotations *see* citations

race, racism 5, 13, 19–20, 31, 52, 92,
    100, 133, 149–50, 177, 178, 183, 191,
    194, 195, 197
The Recruiting Officer (Farquhar) 22–5
reflexivity 184, 185, 201
The Remains of the Day (Ishiguro) 157
repetition 158, 178
Das Rheingold (Wagner) 160–1, 164
rhetoric 9, 12, 17, 31, 33, 38, 39, 41, 46,
    54, 63, 146, 156
Rhetorica ad Alexandrum 158
rhetorical communities 92
"Ride of the Valkyries" (Wagner) 19
Rienzi (Wagner) 132
Ring cycle (Wagner) 103, 109–10,
    113–14, 124, 135–40, 144, 159–6
Robinson Crusoe (Defoe) 30–1
Royal Court Theatre 22–5
Royal Ontario Museum, Toronto

176–204
Royal Shakespeare Company 68, 76

satire 29, 52, 53
self-deprecation 50
settler colonies 183, 206n
sexuality 5, 18, 27, 31, 52, 92, 100
The Shortest Way with the Dissenters
    (Defoe) 121
"Short People Got No Reason to Live"
    (Newman) 176
signifiers, signifieds 64
"signifying monkey" 31
single- and double-voicing 31, 202
skepticism 10, 53
"smiley" 149
speech-act theory 39, 62, 90, 117, 142,
    143, 150, 154
speech-community 92

Tannhäuser (Wagner) 134
teasing 49
television 92, 158, 165, 166, 175, 201
Théâtre de la Monnaie, Brussels 124,
    135–39
theology 44
Third Reich 133
Toronto 22, 141, 143, 176, 179, 183,
    192, 196, 202, 208n
transgression 52
triple-voicing 60

United States (Anderson) 32, 155
United States of America 50, 104, 138,
    206n, 208n

victim, victimization (as terms) 15,
    42–3, 54, 95
Vietnam 19, 76
visual art 5, 6, 10, 13–14, 54, 101–15,
    155, 156, 158, 200–1

Die Walküre (Wagner) 109, 138–39, 163
WaterWorks 143–4
Wayne's World 149
"West as America" 209n
wit 29, 152
Worcester 49, 50, 51, 54, 152
wordplay 142
World War I 76
World War II 6, 76, 102, 135, 160

Printed in Great Britain
by Amazon